S0-BQB-306

RATIONALITY IN THE CALVINIAN TRADITION

EDITED BY:
HENDRIK HART
JOHAN VAN DER HOEVEN
NICHOLAS WOLTERSTORFF

University Press of America

University Press of America,™ Inc.

4720 Boston Way
Lanham, MD 20706

3 Henrietta Street
London WC2E 8LU England

Printed in the United States of America

Library of Congress Cataloging in Publication Data
Main entry under title:

Rationality in the Calvinian tradition.

(Christian studies today)
Papers presented at a conference held Aug. 3–8, 1981 in Toronto, Ont., and sponsored by Calvin College, the Free University of Amsterdam, and the Institute for Christian Studies.
1. Calvinism–Congresses. 2. Rationalism–Congresses. I. Hart, Hendrik. II. Hoeven, Johan van der. III. Wolterstorff, Nicholas. IV. Calvin College. V. Vrije Universiteit te Amsterdam. VI. Institute for Christian Studies. VII. Series.
BX9422.2.R37 1983 230'.42 83–19672
ISBN 0–8191–3616–6 (alk. paper)
ISBN 0–8191–3617–4 (pbk. : alk. paper)

All University Press of America books are produced on acid-free paper which exceeds the minimum standards set by the National Historical Publications and Records Commission.

Co-Published by arrangement with the
Institute for Christian Studies

Contents

Introduction

THESE ARE THE PAPERS OF A CONFERENCE on the theme of "Rationality in the Calvinian Tradition," held in Toronto during August 3-8, 1981, and sponsored jointly by Calvin College, the Free University of Amsterdam and the Institute for Christian Studies (Toronto).

No doubt Calvinism is regularly thought of simply as a system of theology, and the tradition of the Reformed/Presbyterian churches simply as an ecclesiastical tradition. Yet the reform that arose out of Switzerland and its environs in the 16th century was, from its very beginnings, more than this. It was a movement of social as well as ecclesiastical reform. And its intellectual underpinnings were more than purely theological. In particular, from its very beginnings it included certain reflections on the nature of faith, and of reason, and on the relation between them. Of course, Calvinism did not have the articulate philosophical character of Thomism. The positions staked out on these issues were always more intuitive, less developed, more fluid. Yet I think one can safely speak of certain theses on these matters as *characteristic* of the Calvinist tradition. And it is this quality that makes possible a conference on the theme of "Rationality in the Calvinian Tradition."

Let me suggest four or five theses on rationality which, in my opinion, have become characteristic of the Calvinist tradition. (I am not suggesting that all who locate themselves in this tradition would support all of these theses. Moreover, they have occasionally been held by thinkers who would not even locate themselves in this tradition.)

(1) It has characteristically been held that to be (rationally) justified in being a theist, one does not have to accept the crucial tenets of theism on the basis of some argument, or some reasons. A person may well be within his rights if he accepts those tenets *immediately*. And not only may he be within his *rights* in so doing, there

might be nothing *deficient* about his holding those tenets in that way. It may have been *better* not to hold them on the basis of reasons. Indeed, many Reformed thinkers have suggested that it would be worse —perhaps even pernicious—to hold them on the basis of arguments.

(2) Similarly, it has characteristically been held that one may well be within one's rights in believing immediately that the Christian Scriptures are the revelation of God, or the Word of God. This, too, does not have to be believed on the basis of reasons, arguments. One is not doing something intellectually irresponsible if one believes it immediately. Scripture, it was often said, is *self*-authenticating. It does not require external authentication. Indeed, such prominent Reformed thinkers as John Calvin and Karl Barth suggested it would be dangerous to believe on the basis of arguments that Scripture is the Word of God.

(3) It has characteristically been held that sin has darkened our capacities for acquiring justified beliefs and for acquiring knowledge. Reason is, in this way, not insulated from the devastation which sin has wrought in our existence. It is not that sin has affected our will but not our reason.

(4) It has characteristically been held that a specimen of science *(Wissenschaft)* may well be intellectually and scientifically competent and yet not neutral with respect to the Chrsitian faith. It may be in conflict, in tension, with it. Such conflict and tension is not a sign that incompetence has entered the picture (although of course that *may* have happened). The Calvinist has insisted that in the face of an awareness of this conflict, one should re-do the science rather than surrender the faith. He is well aware that this would result in a pluralism of competent science—in a pluralization of the academy. But that, he insists, is our situation in any case. A person's world-and-life view shapes his science. It is an illusion to suppose that competent science constitutes a consensus.

(5) It has characteristically been held that when the Christian engages in science, his activity ought in appropriate ways to be directed by his faith—just as his activity in other spheres of life ought to be so directed. Christ is Lord of all of life.

One will find these theses playing their role in the following papers—in some of them more prominently, in others less prominently. Yet I do not wish to suggest that all the writers of the papers would hold to all of these theses. Indeed, not all of the contributors would want to place themselves within the Calvinist/Reformed tradition of Christianity. Some see themselves more as "sympathizers."

Perhaps one last explanatory comment should be made. Calvinists have regularly made use of, and themselves developed, a wide variety of philosophical perspectives. Yet it can be said that two such perspectives have been prominent in the Calvinist tradition: that of the *common-sense philosophy* which began with Thomas Reid in the 18th century and was especially influential in Scotland and the United States, and that of *neo-Calvinism* which began in the Netherlands at the end of the 19th century. Both of these sub-traditions are given special recognition in the papers that follow; and one of the most interesting features of the conference itself was the interaction of members of these two traditions.

In recent years, rationality has become a lively topic of discussion in philosophical circles. The philosophically informed reader will notice that certain developments in those discussions have enabled the writers of these papers to cast new light on old positions and old disputes which are characteristic of the Calvinist tradition. But it will be clear that the influence has gone in the other direction as well. The emphases characteristic of this long tradition of Christendom have suggested to several of these writers possibilities which their philosophical colleagues in our post-Enlightenment climate have neglected. In short, I think one sees in these papers an interaction between recent philosophy and the Calvinist tradition of Christendom which proves fruitful for both.

Nicholas Wolterstorff
Calvin College
March, 1982

Contributors

William B. Alston is Professor of Philosophy at Syracuse University, New York.

Roy Clouser is Associate Professor of Philosophy at Trenton State College, New Jersey.

John M. Frame is Professor of Systematic Theology at Westminster Theological Seminary, California.

Hendrik Hart is Senior Member in Systematic Philosophy at the Institute for Christian Studies, Ontario.

Paul Helm is Senior Lecturer in Philosophy at the University of Liverpool, England.

Dewey Hoitenga is Professor of Philosophy at Grand Valley State Colleges, Michigan.

Arthur F. Holmes is Professor of Philosophy at Wheaton College, Illinois.

Jaap Klapwijk is Professor of Philosophy at the Free University of Amsterdam, the Netherlands.

Charles Partee is Professor of Church History at Pittsburgh Theological Seminary, Pennsylvania.

Henry Pietersma is Associate Professor of Philosophy at Victoria College (University of Toronto), Ontario.

Alvin Plantinga is the Rev. John A. O'Brien Professor of Philosophy at Notre Dame University, Indiana.

Peter Schouls is Professor of Philosophy at the University of Alberta, Alberta.

Danie F.M. Strauss is Professor of Philosophy at the University of the Orange Free State, South Africa.

Theo van der Merwe is Professor of Philosophy at Potchefstroom University for Christian Higher Education, South Africa.

Albert Wolters is Senior Member in the History of Philosophy at the Institute for Christian Studies, Ontario.

Nicholas Wolterstorff is Professor of Philosophy at Calvin College, Michigan.

Historical Setting

Part One:

Calvin, Calvinism and Rationality

Calvin, Calvinism, and Rationality

Charles Partee

I

I THINK IT IS ONLY FAIR to admit and assert what will soon be obvious in any event—I am not a philosopher. Moreover, I can claim little expertise regarding two-thirds of the topic—"Calvinism" and "Rationality." However, I would like to affirm that I have devoted a good deal of reflection to the works of John Calvin, and am willing to offer my understanding of Calvin on the topic of rationality somewhat boldly, and the conclusions which I draw from that understanding about Calvin and Calvinism somewhat less boldly.

The first problem is to define and delineate the subject. In the case of Calvin, the task of understanding what he meant is by no means simple, yet the dimensions for analysis are exactly proscribed by what he wrote. Moreover, it can probably be agreed that Calvin was a biblical theologian. That is to say, he devoted his major efforts to writing commentaries on the Bible, preaching sermons on it, and organizing a theological presentation of the Scripture known as the *Institutes of the Christian Religion*, all of which taken together offers a way of understanding the Scripture and living the Christian life.

On the basis of Calvin's contribution, a number of people chose to call themselves or were called "Calvinists." In a rough sense, Calvinists are those who accept the term or to whom it is applied, but the correctness of this description depends on the validity of the criteria used to establish it and the accuracy of its application. Obviously, those who followed Calvin did not, and could not, simply replicate his words, but used them in different contexts and extended them to meet new situations. In doing so the question arises whether, and to what extent, these various applications and extensions *renew* or *distort* the tradition as set forth by Calvin, assuming that Calvin's work as a whole is to be regarded as the touchstone of authentic Calvinism.

The concept of rationality, on the other hand, arose independently of Calvin and Calvinism. While the quest for, and conviction of, rationality is an essential part of the Western philosophic tradition, and as such has influenced Christian theology including Calvin, it still cannot be regarded as fixed and unproblematic.

If there is general agreement that Calvin was a biblical theologian, it is also true that his activity took place within the context of Western thought and may be legitimately related to it. Moreover, one could argue that both Scripture and Christian tradition—like the concept of rationality—arose independently of Calvin and that *his* understanding of them all *by being followed* makes the designation "Calvinist" appropriate. I think the designation is clearer in terms of Scripture and theological tradition. For example, one could properly claim to be a "Calvinist" by accepting in the main Calvin's interpretation of Scripture as found in his biblical commentaries. In the same way, one could properly claim to be a "Calvinist" by accepting the *Institutes* as a whole or in good part (however these be defined), and on biblical and theological grounds without being necessarily committed to any precise conception of human rationality. One could simply uphold the commentaries and/or the *Institutes* in general and be willing to discuss specific problems and reservations.

With regard to Calvin and rationality, there is no single work or group of works in which Calvin himself addresses the topic. Thus, one is required to abstract from his writings what his view on the topic is understood to be. Approval of "Calvin's doctrine of rationality," as a whole or in general, then depends on acceptance of the work of the "abstractor" and "systemizer" in a way that acceptance of his biblical and theological views do not.

In a strong sense, one might argue that any "reasonable" reader of Calvin would grasp the "evident" fact that Calvin consciously and deliberately shaped the concept of rationality as a tool for the presentation of the Gospel, and that a commitment to the use of this tool, forged by Calvin himself, is an essential (or important or at least helpful) part of being Calvinistic. However, the paucity of textual and contextual evidence for this position in Calvin's writings makes the proponents of a "Calvinistic philosophy" fall back, I think, on a weaker sense of "Calvinistic rationality." That is to say, while it is *not* asserted that Calvin *himself* developed a complete concept of rationality, he is regarded as implicitly *suggesting* a way of being rational which in its articulation goes beyond what Calvin actually wrote but is considered to remain faithful to his intention. In this situation, exegesis of Calvin's writings is necessary only to indicate the *source of insight*, while the *ground of appeal and defense* is not to the writings of Calvin but to the works of his developers and perfectors.

This is, of course, precisely the issue before us. Is the concept of rationality so developed and defended essentially that of Calvin, or has an unsystematic notion found in selected passages of Calvin's writings been isolated, exploited and exalted as crucial to Calvinism? If the former, then those who can identify, develop and defend this concept of rationality are warranted in calling themselves "Calvinists." If the latter is true, and to the extent that a single and coherent concept of rationality is central to the enterprise in question and therefore to the interpretation of Calvin, then the designation "Calvinist" would seem to be inaccurate and historically tendentious because it is tangential to the work of Calvin himself as a whole. At best, it would be a "courtesy" designation.

In any case, this essay will not attempt to deal *definitively* with the subject of Calvinism as a whole or in part, nor does it purport to offer an answer to the question of rationality. Rather it ventures the first step of trying to ascertain what Calvin himself actually taught concerning rationality. The approach to that objective is based on the assumption that human rationality depends on what is meant by the "human." That is to say, the doctrine of man is the wider context within which the concept of rationality is to be abstracted. Thus, the primary focus of this essay is on Calvin's concept of the human as developed in the *Institutes* and then on the role of reason therein.

II

Calvin's anthropology is, of course, an integral element of his theology, and in dealing with it such topics as the image of God, will and intellect have often been explicated. However, the exposition of these components—while treating important and even crucial aspects of Calvin's thought—almost inevitably distorts the theological context of his anthropology by focusing on and thereby isolating anthropological themes from the theological perspective in which Calvin views them.[1] Doubtless, detailed studies of the various parts of Calvin's theology and critical analysis of the scholarly discussion of them is essential, but these often ignore, or minimize, the way in which the whole modifies the part.

Calvin begins the *Institutes* with a well-known programmatic statement. "Nearly all the wisdom we possess . . . consists of two parts: the knowledge of God and of ourselves" (I,i,1).[2] In the light of that statement, one would, I think, expect Calvin to devote a major section of the *Institutes* to the knowledge of ourselves, presumably including our reason and its use. However, Calvin views our very being as nothing but subsistence in the one God (I,i,1), so that human knowledge is not achieved until one has first looked on God's face. Therefore, Calvin writes that however mutually connected the knowledge of God and the self may be, the right order of teaching requires that the knowledge of God be treated before the knowledge of ourselves (I,i,2). It is surely significant that Calvin does not deal with anthropology in a separate section. This fact would strongly suggest and even demand the conclusion that, for Calvin, anthropology and theology are not separable; to focus on the human apart from God is erroneous not merely in fact but also in principle.[3] Thus, Calvin's anthropology is not merely *tinged* by his theology but *permeated* by it.

If, then, the human self, in even relative isolation from God, is a dangerous heuristic abstraction, it follows that the human being is a "being in relation to God," and this relationship is *dominated by the action of God.* That Calvin's doctrine of God is Trinitarian in form indicates that his theological anthropology will not be different. Thus the investigation of it may be summarized at the beginning as an exploration of the anthropological meaning of being (1) created by God, (2) united into Christ, and (3) filled with the Holy Spirit.

Book I of the *Institutes* is devoted to the knowledge of God the Creator who is revealed to us (1) in the universe and (2) in the Scripture. In dealing with the creation of humanity, Calvin asserts that the knowledge of ourselves is twofold: our originally created and upright nature, and the miserable condition to which we are subjected because of sin. The first he discusses in I,xv in terms of the faculties of soul and the image of God. The second, the fallen condition (which we will consider in the next part), is treated not as the anthropological result of the doctrine of creation *but* as the anthropological introduction to the doctrine of redemption—a kind of factual preface without a theoretically necessary and systematic location (II,i-v).

(1) Calvin thinks it obvious that man consists of body and soul, and that the soul, as an immortal but created essence, transcends the world of the body in knowing God. The image of God extends to the body, but its proper seat is the soul. Thus, the image of God in Adam's original integrity meant the "full possession of right understanding," the "affections kept within the bounds of reason," the "senses tempered in right order" and all human excellence properly referred to the exceptional gifts bestowed upon the creature by the Creator (I,xv,3). To be more precise, "the human soul consists of two faculties, understanding and will." The purpose of the gift of

understanding was to distinguish good from evil, and the purpose of the will was to choose and follow the good and to reject evil (I,xv,7).

According to Calvin, Adam could have remained in this created state, but he fell solely by his own will, thus corrupting the gifts of understanding and will. Calvin admits that it would seem to be more excellent if God had created mankind with the constancy to persevere in the created state, but to argue the point is to quarrel with God about what lies hidden in his plan. It is enough to affirm that man had the ability to persevere if he had willed to do so, but that not willing of his own free choice, he lost the ability to persevere. Yet Calvin insists that the fall contributes to the glory of God (I,xv,8).

While Calvin thinks it is worthwhile to know about the estate of mankind as created, such knowledge of ourselves he regards as of little benefit unless we also recognize our corrupted nature (I,xv,1).[4] That is to say, our original integrity is now contrary to fact and is properly to be described in terms of the renewal of God's image in us which is effected by Jesus Christ.

The two major anthropological themes of the knowledge of God the Creator in Book I are the creation of mankind and God's providence for mankind.[5] Although these themes are treated "reasonably," they are not based on an appeal to their inherent rationality. Calvin explicitly recognizes that reason can conceive a created constancy to persevere—the lack of which he cannot explain other than to assert the mystery of God's hidden plan. Doubtless, Calvin's discussion of the image of God, the will and intellect is influenced by classical philosophy and its appropriation in the theological tradition. But these insights are judged on the basis of Scriptural relevation and most especially in terms of the relationship of the human and divine, a relationship which must include an adequate description of his teaching on Christ, the Holy Spirit and the Church.

III

Having dealt with our original creation, Calvin begins Book II with a consideration of our corruption and the miserable condition after the disobedience of Adam which led to our ruin. Calvin insists that we are perverted in every part of our nature (II,i,8). We are by nature children of wrath (Eph. 2:3). Calvin cautions that this statement must not be understood as referring to nature as created by God, but only to nature as vitiated in Adam. However, our condition is not merely the result of Adam's fault but also of our own, so that

Calvin can say, too, that our "entire nature is opposed to supernatural grace" (II,i,9). The extension of Adam's fall to the entire human race is then not only the divine ordination but the human reality. Moreover, the disobedience of Adam led not simply to the ruin of the human race but "perverted the whole order of nature in heaven and earth" (I,i,5), which means that all creatures are subject to corruption (Rom. 8) because "they are bearing part of the punishment deserved by man, for whose use they were created" (II,i,5).

The absolute condemnation of mankind at least seems complete; but two points should be noted. First, Calvin refuses to give sin an ontological grounding or justification: "it is an adventitious quality which comes upon man rather than a substantial property which has been implanted from the beginning" (II,i,11). Since sin has no ontological reality, Calvin rejects the speculation that God might have forestalled Adam's fall by giving him the grace of perseverance in his created state. Such a thought imputes blame to God the Creator rather than ascribing the defect to mankind, where Calvin says it properly belongs (although a defect in the creature would seem logically to be the responsibility of the Creator).[6] That is to say, Calvin appeals to the mystery of God's will in describing the situation of sin in which we find ourselves, rather than allowing (although he has entertained) rational speculation[7] about what might have been possible for an omnipotent Creator.

Second, Calvin does not teach the *total* depravity of mankind as a principle in the way some "Calvinists" suppose. Calvin asserts that God's image in us was not totally annihilated, although he adds that it was so corrupted that whatever remains is frightful deformity (I,xv,4). This means that no good thing remains in our power. Nevertheless we are obligated to aspire toward a good of which we are empty (II,ii,1), although Calvin does not show how this aspiration is possible in the light of the human situation. Having treated in some detail the perversion of reason and will, it is obvious that Calvin regards human corruption as extensive, in the sense that no part has remained pure and unaffected by sin. Calvin sometimes asserts the adequacy of reason (II,ii,13; II,ii,17) and often asserts its inadequacy (compare Jn. 3:31)[8] but he does not tell us *how* to distinguish them. However, Calvin thinks it would be unfair to God to heap abuse on his creature, although Calvin himself finds a great deal to criticize about the human condition. In any case, mankind is not totally depraved in the sense that one could be no worse, but only in the sense that all have fallen short (from the human perspective: some shorter than others) and all require a total renewal. The fact of sin, then, should not lead simply to our rebuke but to our edification, so that in God's mercy we may recover what was lost (II,iii,2).

Calvin concludes that the created order was such "that the frame of the universe should be the school in which we were to learn piety, and from it pass over to eternal life and felicity" (II,vi,1). However, "after the fall of the first man no knowledge of God apart from the mediator has had power unto salvation" *(Ibid.)*. Therefore, God is comprehended in Christ alone (II,vi,4) until such time as we shall see God as he is (II,xiv,3). According to Calvin, God cannot be known apart from Christ. "[A]ll thinking about God outside Christ is a vast abyss which immediately swallows up all our thoughts." Therefore, those who philosophize about God without Christ are deluded (compare I Pet. 1:20; I Jn. 2:22).

Early in Book I, Calvin had asserted that the knowledge of God is twofold; that is to say, the Lord who shows himself as Creator is also seen as Redeemer in the face of Christ (I,ii,1). In Book II, following the description of sin, Calvin turns to the second element and deals with what God has done *for* us in Jesus Christ. This exposition of the knowledge of God the Redeemer also begins the exposition of ourselves as redeemed persons. The remainder of the *Institutes* is devoted to this discussion. Thus, in an important sense, Calvin's anthropology includes a *threefold* knowledge of ourselves: (1) as created, (2) as corrupted, and (3) as redeemed, although the second is bracketed in an ontological but not an existential sense, if such a distinction may be allowed.

Calvin does not attempt to treat the knowledge of God the Redeemer apart from the existing human condition. Since we are not able to ascend to God, he says "it was necessary [although not of simple or absolute necessity] for the Son of God to become for us 'Immanuel, that is, God with us' " (II,xii,1).

In dealing with our redemption, Calvin seeks to preclude two errors which are important for us to notice. The first error is that mankind as created can be disassociated from Christ, as might be inferred from the doctrine of creation. In opposition to Osiander, Calvin asserts that Christ *was* not created in the image of the essentially righteous Adam, but rather that whatever excellence was engraved upon the unfallen Adam "derived from the fact that he approached the glory of his Creator through the only begotten Son" (II,xii,6).

The second error is the notion that the revelation of Christ is solely and simply the result of God's response to human sin. Calvin believes that "[e]ven if man had remained free from all stain, his condition would have been too lowly for him to reach God without a Mediator" (II,xii,1) and asserts "that in the original order of creation and the unfallen state of nature Christ was set over men and angels as their Head" (II,xii,4). However, Calvin refuses to carry this affirmation into a speculation. The conviction that Christ would still have become man if mankind had *not* needed redemption, Calvin regards as idle speculation since it is contrary to fact. The belief that Christ might have taken on human flesh for the purpose of showing love toward those who are *not* lost, Calvin rejects as a useless inquiry since in fact all are lost. In actuality the fall is set "between man's first origin and the restoration that we obtain through Christ" (II,xii,7).

From an anthropological perspective we do not learn much about ourselves as redeemed in Book II of the *Institutes*. This is to be explained, I think, by the fact that Calvin's Christology is *objectively* presented here. The subjective, anthropological meaning of Christology—that is, faith in Christ—is found in Book III. There Calvin admits the human conflict between doubt and certainty within the "godly heart" (III,ii,18), but faith understands that, in everything, we deal with God. Therefore, "[u]nbelief does not hold sway within believers' hearts, but assails them from without" (III,ii,21). "Accordingly, nothing prevents believers from being afraid and at the same time possessing the surest consolation; according as they turn their eyes now upon their own vanity, and then bring the thought of their minds to bear upon the truth of God" (III,ii,23). However, Calvin unexpectedly objects to what would seem the logical conclusion that if one contemplates Christ, there is sure salvation, but if one turns back to the self, there is sure damnation. The ground of Calvin's objection is that we await salvation from Christ *not* as if Christ were at some distance from us, "but because he makes us, engrafted into his body, participants not only in all his benefits but also in himself." That is to say, Christ does not stand afar off but dwells in us. "We ought not to separate Christ from ourselves or ourselves from him" (III,ii,24). In short, when Christ "illumines us into faith by the power of his Spirit, at the same time [he] so engrafts us into his body that we become partakers of every good" (III,ii,35).

Calvin asserts (epistemologically) but does not explain (ontologically) how sin is able to enter the world which God created. Moreover, he does not distinguish in precise detail between our created nature and our corrupted nature, nor between Adam's sin and our sin. Human reason is not totally destroyed but it is frightfully deformed. Presumably this means that, like a crippled limb, we may and must use it, but we cannot be certain when and where it will fail us. This fact, too, will teach us humility. Indeed, "the foundation of our philosophy is humility" (II,ii,11). It is abundantly clear that the ground of our confidence is not at all in the power of reason, but in the fact that we are not separated from Christ who dwells in us and we in him.

The chief anthropological result of Book II is that in setting forth who the Redeemer is *in himself* and what he has done *for us*, Calvin has prepared the way for developing the theme of redemption *in us*. This conclusion not only reveals the relationship between the Christology of Book II and the Pneumatology of Book III, but points beyond the emphasis on personal redemption in Book III to the focus on corporate redemption (in the Church) in Book IV.[9]

IV

The major subject of Book I (God the Creator) and Book II (God the Redeemer) is clear, but this is not the case with Book III. One can say, accurately enough, that Book I is concerned with theology proper, Book II with Christology, Book III with soteriology and Book IV with ecclesiology. However, these classifications are not exact. For example, Book II and Book IV are also soteriological, as is the section in Book I on providence. We have seen that, in the main, Calvin discusses mankind as created and provided for in Book I; mankind as fallen was treated chiefly in Book II, but theologically and systematically located in brackets between the knowledge of God the Creator and the knowledge of God the Redeemer. From the perspective of anthropology, mankind as redeemed is spread over Books II,vi-IV, and Book II sets the Christological focus. By extension from the titles of Book I and Book II, one might expect that the title of Book III would be some form of the knowledge of God the Holy Spirit. Instead, it is "The Way in Which We Receive the Grace of Christ: What Benefits Come to Us From It and What Effects Follow."

At the beginning of Book III, Calvin indicates that Books I and II dealt in some sense *objectively* with the topics, while the work of God the Father revealed in Jesus Christ the Son, *subjectively* considered, is the domain of the Holy Spirit. Thus he writes:

> As long as Christ remains outside of us, and we are separated from him, all that he has suffered and done for the salvation of the human race remains useless and of no value for us. Therefore, to share with us what he has received from the Father, he had to become ours and to dwell within us. For this reason, he is called "our Head"

> [Eph. 4:15], and "the first-born among many brethren" [Rom. 8:29]. We also, in turn, are said to be "engrafted into him" [Rom. 11:17], and to "put on Christ" [Gal. 3:27]; for as I have said, all that he possesses is nothing to us until we grow into the body with him (III,i,1).

The objective knowledge of God as Creator and Redeemer and of ourselves as created, fallen and redeemed is worthless to us, then, as long as it is "outside" us. That is to say, we must receive the benefits *within us* which the Father bestowed upon the Son for our sake by the secret energy of the Spirit, and these benefits we obtain by faith—which is the principal work of the Holy Spirit (III,i,4).

Earlier in Book I Calvin had affirmed the eternal deity and essence of the Spirit rather briefly and even cursorily (I,xiii,14-15). In Book III he emphasizes not distinctions, but rather relations of the Father, Son, Spirit and us. That is, "God the Father gives us the Holy Spirit for his Son's sake, and yet has bestowed the whole fullness of the Spirit upon the Son to be minister and steward of his liberality." For this reason, the Spirit is sometimes called the "Spirit of the Father," sometimes the "Spirit of the Son" (III,i,2). Moreover, "the Holy Spirit is the bond by which Christ effectually unites us to himself" (III,i,1). Without the Spirit, "Christ, so to speak, lies idle because we coldly contemplate him as outside ourselves . . . but he unites himself to us by the Spirit alone" (III,i,3). And in being united to Christ, Calvin affirms that the Spirit "so breathes divine life into us that we are no longer actuated by ourselves but are ruled by his action and prompting" (III,i,3). In such statements, individual and separate identities of the divine or human are difficult to locate because Calvin does not differentiate sharply between the Spirit and the Father, nor between the Spirit and the Son, nor indeed between the Spirit and the human self. Moreover, it is impossible to decide whether Book III is mainly concerned with the doctrine of the Holy Spirit or the believer's benefits.

In any case, if Calvin had intended to articulate a view of human rationality as an essential component of Christian doctrine, Book III would seem to be the proper, systematic location for its exposition. That is to say, an account would be given of the restoration of the created reason from corruption and of the use and limitations of this "redeemed" reason in some detail.[10]

On the contrary, Calvin teaches that "[T]he foundation of faith would be frail and unsteady if it rested on human wisdom . . ." (compare Eph. 1:13). Human reason can understand neither who God is nor his relation to mankind (II,i,18). Therefore Calvin regards the mixing of human philosophy with Christ as a corruption (e.g., I,x,3) and distinguishes between human philosophy based on reason and Christian philosophy which is grounded on Scripture and the guidance of the Holy Spirit. "[C]hristian philosophy bids reason give way to, submit, and subject itself to, the Holy Spirit . . ." (III,vii,1; cf. II,ii,26).

Calvin indeed places logic *(dialectica)* among the learned sciences which proceed from God (compare Is. 28:29) and affirms that reason separates us from the beasts (II,ii,12; II,ii,17). But human reason can also be called "Satan's logic" (compare Mt. 27:43). Thus Calvin is willing to affirm what seem to be dialectical opposites: divine omnipotence and human responsibility (compare Lk. 24:45), and both God's love and wrath. God bestows grace on a few which could justly be denied to all (III,xxiv,3). If one asks for a reason, the answer is hidden in God (CO 8, 278).

Etienne Gilson correctly observes that what Calvin calls "Christian philosophy" is based on faith rather than reason. Of course, Gilson's own paradigm for Christian philosophy is the relative complementarity of reason and revelation in Thomism.[11] Calvin rejects Thomas' view of nature and grace (II,iii,1), but his reference to the difference between "earthly things" (for which reason is more or less adequate) and "heavenly things" (for which it is not) (II,ii,13) deals with the same issue but without providing, or attempting, a complete framework for its understanding. If Calvin is unable to specify the limitations of created reason in the light of "carnal" reason, he is also unable to specify the use of "redeemed" reason.[12]

There are several ways to account for the omission of a sustained account of the use and limitations of reason in the systematic development of Calvin's *Institutes*. Yet it is obvious that he is concerned about faith, which he declares cannot be obtained by human effort since it is beyond human comprehension. Faith is defined as "a firm and certain knowledge of God's benevolence toward us, founded upon the truth of the freely given promise in Christ, both revealed to our minds and sealed upon our hearts through the Holy Spirit" (III,ii,7). From this faith issues the "double grace" (III,xi,1): regeneration by faith, and justification by faith—both of which "are conferred on us by Christ."

This faith is passive in the sense that we bring nothing of ours to the recovering of God's favor but receive from Christ what we lack (III,xiii,5). "Faith of itself [meaning our human faith?] does not possess the power of justifying, but only in so far as it receives Christ" (III,xi,7). Faith is an earthen vessel but the treasure is the gold hidden in it. Similarly, we should not confuse the pot which does not make us rich with the gold which does. We are not our own but belong to Christ and are united to him. That is, "we hold ourselves to be united with Christ by the secret power of his Spirit" (III,xi,5).

> Therefore, that joining together of head and members, that indwelling of Christ in our hearts—in short that mystical union—are accorded by us the highest degree of importance, so that Christ, having been made ours makes us sharers with him in the gifts with which he has been endowed" (III,xi,10).

The next major section of the *Institutes*, concerned with eternal election and the leading role of God in it, is well-known. Although the doctrine of predestination is scarcely the central dogma of Calvin—as some have thought—it is the culmination of the doctrine of *faith* as Calvin has expounded it. This is not a rational implication or deduction from the doctrine of the sovereignty of God conceived as an abstract principle.

V

The conclusion is, I think, that in his exposition of the knowledge of the human self, Calvin sees no need to develop human verities, including reason, over against (or even systematically within) the truth of God. There is no need to assert human independence over against the sovereign will of God. In short, there is no need to assert man over against God. This is due to the inclusiveness of his conception of our union with Christ, which does not require nor permit demonstration by a chain of reasoning since it is based on faith—the gift of the Holy Spirit.

Calvin regards the human reason—without defining it precisely—as an adequate, although never infallible, tool for making "earthly" decisions based on available (or collectible) evidence and for relating theological items which are revealed in Scripture. Human reason also plays a part in our careful reflection on items revealed in Scripture but not connected in an evident way to all who consider them as they arise separately. Reason is denied as an unrestricted power or ability to speculate (cf. I,xiv,4) accurately into the mysteries of God beyond his revelation. Reason cannot demonstrate relations and conclusions based on the conviction of the conformity of the universe to any canons of human rationality.[13]

If this were a correctable lack of rational precision on Calvin's part, then one might be encouraged to correct it in some fashion. But if the Christian faith involves unresolved, and seemingly unresolvable, logical tensions (or paradoxes, or antinomies) then a "concept of rationality" which excludes them in principle would lead theology into philosophy, and confession into demonstration.

Calvin's own use of reason seems to be eclectic and unsystematic. His "Christian philosophy" uses reason (within limits), but it is based on faith. Thus, to require the development of a sophisticated concept of rationality as an essential part of understanding or completing Calvin's theology, is debatable at best. At least it is obvious that Calvin himself did not provide one. On the other hand, if no one view of rationality is required, any number may be allowed, so long as they are not judged as distortions of Calvin's theology. Like music, a theology may be transposed into a different key or arranged for a different instrument. The acceptance of the sound (for music) or the soundness (for theology) depends on the approval of the audience. And that is the subject of another *étude*.

Notes

1. I have in mind especially T.F. Torrance, *Calvin's Doctrine of Man* (London: Lutterworth Press, 1949), pp. 18, 19, who correctly writes that Calvin's doctrine of man can only be formulated truly from the standpoint of the grace of God in Jesus Christ. However, Torrance then adds that Calvin also points "out the value of thinking of ourselves *apart from grace*" (italics added) which is explained as a didactic device used by Calvin for effect. On this interpretation Torrance can focus directly on anthropological themes (e.g. the image of God in man [4 chapters], the sin of man [3 chapters])—in some sense setting aside their theological context. At the same time, Torrance admits that these "moral denunciations of man, apart from the context of grace, . . . do not stand up to [Calvin's] own investigations" and affirms that God's grace is the context of anthropology. I would argue that to look at Calvin's anthropology apart from its theological context is to see it out of focus.
2. Calvin's *Institutes* in the Library of Christian Classics edition, ed. by John T. McNeill and trans. by Ford Lewis Battles is cited in the text by book, chapter, and paragraph.
3. It is obvious, but perhaps worth recalling, that Calvin was not aware of developments concerning the notion of the separate self with which we are familiar and which, to some extent, determine our interests and questions. That is to say, the Cartesian dualism, the Humean skepticism, the Kantian transcendentalism, and the Freudian critique were all beyond his cognizance. While Calvin most certainly utilized the available anthropological insights of "secular" thinkers such as Plato and Aristotle, it is primarily in terms of Scripture and its understanding that Calvin sought to base his theological anthropology.

4. Calvin criticizes the philosophers for their ignorance of human corruption and its effect on the reason (I,xv,7; II,ii,12).
5. Before Calvin turns directly to our miserable condition, he devotes three chapters to the doctrine of the Creator's providence. Among other things, Calvin says that "God's will is the highest and first cause of all things because nothing happens except from his command or permission" (I,xvi,8). And it is important to notice that God's command, decree, *and permission* seem to be equivalent for Calvin rather than different (cf. I,xviii,1). Calvin's view of providence is a vigorous "Theo-ergism," but—while Calvin asserts them—it is difficult to account for human freedom and responsibility apart from and within his strong insistence upon the action of God.
6. Cf. J.L. Mackie, "Evil and Omnipotence," *Mind*, LXIV, 254 (1955), pp. 200-212.
7. On the subject of Calvin's opposition to speculation, see E.P. Meijerling, *Calvin wider die Neugierde* (Nieuwkoop: B. de Graaf, 1980).
8. Calvin's Commentaries are cited in the text by book, chapter, and verse.
9. Book IV is a continuation of Calvin's exposition of faith in Christ developed in terms of "outward helps" (that is, the church and sacraments) which not only beget and increase faith within us, but gather us together.
10. Calvin does not (!) assert that reason in the redeemed person is restored to its original, uncrippled, pre-fall condition and capacity. The closest he comes is in III,ii,34 where he writes that when we come to Christ, drawn by the Holy Spirit, we are lifted up in mind and heart *above our understanding* so that the soul illumined by the Holy Spirit takes on a new keenness, as it were, to contemplate the heavenly mysteries. This statement, however, is not a defense of the power of redeemed rationality, but an affirmation of the work of the Holy Spirit in interpreting the Word.
11. Etienne Gilson, *Christianity and Philosophy*, trans. by Ralph MacDonald (New York: Sheed and Ward, 1939), pp. 14, 18.
12. Later Calvinists, feeling the need for a clearer concept of reason than that provided by Calvin, returned to the views of Aristotle and Thomas. (See, for example, John Patrick Donnelly, "Italian Influences on the Development of Calvinist Scholasticism," *The Sixteenth Century Journal*, VII [April, 1976], pp. 81-101, and his "Calvinist Thomism," *Viator*, 7 [1976], pp. 441-5.) The notion that the breakdown of the Thomistic synthesis of reason and revelation was a great loss to Reformed Theology is seen in R.C. Sproul (quoted in Jack B. Rogers and Donald K. McKim, *The Authority and Interpretation of the Bible* [New York: Harper and Row, 1979], pp. 197-8), who identifies himself as a "Reformed, Calvinistic, evangelical Protestant" and laments "the loss of the medieval synthesis of Christian theology and philosophy achieved by St. Thomas Aquinas." Quite contrary to Thomas' admiration for Aristotle, Luther remarked in "To the Christian Nobility of the German Nation" that either God had

sent Aristotle as a plague upon us on account of our sins or that the devil had sent him.

13. I regard the second part of the statement in the *Westminster Confession* (I,vi) that "the whole counsel of God is either expressly set down in Scripture *or* by good and necessary consequence may be deduced from Scripture" as fundamentally unCalvinian. This definition seems to replace the medieval view of the sources of knowledge: Scripture and Tradition, with Scripture and Deduction! We must, of course, draw conclusions from and make applications of Scripture, but our deductions, even when they appear to us "good and necessary," are not on the same level as Scripture and do not demand the same commitment nor allow the same confidence.

Faith and Reason in Calvin's Doctrine of the Knowledge of God

Dewey J. Hoitenga, Jr.

THE ESSENTIAL INGREDIENTS—AND PROBLEMS—in John Calvin's doctrine of the knowledge of God are encompassed already in the first seven chapters of Book I of his major work, the *Institutes of the Christian Religion*. By way of a study of these seven chapters and selected relevant material from later portions (especially I,xv; II,i-iii; and III,ii), I try to set forth in what follows both the main ideas in Calvin's teaching and some of the main problems which arise from these ideas. My general conclusion is that Calvin's theory of religious knowledge is not only Christian and biblical, but also broadly Platonic and Augustinian. An interpretation of his thought that leaves out any of these components is therefore bound to be incomplete. More specifically I conclude that Calvin has no well-defined epistemology as such, insofar as he offers no analysis of the relationship between faith and reason and makes no attempt to define such different noetic states as knowledge, belief, certainty, error and ignorance in the way philosophers do.

That Calvin's doctrine of the knowledge of God is *biblical* and *Christian* means simply, but profoundly, that it is informed by the ideas of *creation, fall* and *redemption*. So the main ingredients in his doctrine can be reviewed by looking at three questions. First, what in man's knowledge of God is owing to creation, his being made by God? Second, what in that knowledge is owing to the fall, his original sin and disobedience? And, third, what in that knowledge is owing to redemption, his salvation by the gracious activity of God in his Son Jesus Christ? I turn, then, to an exposition of Calvin's religious epistemology, following the lead of these three questions.

I. Creation

Man is created by God in such a way that his knowledge of God is (1) a result of an inner capacity interacting with his experience of the workmanship of the universe; and (2) connected in a definite way with the knowledge of himself. Let us look at each of these in turn.

A) The Sense of Divinity and *the Workmanship of the Universe*

The Sense of Divinity. "There is within the human mind," says Calvin, "and indeed by natural instinct, an awareness of divinity" (I,iii,i). Here, and elsewhere, Calvin preserves the concept of *nature*, the *natural*, which was his legacy from Greek and Medieval thought. There is about man—and the world—something objectively given: an intelligible structure, and it is good. Calvin thus manifests a continuity with the classical tradition which some of his modern followers sacrifice, when they give up the idea of nature altogether. For example, John Baillie writes: "The truth is that there is in man no *nature* apart from *revelation*. Human nature is constituted by the self-disclosure to this poor dust of the spirit of the living God."[1] This absorption of an ontological idea (nature) by an epistemological one (revelation) is a typically modern development, and it is entirely foreign to Calvin. For him the ontological status of human nature is instead *confirmed* by the revelation in Scripture, which teaches that it is the creation of God.

To be sure, Calvin uses the term "natural" also to describe the present, *fallen* condition of mankind, for a reason that actually enhances his use of the term in its traditional sense:

> Therefore we declare that man is corrupted through natural vitiation, but a vitiation that did not flow from his nature. We deny that it has flowed from nature in order to indicate that it is an adventitious quality which comes upon man rather than a substantial property which has been implanted from the beginning. Yet we call it "natural" in order that no man may think that anyone obtains it through bad conduct, since it holds all men fast by hereditary right (II,ii,11).[2]

In any case, "once this double use of 'nature' is understood, Calvin's meaning at a given place is easily determined by context" (I,ii,3 n.7).

If it is clear, now, that Calvin believes there is a *natural* awareness of God in men, we are ready to ask about its content. Its content is both simple and momentous: "that there is a God and that he is their Maker" (I,iii,1). A question then arises. How does the sense of divinity *(sensus divinitatis)* result in so much—the knowledge both that there is a God, and that he is our Maker? E.A. Dowey observes that the *sensus divinitatis* "is not very closely defined in Calvin's thought." In particular, it does not seem to be a "special organ or faculty of the soul."[3] This seems to be supported by the fact that Calvin does not return to it except for one brief reference to the "seed of religion" when, following Plato, he later describes the faculties of the soul (I,xv,6; see also 2, 7-8). He takes fantasy (perception), reason and understanding to be "the three cognitive faculties of the soul" (I,xv,6). The conclusion is plausible, even though Calvin does not draw it, that *reason* formulates for understanding the content of the *sensus divinitatis, viz.*, the propositions that God exists, that he is our Maker—and others, e.g., that he is majestic, ought to be worshipped, and even, indeed, that he is just *one* being (I,x,3). These are the propositions, then, that constitute the knowledge of God available to all men by natural reason alone—meaning by this, reason in conjunction with the sense of divinity. Granting this much significance to reason in Calvin is supported by his own writings: "The more anyone endeavors to approach to God, the more he proves himself endowed with reason" (I,xv,6). Not only does Calvin thus see no conflict between the knowledge of God and the function of natural reason, he actually regards the knowledge of God as its highest and final purpose:

> Man in his first condition excelled in these pre-eminent endowments, so that his reason, understanding, prudence, and judgment not only sufficed for the direction of his earthly life, but by them men mounted up even to God and eternal bliss (I,xv,8).

Nothing that Calvin says later about the effects of sin on human reason conflicts with this account (II,ii,12-17). When he says in his famous statement that "the greatest geniuses are blinder than moles," he refers exclusively, it should be noted, to the knowledge of *piety* (II,ii,18). Of course, since the fall (and even before the fall), man's natural endowments require the addition of "supernatural gifts" in order to issue in this knowledge of piety. "Stripped" of these by the fall, the "natural gifts" became corrupted and remain so until they are "recovered through the grace of regeneration." This recovery requires the reinstatement of these supernatural gifts (II,ii,12). The distinction between this knowledge of *piety* and a *deficient* knowledge due to the fall is essential to a complete picture of Calvin's teaching; it will be set forth in sections II and III below. The difference between them arises out of the doctrines of the fall and the redemption. These doctrines, however, do not obviate the doctrine of creation (nature), but instead presuppose it.

Although Calvin elaborates the sense of divinity as a knowledge of God which "has been naturally implanted in the minds of men," modern Calvinists tend to interpret it as a "natural revelation" of God within man.[4] T.H.L. Parker supports the point by observing that the *sensus divinitatis*, since it provides knowledge of the existence of God, makes any *argument* for that existence unnecessary. He concludes from this that "the problem of the knowledge of God is the problem of revelation" and not a problem in natural theology, as he claims it is in Aquinas, with whom he sets Calvin in contrast.[5] The conclusion does not follow. What might follow is that the *intuitive* knowledge provided by the *sensus divinitatis* renders unnecessary the *inferential* knowledge presupposed in St. Thomas' "Five Ways." But that is a different question than whether the *sensus divinitatis* is a knowledge of God by nature or by revelation. How then does Parker reach this conclusion? He does so by making the following claim about revelation:

> Revelation implies not only the impossibility of knowledge without it but also the will of God to be known and his ability to make himself known, as well as the capability of man to receive revelation (even if this capability is caused by revelation itself).[6]

But to claim, as Parker does, that revelation implies the impossibility of any other kind of knowledge of God simply begs the question.

At any rate, the introduction of the concept of revelation at this point in the *Institutes* to explain the *sensus divinitatis* is gratuitous. The *sensus divinitatus* is simply a natural knowledge of God owing to the way man is created. It is thus a knowledge that originates differently than the knowledge of revelation. That is how Calvin also presents it. He makes no reference himself to "revelation" in his discussion here. Revelation is a concept he first introduces in chapter v when he discusses the knowledge of God from the "whole workmanship of the universe." Why did he not employ the concept in chapter iii already, if "the problem of the knowledge of God is the problem of revelation"? Apparently he simply saw part of the problem of the knowledge of God as the problem of man's *nature:*

> This conviction is fixed deep within, as it were in the very marrow .... It is not a doctrine that must first be learned in school, but one of which each of us is master from his mother's womb and which *nature* itself permits no one to forget . . ." (I,iii,3, emphasis added).

The Workmanship of the Universe. God's purpose in placing the sense of divinity within man, as well as placing man within a marvelously constructed universe, is man's piety and happiness:

> Lest anyone, then, be excluded from access to happiness, he not only sowed in men's minds the seed of religion of which we have spoken

> but revealed himself and daily discloses himself in the whole workmanship in the universe (I,v,i).

Calvin finds man's actual response so revolting that he spends much of his eloquence upon it:

> How detestable, I ask you, is this madness; that man, finding God in his body and soul a hundred times, on this very pretense of excellence denies that there is a God? . . .
>
> . . . And certainly however much the glory of God shines forth, scarcely one man in a hundred is a true spectator of it! . . .
>
> [Even] Plato, the most religious of all and the most circumspect, also vanishes in his round globe (I,v,4,8,11; see also 12-14).

Calvin's eloquent rhetoric on the greatness and goodness of God in his creation and the stupidity and misery of men who fail to respond to him in piety does not, however, get at one question. How, precisely, does man come to know God from the universe around him? Is it by revelation (a word Calvin begins to use for the first time in this chapter) or by reason? The answer is not very clear from what Calvin says.

It must be emphasized that the knowledge in question, like that provided by the sense of divinity, is not the knowledge of piety. Although that is the purpose of the knowledge, men can (and do) refuse to respond in piety. The point for the present context is that the knowledge of God from the "workmanship of the universe" is like that of the *sensus divinitatis:* both are *naturally* present in all men, in virtue of how God created them. It is a knowledge that persists even after the fall amidst the differentiation introduced by redemption: "This way of seeking God is common both to strangers and to those of his household, if they trace the outlines that above and below sketch a living likeness of him" (I,v,6). How, then, does such knowledge, abstracted from a pious or impious response, arise?

One possible answer is, again, by revelation. Although Calvin uses the term occasionally, in this context, he does not define it. It seems, however, that he wishes to distinguish his occasional use of it here quite sharply from an "inner revelation of God through faith" which differs, as we shall see below, by being inward, verbal and effective in leading men to the knowledge of piety (I,v,14). Revelation in nature, by contrast, is outward, non-verbal and ineffective in leading to the pious knowledge of God. It is outward in that it involves both the workmanship of the universe and man's own nature—insofar as that, too, is a fascinating, intricately designed object in the universe (v,5). Further, this design and order is non-verbal;

it is no "word" spoken, in contrast with the claims Calvin later makes for the revelation in Scripture. Instead, the order and beauty of nature serve as "marks" of his glory; as a sort of "mirror in which we can contemplate God, who is otherwise invisible"; and again, as "evidences . . . that declare his wonderful wisdom," as "signs of divinity" (I,v,1,2,4). Nature bears all these marks, signs and evidences quite simply because it is not God himself, but his creation—an effect of which he is the cause (I,v,6).

God, then, is not literally known *in* his creation, but *from* it—indirectly, as from a sign to what is signified. Such knowledge, I conclude, must be inferential, requiring reason to take a step from the evidence to what is evident. Admittedly Calvin does not himself interpret his language as suggesting an inferential knowledge of God. He wishes instead to convey a sense of the unavoidability and universality of the knowledge: "Men cannot open their eyes without being compelled to see him" (I,v,1). But inferences can be as "compelling" as revelation. Again, "we see that no long or toilsome proof is needed to elicit evidences that serve to illuminate and affirm the divine majesty." His point here must not be misunderstood. When he writes this he is not referring to inference from evidence to what is evident, but to arguments *for the evidences themselves. These* are the arguments that he says are unnecessary, since the evidences "are so very manifest and obvious that they can easily be observed with the eyes and pointed out with the finger" (I,v,9). Those who are trained in "the liberal arts penetrate with their aid far more deeply into the secrets of the divine wisdom. Yet ignorance of them prevents no one from seeing more than enough of God's workmanship in his creation to lead him to break forth in admiration to the Artificer" (I,v,2). I conclude that there is nothing in Calvin's presentation that precludes an inferential quality to the knowledge of God from the workmanship of nature, and much that suggests or even requires it.

Dowey makes much of the "rational quality" of the arguments implicit in Calvin's discussion; yet he interprets the resulting knowledge as owing to revelation.[7] As in the analogous case of the *sensus divinitatis* above, this transformation of a natural, inferential knowledge of God into revelation seems to be unfounded. What Calvin holds is, instead, that men have been created in such a way—with an innate sense of divinity and in the midst of a marvelously designed universe—that they cannot avoid a natural knowledge of God. Reason, a natural faculty, functions either to formulate the propositional content of the immediate perceptions of the former or to infer the existence and power of God from the latter, or both. As we saw above, some writers (Parker, for example) think that an innate awareness of God's existence renders inference and argument unnecessary. It seems instead that they can be combined, judging from Calvin's own addition of the external "evidences" of God in the cosmos to the *sensus divinitatis* within.[8]

B) The Knowledge of God and the Knowledge of the Self

As we shall see in more detail later, the *proper* knowledge of God for Calvin includes both piety (true religion) and human happiness. For the present it is important only to see how the basis for such a doctrine lies in human nature, what God *created* man to be. Perhaps the most far-reaching implication of Calvin's doctrine that knowledge, piety and happiness are one is the intimate connection between the knowledge of God and the knowledge of ourselves—what Dowey, borrowing a term from Paul Tillich, calls the "correlative character of the knowledge of God and man."[9] It is the famous theme with which the *Institutes* opens. It is a theme that is generally traced to St. Augustine; and the similarities between Calvin and Augustine on this point are striking indeed.[10] It is interesting, however, that, although he acknowledges his dependence upon Augustine more often than upon any other church father, Calvin makes no reference in this connection to him. Instead, he refers to the pervasive teaching of Scripture (I,i,3) *and* to "the ancient proverb" of classical thought, "Know thyself!" (II,i,1). It is remarkable that, in addition to Scripture, Calvin turns for confirmation of his main doctrines about the knowledge of God in the opening chapters of the *Institutes* not to the fathers but to the writings of classical pagan authors, especially Plato and Cicero.

The intimate connection between the knowledge of God and self-knowledge in Calvin can be analyzed in two different ways. Calvin seems to hold that there is both a logical (or conceptual) and a psychological (or causal) connection between them. First there is a logical connection. If man's knowledge of God and his chief virtue (piety) are logically connected, there is a mutual entailment-relation between man's knowledge of God and man's knowledge of himself. For what is piety? It is "that reverence joined with love of God which the knowledge of his benefits induces" (I,ii,1). Notice here that, just as Calvin refuses to define our "proper" knowledge of God apart from piety (our right *response* to God), so too he refuses to define piety, this response to God, apart from a knowledge of his *benefits* to us (or, as he says, "what is to our advantage to know of him"). But we cannot know *what* benefits us unless we know who we are—unless we know, that is, what kind of beings we are, what our nature is, what our needs are, and what, in view of these needs, *is good* for us. What is good for us, only God can supply. Hence it is logically impossible for us really to know ourselves, unless we know what good God can be for us, for which we require the knowledge of God; and it is logically impossible for us to know God unless we know what we need, for which we require the knowledge of ourselves.

Second, there is a causal connection between the knowledge of God and self-knowledge. However, says Calvin, "which one precedes and brings forth the other is not easy to discern. In the first place, no one can look on himself without immediately turning his thoughts to the contemplation of God . . . ." For when we look at ourselves, we see especially two things: "the mighty gifts with which we are endowed," which "are hardly from ourselves"; and our "miserable ruin," "the feeling of our own ignorance, vanity, poverty, infirmity, and—what is more—depravity and corruption," which prompt us likewise "to contemplate the good things of God." "Accordingly, the knowledge of ourselves not only arouses us to seek God, but also, as it were, leads us by the hand to find him" (I,i,1). Conversely, "it is certain that man never achieves a clear knowledge of himself unless he has first looked upon God's face, and then descends from contemplating him to scrutinize himself." What we see in God is his absolute goodness and greatness, his glory and majesty. And this leads us to see not only that the "mighty gifts with which we are endowed" originate in him alone as their source, but also that our "miserable ruin" is miserable indeed, and is owing to our own pride and wickedness. Knowing God is particularly required for leading us to this aspect of self-knowledge:

> For we always seem to ourselves righteous and upright and wise and holy—this pride is innate in all of us—unless by clear proofs we stand convinced of our own unrighteousness, foulness, folly and impurity. Moreover, we are not thus convinced if we look merely to ourselves and not also to the Lord, who is the sole standard by which this judgment must be measured.

However:

> Suppose we but once begin to raise our thoughts to God, and to ponder his nature, and how completely perfect are his righteousness, wisdom and power—the straitedge to which we must be shaped. Then, what masquerading earlier as righteousness was pleasing in us will soon grow filthy in its consummate wickedness (I,i,1).

When, further, by piety we also find our *good* in God, through the knowledge of him and ourselves in which piety consists, we shall also have found happiness.

As is clear from the quotations given, Calvin elaborates the intimate connection between self-knowledge and the knowledge of God in the context of the *proper* knowledge of God (I,ii,1). One of the interesting implications of the logical aspect of that connection is that no one, insofar as he has *this* knowledge of God, knowingly does wrong—a version of Plato's doctrine. How Calvin would have discussed the intimate connection for the *deficient* knowledge of God, the result of suppressing truth in unrighteousness, is not clear—although there are many hints in I,iv and similar passages. Presumably the formulation would look something like this. Logically everyone, insofar as he possesses a deficient knowledge of God, thereby knowingly does wrong, and therefore knows his guilt and sin. There is no counterpart to this in Plato. Psychologically, the impious knowledge of God is the cause, and in turn also the result, of man's knowledge of his guilt and misery.

The knowledge of God for Calvin as so far analyzed, then, is the result of an inner sense of divinity combined with inferences made from observing the external workmanship of the universe. Both of these, in turn, are bound up with the knowledge of ourselves. Furthermore, the knowledge of God is *natural* to human beings and *universally present* among them in virtue of *creation*. It would be easy to suppose that such knowledge is one and the same thing with the "proper knowledge" of God to which we have referred, and which Calvin defines already in I,ii; but that would be a serious mistake. It would be a mistake that Calvin does not go out of his way to warn his readers against, for he uses the same term "the knowledge of God" in the titles of all the first five chapters. That the two knowledges should be carefully distinguished is evident, however, from the respective descriptions Calvin gives of each. The knowledge of I,ii ("What It Is to Know God, and to What Purpose the Knowledge of Him Tends") is one and the same thing in the pious response it evokes. The knowledge of God as I have so far analyzed it, with its basis in creation, is not. The former is knowledge not only of God's existence but also of what is to our *advantage* to know him; the latter is knowledge "only that there is a God and that he is their Maker"—it extends only to "a certain understanding of his divine majesty" (I,iii,1). The former, indeed, can be identified with the "primal simple knowledge to which the very order of nature would have led us if Adam had remained upright," and which no one now experiences "until Christ the Mediator comes forward to reconcile him to us"

(I,ii,1). The latter, by contrast, continues to be present in all men after the fall.

Further support for distinguishing between these two knowledges can be found from the way in which Calvin confirms his claim for the presence of the sense of divinity in all men. He does this by calling attention to the universality of religion. The connection he sees is that the *sensus divinitatis* is the *semen religionis* (I,iii,1,2). If the knowledge provided by the sense of divinity were the same as the knowledge of true piety, it could issue only in *true* religion. As a matter of fact, however, Calvin holds that it is the seed of *all* religion. Hence, just as the sense of divinity is *natural*, so too is religion (of all kinds) entirely natural to man. Religion is not "invented by the subtlety and craft of a few to hold the simple folk in thrall," even though "clever men have devised many things in religion by which to inspire the common folk with reverence and to strike them with terror" (I,iii,2).

Just as the *sensus divinitatis* is the seed of religion, so, I think, when combined with man's reflections on the workmanship of the universe it can be taken as the seed of a natural knowledge of God. Of course, this will be less evident among those who resist the sense of divinity. There are those, however, who "foster" it, according to Calvin, even though they be "scarcely one man in a hundred." And even they "degenerate from the true knowledge of him" (I,iv,1). Calvin is so eloquent on this point that his readers frequently conclude that no one, not even "the one in a hundred," can by nature attain a knowledge about God in any sense of the term. But that conclusion hardly follows. All that follows is that the knowledge of "natural theology" which has developed since the fall and apart from revelation is deficient; it is not the knowledge of true piety. Still, it is rooted, like the religions of mankind, in the nature of man.

Here, then, is the complete picture. In virtue of their nature, their natural faculties (including reason), and of the nature of the world—in short, in virtue of *the way God created man and the universe*—all human beings are capable of coming to the knowledge of God. The way in which such knowledge *actually manifests itself* among them, however, is complicated by sin and redemption. All men have fallen from the original goodness in which they were created, and of these, some persist in their fallen ways, while others are being redeemed from their fall by the grace of God. The natural knowledge of God therefore now manifests itself among men in two different ways. In those who are fallen and persist in their fallenness, the knowledge of God is deficient. In those who are fallen but being redeemed from their fallenness, this deficiency in the knowledge of God is restored, at least partially, from the effects of the fall.

II. The Fall

Before turning to the effects of the fall on man's nature and to what characterizes the deficient knowledge of God which results from these effects, we should take a brief look at Calvin's account of the origin and nature of the fall itself. The fall consists in "original sin," which is an "hereditary depravity and corruption of our nature, diffused into all parts of the soul, which first makes us liable to God's wrath, then also brings forth in us those works which Scripture calls 'works of the flesh' " (II,i,8). Although present in all men, original sin stems from the disobedience of Adam, which was occasioned by the work of the devil, and freely chosen in an act of the will (II,i,4-11; iii,5). It is of the utmost importance, given the central role which Calvin ascribes to faith in redemption (Part III below), to observe that he locates the *root* of man's sin and disobedience in *faithlessness* (II,i,4). To discover what faithlessness is, we should first have before us Calvin's doctrine of faith—but that must wait until Part III. For now it is enough to observe that faithlessness does not consist in ignorance. Calvin finds *that* explanation of evil-doing in Plato inconsistent with the persistence of the knowledge of God and of his law after the fall (II,ii,22).

We can seek Calvin's view of the effects of the fall on our natural knowledge of God by looking either at his account of these effects on man's noetic faculties or at his descriptions of the actual knowledge man possesses in his fallen state. In the former, following Augustine, Calvin distinguishes man's "natural" from his "supernatural gifts," which are "adventitious, and beyond nature." The natural gifts include "soundness of mind and uprightness of heart";[11] the supernatural gifts include "the light of faith as well as righteousness, which would be sufficient to attain heavenly life and eternal bliss." The effect of sin, according to Calvin, is "that the natural gifts were corrupted in man" and "that the supernatural gifts were stripped from him" (II,ii,12). Elsewhere he puts it this way: "vitiated as he is in every part of his nature and shorn of supernatural gifts" (II,ii,4). The contrast is significant: reason and will "could not be completely wiped out" since they are "inseparable from man's nature"; but faith, since it is "adventitious," could be—and was—completely "extinguished."

Consider first the loss of faith: the loss is complete and unambiguous; the effect of sin is unbelief—nothing of belief is left. There is, however, a paradox in all this, for it was precisely the loss of faith that was the *source* of the fall; now it is seen as an *effect* of it. Consider next the corruption of reason and the will. A paradox also prevades Calvin's lengthy discussion of the corrupted will, the formulation of which he is content, at one point, to leave in the words of St. Bernard:

> "Thus the soul, in some strange and evil way, under a certain voluntary and wrongly free necessity is at the same time enslaved and free: enslaved because of necessity; free because of will. And what is at once stranger and more deplorable, it is guilty because it is free, and enslaved because it is guilty, and as a consequence enslaved because it is free" (II,iii,5; see also ii,26,27. The quotation is from St. Bernard, *Sermons on the Song of Songs*, lxxxi.7,9).

Calvin's account of corrupted reason is more straightforward. When it comes to "earthly things" like "government, household management, all mechanical skills and the liberal arts," he observes that "no man is without the light of reason" (II,ii,13). In one paragraph, often quoted, he notes how "we can not read the writings of the ancients on these subjects without great admiration," adding only that we recognize "at the same time that it comes from God," and exhorting his fellow Christian believers to learn "how many gifts the Lord left to human nature even after it was despoiled of its true good" (II,ii,15). With respect to "heavenly things," however, the situation is different:

> This spiritual insight consists chiefly in three things: (1) knowing God; (2) knowing his fatherly favor in our behalf, in which our salvation consists; (3) knowing how to frame our life according to the rule of his law. In the first two points—and especially in the second —the greatest geniuses are blinder than moles (II,ii,18)!

The passage is as famous as any in Calvin, and requires a careful analysis, one which will lead us into the second way of seeking Calvin's view of the noetic effects of the fall, *viz.*, his descriptions of the actual knowledge man possesses in his fallen state.

First and foremost, as noted earlier, it must be insisted that the "blindness" of which Calvin speaks here refers to the *proper* knowledge of God, the knowledge of piety, which we have yet to discuss. Otherwise he might be thought to be denying all knowledge of God entirely in fallen man, which is not his intention at all. He grants immediately "that one can read competent and apt statements about God here and there in the philosophers," although he quickly adds, "these always show a certain giddy imagination." More important is his reference to his earlier *sensus divinitatis:* "As was stated above, the Lord indeed gave them a slight taste of his divinity that they might not hide their impiety under a cloak of ignorance" (II,ii,18). It is an important, frequently recurring theme in Calvin that the natural knowledge of God persisting in man after the fall is sufficient to leave him without excuse: "All excuse is cut off because the fault of dullness is within us"; we cannot "pretend ignorance" (I,v,15).

The central question for our purpose here concerns the role of reason in achieving this knowledge, as well as what makes the knowledge deficient. From what I suggested earlier about the function of reason, it is most implausible that Calvin means by its corruption that it can no longer formulate some of the propositional content of this knowledge of God, nor make the required inferences from the character of the universe to the existence and power of God. What reason *chiefly* fails to achieve in its fallen state is, it seems, not conceptualization or inference but the act of *faith*. This is consistent with the distinction Calvin draws between the "natural" and the "supernatural" gifts, *viz.*, that the former are "essential" to man, the latter "adventitious." From that distinction, and from the distinction between reason as a *faculty* and faith as a certain *exercise* of a faculty, we can infer that the corruption of reason (and will), in its most serious aspect, consists precisely in the loss of its ability to believe. The *corruption* of nature is identical in this respect with the *loss* of the supernatural gift, which has the advantage not only of dissolving the dualist language of natural/supernatural, but also of bringing reason and faith into an intelligible relationship with each other.[12]

In what, then, consists the *deficiency* of the knowledge of God that results from the natural activity of reason and will without faith? The deficiency has both a conceptual (propositional) and a moral (practical) component. Fallen man still knows that God exists, that he is the creator, that he is majestic in power and deserving of worship and obedience (I,ii,1). But fallen man does not know that God is Triune and Incarnate in Jesus Christ, nor that he is graciously disposed toward man in his fallen state (II,ii,18). Fallen man is still religious by his very nature (I,iii); however, he no longer worships God as he is, but falsely (idolatry and superstition) (I,iv; xi; xii), nor does he obey God or seek him as the fountain of all good. Instead he fears the divine wrath and even attempts, unsuccessfully, to suppress the "proper knowledge of God," to his own disadvantage and misery.

One mark of the deficient knowledge of God is the tendency to "fly off into empty speculations" about the nature of God. Calvin sometimes seems less impressed with the "droplets of truth" in the writings of the pagan philosophers than with the "many monstrous lies that defile them" (I,iv,1; II,ii,18). Since Calvin's famous opposition to "speculation" is directed not only to fallen man but also to the redeemed, I shall discuss it presently, in Part III.

III. Redemption

The origin and nature of redemption in man consists, insofar as it is a conscious and noetic experience, in the act of faith in Jesus Christ. Before turning to Calvin's definition of faith, a brief account should be given of its origin. Faith arises in man after the fall, according to Calvin, as a gift of God (III,ii,7), by the "grace of regeneration," in the elect only (III,i,1; iii,9), and upon the hearing of the gospel, the Word of God (I,vi), accompanied by the illumination of the Holy Spirit (I,vii). Even before the fall, as we have seen, faith was present in man as an essential ingredient in the proper knowledge of God (II,ii,12). Here we focus only on Calvin's doctrine of revelation and illumination as the special conditions that make faith possible after the fall.

Scripture and the Spirit. We saw earlier that Calvin develops his doctrine of revelation and illumination not in connection with faith (Book III), but in the context of our *natural* knowledge of God as Creator (Book I). Such natural knowledge persists after the fall so that it "is more than enough to withdraw all support from men's ingratitude" which is owing to the fall. But this knowledge is sufficient to lead him back to the proper knowledge of piety. Hence "it is needful that another and better help be added to direct us aright to the very Creator of the universe," which is "the light of his Word" by which he becomes "known unto salvation." The most important difference between that natural knowledge and the restored knowledge, then, is that the latter includes God as *Redeemer*. As for the knowledge of him as Creator from creation, this Word of God also assists, even as a pair of spectacles helps those with weak vision to read the writing of "a most beautiful volume." This is because in Scripture God uses not only the "mute teachers" of creation "but also opens his own most hallowed lips" (I,vi,1). Still, it is in these early chapters of the *Institutes*, and specifically in connection with revelation, that Calvin first introduces the concept of faith: "For by his Word, God rendered faith unambiguous forever, a faith that should be superior to all opinion" (I,vi,2). There is only one earlier reference to faith—as the essence of "pure and real religion" (I,ii,2).

The Scriptures fail to function, however, either as the basis for faith in Christ the Mediator or as the spectacles whereby we can interpret the workmanship of the universe as evidence for its Creator, unless "men regard them as having sprung from heaven, as if there the living words of God were heard." And no one can do this either by considering the "consent of the church" or by "human reasons, judgments, or conjectures" derived from an examination of the qualities and content of the writings themselves. This attitude is fostered only "by the secret testimony of the spirit" (I,vii,1)—not by the "consent of the church." This is a "pernicious error" which makes the truth of God depend on "the decision of men" (I,vii,1). The authority of Scripture is not based on the testimony of the church, nor on human reason. Instead, the testimony of the church is based on the authority of Scripture (I,vii,2). "True," says Calvin, "if we wished to proceed by arguments, we might advance many things that would easily prove—if there is any god in heaven—that the law, the prophets, and the gospel came from him" (I,vii,4). And Calvin himself does just this in chapter viii, insisting at the outset, however, that "it will be vain to fortify the authority of Scripture by argument" (I,viii,1). In fact, "they who strive to build up firm faith in Scripture through disputation are doing things backwards" (I,vii,4).

Faith and Reason. What, then, are the effects of redemption for man's "natural" and "supernatural" gifts? Calvin's explicit answer is that redemption makes up the complete loss of the latter (unfaithfulness is replaced by faith), and restores the former, which were corrupted in the fall. [There is no such restoration of the natural gifts among the faithless, only a "restraint" of the corrupting effects of the fall (II,iii,3,4).] But in what does such restoration consist? Presumably it would consist in *restoring* the ability of reason once again to attain the "spiritual insight" it lost in the fall, especially in "(1) knowing God" and "(2) knowing his fatherly favor in our behalf, in which our salvation consists"—the two points on which Calvin holds that "the greatest geniuses are blinder than moles." Hints in support of such an interpretation can be found in statements to the effect that man will, when redeemed, come "to recognize that we have been endowed with reason and understanding so that, by leading a holy and upright life, we may press on to the appointed goal of blessed immortality" (II,i,1). In this way faith, a supernatural gift, as suggested earlier, could have been directly related to reason and will, natural gifts being a constituitive ingredient in their restoration. Instead of taking that direction, however, Calvin seems increasingly to hold, from the point of his introduction of the term "faith" in I,vi,2 that knowing

God and his benevolence toward us is to be attributed simply to a *replaced supernatural* gift, the gift of faith. The new relationship in the redeemed man between such faith and restoration of the natural gifts he leaves obscure.[13]

Speculation. Why is it that Calvin fails to consider (unfortunately, in my opinion) what seems to be so important a question, arising out of his own analysis of man's powers as they were created by God, corrupted by the fall, and—supposedly—*restored* again by redemption? One aspect of the answer may lie in his well-known opposition to "speculation." It is an opposition that led him on occasion to confuse an "empty speculation" (which he rightly opposes as a sign of the rebellion of fallen man) with a legitimate and necessary type of theological and philosophical inquiry, both among fallen man as well as among the redeemed. Part of his opposition to "empty speculation" is, of course, the mass of false beliefs to which it leads. Still, amidst this falsity are the true beliefs about God which even the pagans have reached, and which Calvin himself freely cites. His deeper concern must be, then, the religious or moral inadequacy of such statements by themselves. When men by "speculation" discover true things about God, the fault lies not in the truth they have discovered but in themselves for not responding piously to the truth. As Calvin says, "It will not suffice simply to hold that there is One whom all ought to honor and adore"; we must also "seek nothing elsewhere than in him" (I,ii,1). The contrast between the two types of knowledge is very clear in a famous passage:

> We are called to a knowledge of God: not that knowledge which, content with empty speculation, merely flits in the brain, but that which will be sound and fruitful if we duly perceive it, and if it takes root in the heart. For the Lord manifests himself by his powers, the force of which we feel within ourselves and the benefits of which we enjoy. We must therefore be much more profoundly affected by this knowledge than if we were to imagine a God of whom no perception came through to us. Consequently, we know the most perfect way of seeking God, and the most suitable order, is not for us to attempt with bold curiosity to penetrate to the investigation of his essence, which we ought more to adore than meticulously to search out, but for us to contemplate him in his works whereby he renders himself near and familiar to us, and in some manner communicates himself to us (I,v,9).

What Calvin is describing here is "the most perfect way of seeking God"; that such a way exists presupposes that less perfect ways exist.

His words here say nothing to the earlier question about whether the deficient way can lead to truths of natural theology which appear in the pagan philosophers. Still the belief persists widely among interpreters of Calvin that his outlook makes no room for natural theology. For example, elucidating Calvin's famous opposition to "speculation," Dowey concludes: "To know God disinterestedly is, for Calvin, a contradiction in terms" (p. 28). The conclusion would be correct if the knowledge of piety were, indeed, the only knowledge of God which Calvin allows. But if Calvin allows another knowledge of God, a knowledge of God that includes true beliefs but is deficient in piety, the contradiction disappears.

Calvin himself, however, appears to forget this all-important distinction in such a way that he seems to cut off *all inquiry* into the nature of God. For example, in elaborating the knowledge of piety, he expresses dismay over philosophers who ask, "What is God? Men who pose this question are merely toying with idle speculations." Why does Calvin think so? He believes:

> . . . it is more important for us to know of what sort he is and what is consistent with his nature. What good is it to profess with Epicurus some sort of God who has cast aside the care of the world only to amuse himself in idleness? What help is it, in short, to know a God with whom we have nothing to do (I,ii,2)?

Here Calvin seems to be led by the intensity of his concern for the knowledge of piety to reject as "speculative" what in some legitimate sense is a "disinterested" question about the nature of God. As a matter of fact, the correct answer to such a question is as pertinent to the possibility of his own knowledge of *piety* as it is to his rejection of Epicurus. Precisely because Epicurus *conceived* God as a remote being unconcerned with the affairs of men, he could not have responded piously to him. Contrapositively, in order to respond piously to God in the way Calvin recommends, one must *conceive* God differently than the way of Epicurus. Hence the question, "What is God?" need not be "idle speculation" at all, insofar as its correct answer is presupposed in his being "piously known." If God is not the "sort" of being Christians say he is, it makes no sense to claim that the "proper knowledge" of him is characterized by piety. And, where Epicurus went wrong, Plato, according to Calvin, went right:

> It is clear, that all those who do not direct every thought and action in their lives to this goal degenerate from the law of their creation. This was not unknown to the philosophers. Plato meant nothing but this when he often taught that the highest good of the soul is likeness

> to God, where, when the soul has grasped the knowledge of God, it is wholly transformed into his likeness (I,ii,3; see also III,xxv,2).

This is just one of the many instances in which Calvin confirms his own teaching by quoting from the very heritage of natural theology which his modern followers believe he undermined.

Plato also recognized along with Calvin the limit of human speculation into the ultimate nature of the good,[14] but this did not lead him to avoid philosophy. He saw no conflict between the religious approach to the good to which Calvin refers and the rational, philosophic, "speculative" investigation of things. That Calvin really wished to see no conflict here either is evident from his *Commentary* on Col. 2:8: "Many have mistakenly imagined that philosophy is here condemned by Paul"; but he only "means everything that men contrive of themselves when wishing to be wise through their own means of understanding . . . . Under the term philosophy Paul has merely condemned all spurious doctrines which come forth from man's head." Still, Calvin was personally disinclined to pursue philosophic questions—even those of great intrinsic interest and of significance for the Christian view of things. For example, "I leave it to the philosophers to discuss these faculties [of the soul] in their subtle way." Partly he wants to avoid obscuring his practical, pastoral aim: "For the upbuilding of godliness a simple definition will be enough for us" (I,xv,6). Partly, too, it appears that Calvin simply failed to appreciate the complexity of those questions that have aroused human interest ever since, in Aristotle's famous words, "men first began to philosophize." He thinks the relationship of body and soul, for instance, "a topic of no great difficulty" (I,xv,2)! Sometimes, however, he seems to sense a danger for piety in the philosophic attitude:

> The pious mind does not dream up for itself any God it pleases, but contemplates the one and only true God. And it does not attach to him whatever it pleases, but is content to hold him to be as he manifests himself; furthermore, the mind always exercises the utmost diligence and care not to wander astray, or rashly and boldly to go beyond his will (I,ii,2).

Here Calvin suggests that the pious mind is not one that inquires, questions, wonders, or seeks to understand, but one that is "content" —precisely because it already knows.

> Because it is persuaded that he is good and merciful, it reposes in him with perfect trust . . . . Because it acknowledges him as Lord and father, the pious mind also deems it right to observe his author-

ity in all things, reverence his majesty, take care to advance his glory, and obey his commandments (I,ii,2).

Since the pious mind is thus persuaded exclusively by revelation, Calvin is led to adopt his "one rule of modesty and sobriety" for all religious doctrine: "not to speak, or guess, or even seek to know, concerning obscure matters except what has been imparted to us by God's Word" (I,xiv,4). Unfortunately, this rule suggests a biblicist cleavage between faith and philosophy. It contributes, together with all of the other factors described above—Calvin's pastoral concern, his disinterest in philosophic questions, his fear that philosophy without piety will lead astray, and his own eclectic and sometimes uncritical, rhetorical use of the philosophic tradition from Plato to Scotus—to a deep ambiguity in Calvin's stance toward philosophy. It is an ambiguity that accounts, I think, for the absence of an identifiable tradition which can be clearly marked "Calvinistic philosophy."[15] In particular, it also accounts for the disagreement and lack of clarity that continues to plague the understanding of faith and reason among various streams of the Reformed tradition.

Two things, however, are clear in Calvin's writings. First, he *locates* the "proper knowledge of God" in the redemption made possible by faith, without, however, connecting that faith to the functions of reason. Second, when he finally *defines* faith in Book III,ii,7, he does it not in terms of belief, but in terms of knowledge—the "proper knowledge" he has already described in Book I, chapter ii. This "proper knowledge of God" as he there presents it, *like* the deficient knowledge of God, has both a propositional and a moral component. Propositionally, in addition to knowing that God exists, that he is Creator of all things, and that he is majestic and deserving of all worship and obedience (propositions Calvin includes as well in the deficient knowledge of God), the man of faith also knows *that* God is Triune, Incarnate and Redeemer (I,xiii; II,xii-xvii). *Unlike* the deficient knowledge of God which expresses itself in fear, distrust, disobedience, and misery, man's "proper" knowledge of God leads him to love, honor, fear, trust and worship God, and also to seek and thereby to find all good in him alone. The correct knowledge of God *is*, in short, both *piety* and *happiness*. "Indeed, we shall not say that, properly speaking, God is known where there is no religion or piety" (I,ii,1).

A footnote to this statement in the Battles translation, as well as the heading added to the section which contains it, interprets Calvin as saying that piety is a "prerequisite" of the knowledge of God, suggesting that piety is a pre-condition, a first step, in acquiring the knowledge of God (n. 1). This does not appear to be Calvin's meaning. He means instead that piety is an essential characteristic of that knowledge; whatever *looks* like knowledge of God but lacks this characteristic of pious response is not, "properly speaking," knowledge of God. That is the point of the opening sentence of each paragraph in the section:

> Now, the knowledge of God, as I understand it, is that by which we not only conceive that there is a God but also grasp *what befits us and is proper to his glory*, in fine, *what is to our advantage* to know him. (emphasis added)

> Moreover, although our mind cannot apprehend God *without rendering some honor to him*, it will not suffice simply to hold that here is One whom all ought to honor and adore, *unless we are also persuaded that he is the fountain of every good, and that we must seek nothing elsewhere than in him.* (emphasis added)

In these sentences Calvin defines the knowledge of God not primarily in terms of its propositional content (although clearly that is *there*), but in *terms of* the religious and moral response that must accompany it. Even to say that this response "accompanies" the knowledge is misleading, for it suggests that (propositional) *knowledge* of God is one thing, and *piety* is another. Calvin's teaching is rather that knowledge and piety are *one* thing. It is what students of Calvin are given to call the "practical," "moral," or "religious" character, and more recently, the "existential" character of Calvin's doctrine of the knowledge of God.[16] Calvin's teaching is thus a Christian version of the Platonic doctrines that knowledge *is* virtue, and that virtue is its own reward (happiness).

It is important to reflect, through all this, on the *centrality* of faith in Calvin's religious epistemology, and especially its conjunction with *certainty*. "Even if [by reasoning] any one clears God's Sacred Word from man's evil speaking, he will not at once imprint upon their hearts that *certainty* which piety requires" (I,vii,4, emphasis added). From this point in the *Institutes* on we can follow Calvin's "quest for certainty" to its climax in the definition of faith as a "firm and certain knowledge of God's benevolence towards us . . ." (III,iii,7). Such knowledge "is so far above sense that man's mind has to go beyond and rise above itself in order to attain it" (III,ii,14). This, incidentally, suggests that the proper knowledge of God is *beyond* even any restored capacities of reason; reason even when restored to its original "nobility" requires the assistance of faith. Again, Calvin's quest of certainty seems to have been satisfied by the discovery that "the testimony of the Spirit is more excellent than all reason." And no wonder, for in this way "God alone is a fit witness of himself in his Word," with the result that Scripture is "self-authenticated" (I,vii,5). Hence:

> . . . we *believe* neither by our own nor by anyone else's judgment that Scripture is from God; but above human judgment we affirm with utter *certainty* (just as if we were gazing upon the majesty of God himself) that it has flowed to us from the very mouth of God by the ministry of men . . . .
>
> . . . Such, then, is a conviction that requires no reasons; such, a *knowledge* with which the best reason agrees—in which the mind truly reposes more securely and constantly than in any reasons; such, finally, a feeling that can be born only of heavenly revelation. I speak of nothing other than what each believer *experiences* within himself—though my words fall far beneath a just explanation of the matter . . .
>
> . . . Let us, then, know that the only true *faith* is that which the Spirit of God seals in our hearts (I,viii,5). (emphasis added)

There it is—an eloquent coalescence, finally, of belief, faith, knowledge, experience and certainty. The noetic states that philosophers from Plato and Aristotle down to Descartes, Locke, Kant and William James (as well as theologians like Augustine and Aquinas) have all tried diligently to sort out and distinguish from one another have been fused together by Calvin in the presence of the revelation of God. Why, to put just one question in focus, did Calvin take faith to be a species of *knowledge*, and not, as Augustine and Aquinas had suggested, a species of *belief*? My own answer at this point is just a guess. It comes back to what I have called his quest—and discovery—of certainty. "Knowledge," as opposed to "belief," just struck Calvin—so goes my guess—as the appropriate way to capture the certainty of the Christian faith.

Whether there is anything to that guess, and whether, indeed, the "fusion of noetic states" in Calvin to which I referred can be justified in light of the efforts of other philosophical and theological traditions to make some distinctions—these questions I invite my fellow Calvinist philosophers to determine. Or will our words, like Calvin's, also "fall far beneath a just explanation of the matter"?

Notes

1. *Our Knowledge of God* (New York: Scribners, 1939), p. 41. For an account of how the concept of (general) revelation came to replace the con-

cept of natural knowledge in modern theology, see J. Baillie, *The Idea of Revelation* (New York: Columbia University Press, 1956).

2. The references to Calvin's *Institutes* will be in the text. Quotations are from the Ford Lewis Battles translation (Philadelphia: Westminster, 1960), 2 vols.
3. *The Knowledge of God in Calvin's Theology* (New York: Columbia University Press, 1952), pp. 50ff.
4. I,i,1, n. 1, p. 35 (Battles edn.); I,iii,1, n. 1, p. 43; see also "Index," under "Revelation," vol. II, p. 1695.
5. *Calvin's Doctrine of the Knowledge of God* (Grand Rapids: Eerdmans, 1959), pp. 7-9.
6. *Ibid.*, p. 12.
7. Dowey, *ibid.*, pp. 73ff.
8. For an interesting theory of the intimate relationship between the immediacy of belief and the discursiveness of reason which could be adapted to Calvin's teaching, see the article by David Burrell, "Religious Belief and Rationality," in C.F. Delaney, ed., *Rationality and Religious Belief* (Notre Dame: University of Notre Dame Press, 1970), pp. 84-115.
9. Dowey, *ibid.*, pp. 18-24.
10. Compare *Inst.* I,i,1; xv,1; II,i,1, with Augustine, *Sol.* I,ii,7 and *Conf.* VII,x,16; xvii,23; X,xx,29.
11. "Heart" often means "will"—see the context here, and also their interchangeability in sect. 27, in II,iii,6-10, and elsewhere.
12. This Augustinian interpretation would contribue to Calvin's oft-confessed continuity with that Saint, who affirms that "we could not believe at all if we did not have rational souls," and that, indeed, "belief itself is nothing else than to think with assent" ("Letter to Consentius"; *On the Predestination of the Saints*, v).
13. For an interesting analysis that shows how Calvin's view of faith and reason can be correlated with Aquinas' definition of faith as "an act of the intellect moved by the will," see Arvin Vos, "Faith: Knowledge or Belief? A Comparison of Thomas Aquinas and John Calvin" (unpublished).
14. *The Republic*, pp. 506-509.
15. There is no ambiguity at all for Catholic critics. E. Gilson's reactions are well known: "There then, is philosophy once again reduced to the Word of God . . . ." *Christianity and Philosophy* (New York: Sheed and Ward, 1939), p. 14; see also pp. 18, 30ff. For a discussion of Calvin's concept of "Christian philosophy" which relates it to both classical and Christian usage, see p. 6, n. 8 in the Battles edition of the *Institutes*. For an earlier effort of my own to understand "Calvin and the Philosophers," see *The Reformed Journal*, VIII, 2, 3 (February and March, 1958), pp. 11-13; pp. 10-14.
16. Dowey, *ibid.*, pp. 24-31.

Bibliography

John Calvin, *Institutes of the Christian Religion*, Battles translation (Philadelphia: Westminster, 1960), 2 vols.

E.A. Dowey, *The Knowledge of God in Calvin's Theology* (New York: Columbia University Press, 1952).

D.J. Hoitenga, "Calvin and the Philosophers," two articles in *The Reformed Journal*, VIII, 2 and 3 (February and March, 1958), pp. 11-13; pp. 10-14.

T.H.L. Parker, *Calvin's Doctrine of The Knowledge of God* (Grand Rapids: Eerdmans, 1959).

Historical Setting

Part Two:

The Scottish Common Sense Tradition and Rationality

Thomas Reid on Rationality

Nicholas Wolterstorff

NOTHING IS MORE CHARACTERISTIC OF MODERN PHILOSOPHY than a recurrent sense of crisis—along with a recurring triumphal conviction on the part of those who newly identify the crisis that they have met and overcome it themselves. The sound of modern philosophy in the West is the ringing of changes on those two themes.

The themes were sounded by Descartes as the beginning of the modern movement. European science is in crisis, said Descartes.

> From my childhood I lived in a world of books, and since I was taught that by their help I could gain a clear and assured knowledge of everything useful in life, I was eager to learn from them. But as soon as I had finished the course of studies which usually admits one to the ranks of the learned, I changed my opinion completely. For I found myself saddled with so many doubts and errors that I seemed to have gained nothing in trying to educate myself unless it was to discover more and more fully how ignorant I was.
>
> Nevertheless I had been in one of the most celebrated schools in all of Europe, where I thought there should be wise men if wise men existed anywhere on earth. I had learned there everything that others learned, and, not satisfied with merely the knowledge that was taught, I had perused as many books as I could find which contained more unusual and recondite knowledge. I also knew the opinions of others about myself, and that I was in no way judged inferior to my fellow students, even though several of them were preparing to become professors. And finally, it did not seem to me that our own times were less flourishing and fertile than were any of the earlier periods. All this led me to conclude that I could judge others by myself, and to decide that there was no such wisdom in the world as I had previously hoped to find *(Discourse)*.

The somberness of Descartes' judgment in this passage on the *scientia* of his day is certainly not in keeping with the sprightliness of his prose. The discrepancy is of course to be attributed to his conviction that the crisis had passed.

> I do not hesitate to claim the good fortune of having stumbled in my youth upon certain paths which led me without difficulty to certain considerations and maxims from which I formed a method of gradually increasing my knowledge and of improving my abilities as much as the mediocrity of my talents and the shortness of my life will permit. For I have already had such results that although in self-judgment I try to lean toward undervaluation rather than to presumption, I cannot escape a feeling of extreme satisfaction with the progress I believe I have already made in the search for truth *(ibid.)*.

These themes of crisis and triumph continue unabated into the twentieth century. By the time we get to such thinkers as Husserl and Heidegger, however, the tone has perceptibly darkened. The scope of the perceived crisis is more extensive than that to which Descartes called attention. Although Husserl, for example, sees the crisis as having its epicenter in *scientia*, it radiates generally from there out into society in general. And although he is convinced he knows what steps must be taken to triumph over the crisis, he is not at all confident that enough will follow him in taking those steps to execute the conquest.

Thomas Reid also did his philosophizing in the context of a sense of crisis—or strictly speaking, of impending crisis. In his case, too, the scope of the crisis which he perceived as threatening was more extensive than that to which Descartes called attention. It was a crisis of faith and of action as well as a crisis of *scientia*. Ironically Reid viewed the basic cause of this threatening crisis as the spreading influence of Descartes' proposed solution to the crisis he had identified. Descartes, said Reid, had introduced the "Way of Ideas." Locke, Berkeley and Hume had followed him. In Hume's hands, the Way of Ideas had led to a blatant form of skepticism. And this, if it gained adherents, would shake society at its very foundations. All of Reid's work is offered as an attempt to forestall, or overcome, that crisis.

In the dedication to his first book, *An Inquiry into the Human Mind*, published in 1764, Reid speaks of Hume as this "ingenious author," and says that he "hath built a system of scepticism, which leaves no ground to believe any one thing rather than its contrary. His reasoning appeared to me to be just: there was therefore a necessity to call in question the principles upon which it was founded, or to admit the conclusion." As for himself, says Reid, he will follow the course of questioning the principles. For "absolute scepticism is not more destructive of the faith of the Christian, than of the science of a philosopher, and of the prudence of a man of common understanding." Reid's philosophizing was shaped by his conviction that he had identified, and perceived how to overcome, the crisis of Humean skepticism.

But skepticism comes in many forms. What did Reid take Hume's form of skepticism to be? Reid saw it as the insistence that we are "to admit nothing but what can be proved by reasoning" (*Inquiry* V,7). That, says Reid, is what "the author of the Treatise on Human Nature" affirmed. And if this is what we affirm, "then we must be sceptics indeed, and believe nothing at all" (*ibid.*). In fact Reid thinks that Hume did not consistently act in conformity with this position, neither in his ordinary living nor in his philosophy. But that is the position he attacks—part of his argument being that Hume *could not* consistently act in conformity with this position.

I think there is considerable ground for supposing that Reid has not gotten Hume's position entirely right. But for my purposes here, that is not an essential issue. There is one issue that *is* important to settle, however. It is *knowledge* that is Reid's primary concern, or is it *justified belief*? A skeptic may contend that we know less than we might have supposed; equally, he may contend that we are intellectually justified in believing less than we might have supposed. Which is the skepticism that Reid proposed to answer?

All the commentators of whom I am aware suggest that Reid is answering skepticism concerning knowledge—although indeed they do so without clearly distinguishing the two forms of skepticism. It seems clear to me, however, that it is skepticism concerning justified belief that Reid is anxious to counter. And since rationality, as I shall be discussing it here, consists of being intellectually justified in one's belief, what we see in Reid's answer to the skeptic is an address to the nature of rationality. The defense of my claim—that the focus of Reid's concern is rationality rather than knowledge—is something that can best be allowed to emerge from my discussion as a whole.

But what, you ask, do I mean by "rationality," and why should rationality be distinguished from knowledge? First, "rational" is a word protean in its meanings. I shall use it, as I have already suggested, in such a way that rational belief is understood as intellectually justified belief. But that just moves the question over one step. What is an intellectually justified belief?

Justification in beliefs, as I understand it, is essentially connected to duties and responsibilities. Justification is a normative concept. In his book *Reason and Belief*, Brand Blanshard remarks that ". . . everywhere and always belief has an ethical aspect . . . . There is such a thing as a general ethics of the intellect" (401). Although I would not speak of *ethics* in this connection, what Blanshard says here seems to be correct. Just as there are duties and responsibilities pertaining to one's treatment of other human beings, so too there are duties and responsibilities pertaining to one's use of the intellect. It is not true that "anything goes" in our actions regarding other persons; neither is it true that "anything goes" in our believings. The justified belief, then, is the belief that is in accord with the norms for believing.

According to this understanding, to be justified in one's believings amounts to doing as well in one's believings as can rightly be demanded of a person. Justification consists in doing one's duty by one's believings. It consists in carrying out one's responsibilities with respect to one's believings. It consists in not believing what one ought not to believe. The justified in the domain of belief is like the permissible in the domain of morality; the morally permissible action is the action in accord with the norms for moral actions; the justified belief is the belief in accord with the norms for believing.

We cannot simply equate the rational belief with the justified belief, however. For although a person may be justified, *all things considered*, in believing something, it may nonetheless not be rational for him to believe it. What is *rational* for a person to believe is what he is *intellectually* justified in believing. And a person may be justified overall in believing something without being intellectually justified in believing it. Conversely, he may be intellectually justified in believing something without being justified overall. Being intellectually justified in believing something amounts only to being *prima facie* justified in believing it.

So what species of justification in beliefs is intellectual justification? Intellectual justification, in my judgment, is tied up with attempting to get in touch with reality, by trying to avoid falsehood in one's beliefs and trying to expand one's hold of true beliefs. In each of us there are certain belief-forming mechanisms. Likewise in each of us there are certain abilities for controlling these belief-forming mechanisms so as to diminish the amount of falsehood in our beliefs and to attain truth. Intellectual responsibility pertains to how we ought to use those governing abilities for the purpose of avoiding falsehood and attaining truth. Each of us is obliged to use those governing capacities in certain ways, toward the goal of being in touch with reality on certain matters; those constitute our intellectual responsibilities. A personal belief that does not represent a violation of my intellectual responsibilities is then a belief I am intellectually permitted to hold, a belief I am intellectually justified in holding. And the beliefs I am intellectually justified in holding are the beliefs that it is rational for me to hold.

But can I be intellectually justified in believing things I do not know? Certainly. Surely Newton was intellectually justified in believing his three laws of motion. In arriving at his acceptance of them he had done as well as could rightly be expected of him in the governance of his belief-forming mechanisms toward the goal of getting in touch with reality. Yet he did not know these mechanisms, for they were not (quite) true, as we now know. And one cannot know what is not true.

At the very foundation of Reid's approach to the topic of rationality is his claim that at any point in our lives we each have a variety of dispositions, inclinations and propensities to believe things —*belief-dispositions* we may call them. What accounts for our beliefs (in the vast majority of cases, anyway) is the triggering of one or another disposition. For example, we are all so constituted that upon having memory-experiences in certain situations, we are disposed to have certain beliefs about the past. We are disposed, upon having certain sensations in certain situations, to have certain beliefs about the external physical world. Upon having certain other sensations in certain situations, we are disposed to have certain beliefs about other persons. Likewise we are all so constituted as to be disposed in certain circumstances to believe what we apprehend people as telling us—the *credulity-principle*, as Reid rather fetchingly called it.

The belief-dispositions which I have cited thus far are all dispositions that produce their effects *immediately*. We do not normally infer, from other beliefs which we take as good evidence, that a person is before us. Rather, upon having certain sensations in certain situations we immediately believe this. Likewise our memory-experiences produce immediately in us certain convictions about the past. Remembering does not consist in going through a process of inferring a belief about the past from other beliefs.

There is, however, another disposition in us about which these remarks are not true. In addition to the features of our constitution mentioned thus far, we are also all constituted in the following way: if we judge that some proposition we already believe is good evidence for another proposition not yet believed, we are disposed to believe that other proposition as well. To this disposition Reid assigned the name of reason. Let me call it the *reasoning-disposition*. What were traditionally called *mediate* beliefs can now be singled out as those produced by the reasoning-disposition, and what were called *immediate* beliefs are those produced by some one of our other belief-dispositions.

Not only does Reid call to our attention the various belief-dispositions we actually possess at a given moment in our lives, he also speaks about the origins of these dispositions. It was his conviction, in the first place, that somewhere in the history of each of us are to be found certain belief-dispositions with which we were simply "endowed by our Creator." They belong to our human nature; they are innate. Their existence in us is not the result of conditioning. It must not be supposed, however, that all such non-conditioned dispositions are present in us at birth. Some, possibly most, of them emerge as we mature. We have the disposition to acquire them upon reaching each level of maturation. Here Reid offers an example:

> Perhaps a child in the womb, or for some short period of its existence, is merely a sentient being: the faculties by which it perceives an external world, by which it reflects on its own thoughts and existence, and relation to other things, as well as its reasoning and moral faculties, unfold themselves by degrees; so that it is inspired with the various principles of common sense, as with the passions of love and resentment, when it has occasion for them (*Inquiry* V,7).

But in addition to our innate, non-conditioned, belief-dispositions, we as adults all have a number of belief-dispositions which we have acquired by way of conditioning. Reid calls attention to a certain range of these as being belief-dispositions induced in us by the working of the *inductive principle*. The inductive principle is not itself a belief-disposition; it is an innate, non-conditioned disposition for the acquisition of belief-dispositions. Here is what Reid says about it: "It is undeniable, and indeed is acknowledged by all, that when we have found two things to have been constantly conjoined in the course of nature, the appearance of one of them is immediately followed by the conception and belief of the other" (*Inquiry* VI,24). And he goes on to say that it is "a natural, original and unaccountable propensity to believe, that the connections which we have observed in times past, will continue in time to come" (*Inquiry* II,9). Here is an example that Reid offers of a belief-disposition inculcated in us by this inductive principle of our native constitution: "When I hear a certain sound, I conclude immediately without reasoning, that a coach passes by. There are no premises from which this conclusion is inferred by any rules of logic. It is the effect of a principle of our nature, common to us with the brutes" (*Inquiry* IV,1).

Reid's thought concerning the workings of the inductive principle can readily be stated in the language of contemporary psychology. What accounts for some of our beliefs is that a process of classical, or Pavlovian, conditioning has taken place. A regular "schedule" has been established in one's experience between phenomena of type A and phenomena of type B; and now one has the disposition, upon experiencing a phenomenon of type A, to believe that there is also a phenomenon of type B. Hence one has acquired a new belief-disposition. It is the disposition to acquire belief-dispositions in this manner that Reid calls *the inductive principle.*

Vast numbers of our non-innate belief-dispositions are not acquired in this way, however, but rather by way of what we would nowadays call *operant* conditioning, working on our native belief-dispositions. In Reid's own thought this comes out most clearly in what he says about the credulity principle. It is a moot point whether the credulity disposition is present in us at birth. But very little maturation is required for it to put in its appearance. "The wise Author of nature," says Reid,

> hath planted in the human mind a propensity to rely upon human testimony before we can give a reason for doing so. This, indeed, puts our judgment almost entirely in the power of those who are about us in the first period of life; but this is necessary both to our preservation and to our improvement. If children were so framed as to pay no regard to testimony or authority, they must, in the literal sense, perish for lack of knowledge (*Essays* VI,5).

It was Reid's view that the working of the credulity principle "is unlimited in children" (*Inquiry* VI,24), in the sense that whatever a child apprehends someone as asserting, he believes. But shortly the principle begins to be "restrained and modified," as Reid puts it. What induces the revision and modification is the discovery that sometimes the principle produces false beliefs in us. "The principle of credulity is unlimited in children, until they meet with instances of deceit and falsehood" (*Inquiry* VI,24). Note how a person's conviction that some of the beliefs produced in him by testimony are false does not *destroy* his disposition to give credence to testimony. Rather, it results in that disposition becoming restrained and modified. The credulity principle becomes more finely articulated.

We can also think of this in terms of modern conditioning theory. The original, unqualified credulity principle is altered by way of operant conditioning. One's discovery, or conviction, that certain of one's beliefs thus produced are false will function as an *aversive* consequence, diminishing to the point of extinguishing the workings of the disposition in such cases. That new, slightly altered disposition is then in turn submitted to the same sort of testing. The person's convictions that some of the beliefs thus produced are false will again function as aversive consequences, and his independent discovery that others are true will function as reinforcing consequences. Then yet another alteration takes place, and so on. Eventually the person is no longer disposed to believe what persons of type P speaking under conditions of type C say on topics of type T, whereas other sorts of testimony he is disposed to believe more strongly than ever (and perhaps more strongly disposed to believe than ever).

I find it surprising that Reid does not emphasize how we are constantly acquiring new belief-dispositions by the working of operant conditioning on our other innate belief-dispositions as well, not just by its working on our credulity-disposition. Reid himself notes in his comments about memory that we tend to place more confidence in our memories according to how vivid or distinct they are. But this is almost certainly a matter of learning. And there is much more that could be said than just this. Other things being equal, one learns to place more confidence in one's memories of yesterday's occurrences than of occurrences in the distant past. One learns to place less confidence in the details of one's memory when one was agitated and upset, than when one was observing carefully and calmly. And so on, and on. In short, one learns gradually that one's memory is reliable on certain sorts of matters under certain sorts of conditions, and unreliable on other matters or under other conditions. This knowledge modifies the belief-dispositions attached to one's memory experiences. The revision can be seen as a selective strengthening and weakening of the original disposition, weakening to the point of disappearance in some cases.

The same sort of thing happens in the case of perception. When, as a child, I rode down a paved road on a hot summer day, I often believed there was water standing on the road ahead, in the distance, because it definitely looked that way. Now I no longer believe that, even when I am in those same circumstances. For I have learned that it *looks* that way, as the consequence of heat waves rising from the pavement, without really *being* that way. In general we could offer this comment. Our native belief-dispositions all go through stages of increasing articulation, as we experience how some beliefs produced by these dispositions are false, and others are true.

Not only does Reid discuss the origins of our various belief-dispositions, he also analyzes, in considerable detail, the workings of our various dispositions. He analyzes the workings of memory, sensation, perception, etc. These, in my judgment, are some of the most interesting passages in Reid's philosophy. For our purposes here, however, we shall have to forego looking into these matters and instead turn to what is usually taken to be the core of Reid's philosophy—namely, his notion of what he calls "the principles of common sense," or "first principles." I judge that Reid's notion of common sense is not, however, at the center of his philosophy. Centrality of place is occupied by his teaching about the nature and origin of our belief-dispositions, and his claim that in this teaching we have an answer to Humean skepticism. What Reid says about common sense is set entirely within this larger context. I do get the impression, however, that nineteenth century members of the Common-Sense school often knew very little about this embracing context.

Sometimes what Reid calls the principles of common sense are those native belief-dispositions essential to being a normal human being. Reid readily admits that there may well be certain madmen who differ quite strikingly from the rest of us in their native belief-dispositions. But we know such people to be abnormal, "ill-formed," "mal-formed." Reid is anxious to assert that it is essential for us as normal human beings to have certain belief-dispositions endowed by the Creator (plus, in the case of the inductive principle, the disposition to acquire belief-dispositions). Such dispositions belong to human nature. And these he calls "principles of common sense." Thus he cites *credulity* as an "original principle of human nature" (*Inquiry* VI,24).

More frequently, however, it is certain *beliefs* (i.e., propositions believed) that Reid cites as examples of principles of common sense, or first principles. Specifically, first principles are those immediate beliefs that all properly formed adult human beings hold and which they inescapably presuppose in their ordinary reasoning and living. (Or, as he sometimes puts it, every man of sound mind is determined to give immediate, implicit, assent to these beliefs.)

> If there are certain principles which the constitution of our nature leads us to believe, and which we are under a necessity to take for granted in the common concerns of life, without being able to give a reason for them; these are what we call the principles of common sense; and what is immediately contrary to them is what we call absurd (*Inquiry* II,6).

In another passage he says "the first principles of natural philosophy" are:

> principles which, though they have not the same kind of evidence that mathematical axioms have; yet have such evidence that every man of common understanding readily assents to them, and finds it absolutely necessary to conduct his actions and opinions by them, in the ordinary affairs of life (*Essays* I,2).

Reid adds that a belief of a person may be a first principle even though he is not aware he holds that belief; he need not believe that he believes it. The belief in question may be what Reid sometimes calls "implicit."

> We may here take notice of a property of the principle under consideration, that seems to be common to it with many other first principles, and which can hardly be found in any principle that is built solely upon reasoning; and that is, that in most men it produces its effect without ever being attended to, or made an object of thought. No man ever thinks of this principle, unless when he considers the grounds of scepticism; yet it invariably governs his opinions. When a man in the common course of life gives credit to the testimony of his senses, his memory, or his reason, he does not put the question to himself, whether these faculties may deceive him; yet the trust he reposes in them supposes an inward conviction, that, in that instance at least, they do not deceive him (*Essays* VI,5).

Reid goes further yet. Not only do people sometimes believe propositions which are first principles without being aware of believing them; sometimes they even deny believing them. They believe that they do not believe them.

> . . . it is another property of this and many first principles, that they force assent in particular instances, more powerfully than when they are turned into a general proposition . . . . Many have in general maintained that the senses are fallacious, yet there never was found a man so sceptical as not to trust his senses in particular instances when his safety required it; and it may be observed of those who have professed scepticism, that their scepticism lies in generals, while in particulars they are no less dogmatical than others *(loc. cit.)*.

I have cited this passage as one in which Reid says that people may deny they believe something which is in fact a first principle, and which is, accordingly, in fact believed by them. What the passage also illustrates, however, is Reid's confusion between first principles understood as belief-dispositions, and first principles understood as beliefs. To the best of my knowledge, Reid never indicates that he is calling these two different sorts of things "principles of common sense." Nevertheless, it does not follow that he confuses them. But I see no other way of construing this passage, as well as a number of others. First principles, he says, "force assent in particular instances." Here he must be thinking of fundamental belief-dispositions, for it is these which, when triggered in specific situations, yield particular beliefs. And it is these that continue to do their work in the skeptic—so we may suppose—even though he *believes* that one or other of them is unreliable. Yet in the very same passage Reid speaks of these principles as "general propositions." It would appear that Reid confused "propositions believed implicitly," with "native belief-dispositions."

Among the examples of first principles that Reid offers are "that the thoughts of which I am conscious, are the thoughts of a being which I call *myself, my mind, my person*," and "that we have some degree of power over our actions, and the determination of our will." Although we may indeed wonder whether everyone does indeed believe these (even implictly), there is no room here for ambiguity. Such principles as these are propositions believed, not belief-dispositions. When Reid cites principles pertaining to the reliability of our noetic mechanisms, then the disposition/belief ambiguity arises. Here are some of Reid's examples of such principles: "that those things did really happen which I distinctly remember"; "that those things do really exist which we distinctly perceive by our senses, and are what we perceive them to be"; "that there is a certain regard due to human testimony in matters of fact, and even to human authority in matters of opinion"; and "that the natural faculties by which we distinguish truth from error, are not fallacious" (*Essays* V,5). We are all disposed, says Reid, upon having a distinct memory experience, to believe that a certain sort of thing happened. We all, in that sense, trust our memory; we all take it as reliable. But it does not follow, however, that we all implicitly hold the *belief that* memory is reliable. Nor does it make any difference to the case Reid wishes to make against the skeptic whether we all implicitly hold such a belief.

Having canvassed Reid's teaching concerning our native belief-dispositions, let us now consider how he uses this material to make his case against the skeptic. The Reidian skeptic, remember, is the person who holds that we are to admit nothing amongst our beliefs but what has been established by reasoning. In other words, Reid's skeptic is the person who holds that we are justified in believing something only if we hold it on the basis of other beliefs which constitute adequate evidence for it. In particular, we must not accept the "testimony" of some noetic faculty until we can infer on the basis of good reasons that this testimony is reliable. "There is nothing so shameful in a philosopher as to be deceived and deluded; and therefore you ought to resolve firmly to withhold assent, and throw off this belief of external objects, which may be all delusions" (*Inquiry* VI,20).

The first point Reid makes in response to the skeptic is the *ad hominem* observation that such skeptics as Hume and Descartes violate this very principle in their philosophizing. Both accept, without having established its reliability, the testimony of consciousness. Reid says this about Hume:

> But are we to admit nothing but what can be proved by reasoning? Then we must be sceptics indeed, and believe nothing at all. The author of the *Treatise of Human Nature* appears to me to be but a half sceptic. He hath not followed his principles so far as they lead him: but after having, with unparalleled intrepidity and success, combated vulgar prejudices; when he had but one blow to strike, his courage fails him, he fairly lays down his arms, and yields himself a captive to the most common of all vulgar prejudices, I mean the belief of the existence of his own impressions and ideas (*Inquiry* V,7).

And about Descartes' argument in the *Meditations*, Reid says this:

> Perhaps Descartes meant not to assume his own existence in this enthymeme, but the existence of thought; and to infer from that the existence of a mind, or subject of thought. But why did he not prove the existence of his thought? Consciousness, it may be said, vouches that. But who is voucher of consciousness? Can any man prove that his consciousness may not deceive him? No man can: nor can we give a better reason for trusting to it, than that every man, while his mind is sound, is determined by the constitution of his nature, to give implicit belief to it . . . (*Inquiry* I,3).

In fact, Descartes really accepts, as properly basic, the testimony of consciousness:

> . . . what appeared to him first of all certain and evident, was, that he thought, that he doubted, that he deliberated. In a word, the operations of his own mind, of which he was conscious, must be real, and no delusion; and though all his other faculties should deceive him, his consciousness could not (*Inquiry* VII,7).

And speaking in general about those who hold the "new system of ideas," Reid says:

> The new system admits only one of the principles of common sense as a first principle; and pretends, by strict argumentation, to deduce all the rest from it. That our thoughts, our sensations, and every thing of which we are conscious, hath a real existence, is admitted in this system as a first principle; but everything else must be made evident by the light of reason. Reason must rear the whole fabric of knowledge upon this single principle of consciousness (*Inquiry* VII,7).

Not only are the great skeptics, Hume and Descartes, inconsistent in their philosophizing, because they fail to construct a system of thought consistent with their profession of skepticism. They, along with other skeptics, fail to *live* in a manner consistent with their profession of skepticism. "I never heard that any sceptic run his head against a post," says Reid, "or stepped into a kennel, because he did not believe his eyes" (*Essays* I,2). But "if a man pretends to be a sceptic with regard to the information of sense, and yet prudently keeps out of harm's way as other men do, he must excuse my suspicion, that he either acts the hypocrite, or imposes upon himself" (*Inquiry* VI,20).[1]

After making these *ad hominem* points against the skeptic, Reid goes on to observe that all normal human beings are so constructed that they *cannot* follow the advice of the skeptic, i.e., to believe a proposition only if they have inferred it from other beliefs which provide adequate evidence for it. We are so constructed, he says, that it is simply not in our power to discard certain beliefs. The skeptic says we *ought to* discard every belief that has not been produced in us by reasoning. Reid's reply is that we *cannot* do this:

> It would be agreeable to fly to the moon, and to make a visit to Jupiter and Saturn; but when I know that nature has bound me down by the law of gravitation to this planet which I inhabit, I rest contented, and quietly suffer myself to be carried along in its orbit. My belief is carried along by perception, as irresistibly as my body by the Earth. And the greatest sceptic will find himself to be in the same condition. He may struggle hard to disbelieve the informations of his senses, as a man does to swim against the torrent; but ah! it is in vain. It is in vain that he strains every nerve, and wrestles with nature, and with every object that strikes upon his senses. For after all, when his strength is spent in the fruitless attempt, he will be carried down the torrent with the common herd of believers (*Inquiry* VI,20).

To argue that we cannot rid ourselves of vast numbers of our immediate beliefs is not, of course, to establish that those beliefs are *true*. Thus Reid's argument is no proof that these beliefs constitute knowledge. I suspect it is Reid's conviction, however, that one is never obliged to do what one *cannot* do. Accordingly, in showing that some of our immediate beliefs are ineluctable he has shown that we are *justified* in holding them. If, in our ineluctable trust in the testimony of our native faculties, we nonetheless fall into error, then "we are deceived by Him who made us, and there is no remedy" (*Inquiry* V,7). Where there is no remedy, there is no irresponsibility. No more can be laid on us as obligatory than that we do the best we can. "Me thinks, therefore, it were better to make a virtue of necessity" (*Inquiry* V,7).

A second argument which Reid launches against the position of the skeptic is that his position is completely arbitrary. The skeptic apparently holds that we are justified in accepting the deliverances of inference without having adequate evidence that inference is a reliable belief-producing mechanism. At the same time we are not justified in thus accepting the deliverances of any other belief-producing mechanism. We may accept the deliverances of our other noetic faculties only if we infer from our other beliefs, which are adequate evidence, that those faculties are reliable. Reid's reply is that this represents an unjustifiable, arbitrary, singling out of reason. What is there about reason that makes us justified in taking it as reliable—without first establishing its reliability—if we are not justified in treating any of our other belief-dispositions this way? All our natural faculties have the same status. There is no relevant difference among them.

> The sceptic asks me, Why do you believe the existence of the external object which you perceive? This belief, Sir, is none of my manufacture; it came from the mint of nature; it bears her image and superscription; and, if it is not right, the fault is not mine: I even took it upon trust, and without suspicion. Reason, says the sceptic, is the only judge of truth, and you ought to throw off every opinion and every belief that is not grounded on reason. Why, Sir, should I believe the faculty of reason more than that of perception; they came both out of the same shop, and were made by the same artist; and if he puts one piece of false ware into my hands, what should hinder him from putting another? (*Inquiry* VI,20)

Reid does admit that:

> . . . when I compare the different kinds of evidence above-mentioned, I confess, after all, that the evidence of reasoning, and that of some necessary and self-evident truths, seems to be the least mysterious and the most perfectly comprehended; and therefore I do not think it strange that philosophers should have endeavoured to reduce all kinds of evidence to these . . . . On the other hand, when I remember distinctly a past event, or see an object before my eyes, this commands my belief no less than an axiom . . . . I seem to want that evidence which I can best comprehend, and which gives perfect satisfaction to an inquisitive mind; yet it is ridiculous to doubt; and I find it not in my power (*Essays* II,20).[2]

Perhaps there is another way of understanding skepticism, however. Perhaps it is the contention of the skeptic that, since *all* of our belief-forming mechanisms are liable to yield error now and then, we are not even justified in accepting the results of inference ("the testimony of reason") unless first we have inferred, from our other beliefs which are good evidence for it, that inference (reason) is a reliable belief-forming mechanism. But if this is the skeptic's position, then obviously we can have no justified beliefs whatsoever; and rather than trying to dislodge him from his position by argument, it is best to walk away, says Reid.

> If a sceptic should build his scepticism upon this foundation, that all our reasoning and judging powers are fallacious in their nature, or should resolve at least to withhold assent until it be proved that they are not, it would be impossible by argument to beat him out of this stronghold; and he must even be left to enjoy his scepticism.
>
> Descartes certainly made a false step in this matter, for having suggested this doubt among others—that whatever evidence he might have from his consciousness, his senses, his memory, or his reason, yet possibly some malignant being had given him those faculties on purpose to impose upon him; and, therefore, that they are not to be trusted without a proper voucher: to remove this doubt, he endeavours to prove the being of a Deity who is no deceiver; whence he concludes, that the faculties he had given him are true and worthy to be trusted.
>
> It is strange that so acute a reasoner did not perceive that in this reasoning there is evidently a begging of the question.
>
> For, if our faculties be fallacious, why may they not deceive us in this reasoning as well as in others? And, if they are to be trusted in this instance without a voucher, why not in others?
>
> Every kind of reasoning for the veracity of our faculties, amounts to no more than taking their own testimony for their veracity . . . the reason why Descartes satisfied himself with so weak an argument for the truth of his faculties, most probably was, that he never seriously doubted it (*Essays* VI,5).[3]

Over and over Reid says it is God who has endowed us with our native belief-dispositions.

> Common sense and reason have both one author; that almighty Author, in all whose other works we observe a consistency, uniformity, and beauty, which charm and delight the understanding: there must therefore be some order and consistency in the human faculties, as well as in other parts of his workmanship (*Inquiry* V,7).

And speaking of perception, Reid says that "now I yield to the direction of my senses, not from instinct only, but from confidence and trust in a faithful and beneficent Monitor, grounded upon the experience of his paternal care and goodness" (*Inquiry* VI,20). So when all is said and done, the person who believes in a good God does, thereby, have a belief from which he can appropriately infer the reliability of his native noetic faculties. But to accept God's goodness as a reason for trusting in one's native noetic faculties is, of course, already to trust one's power of reasoning. And in addition, as Reid often remarks, we all trust our noetic faculties long before, and whether or not, we have this as a reason for doing so:

> . . . a man would believe his senses though he had no notion of a Deity. He who is persuaded that he is the workmanship of God, and that it is a part of his constitution to believe his senses, may think that a good reason to confirm his belief. But he had the belief before he could give this or any other reason for it (*Essays* II,20).
>
> The wise Author of our nature intended, that a great and necessary part of our knowledge should be derived from experience, before we are capable of reasoning, and he hath provided means perfectly adequate to this intention (*Inquiry* VI,24).

I have said that Reid's theory of rationality occurs in the context of his attack on skepticism. Now we have noticed that Reid's attack on skepticism does not take the form of enunciating and defending a criterion of justified belief, and then showing that the criterion proposed by the skeptic is incompatible with his own. That leaves us then with another question. *Does* Reid suggest a criterion of justified belief? Presumably a complete theory of rationality will include such a criterion. Is Reid's theory complete—or at least, complete on this point?

I know of no passage in which Reid explicitly formulates such a criterion. So if he has one in mind, it remains implicit. Here is an important passage to consider in attempting to decide whether Reid is implicitly working with a criterion:

> We give the name of evidence to whatever is a ground of belief. To believe without evidence is a weakness which every man is concerned to avoid, and which every man wishes to avoid. Nor is it in a man's power to believe anything longer than he thinks he has evidence . . . .
>
> The common occasions of life lead us to distinguish evidence into different kinds, to which we give names that are well understood; such as the evidence of sense, the evidence of memory, the evidence of consciousness, the evidence of testimony, the evidence of axioms, the evidence of reasoning. All men of common understanding agree that each of these kinds of evidence may accord just ground of belief, and they agree very generally in the circumstances that strengthen or weaken them . . . .
>
> [These different kinds of evidence] seem to me to agree only in this, that they are all fitted by Nature to produce belief in the human mind, some of them in the highest degree, which we call certainty, others in various degrees according to circumstances.
>
> I shall take it for granted that the evidence of sense, when the proper

circumstances concur, is good evidence, and a just ground of belief . . . (*Essays* II,20).

Evidence for a belief, as Reid here interprets "evidence," is that which produces, or causes, the belief. In the standard case, it is what activates some belief-disposition. (Possibly Reid also has in mind that it is an activating event *of which the person is aware*.) And now what Reid says at the end of this passage is that, for example, the evidence of sense is *good* evidence (*just* ground) for the belief *when the proper circumstances concur*. What does he mean by saying the evidence of sense, when the proper circumstances concur, is *good* evidence for the belief produced by that evidence? Clearly, the evidence in those circumstances is what may be called a *justifying condition* for that belief. For he goes on to say that "all good evidence is commonly called reasonable evidence, and very justly, because it ought to govern our belief as reasonable creatures. And according to this meaning, I think the evidence of sense no less reasonable than that of demonstration." So Reid does not think, along the lines of the skeptic, of justification for a belief as always consisting of other beliefs on the basis of which the belief is held. Instead Reid is inviting us to expand our vision and think in terms of the justifying conditions for our beliefs as evidence of various sorts producing the beliefs under appropriate circumstances.

Now I think it is essential to expand our vision in this way, and to think in general of justifying conditions for our beliefs. But obviously Reid's own suggestion brings questions to mind. Is there, for every kind of event that triggers a belief-disposition, an appropriate circumstance such that if the event occurs in that circumstance, we have a justifying condition? Is it not possible that some events which trigger beliefs never yield justification? If so, which triggering events do provide "just ground" and which do not? Reid says that sensations do. What else? And what are those "proper circumstances" which, for each type of evidence, must concur if we are to have justification? And further, might it be possible to formulate a general theory of justifying conditions which never mentions this business of various types of evidence? A theory of this sort would depart significantly from Reid's approach; for his theory of types of evidence is central to his whole approach. But is such an alternative possible?

I think we must admit that Reid does not answer these questions. What we obtain from Reid is a way of thinking of rationality, and a way of formulating a criterion of justified belief, namely, in terms of justifying conditions. But he does not actually offer a criterion.

We do learn, however, about a number of factors which he would insist must be kept in mind as we try to formulate a criterion. In the first place, Reid seems inclined to say that any event which triggers a belief-disposition that belongs to human nature and has, accordingly, been placed in us by our Creator, constitutes a just ground of belief in the proper circumstances. Whether a belief-disposition has been God-endowed is a relevant consideration. Second, Reid wishes to hold some sort of *ought implies can* principle for the domain of belief. And third, it seems clear, from what Reid says about the credulity principle, that if some triggering event produces a belief in the circumstance where other beliefs suggest the falsehood of this belief, *then* the triggering event is not "just ground" for the belief.

It will have been clear from the foregoing that Reid is firmly persuaded that our epistemic nature has an author, namely God. Reid is like Kant in that he sets his entire epistemology within the context of a doctrine of human nature. He is unlike Kant in that he sees this nature as the handiwork of a creating and beneficent God.

One naturally infers from these convictions of Reid that he regarded it as entirely reasonable, rational and intellectually justified for him to believe that God existed, that God was Creator, etc. And so a question arises: Why did he regard these beliefs this way? What did he regard as the justifying condition for such fundamental theistic beliefs? Did he think we were endowed by our Creator with a disposition to have certain theistic beliefs—that is, with a disposition to have such beliefs immediately? And did he hold that when these dispositions were triggered by "evidences" in the proper circumstances, the resultant beliefs were rational? Or did he think, on the contrary, that if one were to be justified in holding such beliefs one had to arrive at them by good inference—by reason? In short, was Reid a fideist or an evidentialist with respect to fundamental theistic propositions?

It is striking that, in spite of having been a Presbyterian clergyman in the early part of his career, Reid says very little about this topic of the rationality of theistic belief. Indeed, I know of no passage in which he addresses the issue forthrightly. We will have to arrive at his view by inference.

One point to be noted is a matter of omission: Reid never cites any theistic propositions as principles of common sense. And he never explains this omission. One guesses, however, that in his judgment, one could be a well-formed, mature, human being and not believe such propositions. Of course, a Calvinist would respond to this point by saying that sin has introduced a *mal*formation into our existence—one of the results of this malformation being that people resist acknowledging the existence of God. But I know of no passage in which Reid raises this possibility.

In one passage in the *Essays*, Reid remarks that among other contingent propositions must be numbered "all the truths we know concerning the existence of things—the truth of our own existence—of the existence of other things, inanimate, animal, and rational, and of their various attributes and relations" (*Essays* VI,3). But then he goes on to say:

> I accept only the existence and attributes of the Supreme Being, which is the only necessary truth I know concerning existence. All other beings that exist depend for their existence, and all that belongs to it, upon the will and power of the first cause; therefore, neither their existence, nor their nature, nor anything that befalls them, is necessary but contingent (*ibid.*; see also *op. cit.*, VI,6).

To these remarks Reid adds that

> although the existence of the Deity be necessary, I apprehend we can only deduce it from contingent truths. The only arguments for the existence of a Deity which I am able to comprehend, are grounded upon the knowledge of my own existence, and the existence of other finite beings. But these are contingent truths (*ibid.*).

Now when we look into that section of the *Essays* called "First Principles of Necessary Truths" (VI,6), a section in which Reid cites some of those principles of common sense which are necessarily true, although we nowhere find any theistic propositions cited as examples, we do find certain "metaphysical" principles cited, among these being *that whatever begins to exist, must have a cause which produced it;* and *that design and intelligence in the cause may be inferred, with certainty, from marks or signs of it in the effect*. Then a bit later, in the same section of the *Essays*, Reid offers this comment:

> The clear marks and signatures of wisdom, power, and goodness, in the constitution and government of the world, is, of all arguments that have been advanced for the being and providence of the Deity, that which in all ages has made the strongest impression upon candid and thinking minds; an argument, which has this peculiar advantage, that it gathers strength as human knowledge advances, and is more convincing at present than it was some centuries ago (*Essays* VI,6).[4]

So as to have the argument laid out with stark clarity before his readers, Reid later formulates it like this:

> The argument from final causes, when reduced to a syllogism, has these two premises:—*First*, That design and intelligence in the

> cause, may, with certainty, be inferred from marks or signs of it in the effect. This is the principle we have been considering, and we may call it the *major* proposition of the argument. The *second*, which we call the *minor* proposition, is, That there are in fact the clearest marks of design and wisdom in the works of nature; and the *conclusion* is, That the works of nature are the effects of a wise and intelligent Cause.

Obviously any conclusions drawn from all this with respect to Reid's views on the fideist/evidentialist issue must be somewhat speculative. In his published writings Reid does not (to the best of my knowledge) directly confront the issue. Although he never says so, Reid would no doubt agree that children often believe that God exists, that he is our Creator and beneficent Provider, etc., on the authority of some adult; when they do so, they hold these beliefs immediately. Reid might even say that the child would be *justified* in such beliefs. This would simply be a case of the workings of the credulity principle. I think it rather likely, however, that Reid thought the situation of the adult to be different—although exactly *why* he would think it different is not made clear. I think the evidence is that in Reid's opinion, those adults who are justified in their theistic beliefs hold those beliefs on the basis of reason—they have arrived at them by inference. Certainly there is no evidence that Reid shared Calvin's conviction about how we have been endowed with a belief-disposition triggered by our awareness of the rich and intricate design of the cosmos, and which immediately yields the belief that the world has been made by a divine being.

Recently the substance of Reid's lectures on natural theology in 1780 has been published, the text being derived from student notes of the lectures (edited by Elmer H. Duncan; University Press of America, 1981). For the most part, these lectures are an elaboration of the points already made. Near the beginning Reid sets the topic for the entire course of lectures:

> The existence of the Supreme Being is so loudly proclaimed by everything in Heaven and Earth, by the structure of our bodies and the no less curious structure of our Minds and indeed by everything about us, that it may perhaps appear unnecessary to confirm a truth so evident. But when we consider the importance and that there have not been wanting persons who have exercised their uses to weaken its evidence, it will appear proper to consider the grounds on which it is supported and to enquire into the forces of the sophistical arguments that have been urged against it (p. 2).

It is not clear here whether Reid thinks that this "truth so evident" is an immediate belief, or one arrived at by obvious inference. I think, however, that those closing words about "the grounds on which it is supported" tip the scales toward the latter interpretation. This would be confirmed by a later passage in which Reid says that ". . . from the marks of wisdom and design to be met with in the Universe, we infer it is the work of a wise and intelligent cause" (*Lectures on Natural Theology*, p. 51); for Reid quite consistently speaks of "inference" only when he has in mind the workings of reason.[5] Thus it seems that there is one likely interpretation of what Reid saw himself doing in the *Lectures*. He was carefully scrutinizing and defending the inference which, in intuitive fashion, leads the ordinary adult person to God, rather than constructing an argument for a belief which is characteristically arrived at immediately.

What is new in these lectures is the theme sounded in the following passage from the opening paragraph:

> It is no doubt true that Revelation exhibits all the truths of Natural Religion, but it is no less true that reason must be employed to judge of that revelation; whether it comes from God. Both are great lights and we ought not to put out the one in order to use the other. Revelation is of use to enlighten us with regard to the use of Natural Religion, as one man may enlighten another in things that it was impossible could be discovered by him, it is easy then to conceive that God could enlighten Man. And that he has done so is evident from a comparison of the doctrines of Scripture with the systems of the most refined heathens. We acknowledge then that men are indebted to revelation in the matter of Natural Religion but this is no reason why we should not also use our reason here. Revelation was given us not to hinder the exercise of our reasoning powers but to aid and assist them. Tis by reason that we must judge whether that Revelation be really so; Tis by reason that we must judge of the meaning of what is revealed; and it is by Reason that we must guard against any impious, inconsistent or absurd interpretation of that revelation. As the best things may be abused so when we lay aside the exercise of reason Revelation becomes the tool of low Superstition or of wild fanaticism and that man is best prepared for the study and practice of the revealed Religion who has previously acquired just Sentiments of the Natural (*op. cit.*, 1-2).

Here, in characteristic Enlightenment fashion, Reid says that to be justified in accepting the Scriptures as Revelation one must use reason to establish that they come from God—for otherwise "Revelation becomes the tool of low Superstition or of wild fanaticism . . . ." One is not justified in accepting the evidence of Scripture as Revelation, unless by reason one has judged "whether that Revelation be really so."[6] The "testing" that Reid, in his attack on the skeptic, disavows as necessary for our native noetic faculties, *is* necessary for our acceptance of revelation.

My attempt has been to understand Reid's theory of rationality. I freely admit that this, like any other attempt to understand an historical figure, involves a significant displacement of emphasis from that to be found in Reid himself. Such displacement is not only unavoidable but desirable. In wreaking his displacement, the interpreter, of course, runs the double threat of saying what is false, and of saying what is misleading, in the sense that he leads the reader to draw conclusions that are false. I hope that in the particular displacement I have executed, these two threats have been staved off.

Having interpreted an historical figure, one can then proceed in either of two directions. One can ask what his (more or less) immediate successors appropriated from him. Or one can ask what we, in a later and significantly different historical situation, can profitably appropriate from him. Let me conclude my discussion with some comments on this latter point.

One feature of our present philosophical situation is that meta-epistemology has begun to flourish among us. In the past decade or so, philosophers have become more aware than ever before of the structure of epistemological options. As part of this flourishing of meta-epistemology, the concept of foundationalism has been formulated with care, and powerful attacks have been launched against classical foundationalism, whether construed as a theory of scientia, of knowledge, or of rational belief. From their conviction that the classical foundationalist theory of knowledge is untenable, some philosophers have concluded that the concept of knowledge has no application. That seems to me the basic line of argument in Richard Rorty's recent book, *Philosophy and the Mirror of Nature*. Others, on similar grounds, have drawn conclusions about the non-applicability of the concept of rationality. But obviously this is a mighty leap—from the untenability of a proposed criterion for the application of a certain concept, to a conclusion that the concept itself has no application.

In my judgment, one of the most important things Reid offers us in our present philosophical situation is a non-classical foundationalist theory of rationality. In Reid one sees an historical option to the dominance of classical foundationalism in the West.

And as to the character of Reid's option, three things seem to me of primary importance for us in our situation. In the first place, Reid very clearly gives what may be called a theory of *situated rationality*. Rationality is always situational, in the sense that what is rational for one person to believe will not be rational for another to believe. Thus in general we cannot inquire into the rationality of some belief by asking whether *one* would be rational in holding that belief. We must ask whether it would be rational for *this particular person* to hold it, or whether it would be rational for *a person of this type in this situation* to hold it. I think it must be admitted that Reid's increasing emphasis on the principles of common sense tended to obscure from him the fact that his was very much a theory of situated rationality. Yet the realization of that fact repeatedly comes to the surface of his discussion. Although our native belief-dispositions are shared in common, different "evidences" trigger these dispositions in different persons, and different justified beliefs emerge.

Second, Reid, more than any other philosopher in history, set his theory of rationality within the context of a theory of human nature which delved into the actual psychology of the human being. Epistemology in our century has been divorced, until very recently, from any systematic theory of human nature; epistemologists have focused their attention on the evidential relations among propositions. By contrast, Kant's epistemology was very much set within the context of an elaborate theory of human nature. But Kant was radically essentialist in his interests, in the sense that his sole concern in the *Pure Critique* was to develop a theory of the essence of the human being—or perhaps, of the essence of any finite being capable of knowledge. Psychology was irrelevant to Kant's enterprise. Reid, in striking fashion, goes beyond essence to psychology.

Third, Reid's non-classical foundationalist theory is not at all a skeptical theory. It is, on the contrary, a penetrating reply to skepticism. At the same time it is, in contrast to Kant's reply to Hume's skepticism, a theory in which the world is not lost. Fundamental to Kant was the radical claim that only of ourselves can we know the nature, the essence. From this basic tenent, Kant concluded that we can know nothing of reality apart from how it appears to us—not even its essence. This was his reply to Hume's skepticism. In Reid's reply, by contrast, the world is kept.

Although there is much that we in our situation can appropriate from Reid, we still cannot be simply Reidians. For we have learned to work for the formulation of a criterion of justified belief, and we do not find such a criterion in Reid. We find in him a way of approaching a formulation of such a criterion, and we find some considerations to keep in mind as we try to formulate a criterion. But we find no more than that.

In my judgment, however, there is a deeper deficiency than this in Reid's work. His discussion of the sources of belief is too narrow. We live in the shadow of those two great practitioners of the art of suspecting, Marx and Freud, and so for us there is a striking feature in Reid's discussion: he attends only to the "noble" sources of belief. No ignobility enters the picture. The fact that we sometimes come to believe something because it helps us to rest content in our position of economic privilege goes unnoticed. Sometimes we come to believe something because it helps to protect us from the embarrassment of acknowledging our true reasons for acting as we did. This is also unnoticed. Of course, Reid's oversight on such matters as these is scarcely culpable. Marx and Freud were still well in the future.

There was a point, however, at which the relevance of ignoble factors was immediately before Reid. In *Essays* VI,6, in the context of his brief look at the teleological argument, Reid remarked that "in all ages, those who have been unfriendly to the principles of religion, have made attempts to weaken the force of the argument for the existence and perfection of the Deity . . . ." And in the *Lectures* (pp. 58-59) Reid says there are several other arguments for God's existence than the teleological one which "you will find in authors who have handled the subject, but though I would be very far from disparaging these arguments as useless, yet I would despair of convincing a man by these who resists the force of this—such a man is hardened beyond the power of arguments." In these passages Reid sees himself as dealing with a factor of resistance, of "hardening," and clearly he thinks this shapes the beliefs of his opponents. Presumably he has in mind those people who do not want to believe that God exists. But nowhere does Reid do anything with this insight. It does not enter into the structure of his thought.

I can emphasize my point by saying that Reid nowhere recognizes the ways in which sin inserts itself in the workings of our belief-dispositions. He bases his epistemology on those dispositions with which we have been endowed by our Creator. He hardly recognizes how those dispositions are now intermingled with all sorts of dispositions that we have by virtue of our fallenness. In this respect, Calvin and Kuyper were more insightful. Especially relevant, for example, is Kuyper's penetrating passage on "Science and Sin" in his *Principles of Sacred Theology* (Grand Rapids: Baker Book House, 1980, reprinted)[7] and Calvin's discussion on the *sensus divinitatis* becoming a "factory of idols" under the impact of sin. What we need, then, is a blend between Reid's general framework of belief-dispositions, and Calvin's and Kuyper's vivid awareness of these ignoble belief-dispositions that we now have—we who are not only created but fallen.

I have spoken of our situation as one in which philosophers have learned, as part of the rise of meta-epistemology, to question the epistemological vision by which the West has mainly lived—that of classical foundationalism. There are features of our contemporary situation which go much deeper than that, however. We live in a time when the impulses of the Enlightenment have almost played themselves out. In this situation, I sense that people are willing to ask anew about the relation between reason and revelation. Reid's Enlightenment insistence that revelation must be tested by reason no longer seems obviously true to us. Why is it that one must first run an evidential test on Scripture before one is justified in accepting it? Does this not fundamentally subordinate revelation to reason? What then is left of the authority of Scripture? But is it not fundamental to the identity and the direction of the Christian community that Scripture function as canon within it—that it be accepted as authoritative? These are fundamental questions which we, in our situation, must ask anew.

Notes

1. Cf. *Inquiry* VII,7: "When a man suffers himself to be reasoned out of the principles of common sense, by metaphysical arguments, we may call this *metaphysical lunacy;* which differs from the other species of distemper in this, that it is not continued but intermittent; it is apt to seize the patient in solitary and speculative moments; but when he enters into society, Common Sense recovers her authority." Compare *Essays* II,5: ". . . in all the history of philosophy, we never read of any sceptic that ever stepped into fire or water because he did not believe his senses, or that shewed in the conduct of his life less trust in his senses than other men have. This gives us just ground to apprehend that philosophy was never able to conquer that natural belief which men have in their senses."
2. Also, of course, any attempt to *establish* the reliability of some faculties while *assuming* the reliability of others grants the main point: that the justifiability of accepting the testimony of our faculties does not in general await our establishing that they are reliable.
3. Cf. *Essays* VI,6: "We cannot give a reason why we believe even our sensations to be real and not fallacious; why we believe what we are conscious of; why we trust any of our natural faculties. We say, it must be so, it cannot be otherwise. This expresses only a strong belief, which is indeed the voice of nature, and which therefore in vain we attempt to resist. But if, in spite of nature, we resolve to go deeper, and not to trust our faculties, without a

reason to shew that they cannot be fallacious, I am afraid that, seeking to become wise, and to be as gods, we shall become foolish . . . ."

4. Those who assume that natural theology is incompatible with what is now sometimes called "doxological" theology should consider this passage, which follows shortly after the above: "When we attend to the marks of good contrivance which appear in the works of God, every discovery we make in the constitution of the material or intellectual system becomes a hymn of praise to the great Creator and Governor of the world." See also p. 54 of Reid's *Lectures on Natural Theology*.

5. Consider also this passage from p. 52 of the *Lectures:* "From this it is evident that it is no less a part of the human constitution to judge of powers by their effects than of corporeal objects by the senses. We see that such judgments are common to all men and absolutely necessary in the affairs of life, now every judgment of this kind is only an application of that general rule, that from marks of intelligence and wisdom in effects, a wise and intelligent cause may be inferred. From the wise conduct, we infer wisdom in the cause, and from a brave conduct, we infer bravery—this we do with perfect security—it is done by all—they cannot avoid it, it is necessary too in the conduct of life, it is therefore to be received as a first principle. Some, however, have thought that we learn this by reasoning or by experience. I apprehend it can be got from neither of these." See also p. 54.

6. Reid agrees, or comes close to agreeing, with Kant that it is the ethical benefits of theistic belief which constitutes its importance in our lives. The lectures on natural theology begin with these words: "Of all the animals which God has made it is the prerogative of Man alone to know his Maker. There is no kind of knowledge that tends so much to elevate the Mind as the knowledge of God. Duty to God forms an important part of our duty and it is the support of every virtue; it gives us magnanimity, fortitude and tranquility; it inspires with hope in the most adverse circumstances, and there can be no rational piety without just notions of the perfections and providence of God." See also *op. cit.*, p. 125. What is also striking about the passage quoted in the text above is that Reid avoids affirming the medieval insistence that Revelation *adds to* what is accessible to "reason." That fits with the fact that Reid characteristically speaks of God as Creator, Provider, and Judge, but never, to the best of my knowledge, as Redeemer. One gets the impression that on his view, Revelation merely duplicates Reason. Consider this passage: "We must observe at the same time, that there was one nation, I mean the Jews, who had more rational notions of the Supreme Being of his attributes, notions perfectly agreeable to the dictates of reason as we have explained them. Now we can hardly suppose that a nation, barbarous as the Jews were, should have their reasoning powers more refined on this subject than their neighbors, without a Revelation from the Father of Lights. This then may teach us of how Great importance it is, for [us] to attain proper notions of the Deity and his attributes, since so many of mankind, have wandered so far from the truth and so contrary to what reason would dictate to them" (*Lectures*, p. 108). Consider also this: "Hence we

find that the doctrines of Natural Religion have been improved by the Speculations of Theologians and assisted by the representations of Deity given in the Sacred Scriptures. For no where do we find such a completed system of Natural Religions as in the Christian Writers" (*op. cit.*, p. 123). In the passage that follows this, Reid talks about the origins of idolatry. He attributes it not to a sinful resistance to acknowledging God (as does Calvin), but to "the corruptions of human reason, the craft of the priest or the cunning of the politician" (p. 124). "Notions which reason dictates to us and which Revelation confirms" (p. 127)—that seems to me the best summary of how Reid understands the relation between the content of natural theology and of revelation.

7. Consider, for example, this striking passage, only one of many in the section: "He who has had his bringing-up in the midst of want and neglect will entertain entirely different views of jural relationships and social regulations from him who from his youth has been bathed in prosperity" (*op. cit.*, p. 109).

Thomas Reid, Common Sense and Calvinism

Paul Helm

THE SCOTTISH COMMON-SENSE PHILOSOPHY was upheld by many Calvinist theologians, such as Thomas Chalmers (1780-1847) in Scotland, and in the United States, both in the East through the influence of Princeton (where John Witherspoon, a Reidian, had become president in 1768) and in the South through men such as James Henley Thornwell.[1] These Scottish influences upon American Calvinism were reinforced by the arrival of James McCosh (1811-1894) in Princeton in 1868.[2] The general prestige of Scottish common-sense philosophy, or might common-sense philosophy be one native land, where it waned after the mid-nineteenth century, being supplanted by forms of continental post-Kantian idealism introduced by people such as J.F. Ferrier (1808-1864) and Edward Caird (1835-1908).

I

It is not the aim of this chapter to contribute anything to an historical understanding of the rise, influence and waning of Scottish common-sense philosophy and its impact upon Calvinism,[3] but rather to try to formulate answers to two philosophical questions. What was Thomas Reid's view of rationality? And what connection, if any, is there between this view of rationality and Calvinism? Given the existence of Calvinism (a set of propositions about God, man and the world authorized by the Christian Scriptures), what philosophical system or outlook does Calvinism entail? Or, put less strongly, what system is consistent with Calvinism? Might that system be Scottish common sense philosophy, or might common-sense philosophy be one of several such systems? This is different from asking what philosophical outlook would rationally justify or intellectually permit belief in the distinctive propositions of Calvinism. In addressing these questions, attention will be confined almost entirely to Thomas Reid himself. The views of his followers such as James Beattie, Dugald Stewart and Sir William Hamilton will not be considered.

Reid's views on rationality are to be found chiefly in the sixth of his *Essays on the Intellectual Powers* (1785), chapters IV - VII, where he deals with what he calls "first principles."[4] In addition to those references, there are numerous others scattered throughout his writings. On the reasonable assumption that Reid's views did not alter very much over the course of time, we shall look at the relevant chapters in the sixth *Essay* and take up other references only where they add to what Reid says here.

Reid distinguishes between self-evident truths, the grasp of which is intuitive and which are no sooner understood than they are believed (434), and principles, the assent to which requires evidence. All who are of ripe understanding and free of prejudice will, according to Reid, assent to the view that there are self-evident truths in both these senses, although there has been, Reid acknowledges (434), considerable debate as to what such self-evident truths are.

It would be a mistake to think that Reid cannot *argue* for such a position, a mistake that involves a confusion between:

(1) There are self-evident truths; and
(2) *p* is a self-evident truth.

It is possible to argue for the truth of (1) in various ways. For example, (1) could be argued for by showing the philosophical weakness of the position of those who deny (1)—for example, that such a denial leads to total skepticism. But it is not possible to argue, in a parallel way, for the truth of (2), since to argue that (2) is true would be to deny that *p* was self-evident, since any self-evident truth does not need arguing for, and cannot be argued for, but is one whose truth is seen without the introduction of argument.

Reid thinks that the truth of (1) can be established by employing what he considers to be a *reductio*. If (1) is not true, then we are in the intolerable position of having to accept an infinite regress of justifications. That is to say, the process of epistemic justification *could* never come to an end. For Reid holds that any process of epistemic justification must terminate in a set of self-evident truths. Anything else would not *be* epistemic justification. He says:

> We must begin, either with self-evident propositions or with such as have been already proved. When the last is the case, the proof of the propositions, thus assumed, is a part of our proof; and the proof is deficient without it. Suppose then the deficiency supplied, and the proof completed, is it not evident that it must set out with self-

> evident propositions, and that the whole evidence must rest upon them? So that it appears to be demonstrable that, without first principles, analytical reasoning could have no end, and synthetical reasoning could have no beginning; and that every conclusion got by reasoning must rest with its whole weight upon first principles, as the building does upon its foundations (435).

So here is an *a priori* argument for the conclusion that there must be self-evident propositions—namely, that if there aren't any it would be impossible ever to come to a rationally justified conclusion about anything. This is not an argument that is original to Reid and certainly he was not the last to consider and defend it.[5]

Whatever the merits of the argument, it is clear from the above quotation, and from much elsewhere in Reid, that his philosophy is a species of foundationalism. He explicitly uses the metaphor of foundation and superstructure: the self-evident truths form the foundations; those propositions that are justified or justifiable by reference to the foundations form the superstructure. The first principles, the foundations, in some cases lead to conclusions that are certain, in other cases to conclusions that are probable.

> I hold it to be certain, and even demonstrable, that all knowledge got by reasoning must be built upon first principles. This is as certain as that every house must have a foundation. The power of reasoning, in this respect, resembles the mechanical powers or engines; it must have a fixed point to rest upon (435).

Reid further holds, as we noted, that there may be (and have been) disputes about self-evident principles, and that such disputes, when they arise, may be resolved between men who candidly love the truth, by carefully considering the absurdity and ridiculousness of any denial of a self-evident truth (437-8). That is, Reid holds that nature has provided means for settling legitimate disputes about which propositions are and which are not self-evident. To be more precise, nature has provided us with no less than three sets of considerations by means of which disputes about self-evidence may be settled, or at least adjudicated.

(1) The first is that views about such matters are matters of common sense, requiring:

> . . . no more than a sound mind free from prejudice, and a distinct conception of the question. The learned and the unlearned, the philosopher and the day-labourer, are upon a level, and will pass the same judgment, when they are not misled by some bias, or taught to renounce their understanding from some mistaken religious principle (438).

(This reference to common sense brings us to the heart of Reid's views. The meaning and role of common sense will be considered shortly.) (2) Any contradiction of a first principle, a "dictate of common sense," is absurd, and a fitting target for ridicule, even though it cannot be directly refuted by argument. (3) However, although not directly refutable, views that contradict first principles may be argued against indirectly, *ad hominem* and by the employing of *reductiones ad absurdum*, and may be supported by universal consent and by the consideration that such beliefs were held before we had any ability to reason. Such indirect considerations, although not providing absolutely convincing proofs of first principles, nevertheless tend to confirm them and to overthrow their false rivals.

But we can see from this that by "self-evidence" Reid does not mean the property that a proposition has such that as soon as any rational man understands the meaning of the proposition he immediately believes it to be true. He does not mean this because, as we have seen, the intervention of argument—or ridicule—may be required to convince someone that there must be self-evident truths. Nor by "self-evident propositions" does Reid mean merely innate dispositions to believe certain things. For he holds that all men, unless prevented by prejudice or misplaced sophistication, actually hold in common certain propositions about themselves, the external world, the past, and so forth. "Self-evidence" means "self evidence to any rational man not blinded or misguided by prejudice or pernicious philosophical views."

According to Reid there are *contingent* and *necessary* self-evident truths. Although most necessary truths are abstract, there is one non-abstract necessary truth, the proposition that *a supreme being exists*. It is not clear at first whether by calling such a proposition necessary Reid means logically necessary or merely that the existence of a supreme being is ontologically necessary, i.e., uncaused, without beginning, and the cause of the existence of all contingently existing individual things. Reid must mean merely the latter, since he argues later that the existence of God can be inferred from sets of contingent truths. And it seems implausible to suppose that any non-trivial logically necessary propositions are entailed by sets of propositions none of which is logically necessary.

Among self-evident contingent propositions for Reid are: *everything of which Reid was conscious existed* (442); the real existence of what we distinctly perceive by our senses (Berkeley could only deny this, Reid thought, because he did not fully appreciate the logical consequence of his system) (445); and the existence of minds other than our own mind (449).

In the same way there are first principles that are logically necessary, such as the law of non-contradiction and the principle of bivalence. And there are necessary truths in morals and aesthetics (453) and especially metaphysics (454). Among the latter is this principle: "That effects which have all the marks and tokens of design, must proceed from a designing cause" (495). Reid contends that this cannot be learned from experience but is an *a priori* metaphysical principle.

This, in general, is Reid's view of rationality. In summary, his view is foundationalistic and is grounded in common sense. His common-sense principles embrace not only certain basic principles of reasoning in the formal sense, but also an ontology—the existence of the external world, or other minds, of God—and certain epistemic principles. Some further questions now arise. What exact role does the appeal to common sense play in his foundationalism? What is Reid's view of natural theology, his "theology of common sense" as we might call it? And what is distinctive about Reid's common-sense foundationalism that might account for its attractiveness to generations of Calvinists?

It is a notorious fact about the impact of Scottish common-sense philosophy that the phrase "common sense" gave rise to widespread debate and misunderstanding. Two matters in particular need discussing: the ambiguity of the phrase "common sense," and the opposition that Reid himself sometimes creates between common sense and reason, and common sense and philosophy. Let us look at the second problem first.

In the earliest of his books, *An Inquiry into the Human Mind on the Principles of Common Sense* (1764), Reid discusses Berkeley's view of the external world. Reid judges that "the wisdom of *philosophy* is set in opposition to the *common sense* of mankind." Later in the same section he says, "Common Sense and Reason have both one author; that Almighty Author in all whose other works we observe a consistency, uniformity and beauty which charm and delight the understanding" (127). He goes on to say:

> The belief of a material world is older, and of more authority, than any principles of philosophy. It declines the tribunal of reason, and laughs at all the artillery of the logician. It retains its sovereign authority in spite of all the edicts of philosophy, and reason itself must stoop to its orders (127).

Even if we suppose that by "philosophy" Reid means "Bishop Berkeley's absurd and fallacious idealism," there is still a manifest inconsistency here. On the one hand we just noted how Reid wishes to say that common sense and reason are synonyms (or so it seems), while on the other hand he says that common sense is opposed to, or sometimes opposed to, reason and logic. A little later in the same passage he says we must reconcile reason to the common-sense belief that there is an external world existing independently of our consciousness. So there is certainly a difficulty here.

More serious, in view of the centrality of the idea to his philosophy, is precisely what Reid meant by common sense or reason (where the latter is used as a synonym for common sense, first principles, natural principles, or common principles). In order to illustrate the difficulties, we shall briefly discuss five different matters that might be meant by the phrase, some of which Reid does from time to time commit himself to, as we shall see.

(a) A belief is a common-sense belief if and only if it is a proposition which every rational person believes; i.e., common sense is that body of propositions held in common by all rational people. This *might* be the opinion Reid maintained but it cannot be upheld, for presumably among such common-sense beliefs are beliefs about fairly obvious and central matters, such as that there is a mind-independent external world. Yet as we have just noted, Reid and Berkeley held incompatible views on this question. Hence the view that there is an external world, existing independently of any mind, cannot be among the set of common-sense beliefs, and nor can its negation. Hence it follows that in this view of common sense no proposition about the relation of the external world to the human mind can be a member of common-sense beliefs. Further, it seems plausible to suppose that there are many rational individuals who have never considered the question of the mind's relation to the external world, much less taken a view on the matter.

(b) A belief is a common-sense belief if it is a belief about "common matters." Some things that Reid says suggest this is one of the things he may mean by common sense: "It is a bold philosophy that rejects, without ceremony, principles which irresistibly govern the belief and the conduct of all mankind in the common concerns of life" (102). Reid does not tell us, at this point, just what the common concerns of life are, but we can make a pretty good guess—eating, sleeping, traveling, buying, selling—these will be among them. And the beliefs that govern such matters are common-sense matters.

(c) Reid may also mean that a common-sense belief is a belief about a common matter which one cannot help believing. In the quotation just given, Reid mentions principles that "irresistibly govern" belief, and later he refers to the "irresistible torrent" of common sense, and to strong and irresistible beliefs (110). But this criterion is at once too narrow and too wide. It is too narrow because it excludes Bishop Berkeley, and yet for all we know Berkeley could not help believing what he did about the mind's relation to the external world, and he apparently believed quite sincerely that he had the common and the vulgar on his side. And this criterion is too wide because there are many beliefs that people cannot stop themselves having, even beliefs about common matters which seem hardly to provide rational foundations for belief. For example, many people cannot stop themselves from believing that other people are persecuting them.

(d) As a fourth possibility a common-sense belief might be a belief about a common matter that anyone not corrupted with false philosophy cannot help having. Reid seems to take this view when discussing Berkeley and opposing philosophy to common sense, a point we noted earlier. But such a position is a blatant *petitio*, for we cannot rationally dismiss opposing views as false and corrupting without argument.

(e) According to McCosh, what Reid sometimes meant by common sense was "good sense" or "practical sense," that is, sound judgment supported by careful observation. But, as McCosh points out, such common sense could never be a final arbiter of what is true.[6]

What can we make of Reid's view of natural theology, and of what I have called his theology of common sense? He clearly subscribes to the program of natural theology, although there is very little in his writings that can be called an explicit argument within natural theology. The following statement can be made, however. While it would be too much to assert that the proposition that God exists is one of the set of common-sense propositions, nevertheless he claims that "it may be doubted whether men, by the mere exercise of reasoning, might not as soon discover the existence of a Deity, as that other men have life and intelligence" (449). How this can be made consistent with what Reid might plausibly mean by common sense is not clear. Belief in the existence of God is not obviously a common matter, or a belief that most men have or that most men have irresistibly. But we can let that matter pass. Further, the existence of God can be proved using as a premise another proposition of common sense, namely, the proposition "that design and intelligence in the cause may be inferred, with certainty, from marks or signs of it in the effect" (457). This is an inference we cannot avoid (458). "Of how great importance this principle is in common life, we have already observed. And I need hardly mention its importance in natural theology" (460). So the existence of God is something that follows naturally, almost inevitably, from something that is a matter of common sense.

Anyone who reads the work of Reid cannot fail to be struck by the number of times in which he theologizes about the principles of common sense, that is, attributes the authorship of them to God. To give a few examples: "The wise and beneficient Author of Nature . . . hath . . . implanted in our natures two principles" (196). "Shall we say, then, that this belief (viz., in our senses) is the inspiration of the Almighty? I think this may be said in a good sense; for I take it to be the immediate effect of our constitution, which is the work of the Almighty" (329). On memory, Reid says: "Our Maker has provided other means for giving us the knowledge of these things (viz., past contingencies)—means which perfectly answer their end" (341). Yet this belief that God is the author of our common notions is not, it seems, itself a common notion, but is based on a further argument. What argument? Something like the following, perhaps:

(a) *That God exists* is a common-sense belief.
(b) God is by definition the Creator of all that is.
(c) Therefore it is reasonable to suppose that common-sense beliefs are the gift of the Creator.

An alternative argument could be constructed replacing (a) with: *That God exists* is entailed by our common-sense beliefs. Both these arguments appear to be valid.

There are numerous versions of foundationalism in the history of philosophy. What is distinctive about Reid's version—common-sense foundationalism? And what was there, if anything, in the structure of his philosophy that made it attractive to several generations of Calvinistic theologians and apologetes?

I will mention four possible advantages of Reid's common-sense foundationalism. First, it provided a ready reply to skepticism. It was constructed by Reid with that very aim in view, as we shall later note more fully. But other versions of foundationalism also had this aim; for example, the foundationalism of Descartes' *Meditations*. What is distinctive about Reid's foundationalism, and a possible source of its appeal, is that the truths on which all else is to be built are said to be matters of common sense. That is to say, no great amount of theoretical reflection and argument is required in order to arrive at the set of foundational propositions or notions. Thus an appeal of a simple and straightforward kind would be made to those whose primary interest was not philosophical but theological; yet it was an appeal which at the same time evidently had a reputable philosophical backing.

Further, the range, not to say eclecticism, of Reid's foundationalism must not be forgotten. It embraced not merely certain propositions about, say, deductive reasoning and our knowledge of the external world, but also about the existence of other minds, the reasonableness of induction, memory, the existence of God, and certain propositions about morality, "moral axioms" as Reid called them (454). This is a formidable list. The acceptance of such a position is clearly inconsistent not only with global skepticism but with specific skepticisms about, for example, the existence of God, the reliability of testimony (the importance of this is in connection with the appeal to miracles in the validation of the canon of Scriptures, particularly the New Testament), materialism and the obviousness of certain moral principles. Any philosophical position that could deliver on such an impressive list of issues of concern to the theologian and pastor, and deliver with such a small intellectual outlay—an appeal to common sense—was clearly going to have a considerable appeal.

It is likely, then, that the attraction of Reid's common-sense foundationalism lay more in its conclusions, together with the fact that such foundations were secure simply because they were matters of common sense, than in any appreciation of the philosophical detail.

The second possible advantage is connected with the first. A Reidian, whether a Calvinist or not, could make the assumption, as a busy pastor or apologete, that he, his flock, and the enemies of unbelief all live in the same common-sense world. Appearances are not deceptive. They are a good guide, the best guide, to reality. Such a position affords to the one who holds it a considerable tactical advantage. He is able, by an appeal to common sense, to place the onus on someone who wishes to disprove one or more of these common-sense notions. After all, being common-sense notions, they do not actually need proving. And Reid has shown that the appeal to common sense is philosophically in order. Further, the members of the set of common-sense notions reinforce each other to the extent that the apologete is able to appeal persuasively, if not altogether validly, that if one common-sense notion is subverted, what reason is there for holding onto the rest?

A third advantage which might accrue from Reid's common-sense foundationalism is that it is compatible with, if it does not entail, certain other matters that the typical Calvinist of that era valued. In the first place, it is compatible with a broadly inductivist approach to the acquisition of knowledge about matters of fact, both scientific matters and also the data of the Scriptures. As James McCosh explained:

> To the Scottish school belongs the merit of being the first, avowedly and knowingly, to follow the inductive method, and to employ it systematically in psychological investigation. As the masters of the school were the first to adopt it, so they, and those who have borrowed from them, are almost the only persons who have studiously adhered to it.[7]

The Princeton theologian Charles Hodge provides an unmistakably clear expression of this position in the opening pages of his *Systematic Theology:*

> The Bible is to the theologian what nature is to the man of science. It is his store-house of facts; and his method of ascertaining what the Bible teaches, is the same as that which the natural philosopher adopts to ascertain what nature teaches. In the first place, he comes to his task with all the assumptions above mentioned. He must assume the validity of those laws of belief which God impressed upon our nature.[8]

Therefore, the attraction of Reid's position is that from the point of view of the exegete and expositor of Scriptures it is not *obviously* rationalistic. It does not obviously dictate, in an *a priori* fashion, what individual texts and passages of the Bible must mean, in the way in which, say, Immanuel Kant does in *Religion within the Limits of Reason Alone*, nor the way the deists did in terms of their notion of "natural religion." (An investigation of the extent to which Reid-inspired exegesis and exposition of the Scriptures was in fact rationalistic—in the sense that it imposed common-sense categories of interpretation on the textual data—is something that falls outside the scope of this paper. But this point might be worth investigating through the writings of prominent and influential commentators such as Charles Hodge and J.A. Alexander.)

A further matter that Reidism is compatible with, if it does not actually entail it, is the dominant *a posteriori* apologetic stance of English-speaking theology and philosophy since the end of the seventeenth century, best exemplified in the work of Paley and Butler.

It must be stressed that these are merely suggestions as to the intellectual appeal of common-sense foundationalism for successive generations of English-speaking Calvinists. They are based on two sources, the actual uses that Calvinists of that period made of Reid's views, and the affinities between the conclusions of common-sense foundationalism and the work of Calvinist apologetes of that period.

II

Most of the previous discussion has had little to do with Calvinistic theology. To remedy this problem, the remainder of this chapter will be devoted to a consideration of the relation between Scottish common-sense philosophy and Calvinism by setting out and defending a number of rather negative propositions.

(1) There is no strong reason to think that Thomas Reid was a Calvinist. Nominally, at least, Reid was a Calvinist, in that as a minister of the Church of Scotland at that period he would subscribe to the *Westminster Confession of Faith*. But such materials as therc are about his life (and they are rather scanty) suggest that he was a member of the "moderate" party, the party of Hugh Blair and Principal Robertson.[9] They emphasized the preaching of morality rather than the evangelical truths of the *Confession*, and they championed the rights of the patron to appoint a minister to a local congregation rather than the rights of the people themselves. In his only published and extended treatment of a theological theme—the relation of the knowledge and will of God to moral evil[10]—Reid takes up a very mild form of Calvinism, to say the least. His Calvinism is so mild as to be fairly indistinguishable from Arminianism, arguing for philosophical libertarianism and conceding that although "God foresees every determination of the human mind" we can form no proper understanding of this (631). He claims that God's relation to moral evil is that he permits, in the sense of not hindering by superior power, "the abuse of liberty in agents on whom he has bestowed it" (634).[11] Putting all this evidence together we may conclude that Reid was not likely a Calvinist, although it must be conceded that due to the lack of data much of the evidence is negative.

(2) Even if Reid was a Calvinist there is no evidence that he adopted his common-sense foundationalism on account of his Calvinism. It is pretty clear from the available data that he adopted common-sense foundationalism because in his view the only alternative was Humean skepticism. The "great and professed object of Dr. Reid's 'Inquiry' " was the refutation of Hume's skeptical theory. according to Reid's biographer Dugald Stewart (7), and S.A. Grave calls Hume the "vast figure in Reid's intellectual world."[12] Dugald Stewart judged that:

> In the state in which he found the philosophical world, he believed

> that his talents could not be so usefully employed as in combating the schemes of those who aimed at the complete subversion of religion, both natural and revealed (32).

(3) It is possible that others who, like Witherspoon and Chalmers and J.H. Thornwell, were undoubtedly Calvinists, adopted or retained common-sense foundationalism or features of it because of their Calvinism. Perhaps they did, but it is not easy to find much evidence one way or the other concerning this question of fact. What is undoubtedly true is that others who were Calvinists during this period (roughly 1750-1875) did *not* see the need for common-sense philosophy. Here are three examples.

The first is Robert Riccaltoun (1691-1769), an able Calvinist theologian and philosopher, who wrote, among others, *An Inquiry into the Spirit and Tendency of Letters on Theron and Aspasio: with a View of the Law of Nature, and An Inquiry into Letters on the Law of Nature* (1762). This is a reply to Robert Sandeman's critical comments on some of the writings of the evangelical Anglican James Hervey. Riccaltoun spends a good deal of this book denying that there is any kind of natural religion or natural theology, voicing arguments such as this:

> What we have been early taught, and have always from the time we can remember any thing taken for granted, we are apt to imagine purely natural; and because they are really anticipations of reasoning, and exert their strength without it, . . . we thoughtlessly take it for granted, that they rise naturally from the constitution, as instincts do in brute animals.
>
> On the general rules, thus insensibly instilled, the sentiments are formed; and by habit and custom, so confirmed, that, right or wrong, they will maintain their possession against all the reason in the world. This needs no other evidence, than what we have access to observe every day; that men hold the most unreasonable opinions and practises with the greatest tenaciousness, and the most furious vehemence, against all that attempt to undeceive them. But, in truth, all the knowledge of God at this day, or which ever was in the world, must owe its origin to the Revelation which he has made of himself, and the means he has appointed for preserving and continuing it among men.[13]

Thus Riccaltoun denies the possibility of natural theology and *a fortiori* denies Scottish common-sense foundationalism at least to the extent that it implies natural theology.

The second example is "Rabbi" Duncan, the Professor of Hebrew at the Free Church College, formed after the Disruption of 1843 with

Chalmers as its head. In his *Colloquia Peripatetica* he has this to say:

> You tell me that this or that is the voice of Nature, and that we can't help believing it. But does this Reidist solution really satisfy any man? The belief may be false, though we cannot help believing it? . . . Can't-help-myself-ism is to me a very shallow philosophy.[14]
>
> I concur in the main with Reid and Stewart, in the results of their common-sense philosophy, but *not philosophically*. I believe in axioms (including the mathematical and logical laws); in the Senses, which report to me the external world; in Objectivity (including the existence of other minds besides my own); in Testimony (and under this I rank the evidence of a historical Revelation); and in the syllogistic nexus; and besides these I don't know that I believe in anything else. Common sense I believe in, but not in a philosophy of common sense.[15]

Whatever positive views these snatches of conversation suggest, they clearly imply a rejection of the Scottish philosophy of common sense, by a Scottish Calvinist.

The third example is from the United States, in a text by W.G.T. Shedd.

> The true method then of theological studies is to commence in and with the supernatural and to work outward and downward to the natural. The theologian must study his own spirit by the aid of the written word. He will ever find the two in perfect harmony and mutually confirming each other. The supernatural doctrines must be seen in their own light; must bring their own evidence with them, and theology must be a self-supported science.[16]

Elsewhere, in his *Dogmatic Theology*, for example, he does give qualified approval to natural theology, but regards it as having an elucidatory and confirmatory role rather than establishing certain theological conclusions *de novo*.

These three examples are only illustrations. They show that it was possible to be a philosophically alert Calvinist during the period of Reid's influence on Calvinism without subscribing to Scottish common-sense foundationalism. So we are led to the next question. *Ought* these Calvinists to have subscribed to common-sense foundationalism in order to be fully consistent Calvinists?

The only way of properly answering that question is to ask whether there is any logical connection between common-sense foundationalism and Calvinism; whether, say, common-sense foundationalism entails Calvinism, or Calvinism entails common-sense foundationalism. It is exceedingly hard to see how the first option might be possible, to see how the theologically distinctive propositions of Calvinism are entailed by certain common-sense truths, even if we could settle what was meant by "common-sense truths." Perhaps the reverse is more plausible—that Calvinism entails the truth of certain common-sense propositions.

Here one has to be careful to distinguish between Calvinism entailing certain propositions which some accept on Reidist grounds, and Calvinism entailing a Reidist argument for the truth of certain common-sense propositions. Calvinism may well require that certain propositions, normally accepted as true as a matter of common sense, be true without requiring them to be true because they are normally accepted as a matter of common sense. For, presumably, certain propositions also accepted as a matter of common sense must be false. After all, common sense in a rather elastic notion, as we noted earlier.

So in answer to whether Calvinism entails Reidism or *vice versa*, we must offer a tentative "no." But maybe there is a logical relation of a lesser kind. What we might call "full Calvinism" neither entails nor is entailed by Reidism, yet what we might call "Calvinistic natural theology" could be entailed by, and perhaps even entails, common-sense foundationalism. (By "Calvinistic natural theology" is meant "schemes of natural theology held by Calvinists in a way consistent with their Calvinism.")

Many people will be skeptical about such a possibility. Frankly, I am skeptical about it myself. But, for the moment, let us suppose that such a position is possible: one can logically be a Calvinist and yet consistently subscribe to the program of natural theology. Must one be a common-sense foundationalist in order to adopt this position?

The answer is no, as we can see in the following two examples of Calvinist theologians who have subscribed to natural theology. The first is Stephen Charnock (1628-1680). In his *Discourses on the Existence and Attributes of God* Charnock argues (appealing to Romans 1:19-20, as Aquinas had done) that God's existence may be established from reason.[17] He appeals to arguments from innateness and universal consent, and to versions of the cosmological argument:

> Every plant, every atom, as well as every star, at the first meeting, whispers this in our ears, "I have a Creator; I am witness to a Deity." Who ever saw statues or pictures but presently thinks of a statuary and limner? Who beholds garments, ships, or houses, but understands there was a weaver, a carpenter, an architect? Who can cast his eyes about the world, but must think of that power that formed it, and that the goodness which appears in the formation of it hath a perfect residence in some being? "Those things that are good must

> flow from something perfectly good: that which is chief in any kind is the cause of all that kind. Fire, which is most hot, is the cause of all things which are hot. There is some being therefore which is the cause of all that perfection which is in the creature; and this is God" (Aquin. 1 qu.2. Artic.3). All things that are demonstrate something from whence they are.[18]

What is true of Charnock is true of English Puritanism in general. Few, if any, of them would have denied that (as John Arrowsmith put it), "Scripture-Oracles, supposing it sufficiently clear by the light of Nature, that there is a God, make a further discovery of what he is in his Essence, Subsistence and Attributes."[19]

The second example is John Owen (1616-1683). In his *The Reason of Faith* Owen raises the question of how God makes himself known. Here he describes one way:

> He doth it unto our reason in its exercise, by proposing such things unto its consideration as from whence it may and cannot but conclude in an assent unto the truth of what God intends to reveal unto us that way. This he doth by the works of creation and providence, which present themselves unavoidably unto reason in its exercise, to instruct us in the nature, being, and properties of God. Thus "the heavens declare the glory of God . . ." yet they do not thus declare, evidence and reveal the glory of God unto the first principles and notions of natural light without the actual exercise of reason.[20]

So here is evidence that there is only a contingent relationship between common-sense philosophy and the views of Calvinists on the place of reason in the development of natural theology. Not only is it logically possible to be a Calvinist and believe that there is a natural theology—and yet not be a Scottish common-sense philosopher—but many actually *have been* such.

(In highlighting the relationship between natural theology and Calvinism, attention has been focused on only *some* of the allegedly common-sense principles of the Scottish common-sense philosophy, particularly those that involve natural theology. It would require a wider enquiry than is here possible to determine how many other principles that the Scottish common-sense philosophers regarded as matters of common sense were accepted by earlier Calvinists, and on what grounds. But it is likely that many Calvinists accepted many of them, on a variety of grounds, and that some Calvinists accepted some of them.)

But is it not possible that Charnock and Owen had misperceived the *proper* relationship of Calvinism to common-sense foundational propositions? Perhaps so, but how could this be shown? One way would be to show that only the truths of common-sense foundationalism entail Calvinism. But how could this be shown when—to take one example—Calvinism itself entails the truth of certain contingent propositions about the world? An alternative strategy might be to show that whatever entails the truth of Calvinism also entails the truth of common-sense foundationalism. But how could there be any proposition or set of propositions that would entail the truth of common-sense foundationalism, since that doctrine claims there is nothing more basic epistemically than the propositions that form the foundations? It would follow that any putative proposition or set of propositions entailing the foundations would have no more credibility than the propositions forming the foundations. And perhaps these propositions would have less credibility since, according to foundationalism, nothing is as credible as a foundational proposition.

Of course, common-sense foundationalism may be correct, and certain positive conclusions in natural theology may follow from foundationalism. Then we could say that common-sense foundationalism entailed or rendered probable some certain truths which are, logically speaking, a part of Calvinism and logically more basic than other parts of Calvinism. Yet it does not follow that, because a proposition *p* is a logically necessary condition of the truth of another proposition *q*, the truth of *p* has to be established before, and independently of, the truth of *q*. The truth of *This is an orange* depends upon the truth of *This is a fruit*, but it does not follow that one has first to establish that this is a fruit before one can establish that this is an orange.

III

We have tried to answer the question about the relationship between Scottich common-sense foundationalism and Calvinism. In doing so we have seen that the link is at best tenuous and adventitious, and there is nothing about common-sense foundationalism that makes it particularly attractive to Calvinism. Moreover there is nothing about Calvinism that requires common-sense foundationalism. An assumption of this discussion has been that there is a close relationship between common-sense foundationalism and natural theology. We shall conclude with a comment of a more general nature on the relation between common-sense philosophy and Calvinism, and a comment on the relation between natural theology and Calvinism.

We have already noted that the common principles of Scottish common-sense philosophy include logical truths, together with various ontological and epistemic claims. If for the moment we concentrate on the ontological and epistemic claims, it is necessary to distinguish between these as philosophical theories and as empirical truths. Hume was clear on this point:

> Let the course of things be allowed hitherto ever so regular; that alone, without some new argument or inference, proves not that, for the future, it will continue so. In vain do you pretend to have learned the nature of bodies from your past experience. Their secret nature, and consequently all their effects and influence, may change, without any change in their sensible qualities. This happens sometimes, and with regard to some objects: Why may it not happen always, and with regard to all objects? What logic, what process of argument secures you against this supposition? My practice, you say, refutes my doubts. But you mistake the purport of my question. As an agent, I am quite satisfied in the point; but as a philosopher, who has some share of curiosity, I will not say scepticism, I want to learn the foundation of this inference.[21]

But the clownish James Beattie was not clear. Even if Berkeleian idealism is true, Beattie was taking his own course:

> Where is the harm of my believing, that if I were to fall down yonder precipice, and break my neck, I should be no more a man of this world? My neck, Sir, may be an idea to you, but to me it is a reality, and a very important one too. Where is the harm of my believing, that if in this severe weather, I were to neglect to throw (what you call) the idea of a coat over the ideas of my shoulders, the idea of cold would produce the idea of such pain and disorder as might possibly terminate in my real death.[22]

Perhaps part of the appeal of the common-sense philosophy to Calvinistic theologians and pastors (busy educators and preachers, wanting new converts and new congregations) lay in their mistaken view that such a "philosophy" provided an obvious, common-sense, practical, empirical foundation for their activities with the added advantage of being a "philosophy."

And such a view *is* mistaken, for neither the common-sense philosophy nor its sensationalistic rivals offered themselves as theories open to empirical refutation, as Hume knew but Beattie (along with Samuel Johnson) evidently did not. If the Scottish common-sense philosophy is treated as a philosophical *theory*, offering a certain epistemology and ontology, and if we ask of that theory what its relation is to Calvinism, then it is extremely difficult to see how it could be argued that Calvinism requires one particular epistemology rather than another. Doubtless Calvinism *rules out* certain ontologies, such as materialism and solipsism, and certain epistemologies, such as total skepticism, but that is a rather different matter. To rule out p is not to require q. Calvinism, like the Scriptures from which it is drawn, is a theoretically underdetermined affair. Who can say, on theological grounds or on non-question-begging philosophical grounds, that the occasionalism of the Calvinist Arnold Geulincx (1624-1669) is incompatible with his Calvinism, or the youthful idealism of Jonathan Edwards is incompatible with his? There are purely *philosophical* arguments against the theories of occasionalism and idealism, but are there *Calvinistic* arguments against them?

Yet in the case of some of what Reid called "first principles of necessary truths," the position is rather different. The propositions of Calvinism could not be *stated* if Reid's "logical axioms" were not observed. This is not to say that Reid's arguments for the acceptance of such axioms are or ought to be convincing, much less that the axioms entail Calvinism. But they are entailed by Calvinism, at least in the sense that any intelligible and consistent set of propositions presupposes certain rules of intelligible discourse. It would be reasonable to conclude that the relation between Calvinism and ontological and epistemological positions is slacker than the relationship between Calvinism and logic.

Notes

1. On Thornwell, J.L. Girandeau wrote, "He emphatically belonged to that class of thinkers who advocate what is known as the Philosophy of Common Sense, in contradistinction from the class whom he designates as Sensationalists." B.M. Palmer, *The Life and Letters of James Henley Thornwell*, 1875, pp. 541-45.
2. McCosh had been among the ministers involved in the Disruption of the Church of Scotland in 1843. He became Professor of Logic and Metaphysics at Queen's College, Belfast, in 1861. Among his best known writings are *The Method of the Divine Government, Physical and Moral* (1850), and *The Scottish Philosophy, Biographical, Expository, Critical; from Hutcheson to Hamilton* (1874).
3. By "Calvinism" is meant the evangelical Augustinianism articulated by John Calvin in the *Institutes of the Christian Religion* and which finds expression in confessions such as the *Westminster Confession of Faith* (and other confessions modeled upon it) and the *Belgic Confession*.
4. All page references to Reid which are given in brackets in the main text are to *The Works of Thomas Reid D.D.*, ed. Sir William Hamilton, fifth edition, Edinburgh, 1858.
5. Cf. C.I. Lewis: "If anything is to be probable, something must be certain.

The data which support a genuine probability must themselves be certainties." *Analysis of Knowledge and Valuation* (1946), pp. 186-87.

6. James McCosh, *The Scottish Philosophy*, pp. 221-22.
7. James McCosh, *op. cit.*, p. 3.
8. Charles Hodge, *Systematic Theology* (1871-73), Vol. I, p. 10.
9. On the moderatism of Scottish common-sense philosophy, see John C. Vander Stelt, *Philosophy and Scripture* (1978), p. 15. "From the time of Hutcheson, there is a felt and known feud, not always avowed, between the new philosophy and the old theology . . . . It was only in a later age, and mainly through the influence of Chalmers, that the church was prepared heartily to accept what was true in the Scottish philosophy, and to acknowledge its compatibility with the doctrine of salvation by grace." James McCosh, *The Scottish Philosophy*, p. 87.
10. *Essays on the Active Powers of the Human Mind* (1788), Essay IV.
11. Vander Stelt correctly observes that Reid's view of the will is "Erasmian and Arminian," *op. cit.*, p. 26. It is worth noting that although Thomas Chalmers championed many aspects of the Scottish common-sense philosophy, he rejected Reid's libertarianism in favor of determinism which he took from Jonathan Edwards' *Freedom of the Will*.
12. S.A. Grave, *The Scottish Philosophy of Common Sense* (1960), p. 11.
13. Riccaltoun, *op. cit.*, p. 103.
14. John Duncan, *Colloquia Peripatetica* (6th ed.), 1907, p. 2.
15. Duncan, *op. cit.*, p. 63.
16. W.G.T. Shedd, *Theological Essays* (1887), p. 22.
17. S. Charnock, *The Existence and Attributes of God*, originally published (1853), p. 4.
18. Charnock, *op. cit.*, p. 15.
19. *A Chain of Principles* (1659), p. 111.
20. John Owen, *Works*, ed. W.H. Goold (1850-53), IV, 84.
21. David Hume, *An Enquiry Concerning Human Understanding*, IV, II, 32.
22. James Beattie, *An Essay in the Nature and Immutability of Truth* (1770), p. 284.

Historical Setting

Part Three:

The Dutch Neo-Calvinist Tradition and Rationality

Rationality in the Dutch Neo-Calvinist Tradition

Jacob Klapwijk

CALVINISM HAS ALWAYS BEEN A MOVEMENT of much greater scope than the development of a distinctive theology or lifestyle. To put it positively, the reformational aspirations of Calvinism since the 16th century also had implications for human society and culture, and, more specifically, for the status of human rationality and a new approach to philosophical and scientific learning.

When we look at men like Abraham Kuyper, Herman Bavinck, D.H.Th. Vollenhoven, and Herman Dooyeweerd, an important question arises. What has been the contribution of the Dutch neo-Calvinism tradition, which they represented, to finding such a new, reformed approach to rationality? I think that each one of these thinkers has made a unique contribution to the idea and ideal of a truly Christian scholarship. At the same time, we should not neglect the strong differences which become apparent, already in the 19th century, between the views of Kuyper and Bavinck, and later on, between the conceptions of Vollenhoven and Dooyeweerd. These differences were not merely on secondary issues; they concerned the central issues of reason and revelation, of faith and philosophy.

I. Two Basic Convictions

However, it seems to me that there are at least two basic convictions with respect to Christian learning and philosophy on which there has been a far-reaching agreement within Dutch reformational circles. The first is the belief in a divine creation order, that is, the belief that the whole of created reality is subject to the sovereign will of God, the Creator of heaven and earth. This belief entails that the laws and normative structures of reality, including the reality of man and of human *reason*, have in one way or another their ultimate origin in God, and that God himself is not subject to these laws, although he must be viewed as faithful to them. To express this in the language of the reformers: *Deus legibus solutus est*, and at the same time, *Deus non exlex*.

The second basic conviction concerns the religious antithesis. It is the belief that not everything that takes place in God's created world is in accordance with his sovereign will. On the contrary, ever since the fall of man, Satan has wreaked havoc on the whole creation, drawing it into the way of rebellion, folly, destruction and death. However, the second basic conviction holds that this demonic strategy, the signs of which are becoming ominously manifest in our present rationalized and scientized world, is (and shall be) brought to nought by God through Jesus Christ, who, before the eyes of faith, is at work in restoring God's creation, guiding it to its ultimate destination—the kingdom of God. This fundamental opposition between the work of God on the one hand and the devious exertions of the evil one on the other hand, between the realm of darkness and the kingdom of light, comes to expression in the term "religious antithesis." This same opposition is revealed to us even in the first pages of the Bible (Gen. 3:15), where God declares that he will put "enmity" between "the seed of the serpent" and "the seed of the woman," from which in due time Jesus, the true seed, would come forth as the victor.

It must be observed at the very outset that these two basic convictions—the idea of a divine law-order for the creation and the idea of a religious antithesis within the created world—cannot be easily dealt with apart from each other, if indeed it is true that Satan's strategy of sin, as opposed to Christ's plan of salvation, runs counter to God's holy will for his creation. Moreover, we must realize that the idea of God's creation order as well as the idea of a religious antithesis are both highly relevant for (any discussion on) the status and scope of human rationality. Nevertheless, within the limits of this essay, it is impossible for me to deal with both subjects in a satisfactory way. For this reason, I will pass over the subject of the creation ordinances in silence—at least to a certain extent—even though this idea obtained a significant expression in Kuyper's theory of sphere sovereignty, in Dooyeweerd's conception of the cosmonomic structure of all reality, and in Vollenhoven's triadic distinction between God, law, and created reality.

Let me add at this point that while these philosophical positions offer many helpful insights with respect to our problem of the status of human rationality, they also conceal many difficulties. These difficulties come to the fore as soon as we become more specific and begin to ask the following questions. How must we interpret the biblical teaching of God as the sovereign Lord? What exactly is the biblical idea of "law"? How do we (come to) know these so-called creation ordinances? And how must we distinguish between what is due to God's creation order and what is the result of historical development and human (often sinful) positivization? You will understand that in answer to these and similar questions there is anything but a consensus in the reformed community. In fact, the variety of views is very great and extends even to a consistent rejection of the notion of a divine creation order as being rather of Greek than of biblical origin (C.A. Van Peursen).

As I have stated, I will restrict myself in this essay to the second subject, namely, that of the religious antithesis. Within the Calvinian tradition this idea of a religious antithesis is perhaps an even more characteristic contribution of Dutch neo-Calvinism than the idea of a creational law order. But, once again, we must limit ourselves. I cannot deal with this theme in its full breadth; instead, I want to focus on its relevance for human rationality. The problem that I want to dwell on is therefore this: religious antithesis and human rationality—how does the one relate to the other?

II. Calvin on Sin as a Corruptio Totalis

Since the days of Calvin, several questions in this connection have been very urgent. First, is it possible to state meaningfully that human reason in our world is affected or even corrupted by sin in a radical sense of the word? Second, if so, how can we account for and come to terms with the philosophical wisdom of the Greeks and the juridical insights of the Romans? Similarly, how are we to deal with the scientific knowledge and philosophical theories of our modern world, which is to a great extent a post-Christian world, and in its theoretical reflection is based on the principle of a man-centered humanism?

As far as the first question is concerned, I do indeed believe that the human mind is strongly affected by sin and that, in positing this, I am in harmony with the reformers of the 16th century. Luther and Calvin rediscovered in the Bible the totalitarian character of sin. They read, primarily in the letters of Paul, that sin is much more than a human defect; on the contrary, it reveals itself as rebellion against God, as lawlessness, apostasy and unwisdom. In their view it is an evil which festers in man's heart and in all his life. It was John Calvin in particular who in his *Institutes of the Christian Religion* (hereafter, *IR*) taught the "total corruption" of human nature. This view is echoed in the *Heidelberg Catechism* where it is stated that man's nature is "wholly incapable of doing any good, and inclined to all evil."[1]

This doctrine of sin's total corruption of fallen man does not mean, of course, that all sin is equally bad. The Bible speaks of lesser and greater sins and even of mortal sins. This doctrine does suggest, however, that there is no area of life that escapes the grip of sins and, accordingly, none which is not in need of restoring grace through Jesus Christ.

My quoting the *Heidelberg Catechism* is not without reason. This reformed confession of faith has deeply influenced the preaching, the life of faith and the theology of Dutch Calvinism. This Calvinist view of sin as a corruption and perversion which pervades man's total being has far-reaching consequences for our subject. According to Calvin himself, human reason is so darkened that only muddled notions are produced, especially with respect to the highest knowledge, i.e., the knowledge of God. Calvin considers this muddledness all the more remarkable because God, through his general revelation, manifests himself clearly in his whole creation and before the eyes of all men. But because of sin, man is unable and also unwilling to free himself from the prison of ignorance and superstition. Only by the grace of Jesus Christ and through God's special revelation in the Scriptures is man able to come to a knowledge of the truth.

Calvin's position seems to me very challenging, because it turned resolutely against the classical medieval view of scholasticism. According to that view, at the Fall in paradise the original righteousness of man's supernatural being was completely lost. But the consequence of this was not that man's natural being was totally corrupted but rather that it was wounded and weakened. That is to say, the capacities of man's natural being remained more or less intact. Therefore, up to a certain point, man's power of reasoning also retained its self-sufficiency and ability to discover truth. Calvin flatly denies this. "All parts of the soul," he states, "were possessed by sin after Adam deserted the fountain of righteousness"; and he explicitly adds that even the excellent gift of the human mind is not only wounded but corrupted in such a way that it needs, as it were, a new nature (*IR* II.1.9). Thus he can also write that the scholastic *lumen naturale*, the natural light of reason, is "blind" or "extinguished" (*IR* II.1.9; 2.18,24). In other words, Calvin rejects the scholastic distinction of nature and supernature (although not always consistently), because he feels it misjudges the totalitarian character of sin and, for that reason, also the all-encompassing significance of God's saving grace in Jesus Christ.

III. Kuyper's Idea of Antithesis

When the Dutch statesman and theologian Abraham Kuyper rejected the dualism of nature and supernature, he was thinking in accord with Calvin, as he was when in his Stone *Lectures on Calvinism* (1898; hereafter, *LC*) and elsewhere he emphasized the "total depravity by sin" (*LC* 122) and, as its counterpart, the "wide, comprehensible, cosmical meaning of the Gospel" (*LC* 119, cf. 49). And when on this basis he came to speak about a "religious antithesis" and made it a central motive in his worldview he was again, as far as I can see, in the line of Calvin and even in the line of the church father Augustine, who in his book *De Civitate Dei* (hereafter, *CD*) already spoke of a fundamental opposition between the "city of God" and the "earthly city."

However, it seems to me that Augustine went wrong when he then tried to visualize this antithesis in the progress of world history by attempting to describe the story of both cities from the very beginning up to the time in which he himself lived. His interpretation of the antithesis as pertaining to two "groups" or two "communities" within the human race (*CD* 15.1), and as concretized on the one side, for example, in the Assyrian and Roman Empires (*CD* 18.2), and on the other side in Israel (*CD* 18.47) and the Church (*CD* 20.9), was not convincing and, as far as I can see, not permissible. There always remains a mystery in history regarding peoples and persons, a mystery which we have to respect, because it is a divine mystery. World history unfolds itself under the sign of a religious opposition, but only here and there, only at decisive points, does the Bible lift this veil of mystery for us.

It is not without good reason that at this point I referred to the church father Augustine and to the fundamental weakness of his inspiring book *De Civitate Dei.* For I believe a similar weakness is shown in the work of Abraham Kuyper. Kuyper sought to give the biblical antithesis concrete form in the various areas of state and society. He wanted to give the antithesis tangible expression in a manifold of Christian organizations in society. I believe that Kuyper also had other, more acceptable, motives for establishing Christian organizations in the Netherlands.[2] Yet, the motive of giving expression to the religious antithesis was one of them, and again I question whether this "organizational antithesis" does not infringe upon God's mystery and whether, in the case of Kuyper and his followers, it did not inevitably lead to a dangerous identification of the Christian (or, if you will, reformed) cause with God's cause. Although I am sure that Kuyper wanted to see Christian organizations as a means for

Christianizing society, the danger was that they were considered not as deficient instruments but as ends in the struggle for the kingdom of God.

IV. Antithesis and Human Rationality

Kuyper's idea of antithesis had direct consequences for his view of human consciousness and human rationality. The antithesis should be given organizational form even in the unyielding world of science. In following this line, Kuyper dreamed the most daring dreams. At times he saw "his school," the Free University of Amsterdam, as the center of the re-Christianization of the entire Euro-American cultural and scientific world.

For Kuyper there are two kinds of science (in the broad sense of the German "Wissenschaft"): one following from an unregenerate consciousness, the other from a regenerate consciousness. These are two "absolute starting points." The first is that of the Normalists, who proceed on the assumption that the world is normal. The second is that of the Abnormalists, who see the world as abnormal, dislodged by sin, and in need of saving and restoring power through Jesus Christ.

In his Stone *Lectures on Calvinism*, Kuyper concluded that no liaison or reconciliation between these two starting points is possible. On the contrary, the two are in dispute with one another about "*the whole domain of life*, and they cannot desist from the constant endeavor to pull down to the ground the entire edifice of their respective controverted assertions, all the supports included, upon which their assertions rest" (*LC* 133).

On the one hand we can admire the way in which Kuyper took seriously the biblical teaching of the unbridgeable opposition between what the Scriptures call "the dominion of darkness" and "the kingdom of God's beloved Son" (Col. 1:13), and the possible consequences of this opposition for the realm of science and academic learning. Kuyper single-handedly battled the entire educated world of his time, an age which swore by the supposed objectivity and impartiality of all science. Kuyper refused to accept the world of scientific and theoretical knowledge as a neutral given.

On the other hand one must object to the tangible and massive form in which Kuyper, also in the field of science, delineates the religious antithesis and "separates the thinking minds in the domain of Science into two opposite battle-arrays" (*LC* 132). To speak of a reciprocal attempt to demolish each other's scientific edifice is to overstate the case. Science in particular depends on worldwide information and contact; in fact, science represents a universal communication system.

V. Calvin and Common Grace

Of course, Kuyper himself was, as an academic scholar, fully aware of this issue; and to understand Kuyper's view on rationality one should not only read his *Lectures on Calvinism* but also his main scientific work, *De gemeene gratie* (*Common Grace*; hereafter, *GG*), which was published some years later. In developing his theory of common grace, Kuyper saw himself again in the line of Calvin. In this regard he was right, at least up to a certain point.

Although, as we have already seen, Calvin stressed the depravity of human nature, he did not categorically reject all non-Christian thought. Calvin insists that there are still some sparks of light to be found in man's degenerate nature (*IR* I.5.14). This applies above all to human reason. Calvin, in my reading of his Latin text, considers it incompatible with both the Scriptures and common sense to condemn reason to permanent error and blindness (but cf. Battles' translation of *IR* II.2.12). Granted, reason achieves very little where it directs itself to God and heavenly things. It is more competent when it directs itself to earthly affairs. And to these earthly affairs Calvin reckons politics, art and science (*IR* II.2.13). Even science! Calvin, who himself had a great knowledge of classical antiquity, sees "that admirable light of truth" shining in the works of pagan and secular authors, and he declares that reason, even if it is apostate, "is nevertheless clothed and ornamented with God's excellent gifts" (*IR* II.2.15).

Calvin's attitude to all non-Christian culture and science appears, therefore, to be quite subtle. On the one hand, he does not want to depreciate or ignore the gifts which God has distributed outside his church. That would be a deep ingratitude to the giver (*IR* II.2.15)! On the other hand, he does not want to consider these gifts merely in themselves and esteem them as pure human achievements. Calvin continually occupies himself with how these gifts *function* in man. Do they serve to satisfy individual ambition and insight or do they tend to the service and glory of God? It is precisely the latter area in which man on his own falls short. All human gifts are by nature affected by sin. No one can reap glory from them. This applies also to human reason. Human comprehension and understanding, says Calvin, ". . . is an unstable and transitory thing in God's sight, when a solid foundation of truth does not underlie it" (*IR* II.2.16).

Thus already Calvin speaks at times of God's common grace in order to avoid on one hand a denial of human depravity and to avoid on the other hand a depreciation of what God by his Spirit is doing outside the circle of faith. One thing must be kept in mind, however. Although Calvin sometimes speaks of "common grace," he does not use it in a fixed technical sense as Kuyper did. Following the language of the Bible, he can just as easily speak of God's kindness, of his mercy and gentleness (*IR* II.2.17; I.5.14; III.3.25), of his particular grace to all or to a few, or again simply of God's providence (*IR* II.2.14,17).

Calvin also mentions widely divergent motives for God's restraining of sin and his bestowing of gifts of grace. In distributing his blessings to so many people, God is upholding the creation order and caring for the human race (*IR* II.2.16; 3.4; III.14.3), preserving his church (*IR* I.17.7,11), and bringing men to repentance (*IR* III.3.25; I.5.14). Moreover, God does not only want to display his grace or goodness (*IR* III.24.2; 20.15); his holy intention can also be to brand the conscience of the ungodly, to impress upon him his ingratitude and his deserving punishment, and to remove his every excuse (*IR* I.3.1; III.3.25; I.5.14; III.25.9).

VI. Kuyper and Common Grace

Kuyper's position is not quite the same. Kuyper is the one who systematized all of this in the doctrine of common grace. And he distinguished sharply, although not always clearly, between common grace and particular grace. According to Kuyper, common grace and particular grace have a different nature, scope, purpose and ground.

They have a different nature because the content of particular grace is the deliverance from sin and eternal salvation, and the content of general grace is the restraint of sin and temporal blessings (*GG* I 243ff., 265ff.). They have a different scope because particular grace applies to the regenerate Christian, and common grace applies to the whole world and the whole of humanity (*GG* I 8ff.). They have a different purpose because common grace is aimed at preserving the creation order, and particular grace is aimed at a re-creation that in its final fruits (the new heaven and the new earth) to a certain extent transcends the natural creation order (*GG* I 243ff., II 613ff.). Finally, they have a different ground. Kuyper often suggests that the particular grace which is bestowed in the church is based on the reconciling work of Jesus Christ, and that the common grace which is realized on earth in the creation order is *apart from that* based on the care of God as Creator. As if God had different grounds for being merciful to man!

Serious difficulties attend this sharp contrast between common grace and particular grace, between creation and re-creation, cultural activity and salvation of the soul, earthly life and heavenly life. In all of this there is the threat of a dualism, which expresses itself in a divided directedness to the hereafter and to the present. Only rarely does Kuyper know how to connect the spheres of common grace and of particular grace centrally. Yet there are moments when the issue becomes clear to him: the ground for personal grace is the same as the ground for common grace, namely, the cross of Jesus Christ. It is Christ who bears the church *and* the world: to him is given all power in heaven *and* on earth (Mt. 28:18). At such moments he honors Christ as king not only in the sphere of particular grace but also in the sphere of common grace, and he can then confess this kingship in the lofty words: "There is not a square inch of our whole human existence of which Christ, who is sovereign over all, does not say: 'Mine!' "[3]

However, most of the tensions in Kuyper's cultural theology remain. These tensions are also reflected in Kuyper's person. In part his work echoes the mystery of the born-again heart and the sigh of the weary pilgrim who longs for his eternal home. In part he is driven to work with an extraordinary vigor at the unfolding of God's creation in state, society and science. But even here, in the domain of common grace, Kuyper's ideas diverge. At times he sees the creation mandate as a common human task in which Christian and non-Christian stand shoulder to shoulder. Then again he is sure that the great cultural mandate must start from the antithesis and must be translated into a program of organized Christian action in all areas of life, including science and philosophy. One can find a condensation of this train of thought in his book *Pro Rege* (1911-1912).[4]

VII. Common Grace and the Sciences

This brings us back to our main theme again. Thinking, science, and philosophy are grounded in God's creation order. Science is "God's own creation" (*GG* III 495). Hence science is also to be seen as a fruit of common grace. Sin has darkened the understanding, and it follows that all science would end in deceit and self-deception if there were no common grace. God's grace is the reason that men such as Plato, Aristotle, Kant and Darwin (!) have shone as "stars of the first magnitude" (*GG* III 498). The conclusion is that Kuyper can appreciate pagan and profane thought. The appreciation is not added to the account of sinful man, however, but to the grace of God.

Yet Kuyper will also say that science is seriously affected by sin. As a matter of fact, Kuyper's opposition to non-Christian science is much stronger than his appreciation of it, despite his theory of common grace. One can observe this critical approach especially in his *Lectures on Calvinism*, and to a certain extent also in his later work *De gemeene gratie*.

In *De gemeene gratie* Kuyper distinguishes between the natural and the human sciences. He thinks that in the natural sciences a general consensus is, to a large extent, possible because so much depends on an exact observation of the objects. On the other hand, in history, philosophy and the other humanities the subjectivity of the researcher is at stake. Here questions arise concerning the origin, coherence and purpose of things, which cannot be solved through observation or purely logical thinking (*GG* III 499, 508, 512). At this level two kinds of science—regenerate and unregenerate—become possible. Here an antithetical position is needed and a truly Christian science is demanded. The distinctive character of such a Christian science is not primarily determined by the consideration of the data of Scriptures (which is properly concerned with particular grace) but by the consciousness of the investigating subject, who is a born-again man.

Hence Kuyper's position, as far as science and human rationality is concerned, is ambiguous and full of tensions. Science, for Kuyper, belongs to the realm of God's common grace. Therefore here lies a God-given task for the Christian. However, because he tends to separate the field of common grace from the realm of particular grace, Kuyper is hesitant whether he can introduce the principle of religious antithesis. Does the idea of common grace have to function as the basis for appreciating non-Christian conceptions, or does it have to function as the basis for antithetical action and Christian initiative? In *De gemeene gratie*, starting from the principle of common grace, Kuyper tries to limit the antithesis mainly to the higher sciences (*GG* III 515). But when in his *Lectures on Calvinism* he starts from the opposite side and emphasizes the principle of antithesis, he often ignores his ideas on common grace. In the chapter "Calvinism and Science" just a few sentences are addressed admiringly to the "treasures of philosophical light" found in ancient Greece and Rome, legitimized with the argument of common grace (*LC* 121, 125). Yet immediately thereafter Kuyper advocates a comprehensive organizational antithesis in the sciences between the "normalists" and the "abnormalists" and he unfolds a universal program of Christian scientific activity, as we saw before.

In short, Kuyper did not succeed in harmonizing his view on religious antithesis and on common grace, especially not when he dealt with the problem of human rationality.

VIII. The Bavincks on Religion and Rationality

Kuyper's views did not go unopposed. I am reminded of Herman Bavinck, the professor of dogmatics at the Free University. Bavinck was a close spiritual brother of Kuyper, and he was an unconditional supporter of a Christian approach to the practice of science. Bavinck, too, put aside scholastic dualism, which denied the total depravity of human nature, including human reason. Yet Bavinck arrived at a much more moderate judgment of non-Christian thought than did Kuyper. How was that possible? A number of issues should be discussed at this point.

In the first place, Bavinck notes that the antithesis is a conflict of principles, not of persons or of organizations. He therefore cannot follow Kuyper in concluding from two kinds of principle to two kinds of people and two kinds of science. Somewhere he calls this a "metabasis eis allo genos," a shift to another category. For Bavinck, the kingdom of the truth can no more be equated with those who have been born again than can the kingdom of Satan be equated with those who have not been born again; among the former there is in fact much error present, among the latter much truth.[5]

Second, although Bavinck takes it for granted that there is an opposition of *principle* between belief and unbelief, Christianity and heathendom, he states that this opposition is not *exclusively* antithetical: in the heathen religions (see Bavinck's *Gereformeerde dogmatiek:* hereafter, *GD*) "elements of truth" must be acknowledged. Yes, Christianity may be called the "fulfillment" of the heathen quest on the ground of God's general revelation (*GD* I 292ff.).

A different view of the antithesis brings with it a different view of the philosophy of the day! Like Kuyper, Bavinck thinks philosophy is feasible given the basis of God's common grace, which certainly must entail some restraints on lies and errors in thought. However, I think Bavinck views common grace somewhat more consistently than Kuyper as a source of light and truth, because for Bavinck, God's general revelation continues shining, despite everything, in a world estranged from God. For this reason he can describe the philosophy of the day, just as Calvin could, as a *praeclarum donum Dei*, an excellent gift of God (*GD* I 509, 577).

Bavinck adds a third point to this argument. He notes that Christianity did not destroy ancient civilization and philosophy but rather "Christianized" and "sanctified" it. The church fathers themselves, according to Bavinck, came to the view that the existing science "was neither to be rejected as a whole nor accepted as a whole." It is clear that this line of thought must make newer and different demands of Christian philosophy than would a consistent Kuyperian antithesis view. And then especially it must demand that Christian philosophy, given this openness to non-Christian thought, not fall back into scholasticism—something Bavinck wanted to avoid at all cost.

Herman Bavinck's viewpoint was subsequently worked out in greater detail by Johan H. Bavinck, professor of (Christian) missions at the Free University. In his book *Religieus besef en christelijk geloof* (1949) (Religious Consciousness and Christian Faith) and in other publications, J.H. Bavinck shows how ambivalent non-Christian religions and non-Christian philosophies really are. On the basis of an extensive analysis of biblical givens, especially Romans 1, Bavinck states that two things come to expression in the non-Christian religions. In the first place there is present in them the self-manifestation and self-presentation of God. Paul states in Romans 1:20 that God has made known "his eternal power and Godhead"; there is knowledge of God among the peoples of the earth. In the second place, however, there also comes to expression in these religions something that might be called the human suppression mechanism. Knowledge of God is constantly *suppressed* and *replaced*. Paul writes of those "who hold the truth in unrighteousness" (Rom. 1:18) and of those who "changed the truth of God into a lie and worshiped and served the creature more than the Creator" (Rom. 1:25).

In other words, in the view of J.H. Bavinck, it cannot be said that the non-Christian religions, which express themselves even in different types of rationality, are unadulterated apostasy or pure and unmixed idolatry. Rather, it is evident that in their very apostasy and idolatry there is a struggle going on with respect to the truth; they bear witness to both the influence of, and the resistance to, the God who makes himself known to all people.

IX. The Van Peursen-Dooyeweerd Discussion

In the light of our discussion of Kuyper and the Bavincks, it is now possible to make a few clarifying comments on the discussions between the two Free University philosophers Van Peursen and Dooyeweerd, which have partly been published in *Philosophia Reformata* (*PR*).[6] One of the most important points of difference between them is their view on rationality and their evaluation of non-Christian philosophy. As far as I can see, this difference is caused by one fact: with regard to the principle of antithesis, Dooyeweerd shows himself as a disciple primarily of Kuyper, and Van Peursen as a follower of J.H. Bavinck.

Dooyeweerd and Van Peursen both want to give a positive evaluation of non-biblical thinking. However, not only the degree but also the ground of their evaluation differs considerably. Dooyeweerd posits that human reason and therefore all rational and philosophical systems are subjected to the principle of religious antithesis. Most theories are based on an apostate ground-motive, a motive which stands in "radical antithesis" (a word of Kuyper's to the biblical ground-motive (*PR* 25, 144ff.). They can and ought to be appreciated only insofar as they appear to be confronted with undeniable "states of affairs which conform to the law-structures of creation," as he puts it. That is to say, all Christian and non-Christian philosophers, in spite of their conflicting religious starting points, must face the states of affairs which, as it were, impinge themselves upon every man within the structures of God's creation order (*PR* 25, 105ff., 150).

As I mentioned before, Van Peursen does not recognize such a divine creation order, nor does he recognize anything like a "state of affairs," which is based on it. According to him the "affairs" are never static; on the contrary, they are related to the meaning-giving human subject and move always within human patterns of interpretation (*PR* 24, 162ff., 168). Where, then, does Van Peursen find a ground for his appreciation of, and communication with, non-Christian thinkers? In separating faith and reason? That would be impossible, because Dooyeweerd and Van Peursen are both convinced of the impact of religion on human rationality. But for Van Peursen the religious antithesis is not so absolute as for Dooyeweerd. The religious antithesis, God's "no" to sin, is preceded by a religious thesis, God's "yes" to his creation. In line with the Bavincks, Van Peursen emphasizes the *presence* of God in our created world, because God reveals himself to man even within false religions and humanistic ideologies. Not in the general structures of a supposed creation order but in this general appeal of God to every man can the real basis be found for a mutual appreciation and a rational communication between Christian and non-Christian scholars (*PR* 24, 168).

X. The Incongruity of the Religious Antithesis

At this point I would like to evaluate the contributions of Kuyper, along with his adherents and critics, and then to articulate more fully my own perspective on the matter of the relation between religion and human rationality. First of all, it seems to me that Dooyeweerd deserves support when he speaks of incontrovertible states of affairs within reality due to God's creation order. This order impinges upon man even in the use of his power of reasoning. Granted, in the course of life and history man is capable of constantly giving new meaning to reality, but always within certain limits. These limits explain why man in modern civilization does have at least some understanding of what is and has been going on within other civilizations, even in the remote past. Man's capacities for interpreting and re-interpreting reality are, in other words, not unlimited and completely arbitrary. Moreover, even the status of the human being as an interpreting being cannot be understood apart from God, who has obviously created man in this way. If human meaning-giving is possible, this possibility itself presupposes the framework of a divine law order; it refers back to God as the ultimate law- and meaning-giver.

The true significance of Kuyper's teaching on common grace for our subject lies, I believe, precisely on this point of the creation order. With this doctrine Kuyper wanted, among other things, to give expression to his conviction that God, in spite of sin, upholds the world by his "creation ordinances" (*GG* I 62). But as we saw before, Kuyper did not stress nearly enough that God upholds these ordinances with a view to (their fulfillment in) Jesus Christ, thus, with a view to particular grace. One could say that his common grace doctrine is not Christocentric enough, that is, not sufficiently rooted in particular grace.

Dooyeweerd, Vollenhoven and others in the Netherlands have reformulated Kuyper's view of common grace more satisfactorily on a Christocentric basis. Or, phrased differently, they have clearly stated that not only does the earth bear the cross but, first and decisively, the cross bears the earth. The common grace doctrine, once anchored Christocentrically, need not become disconnected from Kuyper's reformational starting point: the biblical teaching of a comprehensive religious antithesis. The common grace doctrine offers in this way the possibility for a more correct evaluation of non-Christian thought.

Nevertheless, in taking this position we should not forget the point that has been brought into the discussion by the Bavincks and by Van Peursen: namely, the point of God's personal presence, or his general self-revelation, even in non-Christian cultures and religions. The theme of God's presence is, to my mind, closely related to the question of the structure of religion in general. I believe that not only the Christian religion but every religion, however primitive or perverse it may be, has an "answer-structure." Religion is religion inasmuch as it is a response to an appeal from the side of God; it is a response to

God's self-presentation in his Word (special revelation) or in his works (general revelation). The answer that man gives in his religion, or in any rational system insofar as it expresses his religious attitude, is always an answer of surrender or of rebellion. Whatever the answer may be, it always reflects the echo of God's call: "Adam, I am here, where are you?"

One can agree with Dooyeweerd that an "apostate religious ground-motive" is at work in non-Christian thinking. However, just as the doctrine of common grace must not be deduced from the teaching of a religious antithesis, so, for the same reason, the idea of God's universal self-presentation must not be deduced from it. It is with a view to Jesus Christ that God upholds his creation ordinances and confronts all men with them. It is also with a view to Jesus Christ that God manifests himself in the heart of all men. And every apostasy, within or without the church, testifies to this self-revelation because every apostasy is a falling away from the living God himself. Every apostasy is a holding down and a twisting of the truth which nevertheless continually confronts man.[7]

In short, there is always a certain ambiguity in pagan religions; the same ambiguity is present in human ideologies: human lie is mixed with divine truth. However, this does not weaken the satanic power of the lie. Rather it confirms its inexcusableness, to speak with Calvin. And at the same time it confirms the superior power of the truth: "For we can do nothing against the truth, but for the truth" (II Cor. 13:8). That is the fundamental *incongruity* which is inherent in the biblical teaching of a religious antithesis.

XI. Openness and Opposition

In order to find a good argument for a positive appreciation of non-Christians, I have argued in support of Kuyper's and Dooyeweerd's ideas concerning a divine "creation order" or of creational "states of affairs." To that end I have also argued in favor of J.H. Bavinck's and Van Peursen's appeal concerning God's universal presence. Let me conclude this point by stating that to me both emphases refer to each other and stem from an original unity. I fear that an exclusive appeal either to universal states of affairs or to the universal presence of God will still ensnare us in a spiritualizing dualism à la Kuyper. For that reason I again draw attention to the teaching of John Calvin, who in the exposition of his *Institutes* never separated God's general revelation from his general grace. Indeed, God's action upon the heart of man and his upholding of creation structures cannot be separated, because God reveals himself to mankind in the visible works of his creation (Rom. 1:20). God's voice and the voice of facts are indivisible.

The voice of truth has sounded again and again in the history of mankind. He who listens has cause for wonderment and bewilderment. We experience wonderment in the working of God's Spirit even in a world of heathenism, secularism, and modern ideologies. And we are bewildered that this working of God is continually warped through human arrogance and guilt, to which a Christian's mind is anything but immune. The Christian finds himself in this delicate situation, especially when he is called to take a stand in the world of scientific learning and rational communication. This situation demands complete openness and radical opposition at the same time. The apostle Paul describes this attitude as follows: "Casting down reasonings, and every high thing that is exalted against the knowledge of God, and bringing every thought into captivity to the obedience of Christ" (II Cor. 10:5). How do these two attitudes—"openness" and "opposition"—and these two activities—"casting down" and "bringing into captivity"—go together?

XII. Reformation and Transformation

I think that bringing these two attitudes together is, for the Christian (even for the Christian scholar and scientist when he is driven by the spirit of the Gospel), largely an unconscious operation. However, because the open-mindedness of the Christian scholar so easily turns into a philosophical adjustment to the wisdom of the world, and his opposition so quickly turns into an unfruitful isolation from this world, let us *reflect* on the position that we as Christian scholars have to take.

It might be helpful for us to recollect a favorite theme of the church fathers, who also wrestled with the problem of rationality in a sinful world: the theme of "despoliation," or plundering. The church fathers recalled how the children of Israel were asked to despoil the Egyptians of their cultural treasures, their silver and gold, when they left the land (Exod. 12:36). As the Israelites made use of the treasures of Egypt, so Augustine and others believed they were justified in making use of the cultural treasures of the classical world, and thus also of its philosophy.[8]

I think that in principle this despoliation theme yields a useful analogy to what can be done with non-Christian theories and ideas. Yet the church fathers did not always keep these points sharply in view: (a) the Israelites had to take the gold and silver of Egypt, using these valuables just for service in the tabernacle of God; and (b) these treasures had to be smelted and refined before they could be used as vessels in the service of God.

What do I mean to say by this? I believe, indeed, that the rational and philosophical ideas of the day, thanks to God's universal creation order and universal self-presentation within and through this creation order, can in certain respects be seen as excellent gifts of the Spirit of God, and we therefore may make use of them. I am personally engaged in the study of contemporary philosophy. But the goal of this study cannot be exclusively to warn against modern thought! On the contrary, I learn from it, and take something of it along with me. Yet I never do so unconditionally. One must always (this is the first condition) devote philosophy, like the gold and silver of Egypt, to the service of God. To state the matter differently: it can never be our purpose just to adopt the valuable insights of non-Christian thinkers, or to accommodate them in some way *to* the content of Christian faith. Such an approach would amount to either eclecticism or scholasticism. No, if we think it possible to make use of the chattels of non-Christian thought—much of it is unusable, some of it execrable —then this is only permissible, I think, to the extent that we are in a position to really fit it *into* or integrate it *into* a Christian, God-directed view of life.

Here I must present the second condition. The above-mentioned fitting into, or integration, can never take place without far-reaching changes. Indeed the insights of philosophy, even of science in general, function for Christians as well as for non-Christians in a broader context of thought, in a total life's view. These insights function in a *Weltanschauung* that is religiously charged and that I would call an ideology to the extent it is in conflict with the Gospel of Jesus Christ. Therefore it is necessary to take the ideas we borrow from others and smelt and refine them like the Egyptian's gold—in other words, purify them of ideology. I may and must enter into communication and discussion with non-Christian thinkers. I may gratefully acknowledge their gifts, God's gifts. Yet I must always extract their insights from the ideological connections present in them, and present perhaps also in myself, which lead men to resist and suppress the truth of God. I have to take these insights and I have to transpose, to alter, to *transform* them. In this way I have to take the gold that comes *from* God and offer it again *to* God.

In conclusion, therefore, I would contend that we who stand in the tradition of the Calvinian reformation, a tradition which had, and still today has, meaning for philosophy, are all committed to the idea of the reformation of philosophy. But the reformation of philosophy is never possible without communication with dissenters. And such a communication means transformation after the model of the Israelites. Thus our program for a reformation of philosophy should at the same time be a call for the transformation of philosophy.

Notes

1. Lord's Day III.8.
2. See J. Klapwijk, "Christelijke organisaties in verlegenheid," in: *Christelijke organisaties in discussie*, pp. 21-66.
3. *Souvereiniteit in eigen kring*, p. 32.
4. See also S.U. Zuidema, *Communication and Confrontation*, pp. 52-105.
5. See R.H. Bremmer, *Herman Bavinck als dogmaticus*, p. 40.
6. C.A. Van Peursen, "Enkele critische vragen in margine bij 'A New Critique of Theoretical Thought,' " in: *PR* 24 (1959), pp. 160-168; H. Dooyeweerd, "Van Peursen's critische vragen bij 'A New Critique of Theoretical Thought,' " in: *PR* 25 (1960), pp. 97-150; C.A. Van Peursen, "Antwoord aan Dooyeweerd," in: *PR* 26 (1961), pp. 189-200. See also: C.A. Van Peursen, "Culture and Christian Faith," in: *Wetenschap, wijsheid, filosoferen*, pp. 32-37.
7. See also J. Klapwijk, "The Struggle for a Christian Philosophy: Another Look at Dooyeweerd" and "Dooyeweerd's Christian Philosophy: Antithesis and Critique," in: *Reformed Journal* 30 (1980), pp. 12-15 and 20-24.
8. St. Augustine, *De Doctrina Christiana* II.40.60.

Works Cited

Augustinus, A., *De Doctrina Christiana* (397-426).

———. *De Civitate Dei* (413-426).

Bavinck, H., *Gereformeerde dogmatiek (GD)*, 4 vols. Kampen: Kok, (1895-1901) 1967.

———. *Verzamelde opstellen op het gebied van godsdienst en wetenschap*. Kampen: Kok, 1921.

Bavinck, J.H., *Religieus besef en christelijk geloof (RB)*. Kampen: Kok, 1949.

Bremmer, R.H., *Herman Bavinck als dogmaticus*. Kampen: Kok, 1961 (dissertation, Free University).

Calvin, J., *Institutes of the Christian Religion (IR)*, trans. by F.L. Battles. Philadelphia: Westminster Press, n.d.

Dooyeweerd, H., *A New Critique of Theoretical Thought*, 4 vols.

Amsterdam: H.J. Paris and Philadelphia: Presbyterian & Reformed Publ. Co., 1953.

———. "Van Peursen's critische vragen bij 'A New Critique of Theoretical Thought,' " in: *Philosophia Reformata* 25 (1960), pp. 97-150.

Klapwijk, J., "Christelijke organisaties in verlegenheid," in: *Christelijke organisaties in discussie, een bijdrage*, ed. by V.C.S.A. The Hague: Boekencentrum (1979), pp. 21-66.

———. "The Struggle for a Christian Philosophy: Another Look at Dooyeweerd," in: *Reformed Journal* 30,2 (Feb., 1980), pp. 12-15.

———. "Dooyeweerd's Christian Philosophy: Antithesis and Critique," in: *Reformed Journal* 30,3 (Mar., 1980), pp. 20-24.

Kuyper, A., *Souvereiniteit in eigen kring: Rede ter inwijding van de Vrije Universiteit den 20sten October 1880*. Kampen: Kok, (1880) 1930.

———. *Lectures on Calvinism (LC)*. Grand Rapids, Mich.: Wm.B. Eerdmans, (1898) 1961.

———. *De gemeene gratie (GG)*, 3 vols. Kampen: Kok, (1902-1905) 1931-1932.

———. *Pro Rege of het koningschap van Christus*, 3 vols. Kampen: Kok, 1911-1912.

Van Peursen, C.A., "Enkele critische vragen in margine bij 'A New Critique of Theoretical Thought,' " in: *Philosophia Reformata* 24 (1959), pp. 160-168.

———. "Antwoord aan Dooyeweerd," in: *Philosophia Reformata* 26 (1961), pp. 189-200.

———. "Culture and Christian Faith," in: *Wetenschap, wijsheid, filosoferen*, Festschrift H. van Riessen. Assen: Van Gorcum (1981), pp. 32-37.

Zuidema, S.U., *Communication and Confrontation: A Philosophical Appraisal and Critique of Modern Society and Contemporary Thought*. Assen: Van Gorcum, and Kampen: Kok, 1972.

Dutch Neo-Calvinism: Worldview, Philosophy and Rationality

Albert Wolters

IN DISCUSSING THE VIEW OF RATIONALITY HELD in Dutch neo-Calvinism, it is important to make a number of preliminary distinctions, and to clarify some underlying assumptions about philosophy and worldview. These distinctions and assumptions have this peculiarity: they play a decisive role both in the writings of the neo-Calvinists under discussion and in the present discussion about them. That is to say, the ensuing analysis of Dutch neo-Calvinism is undertaken by someone who self-consciously stands in the neo-Calvinist tradition. This approach has obvious drawbacks; it may also have its advantages.

A cardinal distinction to be made in this connection is that between "worldview" and "philosophy." This is a distinction of relatively recent date, having first been made in nineteenth-century German philosophy. It is found, for example, in the writings of Wilhelm Dilthey and Heinrich Rickert, although they are by no means the first to adopt it. They contrast *Weltanschauung*, as a pre-scientific view of the world, with *Philosophie*, as its scientific counterpart. The connotations of "pre-scientific," in this context, are: subjective, haphazard and contradictory, arising out of emotional and religious prejudices. "Scientific," by contrast, implies a mode of cognition that is objective, methodical and coherent, founded on neutral and rational principles. Based on this view, the philosophies of the past (since the time of the Greeks) have confused *Weltanschauung* and *Philosophie;* the task now is to develop a rigorously scientific philosophy which will disabuse itself for all *weltanschauliche* elements. Worldview and philosophy, although alike in both offering a view of the totality of things, are basically at odds with each other. In the vocabulary of German philosophy to this day, the adjective *weltanschaulich* includes "unphilosophical" among its connotations.

The English word "worldview" seems to owe its existence to this distinction and contrast in German philosophy. According to the *Oxford English Dictionary*, the word first appeared in English in 1858, as a translation of *Weltanschauung*, presumably because of its implied contrast with a strictly rational philosophy. It does not seem to have caught on in English, however, until well into the twentieth century, in the heyday of neo-Kantianism; in 1917, we find the American theologian B.B. Warfield referring to it as a word newly in fashion.

Whatever its semantic history, the term "worldview" (or its equivalent "world-and-life view") seems to pinpoint a useful distinction between philosophy as a methodologically rigorous academic discipline (a "science" in the sense of *Wissenschaft*), and the common-sense perspective on life and the world, the "system of values" or "ideology," which in one form or another is held by all normal adult human beings regardless of intelligence or education. In this sense, worldview does indeed precede science, and is therefore quite different from philosophy in the strictly theoretical sense.

It is, however, an unwarranted prejudice to regard pre-theoretical common sense as more prone to error and uncertainty than theoretical science, and therefore to depreciate the cognitive claims of worldview as compared to those of philosophy. As a matter of fact, a good case can be made for the epistemological *priority* of worldview over philosophy. That is to say, philosophy (like all scientific knowing) is necessarily based on pre-scientific intuitions and assumptions that are given with the worldview of the philosopher concerned. Worldview necessarily plays a decisive role in philosophy, and the attempt to emancipate philosophy from worldview is doomed to failure.

This is a state of affairs that philosophers do not generally recognize, although historians of philosophy repeatedly point out the role of an underlying worldview in individual philosophers. Werner Jaeger's treatment of Plato in his *Paideia: The Ideals of Greek Culture*, vols. II and III (1943, 1945) may be taken as one example. The technical philosophy of Plato (including, for example, his arguments for the existence of the Forms) is there seen as the expression of a cultural ideal, a vision of men and society current in fifth-century Athens that was not itself theoretical in nature. We may think also of Rudolf Eucken's best-selling work *Die Lebensanschauungen der grossen Denker* (1890), in which he discusses the worldviews of such philosophers as Plato, Aristotle, Plotinus, Spinoza, Leibniz and Kant. Lewis White Beck, in his *Early German Philosophy* (1969), makes a telling case for the role of *Weltanschauung* (Beck's word) in the theoretical philosophy of Immanuel Kant. The same point about Kant is made by G.A. van der Wal in a Dutch work specifically devoted to the problem of the relationship of worldview to philosophy (*Wereldbeschouwelijk denken als filosofisch probleem* [The Hague, 1969]). Van der Wal also explores the role of worldview in the philosophies of Spinoza and Leibniz, and comes to the general conclusion that pre-theoretical worldview and theoretical philosophy are like the two foci of an ellipse comprising all the giants of the philosophical tradition.

If this is so, then philosophers should clearly develop their philosophical thought in direct touch with their own worldview, and not pretend that they do not have one. A good deal of the confusion and lack of communication in philosophy may be due to a failure to recognize the role of worldview in philosophy. Many apparently philosophical disputes may mask differences on a pre-theoretical level which will never be resolved if they are not recognized for what they are. Rather than attempting the impossible task of doing philosophy in a worldview vacuum, philosophers should put their worldview cards on the table and enter the philosophical debate with none of those cards up their sleeve. Moreover, they should explicitly, self-consciously and unapologetically engage in philosophical systematics on the basis of their worldview. (This is much to be preferred over the alternative: doing philosophy in a manner that is implicit, unaware or apologetic.) Such an attitude and practice will not hinder philosophical communication, but foster it.

For Christian philosophers, the obvious implication is that they must seek to orient their philosophizing to a Christian worldview. Or to put the case a bit more strongly and accurately, the Christian must seek to philosophize on the basis of the Christian worldview—that is, the *biblical* worldview. Presupposed in such a formulation is the conviction that there is one Christian worldview, and that it is taught in the Scriptures. We will not argue for either of these crucial points here, but take them as points of departure. It may be useful, however, for our purposes here, to elaborate on the distinctiveness of a *Calvinistic* understanding of the Bible's worldview.

All traditions of orthodox Christendom (those who accept the ecumenical creeds, thus including not only the Greek Orthodox and Roman Catholic Churches, but also the Lutheran, Anabaptist and Calvinistic streams of Protestantism) agree on some basic Christian beliefs. To use a Trinitarian formulation favored by Herman Bavinck, they all agree that:

> the Father reconciles his
> created but fallen world through
> the death of his Son, and re-
> creates it by his Spirit into a
> Kingdom of God.

A Christian's worldview, the pre-scientific overall perspective which he has on life and the world, may be said to be the way he relates this basic confession to the everyday realities of his personal, societal and cultural experience. Distinctive about the Calvinistic understanding of the Christian worldview (building on a long tradition which includes Irenaeus, Augustine, Chrysostom and Tyndale) is that it takes all the operative words of this basic formulation in a universal, all-embracing sense. The *created world* is as wide as our experience, including culture and society, and its *fall* and *reconciliation* are equally cosmic in scope. So the *Kingdom of God* is truly a *re-creation*, a restoration of the entire range of earthly reality to its original goal. Other traditions of Christendom tend to restrict the scope of creation, fall and redemption, and thus to come to some kind of two-realm worldview: one realm where creation applies, and another where fall and redemption apply. The variations that are possible here are described in the well-known book by H. Richard Niebuhr, *Christ and Culture* (1951), where the last chapter elucidates the tradition that is here called "Calvinistic."

Christian philosophy must be oriented to a biblical worldview, and there are different traditional understandings of that worldview. So it would seem that the choice of "understanding" will be decisive in philosophy. This is particularly true of Calvinism, since it rejects a two-realm theory which would allow philosophy to be treated as part of the "natural" realm, unaffected by sin and grace. A Christian thinker whose worldview is dominated by a nature/grace dichotomy will still base his philosophizing on his worldview insofar as "natural reason" must *allow for* an area where sin and grace are decisive. But he will feel much more easily justified in following the current and fashionable manifestations of that natural reason than a Calvinist who denies the existence of a purely "natural" reason.

Here we shall conclude our brief discussion of worldview and philosophy. It remains for us to make a preliminary remark about the concept "categorial framework." This term, which we are adopting from Stephan Körner (see his *Categorial Frameworks* [Oxford, 1974]), refers to something central in both worldviews and philosophies: the most basic distinctions and relations which a person accepts as valid, and which govern his outlook and argumentation. Worldviews and philosophies are both centrally concerned with the fundamental distinctions to be made in reality and with the relations which obtain among the resulting "domains." If Körner is right, such "categorial frameworks" are so important that they establish a person's standards of rationality; they prescribe his *logic*. Consequently, all analysis and argument presuppose and are governed by one's tacit categorial assumptions.

We turn now to a discussion of neo-Calvinism and its worldview, beginning with an historical overview and concluding with a systematic review of the categorial distinctions of its worldview.

The term "Calvinism" (including its compound form "neo-Calvinism"), as here used, refers not so much to a theological system, but to an all-embracing worldview or *Weltanschauung* which has a bearing on the whole of human life. This is the sense in which the word is used in Kuyper's well-known *Lectures on Calvinism*, delivered at Princeton in 1898. It is particularly important to make this point in an English-speaking context, since the term Calvinism is readily equated in the Anglo-Saxon world with a certain view of predestination, or associated narrowly with the so-called "five points of Calvinism." Calvinism as a worldview is comparable to Marxism: it has the same claim to comprehensiveness and immediate applicability.

The term "neo-Calvinism" refers to the revival of Dutch Calvinism in nineteenth-century Holland, chiefly associated with the name of Abraham Kuyper (1837-1920). The term was originally coined by Kuyper's opponents but was accepted by him and his followers, who recognized that their views were a development, not simply a restatement, of the classical Calvinism of the sixteenth and seventeenth centuries. "Kuyperian" is an adjective with much the same denotation as "neo-Calvinistic," as is "reformational," although the latter term again tends to designate a *development*—in this case of Kuyper's basic outlook.

Although Abraham Kuyper was clearly the towering giant of the neo-Calvinistic movement, he was clearly not its only leader. As a scholar and teacher he was certainly matched by Herman Bavinck. There were a number of others, mainly pastors or professors at the Free University in Amsterdam, who helped shape and consolidate the movement. We will briefly review those among the neo-Calvinists who had the greatest concern for philosophy.

Kuyper himself was certainly one of these. He can be described as the romantic genius, a prodigy in both intellectual and practical pursuits. He began as a theologian (trained at modernist Leiden) and spent the first years after receiving his doctorate as a pastor in the national Dutch Reformed Church. Here he was converted to orthodox Calvinism and became a leading voice in ecclesiastical affairs. Soon his influence became national in scope, and he led not only a secession from the largely modernist *Hervormde* Church, but also wrote books on theology, edited a daily and a weekly newspaper, founded in 1880 the Free University of Amsterdam as a specifically Calvinistic institution (where he taught theology and Dutch literature), and became leader and member of Parliament for the Calvinistic Anti-Revolutionary Party. In 1901 he became Prime Minister of the Netherlands, a post which he held until 1904. He was the undisputed leader of neo-Calvinism, a movement which combined spiritual and theological renewal with fresh beginnings on a broadly cultural front: political, social, economic, educational and academic.

Herman Bavinck (1854-1921) was a very different sort of man than Kuyper, although he shared Kuyper's ideals and laid claim to a scholarly reputation which at least equalled Kuyper's. Bavinck came from the circles of the 1834 *Afscheiding*, a secession from the national church which later largely joined Kuyper's forces to form a single Reformed denomination. Bavinck, too, received a doctorate in theology from Leiden, although he never let go of the orthodox faith of his upbringing. After one year as a pastor, he became professor of systematic theology, first for twenty years at the theological seminary of his church at Kampen, then for another twenty years (after the merger of the two churches) at the Free University, where he succeeded Kuyper. He is the author of a magisterial four-volume work entitled *Reformed Dogmatics*, which is currently being translated into English. During the last ten years of his life, Bavinck turned his attention to non-theological disciplines, especially philosophy. His scholarship is characterized by an impressive breadth and balance, and by an ecumenical spirit which allowed him to appreciate and honor the strengths and insights of thinkers of entirely different persuasions than his own.

Next to these two titans, we should mention two other professors of the Free University: Jan Woltjer and W. Geesink. Woltjer (1849-1917) was a classicist who had written his doctoral dissertation on Lucretius, and who maintained an active interest in philosophy all his life. He wrote a number of essays outlining the importance of the *Logos* of John 1 for a Christian understanding of the world. Geesink (1854-1929) taught ethics and philosophy at the Free University, and is chiefly known for his multi-volume popular work *On the Or-*

dinances of the Lord, in which he outlines an approach to philosophy on the basis of a neo-Calvinistic understanding of the Scriptures.

All four of these men were keenly interested in philosophy, but none had the time or training for specialized work in the area. This was left to a number of men of the second generation, who worked out the implications of neo-Calvinism for specifically philosophical questions. Three in particular should be mentioned, although they were by no means the only neo-Calvinists who pursued philosophy with explicit reference to their worldview.

Geesink's successor in philosophy at the Free University was D.H.T. Vollenhoven (1892-1978). Vollenhoven came to study theology at the Free in 1911, at the time when Bavinck's interests were shifting to philosophy. Vollenhoven followed his teacher's interests and wrote a doctoral dissertation in 1918 entitled *The Philosophy of Mathematics from a Theistic Standpoint*. After a number of years as pastor, he received the philosophy appointment at his *alma mater* in 1926, where he remained until his retirement in 1963. Besides original work in philosophical systematics, Vollenhoven is known for his distinctive work in the history of philosophy. Among his most important publications are *Calvinism and the Reformation of Philosophy* (1933) and *History of Philosophy*, vol. I (1950), both written in Dutch.

Vollenhoven's brother-in-law, Herman Dooyeweerd (1894-1977), was professor of jurisprudence at the Free University from 1926 to 1965, and worked together with Vollenhoven on the development of a Calvinistic philosophy. Dooyeweerd's own major philosophical publication appeared in English in the 1950s under the title *A New Critique of Theoretical Thought*. Dooyeweerd is the best known, internationally, of the Dutch reformational philosophers, chiefly because a number of his philosophical works have been translated into English. Other titles include: *Transcendental Problems of Philosophical Thought* (1948), *In the Twilight of Western Thought* (1960), and *Roots of Western Culture* (1979). His own term for his philosophy is "the philosophy of the cosmonomic idea." It takes a unique approach to the history of Western philosophy, and also provides a detailed analysis of reality which notably includes a distinctive view of theoretical thought, human society and history.

A third reformational philosopher, on a par with Vollenhoven and Dooyeweerd, is the South African Hendrik Stoker (1900-). Stoker came to Amsterdam to study under Bavinck in 1921, the very year that Bavinck died. Thwarted in his plans to pursue philosophy at the Free University, Stoker studied under the phenomenologist Max Scheler in Cologne, receiving his doctorate in 1925 (with a thesis in German entitled *Conscience*). He returned to South Africa to teach philosophy at the Christian University of Potchefstroom, where he remained until his retirement in 1964. He stayed in close touch with Vollenhoven and Dooyeweerd, and his philosophy, to which he gave the name "philosophy of the creation idea," closely parallels their mutual concerns.

These three men are the most original thinkers in the reformational movement in philosophy which emanated from the Free University, and which is sometimes referred to as the "Amsterdam School." However, they were not the only ones of the second generation of neo-Calvinists who did work in philosophy. For example, the missionary and missiologist J.H. Bavinck (a nephew to Herman Bavinck) published writings on philosophical topics in his early career, as did V. Hepp, who was Bavinck's successor at the Free University. Hepp delivered the 1930 Stone Lectures on the topic *Calvinism and the Philosophy of Nature*. H. Hoekstra, a Kampen theologian who also lectured in philosophy, had received his doctorate in the philosophy of religion under the well-known Kantian W. Windelband in Heidelberg. None of these theologians, however, made a lasting impact with their philosophical work.

For all their differences in originality, influence and philosophical training, the neo-Calvinists of the first and second generations were united in their basic worldview. We turn now to the basic categorial distinctions which define this worldview and which account for the cohesivenes of reformational philosophizing, in spite of philosophical differences.

As I see it, there are five categorial distinctions that define the unity and distinctiveness of neo-Calvinism as a whole. These are fundamental in the thought of each of the men we have mentioned, although not every distinction is fruitfully developed for philosophy in each of these men. It should be noted that each distinction brings with it a relation between the domains or realities that are distinguished; moreover, the specification of the relation is one of the most important features of each distinction within a categorial framework.

The first distinction is that between *God and creation*. This is of course fundamental to any Christian or theistic worldview, but it appears here in a particularly marked form. Calvinism carries within itself a strong aversion to any tendency toward pantheism or idolatry, any shading of the boundary separating the Creator from his creature. A keen sense of the sovereignty and transcendence of God makes the neo-Calvinist shy away from any view that points to a common denominator for both God and creation, making the difference between them gradual rather than qualitative. By the same token, "creation" becomes the category for all that is not God, including the whole range of visible and invisible reality.

The second categorial distinction is that between *God's creational ordinances and what is subject to these ordinances*. Creation is defined (in characteristically Calvinistic fashion), in terms of a cosmic *law* (decree, statute, word, ordinance), as the expression of God's sovereignty. In the terminology of "cosmo-*nomic*" philosophy, creation is always a matter of "the law-subject correlation." That correlation holds not only in the world of nature (where we all speak readily enough of the "law of gravity" and the "laws of thermodynamics") but also for all other kinds of reality, such as music, politics, business, entertainment, worship and so on. A postulated creational "law" that must be responsibly implemented makes all these areas philosophically accessible *as creation*. This law thus enables philosophy to take seriously the comprehensive scope of creation in the Calvinistic understanding of the basic Christian confession. The distinction between law and subject, understood to apply across the board within creation, is perhaps the most fruitful one for a biblically based philosophy. Although this distinction is developed most extensively in the reformational philosophies of Vollenhoven, Dooyeweerd and Stoker, it is by no means restricted to them.

A third categorial distinction, which cuts across the preceding one, is that between *"earth" and "heaven,"* or between the earthly creation and the creaturely dwelling place of God and the angels. It is important to distinguish here between a broader and a narrower sense of these scriptural terms. The narrower sense refers to heaven as "sky" and to earth as "dry land." Both of these, according to biblical usage, are subdivisions within the earthly creation ("earth" in the broader sense). The latter, called "the cosmos" in Stoker's terminology, is the horizon of normal human experience, and therefore sets the limits of empirical investigation and scientific analysis.

The fourth categorial distinction is that between different stages of *development within the earthly cosmos*. The earth must be formed or developed ("subdued") in human culture so that its creational potential can be historically unfolded or opened up to God's glory. The distinction between "undeveloped" and "developed" is therefore one that is given with creation, and is not the result of the Fall. Man's task of developing the earth is part of God's eschatological plan for his creation, so that human culture is fundamentally recognized as worthwhile, part of creation's movement toward a final consummation. The idea of the "cultural mandate" here militates against any attitude to human civilization and its development that would be quietistic or historically reactionary.

The final categorial distinction is the only one of the five that is the result of the Fall into sin. This is the distinction between *"structure" and "direction,"* or between "the order of creation" and "the order of sin and redemption" (Calvin). "Structure" refers to the created cosmos as it was meant to be; "direction" refers to that cosmos as it is misdirected by sin and redemptively redirected by Christ. Because sin and redemption, in the Calvinist understanding, are cosmic in scope, this distinction holds in principle for all of the earthly creation, including natural, cultural and societal life as well as morality and piety. Here the Calvinist stress on the radical and comprehensive scope of man's Fall, as well as the equally radical and comprehensive scope of Christ's redemption, finds expression in a succinct categorial formulation. At the same time, this fundamental distinction reflects the basic Calvinist intuition that salvation is *re-creation*, that is, that grace does not destroy or supplement, but rather *restores* nature.

Having dealt with the categorial framework of the neo-Calvinists, we can turn now to their view of rationality. We discover that there is widespread agreement among them on the worldview level, but there is a marked development on the philosophical level. We shall deal with each of these themes in turn.

The neo-Calvinists are agreed that rationality is a good creature of God, meant to be developed and cultivated to his glory. The categorial framework of their worldview is clearly in evidence here. Rationality is a creature, which implies that it is not divine (reason may not be deified), is subject to creation norms, and is meant to be developed as part of man's earthly task before the face of God. Because it belongs to the order of creation, it may not be deified—but for the same reason it may not be vilified either, for everything created by God is *good*. However, rationality also participates in the order of sin and redemption, that is to say, it is fundamentally *religious*—under the influence of sin and in need of redemption. In other words, the categories "structure" and "direction" apply to rationality as much as they do to any other part, feature or dimension of the cosmos. Rationality is not religiously neutral.

It is evident how decisively the neo-Calvinists' understanding of the biblical worldview governs their thinking at this point. Clearly they part company here with the doctrine of an autonomous or religiously neutral reason, either in its humanist or its Christian form. It was their distinctive view of the religious nature of rationality, and thus of all science and rationality, which led to the establishment of the Free University in 1880. There, all scholarship was to be guided by "the reformed principles," that is, by a Calvinist understanding of the biblical worldview.

Kuyper explicitly spoke in this connection of *tweeërlei wetenschap*, "two kinds of scholarship (science)." One kind of scholarship arose out of a regenerate heart, and was therefore prepared to interpret the world in the light of authoritative Scriptures. The other kind arose out of an unregenerate heart, and therefore rejected the light of Scriptures. Kuyper consequently called for the reformation of scholarship, for the development of scripturally directed learning.

Bavinck's view of rationality has been analyzed in an excellent work by E.P. Heideman, *The Relation of Revelation and Reason in E. Brunner and H. Bavinck* (1959). Bavinck treats rationality in the light of his fundamental and constantly recurring theme that grace (salvation) restores nature (creation). Christ's redemption therefore means that man's rational powers can be fundamentally freed from the enslaving effects of sin, and restored to their original creational function. Christianity does not lead one to the irrational, but to the truly rational. In this connection Bavinck borrows Calvin's image of the Scriptures as corrective glasses, which allow bleary-eyed fallen man once more to see clearly. The Scriptures allow reason to function once again as it was intended. The biblical worldview must be the Christian's guide in reasoning, both in daily life and in philosophy and science. So Bavinck enthusiastically seconded Kuyper's call for a reformation of the academic disciplines in the light of the Scriptures, and Bavinck increasingly participated in the effort to bring about that reformation in fields outside theology.

The emphasis on the *religious* nature of philosophy also accounts for Bavinck's critique of Scottish common-sense philosophy, with its doctrine of an infallible intuition. In a dissertation written under Bavinck (*The Intuitive Philosophy of James McCosh* [1914], S. Volbeda singles out this feature of McCosh's thought for criticism (p. 386).

Both Kuyper and Bavinck, as well as the other neo-Calvinists of their day, stress the importance of *principles* in the functioning of rationality, and stress this approach in the doing of scholarship. These principles are the axioms or underlying presuppositions which govern theoretical reasoning. They are of a philosophical, and ultimately of a religious, nature. Characteristic of the neo-Calvinist approach to rationality is this stress on philosophical principles as the link between religious commitment and the process of scientific reasoning. In our terminology, the pre-scientific categorial distinctions and relations on the worldview level will immediately reflect an allegiance to revelation (either the Scriptures or some substitute). These distinctions and relations become operative in the scientific enterprise when they are philosophically elaborated. It is clear how important the role is that philosophy, as the "categorial" discipline *par excellence*, assumes in this view. The reformation of scholarship in accordance with reformed principles would depend very largely on the development of a distinctly Calvinistic *philosophy*. It is to this topic that we now turn.

It bears repeating that the unity of the neo-Calvinist movement, at least insofar as this can be defined in intellectual terms, lies in a common commitment to the worldview principles we have outlined. Philosophically, however, there was no such unity, although there was a widespread agreement among the first generation that further clarity and consensus on a Calvinistic philosophy was a task of high priority. Their understanding of rationality reflects the process of development that came about as their philosophy, explicitly geared to their understanding of the biblical worldview, came into clearer focus. That process of development can be roughly categorized by two phases, which I will designate by the labels "neo-Platonic" and "cosmonomic."

The initial attempts to articulate a Calvinistic philosophy, on the part of men like Kuyper, Bavinck, Woltjer and Geesink, were still very much indebted to the tradition of Christian neo-Platonism. This tradition, largely initiated by Augustine and strongly reinforced in the early Middle Ages by the Latin translations of Dionysius the Pseudo-Areopagite, I take to be virtually equivalent to the history of Christian orthodoxy in the West. This tradition is characterized by the idea of "the great chain of being," the cosmic hierarchy of different grades of *ousia*. God is defined as the highest grade of "being" *(summum ens)* and "being" itself, as both "substance" and "essence," and is defined as the objective correlate of rationality *(logos, nous)*. A brief excursus on the history of this scheme may be helpful to put into context the initial neo-Calvinist attempts to give a philosophical account of rationality.

Plato's Forms, characterized as both truly real and truly rational, had put rationality at the center of pagan Greek ontology.

This basic feature was not fundamentally affected by the immanentization of the Forms by Aristotle, or by the pantheistic materialism of the Stoics. Plotinus capitalized on this by bringing together all these major streams of Greek thought (Platonic, Aristotelian and Stoic) into his neo-Platonic hierarchy of being. Plato's two worlds were conceived as two tiers of a five-tier ontology (One-Intellect-Soul-World-Matter). These were correlated with different grades of being (superbeing, true being, two grades of attenuated being, and non-being), which were at the same time different grades of rationality and goodness (evil in materiality, the absence of such goodness). Stoic categories (*logoi spermatikoi*, cosmic *sympatheia*) were drawn on to account for the sensible World, and Aristotelian categories served to elucidate Matter and Intellect (cf. Aristotle's *hylē, noēsis, noēseōs*), as well as to provide the basic ontology of the visible World (the categories, immanent eidē, genus/species). The commanding overall framework remained Platonic (*chōrismos*, participation, intelligible world, virtue as separation and *homoiōsis theō*), with two important innovations: the intelligible world (true being) is equated with the divine Intellect ("ideas in the mind of God"), and the One/Good transcends both.

Augustine read his Bible with the aid of this neo-Platonic framework: the One was collapsed into the Intellect and equated with God, so that the Logos of the prologue of John refers simultaneously to the second person of the Trinity and to the complex of Platonic Forms as the rational archetype and source of created things. Within creation (sensible World), the ontological structure of things must be seen as the ectypical grade of being/rationality designated by the Stoic *logoi spermatikoi (rationes seminales)* or Aristotle's *eidē (formae)*.

This basic ontological framework was bequeathed by Augustine to the Latin Middle Ages during which time it was modified in detail (Pseudo-Dionysius, Eriugena) but never fundamentally challenged. This also holds true for the impact of the rediscovery of the Aristotelian corpus in the thirteenth century. The achievement of Aquinas was possible because the inherited Platonic-Augustinian framework of classical dogmatic orthodoxy was neo-Platonic in character—it had been designed to accommodate Aristotelian categories from the outset. Aquinas in effect *re*-integrated Aristotle into Augustinian Platonism, but Plotinus had already laid the foundations. Aquinas merely strengthened the hold which the neo-Platonic philosophical paradigm has had on classical Christian orthodoxy—a hold which was loosened but not broken by the Reformers, and continues to this day.

The thought of the early neo-Calvinists was no exception to this rule. The basic features of the paradigm are present: God as *summum ens*, the Son or Logos understood as archetypical ideas in the mind of God, creation as the imposition of ectypical *formae* on matter, evil understood as *privatio boni*, the connection of rationality with the image of God, and so on. Herman Bavinck is perhaps most explicit about the connection of rationality with this underlying ontology (see his booklet on *Christian Scholarship* [1904] and his discussion in *The Doctrine of God* [1951]). For him, scholarship was a matter of "thinking God's thoughts after him." Bavinck, more than the other neo-Calvinists, was influenced by the revival of Thomism that was taking place in Catholic circles in response to the encyclical *Aeterni Petris* (1879). Woltjer, too, in his booklet *The Science of the Logos* (1891), is very explicit in his attachment to the traditional metaphysics. Perhaps most telling in this regard is a philosophical dissertation, supervised by Bavinck, which was defended at the Free University in 1917 by H.W. Smit. Entitled *The Philosophy of Nature and Theism*, it simply equated Calvinistic philosophy with a Christianized synthesis of Plato and Aristotle, meaning by this essentially a version of Augustinian neo-Platonism. There continued to be the privileged link between rationality and both reality (true being) and divinity.

Cosmonomic philosophy in many respects constitutes a break with this privileged link, and therefore with the received paradigm. From the outset, Vollenhoven, Dooyeweerd and Stoker sought to reform philosophy in the light of the Scriptures, and they were keenly aware of the dangers of mingling biblical themes with those of pagan or humanistic philosophy (a mingling which they called "synthesis"). They sought to make the categorial distinctions of the biblical worldview *intrinsic* to their philosophical systematics, and not to accommodate them to inherited patterns. Although each started with the classical framework (what they later referred to as "Logos speculation"), they gradually moved away from it, under the pressure of the implications of their worldview. It will be instructive to look briefly at how these implications affected their understanding of rationality.

The God-creation distinction is, of course, one that is common to all Christian thought. But the radicality and primordiality of that distinction in neo-Calvinism, which seeks to capture the force of the Isaianic passages on the incomparability and transcendence of Yahweh, has some unexpected implications. If rationality is *creature*, and there is no creaturely principle of continuity between the Maker and the made, then rationality disqualifies as that principle. There is no rational order that encompasses Creator and creation—not because the Creator is irrational, but because rationality is creature. Accordingly, the reformational philosophers break with the ancient Christian tradition (beginning with Justin Martyr in the second century) which identifies the *Logos* of John 1 with the *logos* of Heraclitean and Stoic paganism. This point is expressed most clearly in some of the early writings of Vollenhoven. Here he systematically discriminates between *Logos* as the sovereign person of the Godhead, and *logos* as one of the dimensions (the reasoning one) of man's creaturehood.

Moreover, once this fateful connection between divinity and one kind of creatureliness is severed, the connection between rationality and "being," as the common denominator of all reality, also becomes problematic. If rationality is not intrinsically divine, how can it possibly reflect "being"—of which it is itself a part? Or how can "being" be the objective correlate of rationality unless the latter *is* something divine which transcends all creaturely being? Against all efforts to absolutize (that is, to deify, to idolize) rationality, the reformational philosophers asserted its *subordinate creaturehood*. Perhaps it is better to say "its *coordinate* creaturehood," since rationality was considered to be on a fundamentally equal footing with all other creaturely dimensions (e.g., morality, spatiality, physicality, aestheticity, etc.). The point was not to depreciate rationality (everything created by God is good), but to put it in its creaturely place.

The law-subject distinction, too, proved fruitful for the reformational appreciation of rationality. For instance, the law, as God's reliable creative command for all creatures, "took over" from rationality (and its correlate, being) the burden of accounting for the constancy, order and unity of created reality. In addition, this second categorial distinction allowed for an analysis of rationality which could honor both its commonality to all men (its law-determined structure is universal by virtue of creation) and its religious diversity (the *direction* of people's response to the law on the subject side is diverse). (We shall presently discuss the structure-direction distinction.) That is to say, the creational law as a transcendental *a priori constitutes* the possibility of rationality, and this is part of the creaturely makeup of all humans, whatever their religious persuasion or commitment.

At the same time, that creational law *prescribes* how human beings, as creatures subject to that law, must respond (they are to observe the law of non-contradiction and all its implications). Sometimes this imperative is not upheld on the subject side, and in many cases religious prejudices may lead to hidden fallacies or to an open flouting of any norm of rationality. Nevertheless, rationality is still structurally common to all men, even though it does not escape the effects of sin or the Fall outside the range of redemption.

Furthermore, the category of the law-subject correlation opens the way to an investigation of the "laws of thought" as specifications of a creational ordinance—one that is both *sui generis* (not reducible to psychic laws, for example, as in psychologism, or to biological ones, as in behaviorism) and linked to other kinds of creaturely lawfulness (e.g., that of numerical reality in mathematical logic, or that of faith in the logic of "God-talk"). Some of these implications, and others as well, are explored in such works as Vollenhoven's *The Necessity of a Christian Logic* (1932) and his *Fundamentals of Logic* (1948).

The categorial distinction between earth and heaven is of limited relevance to the subject of rationality. However, in reformational philosophy this distinction does remind us that rationality as we know it is limited in its application to the earthly cosmos. Our knowledge of heaven must be based on the relatively sparse givens of the Scriptures, not on speculative reasoning that extrapolates from earthly reality. At the same time, human reasoning must not exclude the existence of angels (or demons).

The distinction between "undeveloped" and "developed," the fourth one listed above, also had implications for the cosmonomic philosophers. Part of the historical task of mankind is to exploit the creaturely possibilities of human reasoning. The development of non-Aristotelian logic within the last century is an example of this task. Vollenhoven's dissertation welcomed this evidence of the cultural development of possibilities inherent in man's rational capacity. The "opening up process" that plays such a key role in Dooyeweerd's thought is relevant also for his view of the logical or analytical function of man (his term for rationality). Theoretical thought itself is an example of the opening up of the analytical realm, and Dooyeweerd's system envisages hitherto unsuspected developments in logic. Thus cultural development helps to disclose currently latent anticipations in the analytical function.

The fifth and final categorial distinction, that between structure and direction, has already been mentioned in the law-subject distinction. Clearly this is one of the crucial elements for the reformational concept of rationality. Although the structure of rationality, guaranteed by the constant law-order of God, is a creational given in all rational subjects, direction is not. This is in fact the rationale for the whole enterprise of a scripturally directed philosophy and scholarship. Human rationality, in the sense of the actual process of reasoning (the human response to the creational law for rationality), is never religiously neutral. Vollenhoven, Dooyeweerd and Stoker never tire of emphasizing this point. Fallacies and error (understood as incorrect inferences from the available evidence or from justified premises) manifest the fallenness of human rationality; clearing up muddled thinking is one aspect of the restoration of creation, which is the goal of the Kingdom of God. Rationality gone awry manifests itself in many different ways, according to the Dutch reformational philosophers. One such example is the theoretical absolutization of a creature or creaturely aspect, such as rationality itself. Reductionism is another error: an attempt is made to subsume one kind of creational lawfulness under another. According to Dooyeweerd, this inevitably leads to antinomies and dialectical tensions—theoretical contradictions which by definition are unresolvable.

We conclude this brief survey of neo-Calvinism and rationality with some general observations on rationality in the Calvinian tradition. I think it is important to distinguish between worldview and philosophy when we evaluate differences among philosophers of Calvinistic persuasions. Dialogue needs to take place on both levels, but these levels should not be confused. Many apparently philosophical differences are in reality differences in worldview. The dispute between evidentialists and presuppositionalists in apologetics, for example, seems to reflect a difference on the worldview level. The same holds true for debates about the existence of God or other minds, or the objectivity of values or causality. Until the philosophical discussion reckons with the presence and influence, on both sides, of categorial assumptions which are not themselves of a philosophical kind, communication will be frustrated. To foster and promote communication—a genuine understanding of each other's point of view—the worldview issues must be put on the table.

Furthermore, Christians should recognize that worldview differences can be of many kinds. Christians and non-Christians clearly differ in this regard, but Christians and non-Christians also differ among *themselves*. The differences among Christians in understanding the biblical worldview, even among those who proceed from the assumption that the Scriptures are unitary on this point, are quite significant. Even adherence to the same doctrinal standards does not obviate such differences. (I may affirm in church that man is "totally depraved," but I never think to bring this belief into my philosophizing.) The twentieth century seems to be characterized by a realignment of Christians, not along traditional theological lines, but in accordance with different worldviews: Baptists and Methodists adopt a reformational worldview, Presbyterians and Anglicans take over an Anabaptist perspective, Mennonites and charismatics espouse a traditionally Lutheran two-realm theory, and so on. Among Christian philosophers these differences need discussing, because they play a role in what is said on the philosophical level.

This is not to downplay the importance of philosophical discussion in its own right. Here, too, however, it is useful to distinguish two types of issues: those involving faithfulness to (one's understanding of) the biblical worldview, and those of a more strictly analytical or empirical kind.

If the main points of this essay are granted, namely that philosophy always reflects some worldview and that Christian philosophy therefore ought to reflect the biblical worldview, then an important task of Christian philosophers, especially those who are agreed on their basic understanding of the scriptural world-and-life-view, is to focus on the philosophical implications of that shared commitment. Is it consonant with our biblical understanding that God is treated as *summum ens*, that God the Son is equated with the principle of rational order, that error is treated as sin, that constant standards are presumed to hold for music and architecture? Such discussion can be very fruitful if an agreement on the worldview level can be presupposed throughout.

The other kind of philosophical discussion is of the more traditional kind, where categories and conclusions are tested in the light of the available evidence and commonly accepted standards of analytical rigor. Here, too, worldview considerations play a role, but the given creation in which we all live and move guarantees the possibility of meaningful dialogue, despite fundamental differences in worldview. For the creation speaks with a persuasive voice through both the structure of our rationality, so that we are forced to give due weight to cogent argumentation, and through the evidence of other created things, which we may have overlooked, repressed or misconstrued. Even worldviews may be changed as a result, and our philosophical positions, too.

Bibliographical Note

There is little in English by and about the Dutch neo-Calvinists and their view of rationality. To date, the best resources are probably the following:

Dooyeweerd, Herman. *Roots of Western Culture: Pagan, Secular and Christian Options*. Toronto: Wedge Publishing Foundation, 1979. This is the most accessible of Dooyeweerd's own publications.

Kalsbeek, L. *Contours of a Christian Philosophy: An Introduction to Herman Dooyeweerd's Thought*, Bernard and Josina Zylstra, eds. Toronto: Wedge Publishing Foundation, 1975. This volume contains two useful additions: the "Introduction" by Bernard Zylstra, which sets Dooyeweerd in his historical setting, and the extensive "Bibliography" (pp. 307-345) which lists many English and some French and German publications by and about the Dutch neo-Calvinist thinkers.

Young, William. *Toward a Reformed Philosophy: The Development of a Protestant Philosophy in Dutch Calvinistic Thought Since the Time of Abraham Kuyper*. Grand Rapids, Mich.: Piet Hein Publishers, 1952.

Present Positions on Key Problems

Part One:

The Nature and Limits of Rationality

The Role of Reason in the Regulation of Belief

William B. Alston

i

THE USE OF REASON IS TO REASON. This near-tautology, like others of its kindred, has its value. In particular, it can serve to indicate the way I shall be using the term "reason" in this paper. I shall not be using it as a blanket term for our natural cognitive faculties. Rather I shall understand by "reason" our ratiocinative faculties, our capacity to apprehend logical connections, draw out implications, spot contradictions and incoherencies, engage in trains of reasoning; to arrive at explanations, systematize a body of diverse facts, weigh reasons, arrive at considered judgments, deliberate over alternative courses of action, explicate or clarify meanings, arrive at an interpretation, and so on. In this usage, reason is, in quasi-Kantian fashion, contrasted with intuition or receptivity. The notion of reason comprises our ways of being intellectually active.[1]

Reason, in this very broad sense, undoubtedly has many important functions in the Christian life and elsewhere. (1) There is the search for understanding, itself a many-faceted matter. It includes the attempt, with which philosophy is much concerned, to make explicit the contours of our basic concepts; it includes spelling out the implications of our beliefs and commitments. On another level it embraces all the ways in which we seek explanations. Why did Jim come home from work early? Why are corporate executives more prone to high blood pressure? Why does water boil at different temperatures at different elevations? (2) There is the drive to extend our knowledge, as contrasted with understanding better what we already know or believe. (3) There is the aim at systematization, at seeing connections, at ranging apparently disparate phenomena under a small set of common principles, of seeing a common pattern running through a large number of cases, of reconciling apparent incompatibilities. It is clear that reason in all these respects has much to do in the religious life. Thoughtful Christians have always been concerned with understanding better the Christian faith, with bringing out what it does and does not amount to, what it does and does not commit us to. They have often been concerned to deal with apparent inconsistencies between different Christian beliefs, or between one of those beliefs and something else that seems to be the case. Theologians are professionally committed to constructing an intellectually satisfying system of Christian doctrine. And, it would seem, all this has to be rethought for each age. Occupation is not lacking for reason in the Christian life.

To be sure, there is always the danger that, under the banner of some kind of "rationalism," the ends of rational understanding and rational systematicity will be given a higher priority than wisdom or prudence would dictate. In such instances, we forget Aristotle's admonition that "it is the mark of an educated man to look for precision in each class of things just so far as the nature of the subject admits."[2] Thus we may be led, in a burst of rationalist zeal, to ditch the Christian faith if we cannot understand it in the same way we understand common-sense beliefs or classical physics. And one may hold the Christian faith unacceptable if one cannot resolve all the apparent incoherencies it displays. But what is misguided in these attitudes is not the resolute attempt to reach the goals of reason, but rather the reaction to failure in this attempt. More specifically, what is misguided is the weight one gives that failure in an overall evaluation of Christian belief. It is still legitimate and important to seek understanding and systematization vis-à-vis the Christian faith, insofar as these are attainable.

This last consideration has brought us to another prominent use of reason—the monitoring of belief, the critical epistemic evaluation of belief; determining by critical reflection whether one is *justified* in believing that *p;* whether, as we say, it is *rational* to do so. From a broad perspective this is simply one aspect of the reflective, critical function of reason. Other forms include the moral criticism of character and of conduct, as well as the internal logical criticism of systems of belief, of which we were speaking above. This latter form merges into the function I am calling the "monitoring (regulating) of belief"; for one way to investigate the justification of a particular belief is to inquire into its relations with other things one believes.

The belief-monitoring function is the one on which I shall be concentrating here. It is a function that poses special problems for religious belief, and for Christian belief in particular; and, as I shall be arguing, it is especially liable to a pathological over-valuation of the goals of reason.

ii

Let's begin the uncovering of this over-valuation by noting a close connection between reason as the faculty of ratiocination (and reasoning as its exercise), and having reasons for believing something or for doing something. It is no linguistic accident that the word "reason" and its cognates are involved in both connections. One of the main aims of reasoning is to uncover, evaluate, weigh, and interrelate reasons for believing or for doing. One who reasons much is one who is much concerned with reason.

This being the case, it is understandable that one should come to think that one is rational in believing that *p* only if one has adequate reasons for believing that *p*. Let's trace a plausible line of thinking which yields that conclusion.

We begin with the idea, introduced above, that one of the chief functions of reason is to determine, for any belief one holds or is considering, whether one ought to hold it,[3] whether it is *rational* to do so, or, in the current terminology, whether one is (epistemically) *justified* or *warranted* in doing so. And what does one look into to determine whether one is rational or justified in believing that *p*? One seeks to determine whether one has reasons for believing that *p*, and whether those reasons are strong enough, are *adequate* grounds, for believing that *p*. Reason imposes certain standards on believing, certain tests that a belief must pass in order to be certified as rational. Thus it is rational for one to believe that *p* only if that belief passes the test, only if it is based on adequate reasons.

It would be wildly implausible for one to suppose that a belief is rational only if it has actually undergone rational scrutiny. Clearly no one has the time to subject all beliefs to such an investigation; it would be wholly unjustified to condemn someone as irrational for not having done so. The most that could be laid down as a general requirement is that the belief is capable of passing the test, that there *be* adequate reasons which would be uncovered if such an investigation were launched.[4]

Let's pause for a moment to spell out what it is for a subject, S, to have an adequate reason for believing that *p*. (Where there is a plurality of reasons we will think of them as combined in a single conjunctive reason. This will enable us to speak generally of having *an* adequate reason.)

First, where *q* is an adequate reason one has for believing that *p*, the proposition that *q* must be, as we might say, "appropriately" related to the proposition that *p*, related in such a way as to provide an adequate "ground" or "support" for the supposition that *p*. When we go on to ask just what relations are "appropriate," we run into both obscurity and controversy. At least it is clear that logical entailment is appropriate. If *q* and *p* are so related that it is logically impossible for *q* to be true and *p* false, then the fact that *q* is the best possible reason for believing that *p*. Presumably we will want to count certain kinds of inductive reasons as well. If, in a "scientific" sample of American citizens, 54% approve of the way the president is handling his job, then this provides an adequate reason for supposing that the percentage of American citizens who approve of the way the president is handling his job is not very far from 54%. Perhaps other sorts of relations count as well, but it is far from clear which ones do count, and we are far from being able to give a general formula that will pick out the right ones.

If *q* and *p* are "appropriately" related, then *q is* an adequate reason for believing that *p*, but this does not guarantee that I, or any other particular person, thereby *have* an adequate reason for believing that *p*. If the "appropriate" relationship between *q* and *p* is to put me in the position of *having* an adequate reason for believing that *p*, then I must *have q* in the relevant sense; i.e., I must know that *q* is the case, or at least be justified in believing that it is the case. There may *be* adequate reasons for supposing that more than one person was involved in the assassination of President Kennedy, but if I am not cognizant of those reasons, it will not thereby be rational for me to accept the multiple assassin theory.

Let's formulate a principle that embodies the present view as to what it takes to be rational in believing something.

> (I) S is rational in believing that *p* only if S has adequate reasons for believing that *p*.

This principle is often applied to religious belief.

> . . . everywhere and always belief has an ethical aspect. There is such a thing as a general ethics of the intellect. The main principle of that ethic I hold to be the same inside and outside religion. This principle is simple and sweeping: Equate your assent to the evidence.[5]

I want to suggest that principle (I) expresses an unwarranted "imperialism" of reason, or, as I put it earlier, an over-valuation of a certain function of reason. It takes one sufficient condition for the rationality or belief and inflates it into a necessary condition. No doubt, in many cases what makes a belief rational is that the believer has adequate reason for it, or that he holds it for adequate reason; but there are serious objections, to be canvassed in a moment, if we suppose this is the only way in which a belief can be rational.

Looking back at the line of argument leading to (I), I do not wish to deny that the critical scrutiny of belief is a legitimate and necessary function of reason, although it is easy to over-estimate the extent to which one should engage in it. However, I do deny, for reasons to be given shortly, that the only standard which such a rational scrutiny should employ is the one embodied in (I). If anyone thinks it is obvious that a belief can be rational only by being held for adequate *reasons*, he is being taken in by a verbal similarity.[6]

The basic difficulty with (I) has been repeatedly exposed in the epistemological literature, and here I can be brief. For S to have an adequate reason, q, for a belief that p, S must rationally believe that q. But then, by (I), this in turn requires that S rationally believe some other proposition, r, which constitutes an adequate reason for believing that q. It does not require preternatural insight to see that this drives us either into a circle or an infinite regress. Either the chain of reasons goes back infinitely, adding a new proposition at each step, or it doubles back on itself in such a way that some proposition is supported by that proposition itself. The latter alternative is unacceptable since it involves the unintelligible idea that my adequate reason for believing p could be p itself. The former is unacceptable because of the impossibility of an infinite hierarchy of reasons for a finite intellect.[7]

In order to escape both Scylla and Charybdis, while retaining (I), we are forced into a pure coherence theory. Such a theory seeks to hold onto the view that rationality require adequate reasons, while avoiding either an infinite regress or circularity, by taking the justification of any particular belief to be derived not from the relations of that belief to some other particular belief, but from its place in the total system of belief. In this view the locus of justification, as we might say, is shifted from the individual belief to the total system. There are certain "internal" desiderata for systems of belief, which may be ranged under the rubric of "coherence," and a particular belief is justified to the extent that it plays a role in a coherent total system.

Beginning with Hegel, this ideal of rationality has been elaborated by a succession of philosophers, and an adequate discussion of the program would be very long indeed.[8] For present purposes let the following suffice. A pure coherence theory evaluates systems of beliefs in terms of purely internal criteria—consistency, mutual entailment, the explanation of some items in terms of other items, etc. So long as it does not give some items a privileged position individually (as foundations or as inputs from the world or whatever), these are the only sorts of criteria it has to work with. But if so, there can be an indefinite number of systems that equally satisfy these criteria. This point has been often argued in the literature and I will not pursue it here.[9]

If I were to spell out the arguments outlined in the last paragraph, I am confident they would show we cannot reasonably maintain that a necessary condition for rational belief is that one hold the belief for adequate reasons. We simply cannot work out a satisfactory epistemology on such a basis. We must recognize that what justifies us in holding some of our beliefs is something else. In terms that I will be using from now on, we must recognize *immediate* justification of belief as well as *mediate* justification. Let me pause to explain these terms.

Mediate justification is what we have been calling justification by *reasons*. It is "mediate" because the justification comes through the mediation of other justified beliefs of the subject. Thus we may define mediate justification as follows:

> (II) S is mediately justified in believing that *p*—S is justified in believing that *p* by virtue of some relation this belief has to some other justified belief of S.

Here the relation will include both an "appropriate" relation between the propositions believed, and whatever else needs to be built into the situation to yield justification, e.g., that the belief that *p* be based on the other belief. Immediate justification can then figure as a wastebasket category; it will include any justification that does not derive from a relation of the belief in question to some other justified belief of S.

> (III) S is immediately justified in believing that *p*—S is justified in believing that *p* by virtue of something other than some relation this belief has to some other justified belief of S.

Prominent suggestions as to what can immediately justify a belief include the following:

1. Immediate awareness of what the belief is about (sense-data, mental images).
2. Self-evidence of the proposition believed.
3. In certain special cases, just the truth of the proposition believed (Chisholm).[10]
4. Beliefs about the physical environment may be justified by appropriate visual experiences.[11]

If we recognize immediate justification, we have a chance of escaping the trilemma of infinite regress, circularity, or pure coherence. For each chain of justification by reasons can be grounded in an immediately justified belief, one that does not, in turn, rest on another justified belief. This picture of the situation has been stressed by the epistemological theory known as foundationalism. However, it will not be germane to our purposes here to look into the further theses that have been held under that rubric, nor to investigate the varieties of foundationalism nor the difficulties generated by any of those positions.

However, there is one complication that we must make explicit in order that the subsequent discussion be as realistic as possible. In some cases where beliefs are alleged to be immediately justified, it is recognized that this justification is *defeasible;* it is subject to being overthrown by certain features of the way in which the belief was acquired and/or by the subject's knowledge that these features obtain.

Thus it is often maintained that a perceptual belief about the physical environment, e.g., my present belief that there is a typewriter in front of me (or, if you prefer, my present belief that I see a typewriter in front of me), is justified just by virtue of the fact that it seems to me, visually, that there is a typewriter in front of me. But if this is the source of justification, then that justification is only *prima facie*. For if a certain elaborate system of mirrors were involved in the production of that visual experience, or if I were to realize that this is the case,[12] then I would not be justified in believing there is a typewriter directly in front of me.

Thus an immediate justification may be only *prima facie;*[13] and what overthrows that *prima facie* justification in a particular case may be my reasons for supposing there is something suspicious about that particular perception. We might say, then, that perceptual beliefs are immediately justified, *in the absence of certain kinds of reasons to the contrary*. We find this idea expressed by Roderick Chisholm in an epistemic principle.

> (IV) For any subject S, if S believes, without ground for doubt, that he is perceiving something to be F, then it is beyond reasonable doubt for S that he perceives something to be F.[14]

For that matter, mediate justification can be *prima facie*, too. The fact that my wife told me this morning that she would be away until 4:00 is an adequate reason for me to suppose she will be away until 4:00, unless there is something else I know, or ought to know, which will nullify this evidence, e.g., that she has reason to mislead me about her whereabouts.

Another complication stems from the facts that justification is a matter of degree, and that a given belief may draw justification from more than one source. Thus a belief may be justified both by virtue of the fact that I seem to perceive it to be true *and* by reasons I have for supposing it to be true. My belief that there is a maple tree outside my window may be immediately justified by the fact that it seems to me visually that there is a maple tree outside my window, and it may also draw mediate justification from its relation to various other things I justifiably believe, e.g., that there was a maple tree outside my window yesterday. Thus a belief may receive both mediate and immediate justification. In some cases either alone would be sufficient to justify the belief to a degree sufficient for rational acceptability; in other cases both would be needed to bring it to that level.

Given these complexities we cannot rest content with the notion of a belief *being mediately justified*, or *being immediately justified, überhaupt* where this is understood as "justified to a level sufficient for rational acceptability." The more basic notion is that of a source of justification (to some degree), or of a "contribution" to the justification of a belief. Whether a belief is justified up to a certain level, and how, will depend on a summing up of all the justificatory "contributions" it receives. The simplest way to modify the initial definitions to take care of these points is to add the qualification "to some degree" to the term "justified" in those definitions.

> (V) S is mediately justified, to some degree, in believing that *p*—S is justified, to some degree, in believing that *p* by virtue of some relation this belief has to some other justified belief of S.
>
> (VI) S is immediately justified, to some degree, in believing that *p*—S is justified, to some degree, in believing that *p* by virtue of something other than some relation this belief has to some other justified belief of *p*.

It will be noted that I have left the last occurrence of "justified" in each definition unmodified. I do not want to get into the question of whether the belief that furnishes the reason in mediate justification must be justified up to a level sufficient for rational acceptability in order to serve as the basis for some degree of justification for another belief.

Even with the incorporation of all these complexities, I think the points mentioned earlier suffice to show how we must recognize that some beliefs are immediately justified, at least to some degree, and that this immediate contribution to justification is essential for their epistemic status. If there were time, I would go further and argue that in some cases beliefs are immediately justified to a degree sufficient for rational acceptability, apart from any contribution from reasons. I believe this to be true, for example, with respect to a person's beliefs about his own current conscious states. But apart from that, the objections to (I) mentioned above show that mediate justification cannot go it alone, and some intermixture of immediate justification is required to render the brew palatable. I can be *rational*, i.e., epistemically justified, in believing that *p* without having adequate *reasons* for that belief. This possibility is realized whenever I am sufficiently and immediately justified in believing that *p*.

iii

This suffices to show that the most simple-minded version of rationalistic imperialism, embodied in (I), will not hold up. But imperialism is not so easily stamped out. After the dissolution of the empire, it survives in more subtle forms of economic exploitation. In the present case this post-imperialism may take the following form.

Let's grant that, in a sense, one may be justified in believing that one is angry without having any reasons, much less adequate reasons, for this, and may even *know* this in the absence of reasons. Nevertheless, there is a higher form of justification that does require reasons. Suppose that S is, in fact, justified in believing that *p* by virtue of that belief being based on an experience, E. There are still many questions to examine. Why *should* we suppose that being based on E is sufficient for the justification of that belief? How do we tell what beliefs are immediately justified under what conditions? How do we choose between competing suggestions as to what it takes for immediate justification? Or, most centrally, what epistemic principles of immediate justification should we accept, and on what basis?

These questions will arise for anyone who is sufficiently reflective about the matter, including S himself. I am not saying that S cannot, in any important sense, *be* justified in believing that *p* without being able to give a satisfactory answer to these second-level questions. That would be to commit a level confusion.[15] What I am saying is that one has not fully satisfied the requirements of what we might call "reflective rationality" so long as he is not justified in supposing that the basis on which he accepts the belief that *p is* sufficient to justify this belief. And that means he is not being rational in the fullest sense until he is justified in accepting the epistemic principle which underlies that sufficiency, e.g., a principle of the form: a belief of sort B that is formed on the basis of an experience of type E is thereby justified. So long as he simply accepts beliefs on bases that do *in fact* justify them, he is, of course, justifiably believing what he believes. We could not in the same breath admit that those bases *in fact* justify the beliefs and also deny that he is justified in those beliefs. And let's agree there is a sense in which he is thereby *rational* in so believing.

Nevertheless, in order to satisfy fully the demands of rationality, S must raise questions of the sort cited above, questions concerning the credentials of the basis on which the belief was formed. After all, the unexamined belief is not worth forming. And once he raises those questions, he cannot properly rest content until he has satisfactorily answered them. He cannot consider himself justified, in a higher sense, in forming beliefs on this basis until he has satisfied himself that the appropriate epistemic principle is justified. Thus a person is not *reflectively* justified in believing that *p* until he is justified in supposing that this belief satisfies the requirements of some valid principle of justification.

And what does it take to be justified in supposing that a given epistemic principle is valid? Immediate justification does not seem to be a real possibility here. Such principles do not seem to be self-evident on reflection. Consider, for example, the divergent views as to what it takes to immediately justify a belief about one's own feelings. These include (a) immediate awareness of the feelings, (b) the mere fact that one has the feelings, (c) the mere fact that one believes one has the feelings.[16] These suggestions are in competition with each other. To hold, for example, that (c) is sufficient is to deny that (a) is required. And how do we choose between them? It can hardly be seriously suggested that it is self-evident for one to be correct and the others mistaken. Clearly, the only rational procedure is to subject any such principle to rational scrutiny and accept only those for which adequate reasons can be found. One can *show* that a given epistemic principle is correct only by exhibiting adequate reasons for accepting it; and one is justified in accepting it only if one has such reasons that could be exhibited in order to satisfy oneself or others that the principle is valid.

Thus, once we spell out what is required for *reflective rationality (reflective justification)* we see that reasons must play a crucial role. Now, I might be unreflectively justified in a belief without having reasons. But as soon as I respond to the rational imperative to examine the credentials of putative justifiers, I find I cannot fully satisfy the demands of rationality without having adequate reasons—if not for the belief with which I started, then at least for the principle that the basis of that belief is sufficient to (unreflectively) justify it. For an ideally rational and reflective subject, justifications will always involve reasons.[17]

This is an impressive counterattack on the part of the rationalist. Having been dislodged from his position on the lowest level, he executes an "epistemic ascent," thereby seeking to enforce the necessity for reasons on a higher level. What are we to say of this move?

a.

One may be tempted to use the original regress argument (mentioned earlier) to show that some epistemic principles must be immediately justified if any are to be mediately justified, but this temptation should be resisted. The regress argument does show that in order for epistemic principles (or anything else) to be mediately justified *some* beliefs must be immediately justified. But no consideration as formal as the regress argument can show that the class of immediately justified beliefs must contain beliefs in epistemic principles, or beliefs of any other particular kind. So far as the regress argument goes, the immediately justified beliefs on which the mediate justification of epistemic principles ultimately rests might all be first-level non-epistemic beliefs. In that case, the claim that epistemic principles are susceptible only to mediate justification would be left standing.[18]

But this is a Pyrrhic victory for the rationalist. For the regress argument does show that mediate justification of epistemic principles ultimately rests, like all mediate justification, on the immediate justification of some beliefs or other. So it may be the case that a fully reflective subject would not rest content with an (initial) immediate justification but would seek, and if successful find, a mediate justification for the epistemic principle that underlies that immediate justification. But this will only show that immediate justification presupposes mediate justification, for the fully reflective, at the next step. The consideration just adduced shows that, in the end, the higher level mediate justification itself rests on immediate justification.

So the entire edifice ultimately rests on immediate justification, whatever higher level way-station is inserted to satisfy one's cravings for reflective rationality. Nor will it be of any avail to require *reflective* justification for the immediately justified beliefs on which the mediate justification of the epistemic principle in question is based. For that just gives us a rerun of the whole cycle. When that second cycle has been run through we will be left again with *unreflectively* immediately justified beliefs at the foundation of the entire edifice.

Thus we see that unreflective justification is presupposed by any reflective justification. I can indulge my penchant for being fully reflective only within existing structures which are constituted by the mere *existence* of justifications that simply obtain, without my having reflectively determined this. It is only against such a background that I can gain a limited success in reflectively examining (and perhaps validating) explicit epistemic claims. To summarize simply: unless I am already, as a matter of fact, justified in some beliefs, I will never arrive at the point of being reflectively justified in any beliefs.

b.

This result is in itself a sharp blow to the rationalist's imperialist pretensions. It implies that not everything can be reflectively rationalized; that an ineluctable limit is set on the attempt to subject everything to an evaluation in terms of reasons. But the worst is yet to come. However, at this point we must fill in some additional background and make some important distinctions.

First, what sorts of considerations are relevant to deciding whether to accept a certain principle of justification? To properly go into this we would have to determine how such principles are to be interpreted, whether they are to be taken to be irreducibly evaluative, and so on. For present purposes, let's accept that, whatever else may be involved, a principle that specifies *being based on E* as sufficient for the justification of beliefs of type B, can be supported by showing that beliefs of type B based on E are generally true; conversely this principle can be attacked by showing that this is not the case. Since *epistemic* justification is, as we might say, necessarily truth-conducive, the truth-conduciveness of a supposed justifier is a crucial reason for accepting the claims of that justifier. In other words, the *reliability* of a mode of belief formation is a crucial consideration in determining whether beliefs formed in that way are thereby justified.

Second, we must distinguish between a "theoretical" and a "practical" acceptance of principles. I may be said to accept a principle "in practice" if I regularly act in accordance with it, resist deviations, perceive deviations in myself and others as out of order, perceive compliance as in order, and so on. I accept a principle "theoretically" if I am sometimes explicitly aware of it, assent to it on those occasions, am disposed to affirm it if occasion arises, and so on. Of course, one may accept a principle in both ways.

Here, let's consider an epistemic principle that lays it down that *being based on E renders beliefs of type B justified.* To accept that principle *practically* is to be disposed to form beliefs of type B on the basis of E, to see this procedure as all right, and so on. Let's use the term "epistemic practice" for the complex of behavior that evinces, or constitutes, the practical acceptance of an epistemic principle. Thus we could distinguish a separate epistemic practice for each distinguishable epistemic principle, although it will be more convenient to think of larger units of practice, each of which involves the practical acceptance of a system of related principles. Thus we will speak, for example, of "perceptual practice": the practice of forming beliefs about the physical environment on the basis of sense experience. By contrast, it is a theoretical acceptance that, according to the rationalist, is required for reflective rationality. The fully reflective person is not content to simply engage in the epistemic practices he finds himself involved in, practices that reflect principles which might or might not be correct, so far as he can see. If he is to be fully rational he will disengage those principles, formulate them, subject them to critical scrutiny, consider whether they should be replaced by others, and so on.

Now the justification of principles about which we have been speaking is the justification of a theoretical acceptance. It is this kind of acceptance that requires adequate reasons for its justification. If a person is going to explicitly affirm a non-self-evident principle, he should have reasons to back up that affirmation. The justification of practical acceptance of epistemic principles is another matter. Here we are much closer to the justification of beliefs that fall under the principle. If my current sense experience (plus, perhaps, some background knowledge) justifies me in supposing that there is a typewriter in front of me, then I am *ipso facto* justified in practically accepting some general principle that takes experience of a certain kind (plus, perhaps, a correlated kind of background knowledge) as sufficient for the justification of a correlated kind of belief. This principle is satisfied by the particular perceptual belief in question. For if I were not justified in forming beliefs in accordance with some such principle, then I would not be justified in this belief formation. Because of these differences we may speak of theoretical and practical justifications of P, taking these as short for *justification of theoretical acceptance of P* and *justification of practical acceptance of P*.

Now both principles and practices can be either theoretically or practically accepted and justified. We have been laboring this point with respect to principles, and it is easy to extend the point to practices. If I simply unself-consciously form beliefs according to a certain pattern, I "accept" the practice practically, i.e., I engage in it. And if

I am justified in doing so, the practice is *practically* justified. But if I reflect on this practice, formulate its underlying principles and affirm them, I accept the practice theoretically. And the question then arises whether I am justified in doing so. Despite this double duality, it is natural to think of practical justification in connection with practices, and theoretical justification in connection with principles. In the sequel I shall, for the most part, restrict myself accordingly.

c.

I can make use of these distinctions to explain the worse fate I said was still in store for the rationalist. I have already shown that the mediate justification of an epistemic principle, and so the reflective justification of a given belief, ultimately rests on the unreflective justification of other beliefs. Now I shall show that it also rests on the unreflective acceptance of some epistemic principle, the same or other. Actually, we can see that the mediate justification of an epistemic principle requires a prior unreflective justification of epistemic practices in two directions, so to speak: above and below. Let's begin with the former.

We attain a reflective justification of a belief, B, by becoming theoretically justified in accepting the principle, P, which underlies the unreflective justification of B. But now we must ask about the kind of theoretical justification required of P in order that B count as reflectively justified. Must P be reflectively justified, or is unreflective justification sufficient? In order to avoid the threatened priority of unreflective justification, the rationalist may opt for the stronger requirement. But that only postpones the evil day. For the reflective justification of P requires a justification of the principle, Q, underlying its unreflective justification. If Q = P, the project breaks down because of circularity. To avoid that, let's take it that Q is different from P. But then we are confronted with the same alternative of requiring a reflective or an unreflective justification of Q. Again we will be led by the same considerations to opt for the former. But then again, unless we are to fall into circularity, the reflective justification of Q depends on the justification of still another epistemic principle, O, about which the same problem arises.

It is easy to see that, unless at some point we fall into circularity by appealing to a principle that has already filled an earlier niche, an infinite regress is generated. This problem is unavoidable so long as we continue to require a reflective justification for the epistemic principle that appears at each stage. Thus, on pain of circularity or infinite regress, we must at some point rest content with an unreflective justification for the principle that underlies the justification of some other epistemic principle. No matter how far we push the demand for reflective justification, we will still be relying on the unreflective justification of some epistemic principle. We may fly as high as we like, but only on condition that there is till a sky above us. Reflective justification of beliefs or principles rests on unreflective justification of principles, as well as of beliefs.

d.

Now for the final nail in the coffin: the necessity for unreflectively justified acceptance of principles "below" as well as "above." Let's go back to the point that the mediate justification of an epistemic principle, P, will ultimately rest on some unreflectively immediately justified beliefs. Let's focus on one of these beliefs, B. Since B is only unreflectively justified there will be no epistemic principles figuring in its justification. Nevertheless, as we have seen, B will be justified, for a subject, S, only if S is justified in engaging in a certain epistemic practice of which the formation of B is an instance. S is justified in accepting B only if he is practically justified in practice C, only if he is justified in a practical reliance on C. Imbedded in C will be one or more epistemic principles; for simplicity let's say there is just one, Q. That is, to engage in C is to *practically* accept Q, and S is justified in accepting B only if he is practically justified in accepting Q.

At this point, let's consider the situation both on the supposition that Q is identical to P and on the supposition that it is not, beginning with the former. In this case we have a kind of circularity that requires careful delineation. It is not a straight logical circularity. Since B is only unreflectively justified, P does not appear among its justifiers. Nevertheless there is something radically unsatisfactory about the situation. S has acquired adequate reasons for (theoretically) accepting P only by relying on its validity, only by proceeding as if it were valid. It is only by accepting P in practice that S has come into possession of reasons that tend to show it is valid. And so S is theoretically justified in accepting P to be valid only if he already is practically justified in accepting it.

The kind of circularity involved comes out even more clearly if we think of the matter in terms of practices instead of principles. S has acquired adequate reasons for (explicitly, theoretically) regarding the practice, C, as justified only by using that very same practice to amass those reasons. He has relied on the justifiability of the practice in order to determine whether the practice is justified. His argument for the justifiability of C is cogent only if he was already justified in engaging in the practice. This is as if I set out to test the reliability of an instrument, using other readings from that instrument to check on the accuracy of my initial readings.

We can characterize this kind of circularity generally by saying it consists in the fact that the reasons S has for a conclusion, Y, are such that S would not be justified in accepting them without, at least in practice, assuming the truth of Y. And hence, since the relation of reasons to conclusion does not suffice to justify the conclusion unless S is justified in accepting the reasons, S is justified in believing Y only if he is antecedently justified (at least practically) in believing Y. Let's call this "epistemic circularity," since it has to do with the way in which the *justification* of the conclusion depends on that same conclusion already being justified.[19]

Thus the examination of the first horn of the dilemma, where Q = P, shows that (1) the theoretical justification of P is infected with a kind of circularity, and (2) in any event the *theoretical* justification of an epistemic principle presupposes the *practical* justification of an epistemic principle. And practical justification is all unreflective. Indeed, it is even less reflective than the most unreflective theoretical justification, for here the proposition believed is not even formulated, much less critically examined for its credentials. Hence (2) implies, once more, that reflective justification (involving a mediate justification of an underlying epistemic principle) rests on unreflective justification—in this case the practical justification of an underlying epistemic principle.

Now for the other horn of the dilemma. Suppose that Q is not the same as P. In that case we have a choice as to whether to require theoretical or only practical justification for Q in order that we be entitled to take B as a reason for P. (We did not have this choice where P = Q; to require theoretical justification for P in order that we may attain a theoretical justification of P would be *too* blatantly circular.) Now since the rationalist is seeking to avoid reliance on unreflective justification, his tendency would be to opt for the stronger requirement. However, before pursuing that tack let's note that if he does rest content with practical justification for Q, he is, once more, resting his theoretical justification for an epistemic principle on a practical (and so unreflective) justification for an epistemic principle. In this alternative he is not necessarily involved in epistemic, or other, circularity, but he is subject to the reproach of being willing to settle for mere practical justification for *some* epistemic principles but not for *others*. If practical justification is good enough for Q, we might ask him, why demand theoretical justification for P? But my main interest at the moment is in examining the other element of this second horn, in which a theoretical justification is required for Q.

Here we once again encounter the alternative pitfalls of circularity and infinite regress. Let's remind ourselves of the context in which the present problem is set. We are exploring what is necessary in order that a belief, B, be reflectively justified. This requires that a certain epistemic principle, P be mediately justified. This, in turn, requires that a certain reason, R, be at least unreflectively (theoritically) justified. But then what about the epistemic principle, Q, which underlies the unreflective justification of R? We are now requiring that Q be theoretically justified, and this obviously launches us on a rerun of the mediate justification of P. Q must be based on some reason, T, that is unreflectively justified, by virtue of the practical acceptance of some epistemic principle, X, which is either identical to P or Q, or not. If it is identical, we fall back into (1) epistemic circularity and (2) ultimate reliance on practical justification. If it is different, then we face still another version of the same scenario, generating the demand for theoretical justification for still another epistemic principle.

It is clear that unless at some point the underlying principle is one that has already occurred in the series, thereby introducing epistemic circularity, we are faced with an infinite regress. So the impact of this second horn of the dilemma (Q not identical with P) is as follows. (A) If we rest content with practical justification for Q, we allow that theoretical justification rests on practical justification *and* we choose an arbitrary stopping place for the quest for theoretical justification. (B) If we require theoretical justification for Q, then we are faced with either epistemic circularity and the dependence of theoretical justification on practical justification, or an infinite regress.

e.

I take it that a pattern has emerged from the rather complex argument of sections (c) and (d). The following summary statement may help to throw our results into greater relief. Where Q is the epistemic principle that is practically accepted in accepting R as a reason for the epistemic principle, P, we have the following alternatives.

I. Q = P.
1. The justification of P is epistemically circular.
2. The theoretical justification of P rests on the practical justification of an epistemic principle (in this case P itself).

II. $Q \not\to P$.

A. Only practical justification is required for Q.

1. The quest for theoretical justification for epistemic principles is arbitrarily halted at Q.
2. The theoretical justification of P rests on the practical justification of an epistemic principle (Q).

B. Theoretical justification is required for Q. In that case if an infinite regress is to be avoided either:

1. the mediate justification of P is epistemically circular, or
2. the theoretical justification of P rests on the practical justification of some epistemic principle, at which the quest for theoretical justification is arbitrarily halted.

Thus all the possibilities involve the dependence of the theoretical justification of P on the practical justification of some epistemic principle. This continues the theme of the other two sections—that reflective justification is possible only against the background of a presupposed unreflective justification. Here that note is struck even more strongly, for the presupposed justification revealed in this section is not only unreflective, but practical rather than theoretical. This is a justification which proceeds as if something is the case, rather than a justification which explicitly believes or affirms it.

Furthermore, all the possibilities except (IIA) and (IIB2) reveal an epistemic circularity in the theoretical justification of P. If we rule out an arbitrary stopping point for the theoretical justification of epistemic principles, we can ignore those alternatives. Thus we can conclude that any attempt to provide a theoretical justification for an epistemic principle is going to rest on a justification for some epistemic principle (either the one from which we start or another) that is epistemically circular. For this latter justification depends on reasons that one is justified in believing only by virtue of practically accepting the principle in question. But whatever we say about the circularity issue, the most basic and unquestionable result is that the theoretical justification of any epistemic principle rests on the practical justification of some epistemic principle.

Let me sum up this whole critique of second-level rationalism. The basic thrust of that position is the ideal of fully reflective and critical rationality, which it holds up as the ideal for human cognition. This ideal is realized only to the extent that, for any proposition one accepts, one is not only justified in accepting *it*, but also justified in accepting the epistemic principle, P, which underlies that first justification. It is by way of this second requirement that, it is claimed, a dependence on reasons is involved in every *reflective* justification.

Our scrutiny has revealed three inescapable limitations on the realization of this idea. First, the reasons that constitute the foundation of the mediate justification of P can only be unreflectively justified, on pain of infinite regress. Second, there is an "upper limit" on the reflective justification of epistemic principles. If P is itself reflectively justified, then the subject, S, is justified in accepting another epistemic principle, O, the one that underlies the justification of P. And if O is reflectively justified, S is justified in accepting a still further epistemic principle. Unless we are to suffer either circularity or an infinite regress, there must be, somewhere up the hierarchy, a principle that is only unreflectively justified for S. Third, and finally, there is likewise a "lower limit" on the reflective justification of epistemic principles. Consider the epistemic principle presupposed by the justification of one of the reasons for P. If we require that it be reflectively, or even unreflectively theoretically, justified, we set up a series that engenders either circularity or an infinite regress, unless at some point we are willing to settle for practical justification for some epistemic principle.

These three points reveal three respects in which it is impossible to satisfy the demand that everything one believes be reflectively justified. They point to three loci in one's doxastic system in which reflective justification is unattainable. Furthermore, they not only show that we cannot have unreflective justification everywhere; there is more of a connection than that displayed between the reflective and the unreflective. The point is that we attain reflective justification for one belief at the price of unreflective justification for several beliefs involved in that justification or extensions thereof. Reflective justification is possible only against the background of prior unreflective justification. If I were not at this moment merely unreflectively justified in accepting several propositions, I could not be, at this moment, reflectively justified in accepting any propositions. Reflective justification is a light shining in the darkness, but the light is made possible by sources of energy from the circumambient darkness out of which the light emerges.

I take it that all this reveals serious limitations on the rationalist ideal of the reflective justification of everything by reasons. And it effectively shoots down the pretensions of second-level rationalist imperialism: the idea that once we move to the requirement of reflective justification, we see that, after all, every justification rests on reasons.

iv

Now I should like to draw out a bit further the implications of these points for the justification of epistemic practices. Imbued with the spirit of rational reflection, I come to realize that any given epistemic practice may not constitute a reliable source of truth. Perhaps I am swayed by some of the traditional skeptical arguments. Or perhaps, in more up-to-date fashion, I have been impressed by the cultural or historical diversity of epistemic standards. And I may wonder whether there is any reason why I should prefer my customary practices to those of other times or places. I embark on the project of subjecting all my epistemic practices, along with alternatives, to a rational scrutiny in order to determine which of them are reliable avenues to the truth.

In the above terms, I am trying to convert practical into theoretical justification, for all those practices that are, or would be, practically justified for me; and I am trying to do this across the board. If I am fortunate, I eventually become aware of some or all of the above lines of argument, and I realize that such an unrestricted rationalization cannot be carried through. Indeed, I do not need anything as elaborate as the formulation above to realize that my project has been misconceived. For whatever practice I begin with first, I must have some basis on which its scrutiny is carried out.

Let's say I begin with perceptual practice. I want to determine whether there are adequate reasons for judging sense perception to be reliable. But I cannot carry out this inquiry unless I have, or can get, some possible reasons. In other words, unless I can ascertain some facts, I will not be able to consider, with respect to any facts, whether they provide adequate reasons for the reliability of sense perception. Unless I can be justified in accepting some propositions, I will have no basis for judging sense perception to be either reliable or unreliable.

Therefore, I must rely on some epistemic practice to generate the results I use to evaluate sense-perception. I am practically accepting, practically assuming to be reliable, *some* epistemic practice in order to test the one under examination. If that is the same practice as the one being scrutinized, the procedure suffers from epistemic circularity. If it is a different one, then, by the terms of my project, I cannot accept it without finding adequate reasons for its reliability. But then in this quest, we launch an investigation which, unless it lapses into circularity at some point, will continue endlessly. Thus the original project is fundamentally misconceived. I can investigate the credentials of one epistemic practice only by using one or more practices to do so. I cannot hold all practices suspect while looking into the question of which ones to trust, or while looking into any other questions, for that matter.

It might be suggested that this result holds only for an attempt to evaluate practices in terms of reliability, in terms of theoretical reasons for trusting them, and that we can at least find practical or "pragmatic" reasons for engaging in some practices, without having to use some practice to do so. But this illusion is quickly dispelled. Suppose I decide that I am "pragmatically" justified in engaging sense-perception, because I, and others, have an irresistible inclination to do so, and because by accepting its deliverances I am enabled to cope fairly well with the environment. Well and good. But how do I know this is the case? How do I know that human beings have an irresistible inclination to accept, by and large, the deliverances of sense-perception? How do I know that I cope with the environment fairly well? How do I know that I have an environment, much less one of the sort I suppose myself to have? In supposing that I know these things, so as to use them as practical reasons for trusting sense-perception, I am relying on one or more epistemic practices to provide me with this knowledge. And in this case I am surely relying on sense-perception itself. I would not be in a position to know, or justifiably believe, that I am coping with the environment well, unless I could rely on my observations of the environment.

How, then, is a reflective person to proceed after having realized that the credentials of any particular epistemic practice can be questioned, and that reason seems to enjoin us to settle the question in terms of reasons? Well, the preceding considerations have shown us that this is one of those cases in which the voice of reason, conscience, or whatever, is enjoining us to embark on a fundamentally unfeasible project. Or perhaps it is rather that we were not listening closely enough; we heard the outlines of the message but we missed the saving qualifications. We can, without certainty of failure, look for the credentials of a given epistemic practice. We may or may not be able to definitively settle the question, but failure is not guaranteed in advance. But this is possible only because we are relying on other practices in carrying out the investigation. What we can *not* undertake, with any chance of success, is to hold all practices suspect until their credentials have been established. This would be to refuse to move our limbs until we had tried them out to determine whether they work properly.

How then shall we decide which practices to accept without reasons, so as to be able to put others to the test? If this is a disguised request for reasons, it is an incoherent request. It, too, falls victim to the above arguments. But as a piece of advice, I suppose one cannot do better in this situation than to accede with good grace to the practical acceptance of the practices we find ourselves using. It is hard to find a better starting place than where we are at the moment. What real alternative have we? The above arguments amply show that unless we practically accept some practice(s) at the outset, we cannot make a move in the reflective search for reasons, or in any other cognitive activity. What real alternative is there to humbly accepting the promptings of our nature and relying on the practices we find ourselves carrying out when we arrive at the age of reflection? That is not to deny that modifications can be made in one or more of these practices in order to purify the total doxastic system of inconsistencies and incoherences. But, once again, we will never get to the point at which such purifications are called for unless we begin by practical reliance on the epistemic practices we find most firmly entrenched.

Rationalistic imperialism represents an illegitimate inflation of the rightful function of human reason. The function of reasoning, in the establishment and governance of belief, is to extend, regulate, purify, and systematize the information provided us by our more basic cognitive faculties. Rationalistic imperialism seeks to bring even these faculties themselves before the bar of reason, all at once, and to accept only what passes that test. It is not unduly fanciful to see in this demand an analogue, and more than an analogue, of the basic human sin of seeking absolute control, seeking to install man in the place of God and to sit in judgment over all things. By contrast, in the orientation that emerges from the considerations of this paper, one recognizes human limitations in the cognitive sphere as elsewhere. One recognizes that rational reflection can make a contribution only if it is provided material from outside itself on which to reflect. If we are not, by divine providence or whatever, given reliable data prior to showing that any data are reliable, rational reflection will be in vain.[20]

v

The very general considerations adduced in sections iii and iv only show that we cannot provide adequate reasons for all our epistemic practices at once. They leave open the possibility that we can find adequate reasons for the reliability of a given practice by relying on other practices to do so. Nevertheless, I believe the possibilities along these lines are more restricted than might appear at first glance.

In thinking about this issue there is an important distinction to be drawn between what we might call basic and non-basic practices. A basic practice constitutes our basic access to a given subject-matter —other modes of access either being special forms of it or based on it. Thus sense perception is our basic access to the physical world. We can imagine independent modes of access, but any other way of finding out about the physical world (e.g., the use of instruments or scientific theorizing) is based on sense perception both for its validation and for its practice. Similarly, memory is our basic access to the past.

Now the rational scrutiny of non-basic practices poses no problem; it is done all the time when new instruments are checked for reliability. For non-basic practices we can use the results of the more basic practice on which they rest to determine whether the results they give are generally correct. But for basic practices it is a different story. Attempts to find non-circular reasons for their reliability have been persistently frustrated.

To illustrate this point I shall look for a moment at attempts to justify what I have called "perceptual practice," the practice of forming beliefs about the physical environment on the basis of sense experience in the way we commonly do. I shall be emphasizing the claim that attempts that do not suffer from other defects are epistemically circular; they rely on perceptual practice to obtain the reasons they adduce to support that practice. I shall take it that this is a fatal defect in an attempted justification. If we are allowed to use the results of a practice in order to check its reliability we will have an easy time of it. It is not surprising that the beliefs we get from sense perception should agree with themselves.

To be sure, published attempts to deal with this issue do not fall into so blatant a circularity as that. They do not argue that the beliefs we form from perceptual practice are correct, as we can see from observation. Nevertheless, if the facts they suggest as supporting perceptual practice are such that we have no adequate reason, apart from reliance on perceptual practice, for supposing they obtain, they are guilty of (at least practically) assuming the reliability of perceptual practice in order to argue for its reliability. And so they have nothing to say to anyone who does not already accept that practice.

vi

There is a vast literature that bears on the epistemic status of sense perception. Although it is comparatively rare for a philosopher to pose the problem in the terms we have used (the rationality of engaging in "perceptual practice"), innumerable discussions have a direct bearing on this issue: attempts to prove the existence of the "external world," attacks on skepticism concerning the senses, attempts to show that solipsism is incoherent, attempts to show that the hypothesis of the physical world provides the best explanation of our sense experience, and so on. A proper critical survey of all this would require many volumes. Here, except for a brief historical introduction, I shall confine myself to an examination of two recent attempts to tackle this problem.

As far as our present historical consciousness is concerned, Descartes launched the modern preoccupation with this problem in Meditation VI, where he argued that God would, *per impossible*, be a deceiver if our strong inclinations to trust our sense perception were basically unreliable. Descartes' argument at least has the virtue of non-circularity; he does not rely on sense perception to argue either that God exists and is no deceiver or that we have a strong inclination to trust our sense perception. As the difficulties in his argument have been catalogued repeatedly, I shall pass on. Epistemic circularity is richly illustrated in Locke's arguments for the thesis that our senses give us knowledge of the existence of other things. For example, Locke points out:

> 'Tis plain, those Perceptions are produced in us by exteriour Causes affecting our Senses: *Because those that want the Organs of any Sense, never can have the Ideas belonging to that Sense* produced in their Minds. . . . The Organs themselves, 'tis plain, do not produced them: for then the Eyes of a Man in the dark, would produce Colours, and his Nose smell Roses in the Winter: but we see no body gets the relish of a Pineapple, till he goes to the *Indies*, where it is, and tastes it (*Essay Concerning Human Understanding* IV: 11; 4).

How does Locke know that the possession of a certain sense organ is a necessary condition for having sensory ideas of a certain kind? Clearly, he has learned this by using and trusting his sense perception, and reasoning on such a basis. The premises of the argument were obtained by the use of the practice which the argument is designed to justify.

Epistemic circularity is even more prominent in "pragmatic" arguments for the acceptability of perceptual practice, arguments that flourish more in popular thought on the subject than in the writings of the greatest minds that have addressed themselves to the subject. I am thinking of such considerations as that the practice works, it "pans out." For example, by accepting the deliverances of sense perception and reasoning on that basis, we are able to discover regularities in the behavior of things, which in turn enables us to make accurate predictions and to exercise some control over the environment. Furthermore, people generally agree on what they are perceiving, and this enables us to reach interpersonal agreement concerning the physical environment. And so on.

Once again the epistemic circularity is revealed when we ask how we know that accepting sense perception enables us to make accurate predictions and how we know that people generally agree on what they are perceiving. A moment's reflection will reveal that we come to know this by our observations and reasoning therefrom. We know, or are justified in believing, that Jones' prediction that the apple would fall to the ground was verified, because we saw the apple fall, or because someone else did, or because someone made a reading on an instrument that recorded the fall. How do we know that people generally agree on what they perceive, except by relying on our long experience of hearing what people say about what they are perceiving? We certainly do not learn about these things from an angel or from a crystal ball.

Beginning with Kant and extending through Wittgenstein and Strawson, there have been a number of arguments to the effect that the alternatives to reliance on perceptual practice are incoherent. This has usually taken the form of an attack on solipsism, the view that nothing exists except oneself and one's consciousness. This is relevant to our problem because an obvious alternative to my taking my sensory experiences to be revelatory of a public spatio-temporal world of physical objects is to suppose that these experiences are just modifications of my own consciousness, and that's all. The argument generally takes the form of an attempt to show that an ability to discern physical objects and other persons and to gain knowledge of them is really presupposed by one's ability to attribute experiences to oneself. Knowledge of one's own state of consciousness presupposes knowledge of things other than oneself. The attempt to describe a situation in which one has the former without the latter ends in conceptual incoherence.

I would like to enter into a discussion of one or more arguments of this type, but I will content myself with the following comment. Even if one or more of these arguments should succeed in showing solipsism to be conceptually incoherent, and I do not believe that any of them do succeed in this, the point would remain that only one alternative to our ordinary perceptual practice has been disposed of. There are other conceivable alternatives. How about an epistemic practice in which we interpret the data of sense experience along the lines of Leibnizian or Whiteheadian pan-psychism? How about

Berkelian or Hegelian idealism? And we can have no reasonable confidence in any claim that a certain list exhausts the possible ways of construing sense experience. How can it be rational to suppose that we have already completely surveyed the realm of possibilities open to the human intellect?

Finally, Bertrand Russell, A.O. Lovejoy and others have argued that by attending to certain features of our sense experience we can see that our experience is best explained by supposing it to be produced by external physical objects, via physiological processes in the nervous system. Usually the claim is that our experience exhibits certain kinds of order and regularity, which calls for such an explanation. Some thinkers, in sharp contrast, emphasize the fragmentariness and disorder of our experience as what requires explanation, or possibly supplementation, in those terms. Since these arguments have not been found convincing by many, I shall pass on to the first of the two recent lines of argument I will examine in more detail.

In his book *Reason and Scepticism*[21] Michael A. Slote has made a novel attempt to show that we are justified in supposing our experience to be explained in terms of the physical world, i.e., in terms of the action on us of physical objects, as conceived by enlightened common sense. Slote, unlike the thinkers mentioned in the last paragraph, does not make any claims about the structure, contents, or course of sense experience. He does not claim there are any specific features of our experience that require an explanation in terms of a physical world. Rather he sees his task as finding a way of deciding between three competing explanations that are empirically equipotent, each of which explains all the details of our experience, whatever they may be.

In addition to (1) the familiar physical world explanation, these are (2) the Cartesian idea that our experiences are produced directly by an all-powerful demon, and (3) the hypothesis that they are caused by nothing, but "just happen." His basic idea is that there is a principle of scientific methodology by reference to which (1) can be shown superior, viz., the Principle of Unlimited Inquiry.

> (VII) a. It is scientifically unreasonable for someone to *accept* what (he sees or has reason to believe) is for him at that time an inquiry-limiting explanation of a certain phenomenon, other things being equal;
> b. there is a reason for such a person to *reject* such an explanation in favor of an acceptable non-inquiry-limiting explanation of the phenomenon in question, if he can find one (p. 67).

"Inquiry-limiting explanation" is explained as follows:

> . . . an hypothesis is inquiry-limiting for *s* as an explanation of certain phenomena at time *t*, just in case if *s* at *t* accepts that hypothesis and holds it to be the best and completest explanation of those phenomena available at *t* (and believes in the existence of those phenomena), he ensures the impossibility of his coming to have rationally justified or warranted belief (consistent with his other beliefs) in more and more true explanations of various aspects of or facts about the phenomena in questions (for as long as he continues to accept that hypothesis as true and to believe it to be the best and completest explanation of the phenomena in questions that was available at *t*) (p. 66).

In other words, an exlanation is inquiry-limiting if its acceptance would foreclose the possibility of finding more explanation of facts concerning the subject-matter in question. Slote argues for the acceptability of (VII) as a principle of scientific inquiry on the grounds that science is essentially an attempt to explain as much as possible; and therefore any hypothesis that would imply that no further explanation is forthcoming will, by that fact, receive a black mark. Principle (VII) does not imply that no inquiry-limiting explanation could be accepted; the evidence for such a hypothesis might be so much stronger than its rival as to force its acceptance on us, despite this drawback. The principle only holds that the acceptance of such a hypothesis is unreasonable, *other things being equal*, i.e., if there is some alternative for which the evidence is equally strong that it is not inquiry-limiting.

Slote then argues that, of our three competing explanations, only (1) escapes the stigma of limiting inquiry. It is clear that (1) leaves us a clear field for seeking explanations of particular physical phenomena and of the ways in which particular kinds of experience are physically produced. And it is equally clear that (3) is maximally inquiry-limiting. If all that can be said of our experience is that it "just happens," we are indeed bereft of the possibility of explanation. The case with (2) is not so clear. Slote argues, rather persuasively, that, in hypothesis (2), the only way to seek explanations of why and how the demon produces our experiences as he does, would be to ask him or to receive his messages on the subject. But since, by hypothesis, the demon is engaged in such a massive and long-continued deception, we would have no reason to trust what he says. Therefore (2) blocks any possibility of being rationally justified in accepting any further explanations of the way things go. Hence only (1) is a rationally acceptable explanation of our experience.

If I accepted Slote's invocation of (VII) in this connection, I would have to look more closely at his reasons for holding that (2) falls afoul of the principle. But I feel that the weakness of his position lies precisely in supposing that we can have adequate reason for accepting (VII) prior to, or independently of, engaging in our usual epistemic practices and amassing the fruits thereof. I am quite prepared to acknowledge that (VII) is a sound principle of *scientific* inquiry. But it by no means follows that the principle has any binding force on me if I am trying to decide whether to accept the existence of an external physical world. I can recognize the force of the principle for scientific inquiry because of my understanding of what science is, its goals, *modi operandi*, and so on. But I grasp all that only because I am *au courant* with an "external world" of physical things and processes, distributed in space, enduring in time, and investigated by scientists that form a sort of community. So long as I have not yet decided whether my experience is revelatory of such a world, I do not know anything about all of that, or, for that matter, have any beliefs about it. So long as I am in that "original position" I have no basis for accepting any such principle.

Slote does have an answer to this objection.

> Up to now I have been talking about actual scientific practice and about what "we" experience and have reason to think, in order to point up the validity of the principles I have used to show the (epistemic) reasonableness of believing in an external world. But one does not need to assume that there is an external world or that there are other persons in order to see the validity of these principles . . . .
>
> . . . one can see their validity, I think, merely on the basis of the fact that one has had certain sense experiences of what seemed to be the activities of scientists in a real external world. Upon having such experiences one can see that certain principles of scientific inquiry make good sense and others do not, and if one then comes to wonder whether the external world and the on-going enterprise of science really exist, or even to believe that they do not, that will presumably not cause one to doubt that, *if* there is (were) a physical world with scientific activities going on within it, it is (would be) rational for scientists to adhere to those principles (pp. 87-88).

Let's grant this point, although it is far from clear to me that I would be in a position to make rational judgments about what principles are normative for scientific inquiry if I were in doubt as to whether there is any such thing as scientific inquiry. But even granting that, it does not follow that (VII) holds for what *I* am doing in trying to decide between (1), (2) and (3) as explanations of my experience. Deciding between those alternatives is *not* scientific inquiry. I am not in a position to engage in scientific inquiry until I have recognized a world of physical things and processes, and a community of persons with whom to join in investigating it. Since I am not doing science, why should the fact that (VII) is normative for scientific inquiry (if there is any such thing) have anything to do with what makes one or another choice more reasonable in this situation?[22]

It should also be noted that, like the Kant-Wittgenstein-Strawson line, Slote's argument defends our ordinary perceptual practice by seeking to dispose of certain alternatives. Therefore it is subject to the same point, that even if those alternatives have been eliminated, there will undoubtedly be other possibilities to be considered. Indeed, Slote himself notes one other possible explanation, viz., that one's experiences are produced solely by one's own psychological faculties, working unconsciously. And, again, the more basic point is that it seems to be in principle impossible to have adequate reason for supposing that any list of explanations of a given phenomenon exhausts the possibilities.

Finally, I shall look at a very interesting recent attempt by Richard Brandt, in an unpublished paper, "Rational Belief," to tackle directly the job of giving a non-circular rational justification of our basic epistemic practices. In that paper Brandt writes as follows:

> I suggest we can identify a *policy* for belief-formation or belief-adjudication, composed of *imperatives* for the formation or appraisal of beliefs . . . . In saying we can "identify" a policy for belief-adjudication, I mean that we can pick out one policy among possible policies, and show that it has a unique promise of recommending firm belief only in propositions that are true, firm disbelief only in propositions that are false, and intermediate degrees of belief only in propositions of types the frequency of truth among which is correspondingly great or small (p. 15).

This is a lofty aim. Here is Brandt's attempt to realize it.

> I assume that we do have a conception of a world, or set of facts, independent of our beliefs about it, and that what it is for a belief to be true is that it represents correctly this set of facts. So what we want is a policy that will bring our beliefs as nearly as may be into correspondence with this set of facts.
>
> It could be that no policy can do this job. Indeed, it seems that the job can be done only if at least three conditions are met. The first is that there is enough lawful structure (it could be just statistical laws) in the world so that a sampling of some piece of the world is a clue to the nature of other pieces of the world. The laws might

change, and they might vary from one part of the world to another, but they must have enough range, and be simple enough, so that sampling and inference to other pieces of the world are reliable. The second condition is that we get some input from the world, some touch with fact which can be used as a starting-point for inference and a verifier for inference or proposed laws, not necessarily infallibly since awareness of the touch with fact might itself not be wholly reliable. Candidates for such a status, of course, are how we are being appeared to or what states of feeling we are in or what thoughts are running through our minds; some philosophers would have a longer list. If there are such facts, then at any given time when we are awake we have some samples of the real world at our disposal, for use in theory-evaluation. It is not enough, however, that at any moment *t* we have some contact with the world, for purposes of theory-testing. For instance, even if there is a law of motion we cannot know what it is from just one observation; we need at least two samples. So, if we are to have a picture of the world at time *t*, we need both input from the world at *t* and rather reliable information about inputs at other moments. So there must be some sort of recording device more or less reliable, for information about earlier inputs. So much at least must be the case if we are to attain reliable beliefs about parts of the world currently not observed. I think that in fact there are some further conditions which must be met if we are to get our thoughts into correspondence with the world; the above must do for now.

If these conditions must be met if we are to form reliable opinions about the world, then we can see what roughly the policy with "unique promise" will be, and the sense in which it has "unique promise." It will direct us to form a consistent system of beliefs, since these alone will lead us beyond the content of our inputs. Second, it will direct us to incorporate in this system, at *t*, beliefs about how we are being appeared to at *t;* and to strike beliefs incompatible with these (usually there will be a choice which beliefs to strike, whether lawlike beliefs or auxiliary beliefs about conditions of observation and so on). Next, it will direct us to incorporate the content of ostensible recollections about particular past experiences, or at least most of these . . . . There is no simple rule informing us when a given one or more of ostensible recollections should be rejected or accepted when faced with a complex of lawlike beliefs supported by other ostensible recollections; I have no more precise suggestion than to follow the idealists and say one accepts the alternative least devastating to one's "intellectual world" as a whole (pp. 15-17).

. . . I have said that this policy for belief-formation of appraisal has "unique promise" of leading to true beliefs (etc.). What this means is that the strategy is such that, *if* the world is such, or our relation

> to it is such, that true beliefs about it can be reached by a systematic strategy, then this strategy will lead us to them. Of course there is a world: "I doubt therefore I am" shows this. But given there is a world, if there are inputs which are samples, and there is a reasonably reliable record of what those samples have been, and if the parts of the world are related by laws that are not too complex (etc.), then if we form and test hypotheses involving laws on the basis of these samples, we shall be led to true beliefs, and away from false beliefs, about the world. These conditions may not obtain. If they do not, scientific reflection is idle. But if we want truth (and grasp its practical importance), we had better hope for the best and adopt the policy which will generally lead to the truth if truth is obtainable (p. 18).

Brandt is trying to avoid relying on the output of the epistemic practices he is seeking to justify. Instead of relying on premises about what the world is like, he seeks to determine what it will have to be like *if* we are to have any chance of knowing it, and then considering what practices would give us knowledge of the world *if* it is like that.[23] Nevertheless, in the end he does rely on the very practices he seeks to justify, albeit in a more subtle way. There are two points in the argument at which this dependence can be spotted.

First, why should we suppose that Brandt's three conditions really are necessary conditions of there being a policy of belief formation that can be relied on to lead to the adoption of true beliefs and rejection of false beliefs? Let's look at the first condition: "that there is enough lawful structure . . . in the world so that a sampling of some pieces of the world is a clue to the nature of other pieces of the world." To say that this is a necessary condition for the existence of a reliable policy of belief formation is to say that it is impossible for us to consistently form true beliefs about parts of the world beyond our experience unless there are regularities for which what we do experience constitutes a good sample. And then we would be able to inductively discover those regularities and use them to extrapolate from what we do experience to what we do not.

But surely this is not the only *logical* possibility. Surely there are logically possible worlds in which a cognitive subject has *innate* knowledge of parts of the world it does not experience. And there are logically possible worlds in which ramdom guessing on the part of a cognitive subject is a reliable method of forming beliefs about what does not fall within its experience. So Brandt cannot reasonably claim that this is a *logically* necessary condition of our having a reliable method of belief formation. Is it, then, necessary in some other way?

I would suggest that the most that can reasonably be claimed on this score is that, *as human beings and the world in which they live are constituted*, it is not possible for us to realiably form beliefs about absent parts of the world unless there is enough lawful structure. As things are, other logical possibilities, such as those I was just envisaging, simply are not realized. But how do we know, or what justifies us in believing, that this is the way we and the world are? Obviously, by engaging in the very same practices Brandt is seeking to justify. Epistemic circularity has crept in once more.

Second, suppose we grant Brandt his conditions and look at what he claims our policy must be if we are to maximize our chances of attaining the true and avoiding the false, if the world is as specified in those conditions. The second condition was that "we get some input from the world, some touch with fact that can be used as a starting-point for inference and a verifier for inference or proposed laws." The second part of the policy, correspondingly, "will direct us to incorporate in this system, at *t*, beliefs about how we are being appeared to at *t*." But the question is: why should we identify "how we are appeared to" as "inputs from the world"? And even if we do, why should we restrict the list to ways of being appeared to?

A bit earlier Brandt wrote: "Candidates for such a status, of course, are how we are being appeared to or what states of feeling we are in or what thoughts are running through our minds; some philosophers would have a longer list." Indeed they would. Although Brandt is not very explicit about this, his list of "inputs" is a "subjective" or "phenomenalist" one. Direct realists would take our perceptions of the physical environment to be "inputs from the world." Given the concerns of this essay, we cannot refrain from adding that still other people would regard one's awareness of God acting in one's life as an "input from the world." The basic point is that the mere requirement of *some* inputs from the world does not of itself tell us where to locate these.

Thus even if Brandt's argument for his "policy" were perfectly sound, that Pandora's box would be left wide open. If it is to be shut, if the list is to be closed as Brandt would want it closed, and if he is to have any basis at all for doing so, it will have to come from what he has learned from engaging in the very practices he is seeking to recommend. He will have to argue that the system of beliefs formed in accordance with his policy indicates that being appeared to, etc., are sufficiently reliable inputs from the world, and that there are no other candidates that pass the test. Circularity has once more marred the picture.

This short survey of attempts to provide an adequate non-circular justification of our perceptual practice and other basic epistemic practices indicates that the prospects for doing so are not very encouraging. I take this to bolster the Reidian position that our only recourse, in our condition, is to humbly accept the epistemic promptings of nature, and build on that.

vii

Finally, let's consider briefly the application of these ideas to Christian belief. Consider the widely held position that Christian belief is rational only if based on adequate reasons. This position assumes that no Christian beliefs are susceptible of immediate justification. It supposes that there is no analogue in Christian belief of justifiably believing that there is a tree in front of one just because it looks like there is a tree in front of one. In this essay I cannot go into the question of whether people who hold this position are justified in supposing that religious experience or an encounter with a putative revelation of God cannot play an epistemic role analogous to that of sense perception. But the considerations of this paper do indicate that this possibility should be explored.[24] At the very least, there is the point that a principle like (I), which seems to bar the way, is no more than a paper barrier.

Of course if our rational imperialist were to concede the possibility, he could execute the ascent to the second level already noted. He could say: "But if we are to determine whether that possibility is realized, we must see whether there are adequate reasons for taking religious experience, or whatever, to provide immediate justification for some Christian beliefs." But the considerations of sections iii and iv have shown that we cannot take it without more ado that this is a legitimate requirement. Why shouldn't the practice of forming beliefs about God on the basis of religious experience be counted as a basic epistemic practice along with sense perception and memory, one that constitutes our basic access to its subject matter? In that case we should no more expect to be able to find non-circular reasons for its reliability than for the reliability of perceptual practice.[25] We cannot pursue these suggestions here, but the considerations of this essay indicate that they are ideas that should be explored.

Notes

1. If I were primarily concerned with philosophical psychology, I should have to answer a number of difficult questions to which the above remarks

give rise. Is any mode of cognition wholly intuitive or wholly "receptive"? Does sense perception always involve some, perhaps unconscious, ratiocinative activity? Is the use of *reason* to be restricted to conscious activity? Is seeing that a simple mathematical or logical proposition is true, to be ranged under "reason" or "intuition"? Or should we say that it constitutes an intersection of the two? For the largely epistemological purposes of this paper I can leave all that aside.

2. *Nichomachean Ethics*, I, 3: 1094b 24-26.

3. The application of terms like "ought," "duty," "obligation," and "justification" in connection with belief would seem to be in order only if belief is under direct voluntary control, and there are strong reasons for supposing that it is not. Since the issues we shall be discussing concerning the rationality of belief could all be reformulated so as to avoid this assumption, I shall not pause to discuss the problem of belief and will.

4. In some cases it might be judged that one ought to have undertaken such a scrutiny even though one had not done so, and hence that one is not wholly in the clear, even if one has adequate reasons which would be revealed by a rational investigation. Be this as it may, the only requirement that can be applied across the board is that the belief has what it takes to pass the test were it to be administered.

   We should also note that the requirement might be stated in terms of the belief *being based on* adequate reasons, rather than just in terms of the believer *having* adequate reason. Since all the issues we wish to discuss arise in connection with the latter, weaker requirement, we shall confine ourselves to that.

5. Brand Blanshard, *Reason and Belief* (London: Allen & Unwin, 1974), p. 401.

6. I have not forgotten the earlier admission that there are reasons (sic) for the use of the same word "reason" in both contexts. Nevertheless, as we shall see, these connections between the different uses of the term do not suffice to justify the claim that only reasons can make a belief rational.

7. For statements of this argument see, e.g., Anthony Quinton, *The Nature of Things* (London: Routledge & Kegan Paul, 1973), p. 119; Roderick Chisholm, *Theory of Knowledge* (Englewood Cliffs, N.J.: Prentice Hall 1977), pp. LXIII (1976, pp. 171 ff.).

8. See, e.g., F.H. Bradley, *Essays on Truth and Realty* (Oxford: Clarendon Press, 1914), ch. VII; Brand Blanshard, *The Nature of Thought* (London: Allen & Unwin, 1939), chs. 25-27; Keith Lehrer, *Knowledge* (Oxford: Clarendon Press, 1974), chs. 7 and 8.

9. See, e.g., C.I. Lewis, "The Given Element in Empirical Knowledge," *Philosophical Review*, vol. 61 (1952), pp. 168-175; A.D. Woozley, *Theory of Knowledge* (London: Hutchinson's, 1949), pp. 164-167.

10. Chisholm, *op. cit.*, ch. 2.

11. See the discussion of this in the following paragraph.

12. Epistemologists differ as to whether a *prima facie* perceptual justification may be defeated by the mere fact that something was amiss in the generation of that sensory experience, or whether it is defeated only if the subject knows, or is justified in believing, that something was amiss.
13. We should not jump to the conclusion that all immediate justification is only *prima facie*. It may be, for example, that the justification I have for supposing that I feel tired, when I feel tired, is such that nothing could defeat it.
14. *Op. cit.*, p. 76.
15. See my "Two Types of Foundationalism," *Journal of Philosophy*, vol. 73, no. 7, April 8, 1976, pp. 165-185, and "Level Confusions in Epistemology," *Midwest Studies in Philosophy*, vol. V (1980), pp. 135-150. In addition, if one were to hold that in order for an experience of type E to justify one in accepting a belief of type B, one would also have to be justified in accepting the principle "E is sufficient to justify B"; one would set up an infinite regress. For one has just added *being justified in accepting that principle* to the requirements for being justified in accepting B. But then, by the same reasoning, one is justified in accepting B only if one is justified in accepting a larger principle which includes this new requirement. But then that justification has to be added to the requirements, and . . .
16. See my "Self-Warrant: A Neglected Form of Privileged Access," *American Philosophical Quarterly*, vol. 13, no. 4 (October, 1976), pt. III, for a discussion of these alternatives.
17. The requirements of reflective rationality were developed in terms of beliefs that are unreflectively justified *immediately*. But the argument will work in the same way with beliefs that are unreflectively *mediately* justified. If my belief, B, is justified by virtue of being based on adequate reasons, R, then I will satisfy the highest demands of rationality in believing B only if I am justified in believing that reasons like R are sufficient to justify beliefs like B.
18. For an elaboration of this possibility see my "Two Types of Foundationalism," *loc. cit.*, esp. fn. 13.
19. The case at issue is not the most virulent possible form of epistemic circularity, since here it is a *theoretical* justification of Y that depends on a *practical* justification of Y.
20. The position at which we have arrived bears a striking resemblance to that of Thomas Reid, especially as portrayed by Wolterstorff's contribution to this volume. Consider, for example, the following statement by Reid. "Every kind of reasoning for the veracity of our faculties, amounts to no more than taking their own testimony for their veracity; and this we must do implicitly, until God gives us new faculties to sit in judgment upon the old" (*Essays on the Intellectual Powers of Man*, Cambridge, Mass.: M.I.T. Press, 1969), p. 631.
21. London: Allen & Unwin, 1970.

22. Slote tries to answer this objection as well by arguing that principles of scientific reasonableness are at least *prima facie* principles of epistemic reasonableness generally, and hence apply to every case of deciding what to believe (pp. 85-87). But, so far as I can see, all he succeeds in showing is that it is a *principle of scientific thinking* that scientific reasonableness is, at least *prima facie*, general epistemic reasonableness. If we are not engaged in scientific thinking, this point has no relevance.
23. As Brandt notes on p. 18, this is a generalization of Hans Reichenbach's famous "pragmatic" justification of induction.
24. The earlier discussion of multiple sources of justification indicates that even if Christian belief, or some of it, is susceptible of immediate justification, it is not thereby barred from receiving external support from reasons as well.
25. For an elaboration of this suggestion see my "Religious Experience and Religious Belief," forthcoming in *Nous*, and "Christian Experience and Christian Belief," forthcoming in a book of essays on reason and faith.

On the Nature and Limits of Rationality

Peter A. Schouls

THE SUBJECT OF THIS ESSAY IS AN EXPLORATION of the "Nature and Limits of Rationality." This exploration will involve a discussion of "the legitimate and illegitimate uses of the human ability to analyse, argue and make inferences"; the "uses, canons, methods and products of rationality"; and "the illegitimate claims made on behalf of rationality." Although I can imagine people rash enough to assign such a gargantuan task as this, I cannot believe there would be anyone foolish enough to accept the assignment! I, certainly, want to begin by emphasizing that I do not intend to deal exhaustively with even a single aspect of this task, and that some of it I will touch hardly at all.

1. Problems of Defining Rationality or Reason

Let me use some of G.J. Warnock's statements, in his article "Reason" in the *Encyclopedia of Philosophy*,[1] as a point of departure for what I want to say. Warnock's basic question is "What can reason do?" However, Warnock recommends the transformation of that question "into a question not directly about the 'faculty' of reason itself but about those beings to whom this faculty is attributed." In Warnock's words the transformed question then becomes "What . . . are human beings in a position to do, in virtue of their possession of the faculty of reason? What, by means of reasoning, are we in a position to achieve?" In the brief compass of his article Warnock then offers a succinct discussion of these issues. Two of the themes on which he dwells are the legitimate and illegitimate uses of reason, and the defensible and indefensible claims made on behalf of reason. The transformed question, says Warnock, raises the two further questions of "what reasoning is" and "whether this or that cannot be achieved by reasoning." The first of these is a question about the canons and methods, and the second one concerns the products of reason. An answer to the first question will, says Warnock, be settled "with some degree of arbitrariness."

That the answer to "What is reasoning?" is settled with "some degree of arbitrariness" is a provocative statement which Warnock leaves undefended. I will make this issue a central concern of this essay. I shall argue that the degree of arbitrariness (if it exists) is of minor importance, because the response to "what reasoning is" will in fact be very much determined by "whether this or that can or cannot be achieved by reasoning." I shall argue that the second problem involves human aspirations and decisions, and that the nature of the answer to the first is then indirectly but non-arbitrarily determined in view of these aspirations and decisions.

Let us begin with Warnock's central questions. "What, then, is reason? Alternatively, what is reasoning?" Warnock provides no definite answer but, instead, asserts that "there seems to be no basis secure enough to support a pronouncement that a particular meaning [of the words 'reason' or 'reasoning'], and hence a particular answer to the question, is exclusively correct." Warnock provides no support for the assertion that philosophers have not used "reason" univocally; but that is an assertion which hardly needs a defense. Even a cursory comparison of the relevant writings of, say, Aristotle, Descartes, Hegel, and Marx on this topic will provide more than sufficient material for its support.

In view of this fact of multivocality Warnock then shifts from focusing on the question "What is reasoning?" to that of how a certain philosopher uses "reason." But this shift of focus is not as innocent as it may at first appear it leads to new problems and does nothing to solve the difficulty about definition. For, as we just saw, in view of the multivocality no particular answer to the question "What is reason?" or "What is reasoning?" "is exclusively correct." As Warnock later suggests, "There is, then, no universally agreed or uniquely correct sense of 'reason.' " If there is no uniquely correct answer then it might seem that we are limited to cataloging the various uses of "reason" without passing judgment on the members of this catalogue. That, however, is not where Warnock wants to end up. As he writes in his final paragraph:

> . . . the philosopher who produces an argument against high traditional claims for, or traditional characterizations of reason is, in so doing, exercising reason to the best of his ability . . . . Thus, to dissent from [e.g.] rationalism as a philosophical doctrine is certainly not to disparage reason; the man who values, and shows that he values, reason is not he who merely pitches reason's claims exceptionally high

but, rather, he who attempts, by painstaking reasoning, to determine how high those claims may justifiably be pitched.

That leaves us with a picture which is far from clear. Evidently we should see reason as that which is exercised by someone whenever the product of the exercise is something which we can, to some degree at least, understand, and the only useful or possible definition statements about reason are about extent only. A claim about this extent made by anyone whose claim we can understand is then a claim which is, to some degree at least, correct. Whether it is "uniquely correct" we cannot determine because it is precisely about this extent that there must remain philosophical controversy. While suspending final judgment about the nature of the extent, we can only criticize the positions of others when they attempt to fix precisely the limits of this extent.

One problem with this position is that (in the meantime) what is presumed to be reason, is being used; and the way in which it is being used (or has been used by others) is left unexamined. Something that is "external" has come to occupy our attention; rather than discuss what we take to be reason and its procedures, we discuss uses of what we take to be reason. In doing so, we disregard its procedures. Rather than deal with the nature of rationality we focus exclusively on its extent or limits. But suppose the issue of extent is itself determined by prior decisions—prior decisions which, indirectly through one's resulting view of extent, come to determine the nature of reason (which is being discussed in terms of extent). In that case Warnock's procedure is unsatisfactory. It is unsatisfactory if the decisions in question are themselves related to the ambitions or aspirations of the one who thus fixes or determines this extent. For when the answer to the question "What is reasoning?" is settled in terms of extent (where extent is itself determined by aspirations and decisions), the answer to the question is far from arbitrary. Moreover, what one person can accept of some other person's definition of "reason"—whether in terms of "uses of," "canons, methods, and products of," or "claims made on behalf of" rationality—is not arbitrary either. This acceptance is determined by the degree to which there is a sharing of human aspirations, and by the degree to which two people share the way they come to a realization of such aspirations.

It seems to me that something may be said for the supposition I just made. Thus I take it that a discussion of "legitimate and illegitimate uses of the human ability to analyse" involves questions about human ambitions and decisions, about the extent of the ability to analyze, and about the nature of that ability. And I take it that we may profitably deal with these questions in the order in which I just placed them.

Some readers might offer an objection here: if, instead of beginning with a contemporary view, I begin with a more traditional one —say, such founders of modern philosophy as Descartes and Locke— then the picture will be different. For Descartes and Locke, it might be objected, the limits of rationality are determined by the nature of reason or of reasoning, rather than *vice versa;* and the criteria by which we settle whether a claim made on behalf of rationality is legitimate or not are determined strictly by the nature of reason. Moreover, one might object that, given their view of the nature of reason, questions concerning its legitimate or illegitimate use simply cannot arise for them. For they hold that reason, taken by them to be given by God, is the "candle of the Lord," the "Light of Nature." It is believed to be given by God to light man's path wherever he goes, and it is taken to be fully adequate for that task. Finally, it might be said that although Descartes and Locke would concede it possible to make wrong use of the products of analysis, wrong use of reason itself is for them an impossibility; for wherever reason can be used, it may or ought to be used, and wherever reason ought not to be used, it cannot be used.

Just a bit of probing of this position should, however, lead us to recognize that it leads to problems not all that different from those pointed to earlier. Both Descartes and Locke hold that if we take reason to be capable of shedding light on our path because it is given by God for that very purpose, then we can take reason to be absolutely trustworthy in the context of all human affairs. As Locke might phrase this: in view of the nature of God, he would not deceive us with respect to what reason tells us. Or as Descartes might phrase this: given the nature of God, he could not deceive us if he would with respect to what reason tells us. Reason becomes that aspect of man to which man has to submit if he wants to live responsibly. Man, then, is responsible for listening to reason, but man is not responsible for what reason says. He need not evaluate what reason says, for reason cannot but speak the truth, and so reason itself is the criterion for what is and what is not the right way to go.

Many Christians (in addition to Descartes and Locke) adopt a position similar to this. They then argue somewhat as follows: God created man, and whatever God creates is good. Man fell into sin, and although it may be a mystery how God's handiwork could turn to evil, we at least know that sin does not impair our natural faculties as such. Sin is only to be found in the *use* we make of our God-given native capacities—by which they mean that sin is to be found in our misuse of whatever reason, for example, gives us. Our natural faculties, not having been impaired by the Fall, still function as they ought to, and the product of their functioning is to be accepted as a good gift from God.

One might hold that this position "begs the question" precisely because of the assumption that a certain ability, which man is supposed to possess, is thought to be God-given. Only if we fail to recognize that the nature of this ability may be determined by man's aspirations and decisions can we hold that corruption is to be found only in the use of the products of our native capacities. But once we recognize that the ascription of a capacity of a certain type may be determined by human aspirations, then we cannot simply hold that we have responsibility only for its use, or only for our use of its products. And I hold that the nature of the capacity traditionally (i.e., also by thinkers like Descartes and Locke) ascribed to man is determined by human aspirations and decisions.

2. An Illustration from Early Modern Philosophy

There is no generally accepted definition of reason or of rationality. I have asserted that such a generally accepted definition is absent because definitions of reason are in the end determined by a person's aspirations. I will now support these assertions by means of an illustration. In the course of this illustration I will have a further opportunity to say a few things about "legitimate and illegitimate uses of the human ability to analyse," about "the uses, canons, methods and products of rationality," and about "claims made on behalf of rationality."

For a number of reasons I think it best to cast my illustration in terms of early modern philosophy. One reason is that philosophers like Descartes and Locke set the parameters for much of subsequent thought; their way of proceeding is often still ours, or is one from which we still struggle to escape. Moreover, Descartes and Locke are also influential in the Calvinian European-continental tradition. (Although it publicly resisted Descartes' influence in its earlier stages, this tradition has hardly remained free from Cartesian rationalism in its subsequent development.) And Scottish common-sense thinking is not really imaginable without Locke, who invented the notion of common sense as it came to be used by subsequent English-speaking philosophers.[2] Finally, both Descartes and Locke were adherents of the Christian religion (although, of course, in different camps, with Roman-Catholic Descartes far more tolerant of Protestantism than

Calvinistic-Anglican Locke ever was of Roman Catholicism). All of these are reasons which, in various ways, bring these thinkers closer to us. I will therefore use the work of one of them, Descartes, as my illustration.

Whatever rationality may be, I hold that it is a part of creation and that, as something created, it is limited. This is a statement with which some rationalists would likely agree, although Descartes would, of course, say that rationality is limited only if we consider it as it is manifested by a part of creation. He would say it is also unlimited because the Creator possesses, without limitation, that with which he has endowed some of his creation in a limited manner. Reason, for Descartes, is one of those things whose nature does not change whether it is present as a finite or as an infinite capacity. Therefore the results obtained through reasoning are absolutely trustworthy, and so the supreme norm for the conduct of human life is to be found in the dictates of reason. Reason tells man what is the essence of whatever is created, and what is therefore the essence of man; it tells him what is the purpose of his creaturely being within the whole of creation. Reason also tells man how to come to fulfill the purpose of his being, and so reason is, in effect, itself the tool—the only tool available to man—to attain such fulfillment. For a Cartesian, all of these are legitimate claims made on behalf of human rationality. Whatever degree of agreement there may exist between myself and a Cartesian rationalist, I doubt whether any of it survives beyond the first sentence of this paragraph.

For Descartes, the greatest need which the philosopher can fill is to do away with insecurity, with lack of certainty. Or to put it positively, the greatest service which the philosopher can provide is to show the path to security, to absolute certainty. Man desires security, and the recurrence of skepticism is little more than a backhanded proof that the desire for certainty expresses man's deepest need or highest aspiration. For whenever it was believed that certainty had been found, there was always someone who, in a compelling way, asked the question "But are you sure?" The very recurrence of this question is indicative of the fact that security is man's deepest need. That it kept recurring in a compelling form points to the fact that man's highest aspiration was for absolute certainty.

Descartes also asked this question and he answered it in a way which, he thought, would at least in principle do away once and for all with human insecurity. Of his *Meditations* he says that they are "arguments by which I, first of all men, upset the doubt of the sceptics" (*HR*2, 336).[3] In the *Meditations* it is reason that shows how the products of reason may be trusted absolutely.[4] Central to Descartes' attempt to attain certainty is *individual autonomy (certainty is to be found within the self)* or *individual freedom (certainty cannot be found in terms of any "givens" that we must accept and that originate beyond the self)*. And the outcome of such certainty is mastery of one's destiny through becoming "master and possessor of nature" (to use words from the *Discourse on Method, HR*1, 119). Certainty is attained through, and is founded on, reason; and mastery—which is the practical extension of this certainty to all areas of life—is established by means of reason.

If the story of man's Fall as related in the third chapter of Genesis is a story of individualistic self-assertion and of egocentricity, and if the prospect of "being like God, knowing good and evil" is one of ambition to have the supreme standard for human life emanate from the creature rather than the Creator, then the Cartesian program and view of rationality implicitly constitute a powerful reenactment of the Genesis story.

In view of this role which reason is to play, what must reason be like? Or, for Descartes, what is man like? How are we to view man, who does not just possess the ability to analyze, argue, and make inferences, but who is to be defined in terms of this ability, this man who does not merely possess reason but whose essence is constituted by his rationality?

I will try to answer these questions by focusing on what I have identified as a central point in Descartes' attempt to attain certainty—on individual autonomy or on individual freedom. From my formulation above it will be clear that I see the words "autonomy" and "freedom" as roughly interchangeable; they are merely different sides of the same coin. Dealing with the one will therefore go a long way toward dealing with the other. Let me begin with Descartes' notion of individual freedom.

2(a). Certainty and the "Given"

Descartes asserts that certainty is not to be found in what does not originate within the self, so individual freedom is central to his attempt to attain certainty. Explication of this relationship between freedom and certainty will allow us to come to grips with the Cartesian notion of rationality, both its extent and nature.

The second part of Descartes' *Discourse on Method* closes with a statement on the prerequisites for doing scientific work. These are: overcome partiality, observe life, and obtain facility in the method.

The attempt to overcome partiality focuses especially on the task to make oneself free from all kinds of preconceptions. Overcoming partiality is to result in the kind of disinterestedness that enables one to distinguish between opinions or beliefs held because of the cultural epoch or geographical area in which one happens to live, and beliefs or items of knowledge accepted on rational grounds. To observe life has a double reward. It is, first, an aid to overcoming partiality. Experience of the fact that manners, customs, and opinions which in one country may be signs of sophistication are elsewhere deemed inconsequential or even silly is an important step on the way toward disinterestedness. Second (and quite important but not directly relevant to my topic) is that the observation of life provides one with a stock of exeriences which can come to form starting points for analysis at various stages in one's scientific work. Finally, facility in method is needed for the simple reason that method is always necessary for finding out the truth.

To observe life is a prerequisite for doing scientific work. On the other hand the very fact that we need to observe life in order to overcome partiality is for Descartes an indication that life itself has spoiled our ability to do scientific work. We need to observe life to come to recognize that the very process of growing up in a certain place at a certain time has saddled us with beliefs peculiar to that place and time. To use Descartes' words:

> . . . since we have all been children before being men, and since it has for long fallen to us to be governed by our appetites and by our teachers (who often enough contradict one another, and none of whom perhaps counselled us always for the best), it is almost impossible that our judgements should be so excellent or solid as they should have been had we had complete use of our reason since our birth, and had we been guided by its means alone. (*HR*1, 88)

Our teachers "often enough contradict one another." In this they only reflect the world around them in which there are "many conflicting opinions . . . regarding the self-same matter, all supported by learned people"; a world in which philosophy, although "it has been cultivated for many centuries by the best minds that ever lived," is nevertheless a discipline in which "no single thing is to be found . . . which is not subject of dispute, and in consequence which is not dubious" (*HR*1, 86). Descartes' observation of life, his confrontation with the bewildering variety of opinion and doctrine which man can encounter, did not lead him into skepticism about man's innate capacities or into a thoroughgoing relativism. Instead his intellectual pursuits prompt him to assert the absoluteness and universality of truth, an assertion which rests on an implicit doctrine about the extent and nature of reasoning: never mind "how many conflicting opinions there may be regarding the self-same matter . . . there can never be more than one which is true." If only we had possessed "complete use of our reason since our birth," so that we would not have been submitted to the biases of our teachers and to the murky controversies of our tradition, we would not now have our natural light obscured and would live in the realm of truth. For, as he writes somewhat later in the *Discourse*, since there is "but one truth to discover in respect to each matter, whosoever succeeds in finding it knows in its regard as much as can be known."

To illustrate this point, Descartes introduces the example of a child "who has been instructed in Arithmetic and has made an addition according to the rule prescribed; he may be sure of having found as regards the sum of figures given to him all that the human mind can know." Crucial, however, is that the addition be made "according to the rule prescribed." This rule is a specific application of the general method, of "the Method which teaches us to follow the true order and enumerate exactly every term in the matter under investigation" and which, if followed scrupulously, gives "certainty" in the sciences (*HR*1, 94).

At the very end of the first part of the *Discourse*, just before Descartes turns his attention to the articulation of the methodological precepts in the second part, he writes:

> . . . I learned to believe nothing too certainly of which I had only been convinced by example and custom. Thus little by little I was delivered from many errors which might have obscured our natural vision and rendered us less capable of listening to Reason. But after I had employed several years in thus studying the book of the world and trying to acquire some experience, I one day formed the resolution of also making myself an object of study and of employing all the strength of my mind in choosing the road I should follow. This succeeded much better, it appeared to me, than if I had never departed either from my country or from my books.

Study of the great book of the world helped to overcome partiality, which made his natural vision clear; this, in turn, allowed him to succeed much better in studying himself. The result of this self-study is presented in the *Discourse*'s second part. This result is the method to be used in whatever area reason tells man he can attain truth—which is everywhere. For, as the Introduction to the *Principles of Philosophy* suggests, the method extends to "all things with which we come into contact" (*HR*1, 213). Clearing the natural vision, or freeing oneself from the bondage of habit rooted in sense and in education,[5] will lead reason to become conscious of its own operations unhindered by sense or prejudice. Indeed the method articulated is nothing but a statement of how the mind goes about its business in its successful pursuit of truth. And whereas the proper object of reason is truth and its proper activity is the pursuit of truth, the methodological precepts constitute a self-portrait of reason.[6]

One result of the consistent application of the method is the "principles" which Descartes published as his *Principles of Philosophy*. And one of the "fruits" of these principles is "that the truths which they contain, being perfectly clear and certain, will remove all subjects of dispute, and thus dispose men's minds to gentleness and concord." This is in sharp contrast to "the controversies of the Schools" which "by insensibly making those who practice themselves in them more captious and self-sufficient *(plus pointilleux et plus opiniastres)*" are therefore "possibly the chief causes of the heresies and dissensions which now exercise the world" (*HR*1, 213). Gentleness and concord will be the lot of those who practice themselves in Descartes' principles.

The context of this passage emphasizes the point that such practice consists in working at the foundations of the sciences. The emphasis on method is not surprising for it is only the unhampered exercise of reason which, according to Descartes, can lead to concord. Practice in working methodically leads to peace and tranquillity rather than to dissension and opinionatedness. Unanimity, which is not a criterion of truth but may still function as a mark indicating its presence,[7] comes about once partiality has been overcome. And the method for gaining truth becomes available to man through what might be called reflexive awareness of the way the mind works in its successful pursuit of truth—that is, when it is taken to be functioning unhampered by prejudice. Meeting these prerequisites for doing scientific work—namely, overcoming partiality and obtaining facility in the method—will allow one to break away from insecurity and cultural relativism into the realms of certainty and of absolute truth.

Making clear how radical these seemingly innocuous prerequisites really are will bring into clear focus my prime contention: central to Descartes' attempt to attain certainty is the notion of individual freedom expressed in the conviction that certainty cannot be found in any "givens" which one must accept and which originate beyond oneself. At the same time I should be able to make more explicit how all of this relates to the extent and nature of human reason.

First, we should note that Descartes' position may be said to be one of "anti-trust." By this I mean it is clear that, for Descartes, in order to be able to act rationally we must separate ourselves from all that is past and from most of what is present. He recognizes that such a separation is not easily achieved, that life itself seemingly militates against it. For we are brought up by our elders, educated by our tutors; and the parent/child as well as the teacher/student relationship demands from the child or student a closeness and trust, and the will to follow. We are sentient beings, and the senses force the world upon us. We have acquired the habit of trusting what we have learned and of trusting what our senses teach us; and we recognize that it is this habitual trust which is necessary for the very lives we lead.

There is nothing in these statements with which Descartes would quarrel. Instead, he himself makes these points in many different ways. While, for example, we immerse ourselves in the universal doubt of the *Meditations* in order to try to take radical distance from all that is past and present, we are not in danger of losing our life, he says. As long as we don't know any better we will, in our practice as distinct from our thought, trust the "teachings of nature" and live by the moral precepts held dear by our contemporaries. While we do not yet possess a rational system of knowledge, "we should not doubt those things that appear to be true in what concerns the conduct of life," as long as we do "not hold them to be so certain that we may not change our minds regarding them when obliged to do so by the evidence of reason" (*HR*1, 207; see also *Principles* I, 3). But it is the "evidence of reason" which will determine whether or not such precepts will be retained. The radical distance created in the *Meditations*' realm of theory—where, in words from the *Discourse*, "I rooted out of (*i.e.*, *déracinois*) my mind all the errors which formerly might have crept in" (*HR*1, 99)—frees reason from bondage to prejudice, from the habit of trusting what does not originate with reason itself.

It is no exaggeration to say Descartes' view holds reason to be in bondage to such prejudice. This is, in fact, an understatement. In the First Meditation, for example, we read:

> . . . these ancient and commonly held opinions still revert frequently to my mind, long and familiar custom having given them the right to occupy my mind against my inclination and rendered them almost masters of my belief; nor will I ever lose the habit of deferring to them or of placing my confidence in them, so long as I consider them as they really are, i.e. opinions in some measure doubtful, as I have just shown, and at the same time highly probable, so that there is much more reason to believe in than to deny them. That is why I shall con-

> sider that I am not acting amiss if, taking of set purpose a contrary belief, I allow myself to be deceived, and for a certain time pretend all these opinions are entirely false and imaginary, until at last, having thus balanced my former prejudices with my latter . . . my judgement will no longer be dominated by bad usage or turned away from the right knowledge of the truth. (*HR*1, 148)

The ancient and commonly held opinions which are here rejected because they are in some measure doubtful are those that express our habitual trust in the senses to give us our everyday, non-scientific, yet dependable knowledge of our surroundings. These opinions express our habitual trust in the deductive power of the mind to give us scientific knowledge in applied sciences, such as medicine, as well as in what Descartes takes to be purely theoretical sciences, such as mathematics. It is because of the questioning of the deductive power of the mind that I take it to be an understatement to say that reason is in bondage to prejudice. Here the question is whether deduction may in fact be called "reasoning," that is, whether it in fact gives me results which are certain. Everyday sense-based "knowledge," as well as "knowledge" deductively obtained, hardly seem candidates for the label of "prejudice." One would be more inclined to accept them as knowledge and oppose them to the prejudice or opinionatedness of those who accept "the tradition."

But the very fact that without more ado we are inclined to accept as knowledge the givens of the senses and the products of deduction in itself is proof of the power that uncritically-held beliefs hold over us. For if we ask why we place this trust in sense or in deduction, the answer is apt to take several common forms: it has served me well, everyone does it, my parents and teachers taught me so. Because none of these answers contain or even point to clear principles which are indubitable to reason, their assertion merely betrays dogmatic conceit. Descartes would take their very matter-of-factness as an indication of the extent to which reason is in bondage to prejudice.

For Descartes, certainty is not to be found in any "givens" which originate beyond the self, nor is certainty to be found through reason alone. Therefore he believes that man possesses the freedom to do away with what one might call the "given" universal order. This "doing away with" I have described as an exercise of freedom. But, for Descartes, it may just as legitimately be called an act of reason. For, whatever cannot be seen as absolutely indubitable is rejected, or the acceptance of such things is called irrational, precisely because their validity is not absolutely certain, or at least not entirely a product of reason. Only what is certain is rational, and only what is rational is real as far as scientific purposes is concerned.

And so Descartes begins by rejecting the trustworthiness of both everyday and scientific "knowledge." This rejection leads him to declare the non-existence of that about which such "knowledge" is taken to be: things in the world and the relations between and among these as well as their relation to their Creator; the world itself; and the Creator himself. Only reason, the power to search for and recognize certainty, remains. This power is one that breaks continuity with the present and allows no links with the past. It functions atomistically and a-historically. For Descartes, to act rationally always involves the institution of a new order, always beginning *de novo*. Whatever topic I, as a rational being, consider, "I shall be . . . obliged to write just as though I were treating of a matter which no one had ever touched on before me" (*HR*1, 331).

2(b). Certainty and the Individual

And now I am already well into the other point I wanted to discuss: central to Descartes' attempt to attain certainty is individual autonomy, the conviction that certainty is ultimately to be found only within the self. The connection between this point and the nature that Descartes ascribes to rationality is now easy to state.

In Descartes' estimation, to understand is to be certain; and "certainty" pertains only to the self-evident and to the necessary. Thus the area of what is self-evident and of what is necessary indicates the limits of rationality. Therefore, claims to knowledge are legitimate only when a person grasps what is epistemically atomic or what is a first principle (in either case, what is known *per se* or is self-evident). In addition, these claims are legitimate only when a person grasps necessary connections between or among self-evident items or between or among clusters of concepts which are themselves in turn grasped as having necessary connections between or among themselves. Only such claims to knowledge are legitimate, for only such claims carry the stamp of certainty imprinted by the indubitability of what is known *per se* or by the recognition of the relation of necessity of what is known *per aliud*.

And so if I am to understand, I must, according to Descartes, start with the grasping of epistemic atoms or first principles. And that entails that if I am to understand I must understand for myself, radically so. To adopt words from the opening paragraph of the First Meditation, someone else's "firm and permanent structure in the sciences" is of little use to me for I will not be able to understand it unless I myself "commence to build anew from the foundation." And no foundation, no certainty, is given; the foundation has to be established. Whoever wants to understand will first have to establish his own foundation. Descartes' aspiration for certainty leads him to a doctrine of reason which is explicated in terms of "analysis" and "synthesis." We cannot synthesize and attain certainty in the resulting structure unless we put together what is itself beyond doubt. And we cannot obtain such foundational items which are beyond doubt unless, through analysis or reduction, we destroy the "given" universal order, until no order remains but that of necessary connections clear and apparent to the intellect—to each individual's intellect. So Descartes' aspiration to certainty leads him into radical epistemic individualism or radical epistemic autonomy.

The very first precept of Descartes' method—and we must remember that the precepts of this method together are meant to constitute a self-portrait of reason—is "to accept nothing as true which I did not clearly recognize to be so: that is to say, carefully to avoid precipitation and prejudice in judgements, and to accept in them nothing more than what was presented to my mind so clearly and distinctly that I could have no occasion to doubt it" (*HR*1, 92). Avoidance of precipitation calls for suspension of judgment, for withholding trust from what I may have earlier accepted as trustworthy. That case in which judgment has been suspended then needs to be submitted to analysis, i.e., needs to be "divided up . . . into as many parts as possible" (as the second methodological precept characterizes the nature of analysis) so we may come to see whether it rests on a foundation of items which are self-evident. It is through suspension of judgment that I am to stay clear from prejudice, from the kind of prejudice which, as we have seen, consists in accepting a belief as an item of knowledge although I have not constructed that item on a foundation of clear and distinct and, ultimately, self-evident knowledge. Suspension of judgment is motivated by doubt, by lack of certainty. Anything given in experience (of whatever kind) is complex, and as such it is neither clear nor distinct to reason, and hence dubitable. Analysis of what is experienced as complex is pushed by doubt to its extreme, which is found in the self-evidence of what is utterly simple. The intellectual grasping of such an item, says Descartes, is accompanied by the experience of absolute certainty.

Descartes holds that to be human is to be rational, and to be rational is to possess the powers of analysis and synthesis. The nature of reason does not change from person to person; it is universally the same. Egocentricity and individualism do not, therefore, entail solipsism and subjectivism. These points Descartes makes in many different ways. In the Preface to the *Principles of Philosophy* he writes that ". . . the principles are clear and nothing must be deduced from them but by very evident reasoning," and anyone has ". . . sufficient intelligence to comprehend the conclusions that depend on" these principles. If those who reflect on the issues which Descartes discussed in his *Principles* do not reach his conclusions, then he explains this either in terms of the permeating influence of "habit" or "prejudice," i.e., lack of freedom or method. In either case those who come to different conclusions have not really reflected, have not acted rationally.

How do we know whether we have acted rationally? According to Descartes we act rationally once we accept nothing as a primary given. We act rationally as long as we limit ourselves to reducing whatever is "given" to what is known *per se* and as long as we limit ourselves to combining only those foundational elements which, once placed side by side, show themselves to be necessarily related to one another. The latter is a process which, of course, is taken to continue beyond such foundational elements in terms of comparing the resulting "clusters" of concepts with other simple concepts or other such clusters. It is a process which, Descartes believes, will go on indefinitely, and so man is forever on the way to creating greater and greater security for himself in his mastery over nature by means of science.

The former (reduction or analysis) is a process that stops once indivisibility or self-evidence has been reached or, alternatively, once it is recognized that reduction to self-evidence cannot be carried out. In the latter case what is "given" remains unintelligible and is taken as non-existent insofar as it cannot become the object of scientific knowledge. Even if we are successful in reducing the "given" to what is self-evident, we still might be unable to carry out composition through connections which are seen to be necessary. Then we must stop and "spare ourselves superfluous labour"; we must stop if "our understanding is not sufficiently well able to have an intuitive cognition" of such connections. (The quoted phrases are from the heading of Rule 8 of the *Rules for the Direction of the Mind*, *HR*1, 22.)

The nature and extent of rationality are now clearly indicated. Both this nature and this limit are connected with man's aspirations. For I am to acquire a new habit, "the habit of never going astray." This habit I acquire when I make it my duty "firmly to adhere to the resolution never to give judgements on matters whose truth is not clearly known to me." It is in acting out this duty "that the greatest and principal perfection of man consists" (*HR*1, 178).

To act rationally is to act in terms of analysis and synthesis. Judgments made outside the bounds of methodic procedure are not based on knowledge; they are likely to be erroneous and are irrational acts. To err or not to err is entirely within each man's power. When a person strictly adheres to the precepts of the method, then he acts rationally, he cannot err, and he cannot fail to find security.

This new habit is not, in Descartes' opinion, to be called a prejudice. Of the *Principles of Philosophy* he writes "that in studying these Principles, we shall little by little accustom ourselves to judge better of all things with which we come in contact, and thus to become wiser" (*HR*1, 213). The *Principles* he holds to be the product of strict methodic procedure. Wisdom, therefore, is taken to have its roots not in tradition, culture, or community, but in individually experienced freedom or in individually practiced methodic procedure. Wisdom is held to have its roots in egocentricity, in subjectivity, in an individual's epistemic autonomy.

Notes

1. Vol. 7, pp. 83-85.
2. This invention of "common sense" is considered by Gilbert Ryle to be Locke's greatest contribution to philosophy. Cf. Ryle, G., "John Locke," *Critica* (vol. I, no. 2, 1967), *passim.*
3. Unless otherwise stated all the page references to Descartes' works are to E.S. Haldane and G.R.T. Ross, *The Philosophical Works of Descartes*, vols. I and II (Cambridge, 1911), abbreviated as *HR*1 and *HR*2.
4. A detailed discussion of the structure of this argument I have presented in chapters IV and V of *The Imposition of Method, A Study of Descartes and Locke* (Oxford, 1980).
5. Freeing oneself from "sense" and "education" is the way in which Descartes often expresses his doctrine that certainty cannot be found in terms of "givens" which originate beyond the self.
6. For a detailed argument to justify the picture sketched in these two sentences, see *The Imposition of Method*, chapter III, part 1.
7. See Kenny, A.J.P., *Descartes, Philosophical Letters* (Oxford, 1970), p. 66.

Present Positions on Key Problems

Part Two:

Commitment and Rationality

Commitment and Rationality

Arthur F. Holmes

THE SUBJECT OF COMMITMENT AND RATIONALITY is complex. To begin with, it is larger than the *logical* relationship of Christian control beliefs to theory criticism and formation, which Nicholas Wolterstorff has so helpfully set before us in *Reason Within the Bounds of Religion*. Christian commitment (which I shall abbreviate as CC) includes specific beliefs, but it also includes other rational activities and states, and non-cognitive states as well. The term is well-chosen if it is to embrace Dooyeweerd's emphasis on the heart of the believer, for more than a set of presuppositions is involved in CC. "Presuppositions" suggest propositions from which we deduce a Christian philosophy in purely formal fashion, as Gordon Clark has claimed.[1] I have preferred the term "perspective,"[2] claiming that all philosophy (not just Christian thought) is "perspectival" insofar as it sees things from a holistic life-world standpoint that centers on some religious or quasi-religious commitment.

Thus, I am addressing the relation of religious commitment to rationality, but I shall also need to look at its relation to other elements in one's overall perspective that influence rational activity. In the concluding section of this chapter, therefore, I shall address the relation to religious commitment of universal basic beliefs (of the sort Scottish realists affirm) and of the conditions evoking them.

Meantime rationality (which I abbreviate as R) must be defined. Unless otherwise specified, I take R in a broad sense to include any variety of cognitive awareness or activity: perception, reflection, description, explanation, understanding, analysis, argumentation and whatever. It should be noted, however, that Thomas Reid uses it in the narrower sense (*r*) of logical argumentation and proofs of the kinds 18th century philosophers sought. And the recent volume *Rationality and Religious Belief* (ed. C.F. Delaney) also seems to address *r*. R, however, includes *r* but it is not confined thereto.

I will begin by identifying some apparent functions of CC in relation to R, and of R in relation to CC, much of which could be said of other religious or quasi-religious commitments as well. Then I will elaborate the whole-part nature of this relationship in the light of three ways in which it is expressed: belief and knowledge, practice and theory, subjectivity and objectivity. Employing that whole-part model, I finally explore the relation of CC to more universal aspects of "perspective," with an eye to the relation of universal basic beliefs to Christian belief.

I. Functional Descriptions

1. *CC arouses interest in R.* I take this to be self-evident. One has only to consider the history of Western thought, as well as his own motivations and the intellectual biographies of others.
2. *CC mandates R.* Implicit in the creation mandate and its cultural responsibilities are science and philosophy. Explicit in the New Testament is the responsibility to give reasons for the hope we possess.
3. *CC affects R's selectivity and perceptivity.* What intellectual interests we choose to pursue depend in measure on beliefs and values inherent in CC, and become a matter of Christian stewardship and strategy. Likewise CC alerts one to certain phenomena and problems, which may not be as evident to others: e.g., the effects of human pride, and the self-deceptions of reason. And as Wolterstorff points out, Christian control beliefs affect theory selection and formation. Reason is therefore not religiously neutral, not autonomous.
4. *CC includes cognitive content.* As Roger Trigg says, "If what I am committed to can be stated, . . . [it] will be based on beliefs that are objectively true or false and which are not merely valid for me and those who agree with me . . . . It can be understood by those who do not hold it and can therefore be rationally scrutinized."[3] Trigg is objecting at this point to Wittgenstein's exaggeration of the logical differences between Christian beliefs and belief in ordinary historical facts. The former, Wittgenstein claims, are not empirical propositions, for they are about a whole way of life. They function more like pictures constantly in my thoughts than like empirical referents.[4] While Wittgenstein is trying to avoid the reductionism that equates CC with purely empirical belief, followers (such as E.B. Braithwaite and D.Z. Phillips) fall into an opposite reductionism that guts CC of cognitive beliefs altogeth-

er. Trigg objects that CC involves claims to truth that are logically prior to that commitment; he says the believer has a fundamental interest in truth or falsity of these claims.

5. *CC is more than assent* to the truth of its cognitive content. Wittgenstein is correct in saying it involves an entire form of life, a view of things that affects attitudes, conduct and lifestyle. My term "perspective," as distinct from the term "presupposition," has similar intentions. CC contributes more than a set of propositions which we affirm. It (and any other life commitment, too) provides a whole way of seeing things, of experiencing and approaching life, an intensity and extent of belief that has both cognitive and affective dimensions. Conversion changes one's entire form of life.[5]
6. *CC gives unity to R.* The cognitive content of CC does not just inform R at miscellaneous points, but gives it a theocentric, indeed Christocentric unity. It helps us articulate an overall world-view that is unified within the God-creation distinction and relationship, which is revealed most fully and dramatically in Jesus Christ. The rational ideal of the unity of truth is satisfied by the completely coherent understanding that results.
7. *CC grounds creaturely confidence in R.* Within the context of this world-view, with the absolute dependency it stresses of creature on Creator, the autonomy of reason has no place. Rather, R is seen as a gift of God, an endowment that should be respected and valued, so that epistemic confidence is justified. On the other hand, within the same world-view, human finiteness and fallenness limit what R can and does achieve. Epistemic modesty must therefore combine with epistemic confidence to create a proper "creaturely" attitude of epistemic dependence on God, his revelation and his grace.

In view of the above, what then is R's function in relation to CC?

8. *R apprehends CC's cognitive content.* This much at least is prerequisite to CC.
9. *R articulates CC's cognitive content.* This is presupposed in the church's preaching of God's Word.
10. *R expounds and elaborates on CC's cognitive content.* This is the theological task. It includes the correction of misunderstandings and misemphases. This, like all other functions of reason, is subject to the objective control of the Scriptures and the canons of reason (which stand as God's laws over our thinking).

11. *R explores the justifiability of believing CC's cognitive content.* I do not say R *must* justify CC's content, but rather I make the more modest claim that it explores the justifiability of that content. If it should turn out that in principle justification is possible, then presumably R would proceed to attempt it in practice.
12. *R pursues cultural tasks mandated, illuminated, and informed by CC*, which are less directly involved with theology than functions 8-11.

Of these functions, 11 is the most debatable. The Scottish realist theologian Charles Hodge says bluntly that reason judges the credibility of a revelation: the self-contradictory is incredible and cannot be believed, and reason also judges the evidences of a revelation. Faith's assent, he believes, is "produced by evidence."[6]

Before writing this criticism off as Enlightenment rationalism's autonomy of reason, we should note Hodge's insistence that these are *God-given* functions for reason. As a Scottich realist he maintains that we are forced to believe some things because God has impressed "laws of belief" upon our nature. Some basic beliefs, he holds, are therefore universal. Since some other beliefs are indigenous to CC, the question remains as to their relationship to the universal. Do universal beliefs contribute to the credibility (or incredibility) of Christian beliefs, and how? Can faith really be produced by evidence, if R is selective and its perceptions are already affected by one's particular faith and its life-perspective? That is to say, if our perception of universal beliefs is itself variously affected by different commitments, can universal beliefs be logically compelling? Here the question of R's neutrality arises: are there presupposition-less and value-free sciences? Is philosophy (as Hodge claims) "knowledge by reason alone"? Functions 3, 4, and 6 (at least these) seem to preclude it. But what then is the relation between universal and Christian beliefs?

II. Whole and Part

The functions we have described suggest that R arises within life's more holistic commitments. CC arouses, mandates, affects and grounds R. It includes a cognitive content that unifies R's thinking. R meantime serves CC; it apprehends, articulates, expounds, and it pursues CC's cultural mandate. All this, I think, is in the Kuyperian spirit. But parallels exist in Scottish realism, which also has its whole-part relationship: common-sense belief (part of R in the large sense) is neither separate from life nor autonomous, but is part of life itself. The laws of belief that govern it are rooted in the way God made us and the world. R is in effect precommitted. Our being-in-the-world, like our being-before-God, arouses, mandates, and affects R. CC affects R; but so, too, does our tacit commitment to human life generally.

In order to spell this out more clearly, I shall consider the whole-part relationship of belief to knowledge, of practice to theory, and of subjectivity to objectivity. Belief, practice and subjectivity are cognates of CC while knowledge, theory and objectivity pertain to R.

1. *Belief and Knowledge*

In classical philosophy, at least until the time of Hume, belief was regarded as low-grade rationality, to be distinguished from knowledge by its lack of either intuitive or logical certainty. Belief may suffice for some purposes but not for science. Belief is fallible, having at best an empirical basis and perhaps just an emotive or conventional one. Knowledge is infallible, and it alone ensures access to eternal truth.

This classical disjunction considers belief simply as a cognitive state, not as a life-commitment, and it thinks of reason as above such uncertainties. Demonstration and contemplation of eternal truth are reason's ideals. In biblical usage, on the other hand, no such distinction is made. By Platonic standards, "I *know* whom I have *believed*" is a curious mixture of terms. Belief here is a holistic commitment within which cognitive confidence appears. Neither the Greek reduction of belief to cognition, nor the post-Wittgensteinian elimination of cognitive content from commitment, is acceptable.

The Scottish realists seem to recognize this, too. Consideration of the *bases* of belief shows it to be more holistic than reason, in the narrow sense. Reid places his basic beliefs not in the province of reason but in that of common sense, claiming they are so necessary in the conduct of life that a man cannot live and act without them.[7] Cognitive content (R) is part of a universally human life-perspective, and is evoked by the kind of commitment that human existence itself requires.

Other examples come to mind. John Henry Newman's *Grammar of Assent* distinguishes certainty from certitude, the former being a purely logical matter while the latter, still drawing on evidence, is a more holistic state of personal conviction and confidence. William James' famous essay "The Will to Believe" also finds larger grounds for belief, when evidence and argument are indecisive. Interesting parallels appear in G.E. Moore, whose similarities to the Scottish realists have been well documented by Alan White.[8] And when Kierkegaard for his part complains that the age of reason is without passion, the passionate belief he wants is a whole-hearted, whole-personal commitment. An age without passion, he says in *The Present Age*, is an age without values. Man neither lives nor believes by reason alone, but by what he most values, with his whole heart.

My point is that the whole-part relationship of belief to knowledge fits not only the CC-R relationship but also the relationship of human existence to more universal kinds of cognitive belief.

2. *Practice and Theory*

Again the Platonic model has shaped our thinking. Reason, for Plato, is theoretical, detached from the world of particulars, and it contemplates unchanging universals for their own sake. *Theōreō*, of course, has to do with contemplative knowledge and is used, significantly, to describe spectators who watch but do not participate. Dewey aptly spoke of the "spectator theory of knowledge."

The Cartesians developed a different philosophic method, but the theoretical ideal still prevailed. While Descartes included willing, doubting, understanding, and other such cognitive activity in his *cogito*, his philosophy functions with a more limited notion of reason as thinking clear and distinct ideas and deducing logical conclusions. Yet for all *practical* purposes, much of what he tried to prove theoretically was already beyond any serious doubt.

Bacon's method and his "knowledge is power" pointed in a more practical direction. Eventually Hume and Kant called into question the classic disjunction of theory and practice. Purely theoretical thought, they both argued, fails. A more holistic approach is needed. Said Hume, ". . . be a philosopher, but be still a man"; and Kant observed the demands of practical reason on the man who acts. The Scottish realist concurs.

We have, then, two models: the Platonic and Cartesian disjunction of practice from theory, and the whole-part model that sees theory as one function arising in the practical context of life itself. Two extremes arise. On the one hand, the "pure theory" extreme fosters an elitist attitude to theoretical thought. It fails to recognize that creaturely rationality exists in order to serve, and it lacks epistemic modesty—all this in addition to epistemological problems which the Cartesian project faces. On the other hand, a "purely practical" approach can become relativistic when, in the case of Dewey, it relates all inquiry to particular problem situations without paying attention to universalities in human life and practice. Similarly, in the case of Marx, theory becomes an ideology at the service of social revolution. From a theistic standpoint, this is too anthropocentric; our particular human ends become the focus of theory as well as of practice.

I find a less objectionable whole-part model in the writings of John Macmurray, a model more closely related to Kant than to Dewey or Marx. Action is the primary and all-inclusive concept, while R is derivative and abstract. A theory of knowledge presupposes and is part of a theory of action.[9] More recently, Nicholas Wolterstorff has distinguished three kinds of justification for theoretical work: the Pythagorean, in which theory has moral value for the thinker; the Baconian, in which theory gives us power to change the world; and the Aquinian, in which theory is justified by the worth of its object, the eternal and ultimately the divine. Wolterstorff argues that the question must be resolved by what we say about the scholar's task in the present condition of God's creation. That task is part of our overall calling. Theory is a part of praxis as a whole. We are first responsible agents who act. Theoretical work is part of that responsibility, serving the same overall ends as any other kind of action.[10]

Action and practice are grand and somewhat vague notions. Wolterstorff properly relates theory to man's overall life-project, which he defines in biblical terms as contributing to "justice in shalōm." But there are other universals, too. Theory serves universal "action spheres" common to humankind: economic, political, aesthetic, sexual and familial, and so forth. Human action, in other words, is not an unstructured variable, but reflects universal structures of human existence within the structures of God's creation. Human action pursues mandates that God has ordained for our relationship to nature, to other persons, and to ourselves. Theory also operates within these parameters, controlled not only by cognitive beliefs but also by the objective structure of universal action spheres of which it is part. We are responsible in our economic, political, aesthetic or other theorizing—just as much as in our other activities—to the ends God has ordained.

The whole-part relation between practice and theory, then, lays responsibility on the theoretician to consider not only objective structures revealed in experience but also God's purposes for economic, political, familial, aesthetic and other activities. R is thus a function of CC.

3. *Subjectivity and Objectivity*

The same pattern applies here as in the two previous formulations: in an effort to avoid the pitfalls of relativism and subjectivism, classical epistemology demanded a purely objective knowledge devoid of subjective elements or influence. This ideal was most pronounced in the Enlightenment, as seen in Locke's *tabula rasa*, for example. When objective facts and scientifically controlled observations took over, positivism became king. And many empiricists still seek a hard core of objective data on which foundationalist proofs can be built.

Realistic theories of knowledge might seem to tend in the objectivist direction. This was clearly the case for American neo-realism with its objective relativism, but not so with other theories. Scottish realism based its laws of belief on the constitution of the human subject. Critical realism, in the cases of Santayana and Whitehead at least, reverted to something visceral in addition to the ideas we intuit and objectify. Universal aspects of human subject-hood are involved.

More relative aspects are also involved, as recent work in the sociology of knowledge, the philosophy of science, and hermeneutics has made plain. One such variable, of course, is CC (or its alternatives). This is the holistic response to God of a human subject, and it influences his thinking, his selectivity and perceptivity. Individual as well as universal subject-hood must be considered.

Complete subjectivity is neither desirable nor logically implied. Fair consideration of all sides of a question, honest judgments, and careful assessment of evidence are morally obligatory, to whatever extent they are humanly possible. Individual prejudices and ignorance can be at least partly transcended, but the generic concerns of human subjects are with us always. And this is a good thing because it keeps us, as Kierkegaard remarked and Scottish realism implies, from endless indecision whenever any shade of incompleteness or of logical uncertainty persists.

Some alternative is needed in epistemology other than the extremes of complete objectivity and complete subjectivity. We can take a first step toward such an alternative by adopting a distinction I have drawn elsewhere[11] between two very different senses of objectivity and subjectivity that are often confused: the metaphysical and epistemological. Metaphysical objectivity is the objective reality of a state of affairs, independent of whether we know anything about it at all. Thus sticks and stones and cabbages and kings exist objectively, and so does God, and so do certain structures of his creation. But unicorns and centaurs have no such metaphysical objectivity, at least in the sense of reality we apply to cabbages or dogs. They exist only in our imagination and myths, in our minds, dependent on their being known. Their status is metaphysically subjective.

On the other hand, epistemological objectivity is the knower's attitude of detachment, unconcern, uninvolvement in regard to an object of his inquiry. Epistemological subjectivity is his involvement and personal concern with whatever he may consider.

The distinction pays dividends. Some rationalists are concerned that any admission of subjectivity is a denial of metaphysical as well as epistemological objectivity, but that is certainly not the case and does not logically follow. My knowledge of what is independently real may well be subjectively influenced and may involve me passionately, but that does not affect its metaphysical status. Metaphysical objectivity and epistemological subjectivity are quite compatible with each other and come ready-mixed all the time. Fears to the contrary are unfounded.

Yet again, concern is voiced that once we admit subjectivity, all objective controls are lost. Objectivity and subjectivity, both in the metaphysical sense, may indeed be incompatible and mutually exclusive, but not in the epistemological sense. Objective controls do still operate—public evidence and logical arguments, for example—at the same time as subjective influences like personal commitments and predispositions, fears and hopes. And these controls can help us clarify our commitments, resolve our fears, abandon some hopes, and otherwise change our minds. Knowing is in every case an individual mix of subjective and objective factors.

Subjectivity need not be a liability for R, because there is significance in those areas of need and value which all human beings experience. Our physical needs show subjectively the reality of our bodies and cry out for the reality of a physical world of which we are part and on which we depend. And it counts epistemologically that our inner being yearns for other persons, and that togetherness and empathy reveal us to one another for what in reality we are. Epistemologically it is significant that our hearts are restless, as Augustine observed, until they rest in God. Subjectivity is an asset as well as sometimes a liability in knowing.

Michael Polanyi, scientist turned philosopher, speaks of a tacit dimension and of personal factors in science and knowledge. We always attend, he says, *from* something (the proximal) *to* something (the distal), and the former influences how the latter appears to us, what meaning it conveys, and how it is related to everything else.[12] Subjective and peripheral factors, in other words, focus attention and elicit belief.

Subjectivity, I suggest, represents the whole of our being, out of which we think and with which we believe and seek to know. Objectivity is a move we make in reflection by temporarily and partially transcending what we are and holding our lives and the demands of our being in abeyance. But we seek this objectivity because of what we are subjectively, because of the truth we need and want and value. The same pattern holds here as with knowledge and belief, and with theory and practice: knowledge with certainty, along with theory and objectivity, while unduly elevated in the Greek and Enlightenment traditions, represent one important part of things but not the whole. The necessities of our existence as human subjects require more; a man's life does not consist in the abundance or scarcity of objective and logically certain theories he possesses. Subjectivity is more holistic than objectivity and yields a fuller knowledge.

III. Universal and Particular Beliefs

We have now come to a preliminary conclusion that is crucial to what follows: the whole-part relationship between commitment and rationality applies to generic, human life-commitments as well as to something as specific as CC. In one case the universal basic beliefs evoked are essential to universal humanness, and in the other case more specific beliefs evoked are essential to specifically *Christian* commitment. Both in effect are perspectival beliefs, from the perspective of a life-world: in the one case the perspective of the universal human life-world, and in the other case a particular additional perspective. On the one hand, the Scottish realist stresses the universal; on the other hand the Kuyperian stresses the particular; but both agree that belief is rooted in the inner heart of one's human existence.

John Calvin sounds at one juncture like a Scottish realist:

> The manifold agility of the soul, which enables it to take a survey of heaven and earth; to join the past and present; to retain the memory of things heard long ago; to conceive of whatever it chooses by the help of imagination; its ingenuity also in the invention of such admirable arts,—are certain proofs of the divinity of man.[13]

He traces universal cognitive activities, (R) to the nature of man, thanks to the Creator. Granted that reason is partly debilitated by sin and retains more ability in things "terrestrial" than in "celestial things," the light of truth is still admirably displayed in its works.[14]

Note the similarity to this, and to Calvin's *sensus deitatis*, in Thomas Reid's arguments. God so constituted the mind, says Reid, that we believe without proof that external objects exist; we believe memory tells of a past; we believe the causal principle and the axioms of geometry; we believe there is a distinction between right and wrong, and that God exists—in the general sense of a Being on whom we depend and to whom we are responsible.[15]

So sure is Reid of this, that a man like Descartes who doubts his own existence:

> . . . is surely as unfit to be reasoned with as a man that believes he is made of glass. There may be disorders in the human frame that produce such extravagancies, but they will never be cured by reasoning.[16]

These beliefs which we know so surely to be true, moreover, are spontaneous interpretations of experience rather than logical inferences. The appearance of a sign is followed by belief in the thing signified: a sensation by belief in its present existence or a remembrance by belief in its past existence. Yet imagination is not accompanied by belief at all. This is all due to the human constitution, a matter of common sense, not reason, and it is common to all men. Our very nature evokes beliefs and bears witness to their truth.

Parenthetically, Pascal's "the heart has its reasons that reason does not know" is somewhat similar, too. Pascal says the "heart" believes much the same things as Reid affirms and, if I am not mistaken, "heart" for Pascal refers to the inner constitution of man. Universal belief-evoking conditions of a holistic sort make such beliefs practically unavoidable. Calvin, Pascal and Reid seem to concur at least in that regard.

1. In principle I also concur, but with qualifications. First, the existence of an external world is more readily accepted as a universal basic belief than is its nature. The existence of some natural order is clearer than the exact nature of its causal relations. The existence of some ultimate reality, with which we must reckon, falls significantly short of the existence of a personal God to whom we are responsible; indeed, the seed of religion in humankind comes to fruition in vastly misshapen ways. The practical and holistic demands of human nature and existence may require belief that things and other people exist, but what we believe about them is shaped as well by cultural, scientific, historical and psychological influences. Existence is surer than essence.

Second, the Scottish tradition therefore seems to extend unduly the scope of universal basic beliefs rooted in our inner constitution. My inclinations are more modest. The law of non-contradiction is essential for meaningful discourse and action, as Aristotle's negative demonstration shows. Likewise something like a principle of induction is needed. But these are formal principles without much material content. We can add the existence of external objects with properties of some uncertain sort and in a coherent arrangement for some reason or other. I can include my own existence and my mental states, and the existence of other persons analagous to myself who share the world I inhabit. We can add that we are able to communicate one with another, and have a part in ordering our lives together.[17] And I would include the belief that something is basic to all this, whatever it is, and that I have to reckon with such an ultimate reality in the final analysis. But I am not sure that anything much more specific than this will qualify for tenure as a universal basic belief. The existence of a personal theistic being may indeed have been a basic belief for unfallen man, but it is not as for fallen people. God-substitutes fall tragically short.

Third, Reid proposed that his universal basic beliefs were first principles from which reason could deduce the other knowledge it seeks. Hodge's claims depend on it. For this "foundationalist" position, reminiscent of Plato, Aristotle and Descartes, I have limited hope because of the limited scope of universal basic beliefs. Problems also arise with the intrusion of different scientific paradigms or different religious and world-view perspectives, or whatever. Yet all is not thereby lost to reason: more modest claims remain.

2. But someone will object that if reason is not autonomous, neither are universal basic beliefs theory-neutral and independent of religious commitments of one sort or another. Several replies are possible.

(a) As Reid sees it, universal basic beliefs are pre-theoretical, rooted in the demands of the human constitution rather than in reason. They are evoked by human biological, psychological and social conditions that are both universal and essential to our humanness. Thus, accepting these beliefs in their rudimentary and pre-theoretical form is significantly different from accounting for them in some theoretical way. The rationalist may even accept them in practice while doubting or denying them in theory (this is the paradox that puzzled G.E. Moore). But the theist has good theoretical reason for neither doubting nor denying them, if he believes like Reid that God made us and our world in this belief-evoking way, and that God does not deceive. Regardless of whether accepting these beliefs is a religiously neutral practice, justifying them is not.

(b) Yet universal and particular beliefs are not mutually exclusive of each other. Universal belief-evoking conditions function in particular historical and cultural ways. Particular belief-evoking conditions are variations within universal conditions. Together they provide a common matrix for belief. Our common humanness in a common world not only evokes the universal belief that, for instance, external objects and people exist, but our commonness also calls for more particular beliefs about things and people. It not only evokes belief in some ultimate reality with which we must reckon, but it also needs more specific beliefs about ultimate being that can illuminate and guide our life and thought.

Universal basic beliefs are in practice unavoidable by any human subject. They are necessary but insufficient for what any of us need to think and live. *That* we act implies universal beliefs. *How* we act depends on what specific content these beliefs are given. We need beliefs in every sphere of human action (the economic, familial, political, aesthetic, etc.) in order to find order and direction to our activity in those spheres. It is here that other than universal belief-evoking conditions intrude, not only specifically religious, but also historical, cultural, psychological and scientific conditions. The universal remains hungry for the more specific, which the universal alone cannot supply. Believing there is a natural order, we need to know what it really is like. Believing there is an ultimate existent, our hearts are restless until they can rest in something more.

While some rudimentary outlines of universal belief may be theory-neutral, therefore, I suggest that nobody holds merely rudimentary outlines. Universal beliefs turn out to be loaded differently for people of differing perspectives. Reid's are loaded with a Christian perspective influenced by 18th century science; our perspective is much different. Doubtless the influence of CC varies in degree, as Emil Brunner points out, so that ideas of matter and causation are less affected than ideas of man and God.

3. What, then, can we say about the relation of universal to particular beliefs, especially those inherent in CC?

(a) Universal beliefs provide the backdrop, the context for particular beliefs. He who comes to God must believe that God is. And he who confesses that Christ is come in the flesh must believe that an external world of things and people exists. Universal beliefs are prerequisite to Christian belief: they do not logically imply it, but they remain necessary even if not sufficient.

(b) It follows that just as universal basic beliefs are articulated in some particular historical form, so, too, that particular historical form provides the vehicle for articulating distinctively Christian beliefs (functions 9 and 10). What sort of a physical world did God create—Aristotelian or Newtonian? How do we understand the nature of persons? How does this affect our God-concept? The articulation of theology has been influenced by how we answer questions such as these. Scientific and other variables influence human thought, including thought in Christian perspective.

(c) From the relation of Christian to universal basic beliefs it also follows, I think, that while CC unifies R's understanding, what it unifies includes universal basic beliefs particularized in historical ways. A Christian world-view is incarnated accordingly in particular historical forms, and Christian philosophy emerges as a somewhat pluralistic tradition. The Kuyperian and Scottish traditions are not alone: we might also give a place to Cambridge Platonism or to Jonathan Edwards.

(d) Even apart from the foundationalist hope, universal basic beliefs contribute to the justification of Christian beliefs in at least two ways. First, they eliminate some options. Solipsism, for example, is not just one more position alongside other particular beliefs to be examined. Solipsism contradicts universal basic beliefs, yet any discussion of it would in practice affirm them. It is in practice self-contradictory. Nihilism of the sort that denies any intelligibly structured reality or world order also stands in contradiction to universal basic beliefs. Yet one cannot live or think consistently that way: in practice one has to affirm what nihilism denies. But if the denial of any structured reality is in practice self-contradictory, then the affirmation of some structured reality is necessarily correct.

Again, if we take seriously our universal basic beliefs about intersubjectivity, then certain extremist political views are eliminated. For if I have direct self-awareness along with an empathetic awareness of other persons analogous to myself in a world analogous to my own, then the respect I claim for myself as a person must logically be claimed also for other persons. On the one hand, then, any extreme totalitarianism that disrespects the value of persons is humanly unacceptable, as is any extreme individualism that ignores the good of others and the common good. Universal basic beliefs thus place limits on what positions we might as humans and as Christians consistently adopt, and argue against some of the insanities of the age—as Socrates argued against Thrasymachus. If particular beliefs are indeed evoked as something specific that we need to think and live with, then beliefs that with consistency are "un-think-with-able" (as is nihilism) or "un-live-with-able" (as is solipsism) are ruled out.

Second, universal basic beliefs allow other possible options. They serve as control beliefs, eliminating some alternatives but still allowing a variety of possibilities. No single economic or political theory is implied, nor just one view of God or man. Do universal beliefs then contribute at all positively to the justification of Christian belief? Assuming that the deductive and inductive inferences of foundationalism cannot do the job, we need a logic of "adduction"; for Christian (and other particular) beliefs are, as it were, adduced or proposed to fill a theoretical and practical need unsatisfied by rudimentary, universal, basic beliefs alone. One approach might be sought in forms of functional description 3: CC affects R's selectivity and perceptivity. That is to say, Christianity gives to R a peculiarly revealing kind of specificity, alerting R to important considerations which might otherwise be omitted. This is a telling point for CC. It means that while universal beliefs are in practice not a neutral check on CC, they combine with particular beliefs to form an inclusive and coherent scheme.

Consider also functional description 10: R expounds and elaborates on CC's cognitive content. Thereby it exhibits CC's consistency and plausibility, and removes mistaken objections.

Consider also functional description 12: R pursues cultural tasks mandated, illuminated and informed by CC, thereby exhibiting CC's eminent "think-with-ability" and "live-with-ability."

And consider functional description 6: CC gives unity to R. Insofar as other commitments might also unify R, this becomes a matter of degrees of coherence. Does CC unify R to a greater degree, more naturally, or without arbitrarily forcing things where they do not fit? Does CC unify R more "livably" and "thinkably" in terms of the practical demands of life and thought? Does CC really satisfy in a unified way the practical and theoretical needs which call for more than rudimentary universal beliefs can give?

But this brings us back to the whole-part relationship of practice to theory and of commitment to rationality.[18] Parallels exist between universal and Christian beliefs in this regard, in that both arise under belief-evoking conditions of a holistic sort. The witness of the Holy Spirit and the divine calling are, after all, addressed to the whole person in the very heart of his being, and faith is the holistic response of the heart. In this light, consider the following list of terms I have used or referred to in this paper, and how some of them at least might apply to the context of Christian as well as of universal beliefs:

form of life
perspective
life-world
God-given functions of reason
laws of belief impressed upon our nature
certitude
practice
praxis
universal action spheres
structures of human existence
Moore's paradox
the heart has its reasons
Aristotle's negative demonstration
common-sense beliefs
universal aspects of human subject-hood
belief-evoking conditions
the holistic life-context of the human subject and human action
think-with-ability
live-with-ability
whole-part relationship

I have toyed with various "umbrella" labels for this kind of life-demand to which such language refers, and I suggest "practical necessity": "practical" in the holistic sense that embraces in a unified fashion the demands of every aspect of our being, acting and thinking in this world; "necessity" in the sense that it is unavoidable without contradiction between practice and theory. Practical necessity is the demand of the whole on the part, of life on thought. A belief would be a universal practical necessity if the consistent practice of our humanness depends on it. And a belief would be a practical necessity for CC in particular if the consistent practice of CC depends on it. And plainly the consistent practice of CC depends in part on the same beliefs as does the consistent practice of humanness generally.

This should be spelled out more fully, so I will offer two suggestions. Years ago, I suggested that we distinguish between "necessary beliefs" and (alluding to Hume) purely "customary beliefs," the former molded by essential human factors, the latter by accidental factors. The former "represent certain root needs" and basic "commitments" which no man can avoid whatever his place in history or culture, and whatever his philosophical position.[19] Again, it seems to me that practical necessity relates not only to the demands of life and thought in general or as a whole, but to the demands that every universal, human, value area and action sphere (economic, familial, ethical, political, etc.) make on life and thought. Universal basic beliefs alone do not satisfy those demands—they provide too rudimentary an outline for living and thinking effectively. Christian beliefs are necessary, I suggest, as an essential part of a Christian commitment to the God whose word of grace speaks to every area of values and action and fleshes out universal basic beliefs in those areas in a coherent and livable way. This is much more specific than coherence *überhaupt:* it is a meaning-giving and life-directing capacity that could be perceived in particular disciplines and particular human enterprises.

A CC that unifies all this is one about which, as Pascal said, the heart has reasons (R) of its own that reason in the narrow sense does not know.

Notes

1. See his "Wheaton lectures" in *The Philosophy of Gordon H. Clark*, ed. by Ronald H. Nash (Presbyterian and Reformed Publishing Co., 1968).
2. *Christian Philosophy in the Twentieth Century* (Craig Press, 1969).
3. Roger Trigg, *Reason and Commitment* (Cambridge University Press, 1973), p. 166.
4. See Wittgenstein's *Lecture and Conversations on Aesthetics, Psychology and Religious Belief*, ed. by Cyril Barrett (University of California Press, 1966), pp. 53-72.
5. Cp. T.S. Kuhn's comparison of a revolutionary change in scientific paradigms to a religious conversion. His discussions of the sociology of science, as well as similarities to Wittgenstein's "forms of life," merit consideration in regards to the relation of CC to R.
6. *Systematic Theology* (1871; Eerdmans Publishing Co., 1952), vol. I, pp. 50-55.
7. *The Works of Thomas Reid, D.D.*, ed. by Sir William Hamilton (James Thin, 1895), vol. I, pp. 108, 230, etc.
8. Alan White, *G.E. Moore* (Blackwell, 1958), pp. 192-199.
9. *The Self as Agent* (Faber and Faber, 1957), especially ch. 4.
10. "Theory and Praxis," *Christian Scholar's Review*, IX (1980), 317.
11. *All Truth is God's Truth* (Eerdmans, 1977), ch. I.
12. See Polanyi's *The Tacit Dimension* (Doubleday, 1966).
13. *Institutes of the Christian Religion*, trans. by John Allen (Eerdmans, 1949), vol. I, p. 67. Calvin's uses of logic are discussed by R.H. Ayers in "Language, Logic, and Reason in Calvin's *Institutes*," *Religious Studies* XVI (1980), 283.
14. *Ibid.*, pp. 292ff.
15. *Op. cit.*, pp. 191ff.

16. P. 100. Cp. Wittgenstein, *On Certainty* (Harper Torch Books, 1972), pp. 674-675, and p. 344: "my life consists in being content to accept many things."
17. See Alfred Schutz, *The Structure of the Life-World* (Northwestern University Press, 1973).
18. I am indebted to Professor Galen Johnson of University of Rhode Island for discussions that helped to clarify the final part of this paper.
19. "Moore's Appeal to Common Sense," *J. of Philos*, LVIII (1961), 197. Cp. my *All Truth is God's Truth*, ch. 7, where I argue that the law of non-contradiction and principle of induction are "practical necessities." In larger scope see E.J. Carnell on a "third way of Knowing" in *Christian Commitment* (Eerdmans, 1957) and *The Kingdom of Love and the Pride of Life* (Eerdmans, 1960) with its more psychological orientation.

The Articulation of Belief: A Link between Rationality and Commitment

Hendrik Hart

WHAT IS THE RELATIONSHIP BETWEEN RATIONALITY and commitment? In this essay I will discuss some conceptual elements of one possible framework for dealing with this question. In particular, I want to explore some concrete, functional dimensions of that relation. This material will appear in the second major section of this paper. Before I can begin this discussion, however, I will need to deal with some preliminary matters.

First I will offer an indication of the type of problem I have in mind. I hope this will help establish that the seemingly abstruse theoretical discussions in the final sections of the essay do relate to well-known, philosophically interesting and important problems. Following this introductory material I will provide a summary of the approach I have in mind. In this way the proximity of the problems to the solutions offered, presented at the beginning of the essay, will help to integrate my project.

Because my approach differs from the philosophizing currently *en vogue* among English-speaking philosophers, I will need to clarify some things. For this reason I will first present what I find the relevant historical background material to the current debate on rationality in relation to commitment. I will also summarize elements of my own views, which may help readers understand better what I intend to say. This summary will outline my use of some key terms and my understanding of a few contextual issues. Finally, I will also mention some of the complexities of the discussion, in order to share an awareness of the difficulties I had to face in coming to terms with material for this essay.

The second main section has three sub-sections. These will outline the mutual support that reason and commitment provide for each other. The first sub-section will deal with rationality as it is rooted in faith. The second will deal with the priority relations between faith and reason. The third sub-section deals with aspects of one common Christian faith for all believers who subscribe to it.

1. Preliminary Discussions

I need to construct a bridge from my way of perceiving things to the more customary conceptual frameworks of current philosophy in the English-speaking world. Hence a discussion of some contextual issues is in order at this point.

Some Perceptions of the Problem

My analysis of the faith-reason problem in this essay lies mainly within the context of what has been written by Calvinists. Among Calvinists there have been two principal points of view for dealing with Christian faith and its relation to rationality. One point of view has been influenced by the Reidean common-sense tradition, and the other is familiar to us from the work of continental theologians such as Barth, Bavinck or Kuyper.[1] The most prominent difference between them is this: the common-sense-oriented thinkers ascribe a greater independence to rationality than do the continental scholars. I believe these two traditions have made significant progress in discussing the relation of rationality to our shared faith. In the last twenty-five years they appear in fact to have come to an agreement on at least two crucial points: reason is not religiously autonomous (in an Enlightenment sense), and there is more to knowledge than simply its discursive, inferential, rational dimension.

However, I believe there is still much work to be done in order to make these agreements *operational*. For example, I tend to react to a philosophical position not merely on the basis of how its author *articulates a concept* of that position; I react even more on the basis of how the author *works philosophically with* that position. And in the context of my concerns I am interested in what we *do* with reason, particularly in relation to the various issues surrounding the traditional faith-reason dilemma.

As a result, I am prompted to ask many questions. How should we view rational or natural theology? What is meant by reason, when contrasted with faith and revelation? Why is religious belief not rational in the traditional sense? What do we say about a distinction between confessional language and propositions? Can we make something of what may be called Calvin's exceptional position on faith as knowledge, rather than faith as belief? What are the implications when knowledge in turn is treated as some sort of belief? Could faith just be knowledge as belief, in distinction from knowledge as perceptual or knowledge as conceptual? What do we mean when we say God is rational? How can we truly infer things about God if our language about him is not univocal? If reason, for the Calvinists, is under the judgment of revelation, can reason also judge revelation in some sense? Arguments are logically compelling, but is it also necessary to say, on the basis of argument, that God *must* such and so? *Must* God anything at all? Who or what makes him? I have had these practical philosophical *consequences* of a view of rationality in mind as I explored my approach to *commitment in relation to rationality*.

To repeat, other Calvinists and I share the *thesis* that reason is not religiously autonomous, and we *argue* the *proposition* that knowledge is more than rationality. But do we also live with these shared views in a practical, unified way? Perhaps a brief look at earlier philosophers might help us here.

After the Greeks rejected the ultimate authority of the myth as an organizing principle of their society, they began to look for community, certainty, authority, truth and so forth in reason. In the Middle Ages, scholars temporarily challenged this position. They balanced the position of reason with their belief in the ultimate authority of revelation. This Medieval synthesis between the authority of dialectic and the authority of revelation had been established in the struggle between the universities and the church. After some time, however, it appeared this synthesis had failed to satisfy the thirst for certainty and truth in Western thinkers. The attempt was only partially successful, and it was largely limited to the life of faith. Descartes re-established the ultimate authority of reason in our culture, not primarily through *argument* but through the *proclamation* of reason's virtues. He ushered in our modern tradition. From Descartes to Hume a new climate was now established. A rational justification of knowledge took the place of the Medieval synthesis; a rationally unjustified belief in reason became the origin of certainty, truth and authority.

Until very recently the modern commitment to rationality went largely unchallenged in such movements as rationalism, positivism or scientism. In these movements attitudes such as foundationalism or evidentialism indicate the presence of an almost hidden commitment to rationality. Calvin and some of his adherents were wary of reason precisely because of this commitment. Other Calvinians, notably those influenced by Thomas Reid, were much less suspicious of reason. Nevertheless, they *also* challenged any facile or narrow rationalism. Reid was quite aware that it was unreasonable to demand that all knowledge be rationally justified, except the epistemic claim itself that knowledge would be knowledge only if it were rationally justified.

This problem is especially acute today because the difficulties of relying on reason are becoming more apparent. As inheritors of the Calvinian tradition, how can we come closer to understanding what the proper place of rationality is in our *lives?* Surely we need to take a closer look at how we treat reason in relation to faith, the Bible and God, i.e., in the traditionally contentious areas.

I have doubts about some of our opinions concerning the proper uses of reason. They seem not to stem from a careful and critical investigation of reason based on the religiously ultimate point of view of revelation. Instead, some of these opinions appear to come to us via the tradition of a community that is religiously committed to the ultimacy of reason.[2] We *have* taken our distance from that tradition in some ways. I am thinking of Plantinga's efforts, for example. Commitment to reason, he argues, is self-referentially incoherent. Similarly, Alston says reason cannot be rationally justified.[3] Plantinga has also tried to argue that belief in God is rational after all; it is properly basic. These efforts, however, may keep us too tied to the problematics of the Western tradition. Do they allow us to discover the internal problems of the very approach we inherited from the tradition of commitment to reason? Why do we differ so sharply on whether it is proper to argue about God?[4] Why is there so much controversy about the very use of the term *rational?*

Let me take up this matter of the term *rational* for a moment. It has a burden of meaning carried over from traditions committed to rationality. For this reason I think we should use it with care. Is it really true, for example, that we can innocently use this term to describe the *norm* for the *cognitive* enterprise? But why should we use *rational* in that case? Why should the norm for good belief or knowledge not require that it be socially relevant, just, liberating, sensitive or whatever else? Why just *rational?* The use of *rational* to name *the* cognitive norm may tempt us to slip back into seeing knowledge as *narrowly* propositional. When we use the term *rational*, and we say we have nothing in mind narrowly connected with reason as argument and inference, we may at least be *historically* insensitive. Traditionally, rational justification meant validation before the high court of reason.[5]

I believe this problem is more than terminological. Today the justification of *knowledge* is usually taken to follow the line of the justification of belief or the formation of true belief. But in this connection we often see how truth, belief and knowledge are all conceived exclusively in relation to propositions. And that lands us right back in the dangerous realm of a narrow propositional view of knowledge.

Perhaps we should pursue this problem further. Is believing an assent to propositions? If we regard knowledge *as* belief and belief *as* propositional, we cannot also claim that knowledge is wider than propositional. There is a well-known difference between understanding a proposition and assenting to it. But if this is the case, why do we connect belief or assent only with propositions? Can belief not simply be a species of faith which only in some instances is related to propositions? And if so, was it so strange for Calvin to see faith as knowledge, if indeed knowing is sometimes believing and believing is a sort of faith?

There is another point here. If knowledge is more than an assent to propositions, then even if beliefs are propositional, the justification of belief would not be the same as the justification of knowledge.[6] At the same time, if rational justification is justification by reasons, then justification of belief would be meaningful only for propositional beliefs. It would not be meaningful for other forms of faith which, not being propositional, would hardly be candidates for inferential justification.

Preview of My Approach

Let me now briefly summarize how I will address these concerns in the second major section of this essay. There I conceive of *knowledge* as broadly as possible. In this regard I agree with what Alston says about knowing God. He says our awareness of God, our understanding of both God and God's will for our lives, requires total involvement and living commitment, spiritual practice as well as rational cognition.[7] However, I hasten to add that in my view this requirement holds for the knowledge of anything whatsoever. So I use the term *knowledge* to refer to the integral and coherent unity of all the many dimensions of experience. Some of these dimensions we easily recognize, such as perception, conception and belief. But I could also mention some less acknowledged dimensions, such as the ethical, political, social or economic sides of knowledge.

The conceptual dimension of knowledge I will designate by the term *rational*. I believe I am historically and systematically justified in saying rationality is associated with concepts and propositions, inference and argument, syllogistic processes, conclusions and premises, and with reasoning and analysis. And I mean to include *process* as well as *result*, i.e., forming as well as holding a concept, arriving at as well as understanding a proposition, having a reason as well as reasoning or giving reasons. I will use the terms *rational, rationality, reason* (when meaning the human faculty as well as the ground for an argument), *reasoning* and *reasonable* exclusively to refer to this area of human knowing and knowledge. My use of *rational* as a form of commendation, a norm, is derived from this. Thus, all the phenomena in this realm of knowledge that are appropriately formed are called *rational*, in the sense of both *being* of this kind *and* being that *successfully*. All phenomena that *are* of this kind but do *not* meet the appropriate *standards* are *irrational*. Thus, feelings, emotions and faith are *not* irrational, whereas faulty arguments, ill-formed propositions, etc., *are* irrational.

All knowledge, as I conceive of it, has rational dimensions; it is *in part* conceptual, propositional, inferential and discursive. But it is *also* sensitive in its perceptive dimensions, symbolic in its semantic dimensions, aesthetic in artistic knowing, fiduciary in its credulity dimensions. In all knowing, all levels of knowing are involved, and these are all involved coherently with one another. This can easily be seen if we call to mind, for example, that concepts have perceptual foundations, that in order to become operational they must be believed, and that many things will never be believed if they are seen to have unjust implications. But to know something is always more than knowing *that* it is such and such. Even true knowledge of something, i.e., knowing something truly, is more than knowing *that* it is true *that* it is such and such.

In our work we sometimes overrate the rational dimension or act as though that is all we need. Sometimes we think knowledge is not justified unless it is rationally justified. In these instances we are influenced by conceptual attitudes fostered in rationalism, evidentialism, foundationalism, positivism, scientism, etc. I take all of these to contain variations of the same basic attitude: a religious commitment to rationality or to absolutized, conceptual knowing. But in that case, what about the sociology of knowledge, the politics of science, the ethics of research, the communality of a paradigm or the commitment involved in our attachment to certain basic propositions? These all point to a need to pay more attention to dimensions of knowing *other* than the rational. We must develop a comprehensive view in which we try to understand the structural coherence of all of these dimensions.

Philosophers tend to look at *truth in knowing* primarily as a propositional matter, and consequently they favor a correspondence view over a coherence view. But if we take into *active* account what others may say about aesthetic or artistic truth, about intuitive or imaginative truth, about doing the truth or being in the truth (trying to take these as much more than mere metaphors), and we place this in relation to a contextual or integral view of knowledge, then the coherentist view of truth may well commend itself to us also.

Having said all this, however, I want to stress again that I do indeed recognize a rational dimension to knowing—in fact, to all knowing. In many cases that dimension *legitimately dominates* our knowing, and we may then simply speak of rational knowledge (recognizing that even *it* has many *other* dimensions). Naturally, we will then have to make up our minds when we speak of intellectual, epistemic or cognitive concerns, whether we then mean this rational sort of knowledge or whether we mean all knowing. But in any case there *is* rational knowing, and there must be rationality in *all* knowing. And both rational knowledge and that rational dimension of knowledge must conform to norms for rationality, norms that are particularly investigated in what we call the study of formal logic.

In this essay I am especially concerned with the role of rationality-in-knowledge in relation to faith, belief, commitment or credulity-in-knowledge. *Each*, I will argue, has priority in a certain context and of a certain kind. Each can be called fundamental, basic, prerequisite or a ground. Each has a unique role that the other cannot play. Given this premise, I will argue that faith knowledge, which has *its* own uniqueness in questions of ultimacy and finality and originality (especially as grounded in revelation), does have a proper right to prescribe to reason. Rational knowing can legitimately accept some of faith's deliverances on ultimate matters without justifying them rationally beforehand. Thus, the confessed meaning of divine revelation, especially in Scripture, can legitimately be called upon to *lead* inferential procedures. This might be called a contribution from the Kuyperian/Calvinian camp. For this reason the Kuyperian/Calvinian does not trust natural theology because in his view it makes deliverances of faith dependent on deliverances of reason. Where certainty, truth and knowledge must all be finally justified rationally, or must be grounded in basic rational propositions, there the Kuyperian/Calvinist sees a confrontation with demands of a commitment, i.e., a religious surrender, to rationality. Yet rationality, in that case, itself does not require rational justification and, in not requiring this, hides its own commitment from itself. Such commitment has led to distortions in our view of knowledge and even in our view of rationality itself.

So I will argue instead that rationality must be rooted in a commitment and directed by a commitment outside of rationality. Faith gives reason the ultimate word on what is ultimately true. Faith directs reason to what is finally real and to what is originally real. When we try to understand what we believe, however, reason does tell faith just what is *conceptually* possible and necessary to think. Yet reason is correct only when directed by faith, even when it understands faith. At the same time, faith is understandable only when, even in our final surrender, we stick to what is legitimately conceivable.

It is important to appreciate that faith knowledge and rational knowledge are somewhat different. Although each has elements of the other, each also displays an ultimately irreducible difference. Faith knowledge does have rational elements, for example, but we cannot finally judge it on the basis of whether it is rational. Faith knowledge, being what it is, transcends rationality, even in its own confessional belief content. Thus, even the belief content of faith in an important sense can be grasped in faith only, and it transcends understanding. On the other hand, rational knowledge, genuine propositional knowledge, does need to be judged on the basis of its rationality. But rational knowledge, I will argue, is primarily our understanding of propositional phenomena. Therefore the acceptance of rational knowledge in belief should usually have rational grounds. Yet, in spite of that, we know that many propositions are basic in any rational-noetic system. They are accepted, not on the basis of their rationality, but on the basis of being rooted in other dependable dimensions of human knowledge, such as perception, memory, etc. Among those other dimensions is that of faith. By implication, our basic propositions will include some that are in our rational-noetic system on the basis of our faith. They are creedally-based propositions, just as others are perceptual propositions or memory propositions.

Among the basic propositions there will also be some creedally-based propositions that are crucial to a Christian commitment. I believe these must always function as control beliefs for our entire rational-noetic system. Since these creedal propositions that are basic and also function as control propositions are founded in faith, faith ultimately controls all rationality, without itself being rationally justifiable.

Historical Background

At this point it may be helpful to sketch briefly some of the main features of how I understand the faith-reason problem to be rooted in our Western intellectual heritage. The intellectual history of our civilization has left us with a legacy of ideas, I believe, which are the catalyst for the revived, contemporary interest in rationality and commitment. One conviction crucial to this legacy is that there is a faith-reason problem, due to a conflict between the two. Even if we should characterize it as a pseudo-problem, historically it has produced tension and conflict. Consequently, the problem commands our attention. The existence of this problem is closely related to the ideas just mentioned that help to revive our interest. I am thinking here of the idea that the rational order is the ultimate order of all things or that rationality is the common nature of all order. Similarly, we might take the idea that knowledge is predominantly rational, or the idea that certainty or truth are best understood from a rational point of view.[8] All of these ideas I take to be components of a single conviction: reason is autonomous.

By the autonomy of reason I mean that reason is both a law unto itself and the justification for all knowledge or even reality, and that reason itself is purely rational and independent of anything else. So by autonomy of reason I mean much more than that reason or rationality has a structure of its own or a nature of its own which must be respected. The doctrine of the autonomy of reason, either in knowledge or in all of reality, stipulates that reason recognizes no authority except its own. In our culture, acceptance of this has led to the rejection of any notion of faith as genuinely cognitive, authentically true or inherently certain.[9] Reason has itself become the main or even sole source of truth and certainty.[10]

In the past few decades, however, the doctrine of the autonomy of reason has become suspect; many thinkers regard it as an unexamined dogma which has been uncritically accepted. There are suggestions today that the idea of the autonomy of reason, in spite of its implications for the rejection of faith, is itself held in faith. Many of those who have come to this conclusion now view rationalism as a commitment to rationality in which commitment as such is rejected. Such a commitment is, of course, antinomous.[11]

This discovery has for the first time in centuries opened an important discussion: what is the relationship between rationality and faith or commitment?[12] This newly opened discussion is taking place against the background of an intense exploration of the nature of rationality. In part this inquiry is the result of the declining trust in reason in our tempestuous times. Current discussion about rationality has, as a result, produced a great volume of literature and prompted numerous conferences.[13] But just what is meant by reason or rationality is still in dispute. There is a wide spectrum of controversy about concepts of rationality; unabated rationalism lies at one extreme, and a founding of rationality in commitment at the other.[14] In between we see various shades of concepts, all aligned in colorful array. Only one thing seems clear: we are in the midst of a significant crisis regarding rationality.

For the time being no one has offered an alternative view that can count on broad acceptance. Even though almost everyone recognizes the problem, aspects of dogmatic faith in reason often prevail; they prevent us from making a clean break with problems of the past. What one school may call the main problem to be solved may be regarded by another school as the one thing to be salvaged.[15]

Deeply ingrained habits of viewing reason and knowledge in particular ways still seem to hinder us. As a result, we cannot seem to dissolve our commitment to rationality in our analysis, even when in theory we reject rationalism as a dogmatic faith in reason.[16] For example, some sort of faith—namely belief—has been domesticated within analysis ever since Hume's time. But religious faith is still suspect to believers in rationality. Consequently, the acceptable beliefs often turn out to be no more than the rationally authorized acceptance of propositions.[17] However, no matter how strong the bonds of rationalistic paradigms may still be, and in spite of the absence of generally accepted new approaches, the old defences are crumbling. Here and there commitment is given a place in analysis.[18] There are even those who posit the thesis that knowledge can be locked within the bounds of rationality or analysis or logic only at the cost of turning knowledge into ignorance.[19]

On some crucial philosophical matters, clear and precise thinking now seems impossible. For example, the philosophical foundations of all clear thinking may themselves not be clearly nor precisely conceivable.[20] Reductionism and the totalization of partial concepts is now generally suspect.[21] At the same time, totality views and integrational pluralism are stressed by many.[22] In view of these developments, the very meaning of rationality is being investigated anew.

With the discovery that belief, faith or commitment may well have something to do with rationality, we have ushered in many important questions. What is commitment? To what are we committed? Is commitment permissible within reason? How is commitment related to rationality? Are there things to which we cannot be committed? These have become, for some thinkers, pivotal questions of philosophy.

Elements of My Views

Before I can deal with some of those questions I need to set forth a few of my assumptions and explain my use of certain terms. I should also indicate the complexity of the problem. This will provide the proper context for the few specific concepts with which I will be dealing.

As I noted earlier, history has left us a legacy of ideas rooted in the belief that reason is autonomous. This belief is itself founded on a commitment to rationality, which in turn is characterized by the rejection of all commitment. (As we have seen, commitment in this legacy is understood to be irrational and therefore unacceptable as genuinely cognitive.) The view I will explore here runs quite contrary to this theme. I will suggest that all rationality is necessarily founded on commitment.[23] Indeed, I believe we maintain our commitment even when we explore the nature of the relationship between rationality and commitment. There is certainly a distinction between my (open) commitment to divine revelation and the (hidden) traditional commitment to the autonomy of reason. And this makes all the difference when we begin to explore certain questions. For example, a person committed to reason (say, a rationalist) and I may both agree on the progress of science, the close relation between rationality and order, and the stability of order. But we would not draw the same conclusions based on shared premises. I would not say order is rational either in origin or in nature. Nor would I say reason imposes its order on nature or experience.

Similarly, we may agree that rational knowledge is a peculiar kind of knowledge, with a character all its own. But I would not say this makes reason autonomous. I will grant that no proper human knowledge is either a-rational or irrational. But I do not think knowledge is always and primarily rational or solely rational. I even support another contention about typically rational knowledge, namely that it requires us to take distance from factors of subjectivity and individuality. But I do not believe rationality can ever have a neutral position with regard to commitment. I reject all of these interpretations of apparently shared givens. This is to be expected, given my views on commitment to rationality. Because I reject such a commitment, I also reject the interpretations following from that commitment.

My own commitment in philosophical matters leads toward strong basic beliefs in order, coherence, integration and totality. These beliefs convince me that rationality must be reintegrated into knowledge.[24] Such a reintegration will, in turn, lead to new ways of looking at such fundamental concepts as knowledge, rationality, commitment, truth and proposition. All of these play a crucial role in the relationship I will explore. So, for the sake of clarity, I will first indicate how I will use these terms.

Clarification of Terms

(a) *Knowledge* will perhaps be the most difficult term to grasp. As it is we have several expressions to identify different sorts of knowledge. *Knowledge that, knowledge how, acknowledgement* and *recognition* are some of these. I will use *knowledge* as a non-specific term; it will include and embrace all of these. When I refer to knowledge I mean the integration of all human functions of consciousness, and I do not differentiate much between knowledge and experience. Unless otherwise specified I use the term *knowledge* to refer to people's conscious, aware, dispositional relationship to God, themselves and the rest of creation. Such knowledge comprises our whole, integral experience; it relates to the totality of the known in its coherence.

In effect, we are talking here about a many-sided pattern of seemless unity. The elements of this pattern are functional dimensions of human experience, such as observation, language, rationality and trust, to name only a few. These functional dimensions have complex natures. Because knowledge always occurs in specific contexts, the many dimensions are present in specified configurations. In these, all dimensions play a role, even though different dimensions of the pattern dominate, depending on the needs and structure of the context.[25]

All knowing is, in its integrality and wholeness, concentrated and rooted in a person's stand before the ultimate. The person *in toto* is *coram Deo* and called to be in the image of God. The human self or person, one might say, indicates the undifferentiated root of knowing in the image of God (the fear of the Lord). Knowing is concentrated in the self. If it is true knowing, it is the same as what in the Bible is meant by life or obedience. It is, one might say, the mystery of subjectivity as human subjectivity in the covenant of creation.

(b) *Rationality* is one of these constituent dimensions of knowledge; it is a functional complexity. When it dominates, we have knowledge *that*, i.e., conceptual knowing or analytical knowing. Rational knowledge is dependent primarily on inference and guided by logical rules; it yields concepts, propositions, general information, theories and the like. Rational knowing is our *understanding* of structures, our grasp of general patterns, our insight into laws, kinds and properties. It is intellectual knowledge. It gives knowing its clarity, distinction and precision.

Rationality is a dimension of all knowing, but not all knowing is rationally dominated. Rational knowing, as it is developed in the scholarly, academic institutions of our culture, is scientific or theoretical knowing.[26] Of course, typically rational processes such as reasoning or arguing, for example, do not occur only in science. Inferences are made by all of us each day. And the contexts of the situations in which we infer will, in turn, tend to influence the validity of the process.

Thus, a judicial argument will be quite different from a mathematical one. Similarly, the reasoning of an artist will not be the same as the deductive procedures followed by a formal logician. All of these will have to be logical or rational. Yet different types of logicality will certainly be evident in different contexts. Nevertheless, in all contexts we will recognize the rational element as the grasping of general structure (order, the nature or essence of things) which is sometimes called rational intuition. And we will also see the development, clarification, correction and expansion of this grasp through processes which must follow canons of inferential procedure.

(c) *Fiduciary* functioning is another dimension of all knowing; it gives knowledge its certitudinal character. This function is prominent is trusting, believing, accepting and relying, all of which are necessary if anything is to be known. Where this dimension dominates, we speak of knowing as faith. Only in faith as fiduciary knowing can we know what is fundamental and ultimate. Belief is part of the complexity of this dimension.[27] Just as understanding is rationally dominated knowing, so faith is commitment-dominated knowing.[28]

(d) *Truth*, in the context of this approach, can be understood if we integrate a variety of traditional emphases, all of which relate to the multi-faceted nature of knowledge. In this way, truth is seen to be both subjective and objective. It has elements of correspondence and coherence. And finally, it is perspectival.

Truth of understanding, for example, shows correspondence. Truth of commitment shows coherence. Truth as true knowledge is perspectival. When we see the order of creation as the condition for truth, we see truth in its objective form. When we say subjection to that order must be accomplished in truth, we see truth in subjective form. Truth as known or true knowledge, however, can never be understood from just one of these vantage points. All knowledge, not only rational knowledge, can thus be true. And all truth will have a measure of correspondence to it. Truth is always integral, although certain dimensions may stand out, depending on the context.[29]

(e) The term *proposition* needs to be explained carefully. I will refer to what I will mean in all instances of its occurrence in this essay. As well, I will mention a variety of semantic situations in which this constant meaning shows up. I will not use *proposition* to refer to a semantic performance of any kind. Instead, it will designate what may be referred to, by or in semantic performances of some kind. In this way, some semantic act may directly assert, indirectly imply or in some way suggest a proposition. But the proposition itself will be a conceptually grasped relationship between general or structural states of affairs. It may also exist between such states of affairs and a concrete, individual entity, event or relationship. So I distinguish between (1) a state of affairs, (2) our conceptual grasp of that state of affairs, and (3) our semantic reference to conceptually grasped states of affairs.

I will use both *concept* and *proposition* to refer to the second kind of reality. In the concept we only grasp general states of affairs. In the proposition we grasp such states of affairs in relationship either to other such states of affairs or to concrete, individual particulars. Concepts and propositions are our primary logical, analytic or rational entities. In reasoning, analyzing, thinking and the like we develop our conceptual and propositional grasp of reality, which is only one dimension of our knowing reality. In our conceptual hold on reality we grasp the order or structure of reality (nature of things) either in terms of that order (mostly in theory) or in relation to our ordinary world of concrete things, events and relations (mostly in everyday affairs).

I distinguish sharply between understanding a proposition (primarily a rational matter) and believing a proposition (primarily a fiduciary matter). An understanding or a conclusion differs markedly from a belief. A belief need not be a believed proposition, whereas a proposition must always be understood. A proposition *is* no more than an understanding, i.e., a conceptual or intellectual grasping.

This is certainly a lengthy description of my use of the term *proposition*. However, I should also like to describe the various semantic ways in which a proposition may surface. Concepts and propositions, like reasonings, can only surface in semantic ways. Only when these semantic performances have one, specific, intended function—that of voicing conceptual or propositional understandings—will I refer to these performances as propositional language. Such language could be of many kinds. It could be theoretical or non-theoretical, i.e., it could surface in everyday language or in the realm of science or scholarship. In either situation, it could be narrowly rational or logical in nature, and it could also be biological, artistic or whatever. In short, even in the directly propositional language world there is a great variety. Most of this variety, however, can be recognized by its subject-predicate form, its definitional nature, its classifying function or its assertive character. I do not use a special term to name these sorts of propositional language forms, however. Nevertheless, *statement* would cover most of what I have in mind. But I do not use *statement* only for this purpose.

In addition to this great variety of directly propositional language, there is an added factor. All semantic behavior, or almost all of it, has propositional implications and conceptual assumptions. The ability of language to communicate will always depend on whether two subjects understand what language refers to, i.e., univocity. And this is made possible by our shared conceptual grasp. So, even though only some language is directly, intentionally and explicitly propositional, all language is propositional in some way or other.

Supporting Concepts

The preceding definitions show how certain key terms will be used.[30] Now I will outline certain basic beliefs that play a role in what follows.[31]

(a) *Order and Existence.* My philosophical commitment leads me to assume a particular correlation. On one side it has the empirical world of concrete, existing entities, with their functions and in their functional interrelationships. On the other side it has an ontic order of laws, or principles, to which existence is subject. That order holds universally for existence, while existence is individually subjected to it. Order gives general structure to existence. And we can explicitly know structure because our knowledge has a rational dimension. So I use *existence* to indicate less than what is real. Order, too, is real, although it is not the same as existence, which is subjected to order.

(b) *Structure and Direction.* The order of reality is the fundamental condition for existence. Order assigns to existence its structural limits of possibility and necessity. Nevertheless, this structural determination by order should not be viewed deterministically. There is room for subjective existence to be individually underdetermined. Within that "room to move" (the ontic foundation for structural freedom) it is possible to move in the direction intended in the order (good) or in another direction (evil). There are creatures capable of consciously participating in the directional decisions in creation; these are spiritual creatures who are directionally free to do good. No one is directionally free to do evil, even though the structural "room to move" apparently provides space for evil.

(c) *Unity and Diversity.* All existing entities are individual units of subjectivity. They are whole functors; they are integrally one in the coherent diversity of their many functions. Existing entities have functions, i.e., there are functors and functions. And the relations between functors, between functions, and between functors and functions, are all functional relations. No function is a separate entity; it is always the function of a functor. No relation is a separate entity, either.

(d) *Humankind.* All humans are created as members of the body of humankind. Humanity is called to be one in spirit, yet diverse in its individual members. God intended to be present on earth in the human community. We see his presence in the image of God and the incarnation of Immanuel.

Humans, in their entirety, are in one sense spirits, i.e., the only earthly creatures capable of knowing and receiving God's Spirit (through whom God directs creation). In this way we are co-directors of creation, helpers of God in guiding the world to its intended destiny. We become co-responsible for leading creation into obedience to the Word (through whom God orders creation). In humanity the structure and direction of creation can be subjectively one, as they are one in Word and Spirit.

Humans, in their entirety, are in another sense bodies, i.e., the integral unity of a diversity of irreducible functions: material functions, life functions, sensitive functions, rational functions, moral functions, etc.

(e) *God.* God is the Sovereign Creator of the universe and its order. God transcends everything created; there is nothing God has not created. God is neither a creature, nor subject to the order for creation.

Complexity of the Issue

It will be clear by now that my approach to the relation between rationality and commitment differs markedly from an approach taken from the analytic position, for example. In order to remove as many obstacles as possible from the pathways of communication, I will now give some indication of how complex the relationship between reason and faith appears to me.

(a) I am faced with a perplexing problem in this essay: my use of traditional terms for key concepts is almost impossible. Words such as *knowledge, truth, reason* and *faith* have long established meanings.

These are deeply ingrained in our listening and speaking habits. Yet I believe some very basic positions have to be challenged here. This may be a way to give new meanings to these terms (although we might not expect them to be heard by ears used to traditional meanings).

Analytic philosophers will be conditioned to understand the term *knowledge*, when used in a philosophical discussion, to refer to discursive, conceptual knowledge. They may admit there is more to knowing than conceptual knowing, but in their philosophical practice this admission makes little difference.

For me, however, all dimensions of human experience, of our concrete being in the world and all aspects of living are present when I deal with knowing. *Knowing x* will, for most analytic philosophers, mean being well (i.e., truly) informed about *x* and understanding this information. In my philosophical dealings with knowledge, however, this narrow definition will be only a moderate help in knowing *x*. To know anything truly, I require an active relationship with it.

(b) The actual practice of many contemporary English-speaking philosophers is to understand the term *belief* primarily, or only, as associated with the acceptance of propositions. So belief tends to function as a term whose meaning lies primarily *within* rationality. Thus, Wolterstorff understands rationality as the norm that justifies any belief.[32] However, there is a long tradition that associates *belief* with religious faith. That tradition, in turn, has always strongly dissociated such faith from rationality. Thus, in an exploratory essay such as this one, we always run the risk of confusing meanings, even when terms are well defined.[33]

(c) In my own usage, I insist on distinguishing faith or commitment (and its belief content) from religion. I do this because there is on the one hand the religious or spiritual drive of *all* human experience. (Our being is being before the face of God, and therefore we are totally responsible for being God's representatives.) On the other hand there are clearly identifiable acts of faith such as prayer, worship, etc., which differ from other kinds of experience. The rational dimension of experience is as religious as the trusting dimension, even though these two dimensions are mutually irreducible.

(d) An expression such as "believing in God" has a very complex meaning. It is God *whom* we believe, and we can believe him only because we are *in* him.

(e) As mentioned earlier, in exploring the relationship between rationality and commitment, our commitment itself is never in question; in fact, it is actually involved in the development of the exploration. However, because commitment is itself not a function of rationality, the content can never be fully stated in a proposition, nor can it be adequately defined propositionally. Thus the exploration is rational, but the rationality in question is committed rationality; it is both conditioned by its commitment and incapable of defining that commitment.[34]

(f) In our Western tradition, any proposition can be entertained, by reason, as a possibility. But commitment has a core, an ultimate commitment, which is directed to an ultimate origin. That origin is outside commitment and is also the origin and foundation of commitment. The origin dictates to commitment (i.e., reveals authoritatively) what can (must) and cannot (must not) be believed. If we are committed to reason, we must accept or reject different propositions than if we are committed to God in Christ.

Let us take this statement, for example: "Scripture might not be true." A rationalist could certainly entertain that proposition. For a Christian, however, there is no possible evidence on which we can decide this issue. As a canon, Scripture is the ultimate test for all truth, especially for all testimony concerning Scripture. If we accept evidence to the contrary, then we do not accept the canon and we cease to be Christians. Although some beliefs (such as the one here discussed) of rationalism are incompatible with Christian commitment, they have nevertheless penetrated deeply into the Christian intellectual community.[35]

(g) Christian commitment has been articulated in many different statements of faith.[36] In some of these the sovereignty of God is central. However, we could also organize our confession in a different way; for example, the central element could be the love of God. And that could still be biblical. No particular conceptual scheme will comprehensively fit Scripture. Nevertheless, every confession commits Christians to some ultimate, essential and basic beliefs.

2. *Exploration of the Relationship between Rationality and Commitment*

Christians should never be ultimately committed to rationality. Consequently, their belief in propositions might ultimately have to be founded in functions of faith. These functions, in turn, are not of a rational nature and cannot be rationally demonstrated.[37] Further, such functions of faith would then be grounded in commitment. The question therefore arises whether any proposition could ever be the ultimate basis for other propositions, if even the most basic propositions have other non-propositional grounds and foundations. This same question arises from another angle. Gödel's incompleteness theorem also appears to point to the non-ultimacy of every proposition. Rational incompleteness may be the price we pay for rational consistency. This raises a further question: if there is a relationship between conceptual or propositional functions on the one hand, and non-conceptual faith functions on the other, then can we determine a priority in that relationship? Finally, are there elements of either rationality or faith that must be common and constant for all Christians? In more conventional language we can thus pose three problems: (1) Is reason rooted in faith? (2) Does faith have a priority over reason or vice versa? (3) Does faith have constant elements that are common to all Christians—elements that give universally recognizable contours to Christian thought for all its followers?

Is Reason Rooted in Faith?

Many philosophers are familiar with literature discussing the epistemological and ontological implications of Gödel's incompleteness theorem. Against that background I will offer the general thesis that no formal rational-noetic system can be internally self-contained, i.e., not all of its necessary grounds and foundations can be contained within such a system.[38] If this is valid, it certainly seems applicable to the total rational-noetic system of any person or group.[39] A consequence of this thesis would be that, in order to be grounded, the basic concepts or propositions of a rational-noetic system need a non-conceptual ground or foundation. Such a foundation cannot be conceptual or propositional, because all conceptual or propositional bases are rational and noetic in nature, i.e., they belong to the system which cannot be self-contained. And no system can be validly self-attesting; it cannot be its own ground.[40] Further consequences would be that true knowledge cannot be exhaustively rational, and that truth cannot ultimately be merely rational in nature.[41] For it is precisely the truth of any system that, according to Gödel's findings, is not fully demonstrable within the system.

Someone might say we could rationally assure ourselves of the truth of basic propositions either by being committed to them or by observing and verifying them. But this objection could easily be countered. In the first place, an ultimate commitment to basic propositions is unacceptable for a Christian. It is a rationalistic commitment. Second, the observation of propositions is impossible anyway—most certainly in the case of basic propositions. Further, neither commitment nor observational procedures are rational, i.e., inferential, procedures. As such, they too would lie outside the boundaries of a rational-noetic system.

What does all of this indicate? In the first place, we know that inductive procedures and observation, or empirical verification, are ultimately unable to insure the truth of any empirical proposition. We may be persuaded that inference needs to be anchored in observation procedures in order to be in touch with reality. Yet observation is unable to establish the truth of an argument with any certitude.[42] And formal inference, according to Gödel, remains within the boundaries of a rational-noetic system; it is ultimately incapable of establishing the final truth of that system. So we need to look for another basis outside of observation, inference and rational-noetic systems. On such a basis we could then try to establish the truth of a concept, proposition or system. Some contemporary literature points us in the direction of faith or commitment.[43] Commitment does meet the requirement that it lies outside the inner limits of rationality. Might it be possible to connect them? A possible link could be the phenomenon of articulation, which is evident both in the case of conceptualization (rationality) and in the case of belief (fiduciary knowing). Belief, in turn, not only accepts propositions but also grasps the ultimate. We can articulate our faith (in creedal statements) and we can also articulate our understanding (in propositional statements).[44] We can express both our confessions and our conceptions in words and sentences. And both kinds of articulation can be the content of belief. Does this provide a suitable link for us? Does articulate belief, linked to both faith and rationality, link the latter two?

To answer this we first need to see how faith and understanding can both reach out to many different realities. We can understand much more than concepts. Although we may do all of our understanding through concepts, they are mostly directed to other realities (themselves non-conceptual), such as physical reality, human social reality, feelings, etc. The same goes for faith. We do not believe only *in* God, nor do we believe *only* God. We can also believe propositions, for example. Accepting a proposition (in belief) must have some (ultimate) ground. The proposition will recommend acceptance on its own ground only to a rationalist. Self-evident propositions are evident to reason only through commitment to reason.[45] Perception is not ultimate either, except for an empiricistic, ultimate commitment to sense data.[46]

So we need a grasping in faith, not in concept, of something that provides us with an ultimate foundation, outside of reason and propositions, on which we can ground our rationality and our propositions. The grasping of this reality will have to be related to the propositions and concepts of our rational-noetic systems in order to give them truth. Thus we need statements that articulate what we grasp in faith (believed creedal grounds), placed in relation to statements that articulate what we conceive (understood propositions and theories). And we must remember that both kinds of statements can be statements in which we articulate what we believe.[47]

Why do we need a creedal statement that articulates something (even if it still does not articulate a proposition)? And are there any such statements? Is there language, assertive language even, that is non-propositional? We need a statement because through it we can bring what is basic to rationality (a basic propositional belief) in touch with a ground (a creedal belief) which is not itself rational even though it must be relatable to what falls within the confines of rationality. An assertive articulation is one way to establish a link between a rational system and its extra-rational ultimate grounds and foundations.

This presents us with a perplexing problem: are there statements or assertions that may appear to be propositions yet are not truly propositions? Is it possible that some propositional analogues exist, whose real nature is not propositional but creedal, not rational but fiduciary? I believe this is the case. I believe that many statements about the ultimates of our faith (confessional or creedal statements) do not assert a proposition we believe; they are statements in which we articulate what is grasped in faith, i.e., creedal beliefs of commitment. Propositions are grasped conceptually; they are understood rationally; they are asserted semantically. And when they are accepted, we say they are believed. But belief attaches itself to more than just propositions that are rationally understood. It also attaches itself to what is ultimately grasped in faith concerning the ultimate.

Let us look at an example. As Christians we confess that God is our father. This confession can never be taken merely as the assertion of a genuine proposition. If it were just a stated proposition, it would have to be an articulation of a grasped instantiation of a certain order. But then it would also have to be open to normal inferential procedures. *If* anything is to be a father, we must inferentially assert, *then* it *must* also be a male. However, the Christian faith does not make such a confession; in addition to being our father, God is not also a male person. When we say *that* we believe *that* God is our father, we state in proposition-*like* language what in fact is not a grasped general structural relation (concept or proposition). Rather, we are stating a belief in something grasped as ultimate. God is the origin of all order. God, therefore, is not subject to order, does not instantiate order as a creature would. Creatures that would be fathers *must* be male persons; they are bound to the natural or created order, so they must be male by natural necessity. But we do not know God to be bound. Consequently, our concepts (intellectual grasp of order) do not apply to God (origin of order) in the same way they would to a creature (existing in subjection to order).

We do grasp in faith what God reveals to us. Since God does this in creaturely ways, our grasp in faith of what we believe is also dependent on the way we grasp these creaturely ways in concepts. And in this way our concepts do apply (indirectly as elements for the understanding of our faith) to God. When we articulate what we grasp in faith (in believed assertions that are proposition-like), we also enable ourselves to relate what is grasped in faith to what is grasped conceptually.[48] We have, then, two articulated beliefs related in two statements. In this way a rational-noetic system can be given a ground outside itself in statements that are confessed. This happens even when the rational-noetic system itself plays a crucial rôle in allowing faith to grasp the ultimate through understanding.[49] (I will take this question up again in a moment.)

Why is it necessary that the ultimate ground for rationality be grasped in faith? The reason is fairly straightforward; the ground we need has to refer us to an original or ultimate foundation, one that has no foundation but is the ultimate or original foundation for everything else. What we need is an ultimate grasp of an ultimate ground or foundation. The human function in which we reach out ultimately to what is ultimate is the trusting function of faith or commitment.[50] Faith grasps the foundation of ultimate certitude. Faith statements point to mysteries beyond our finite knowledge. Faith, says a Calvinian confessional document (the Heidelberg Catechism), is a certain knowledge. In faith we acquire certitude by surrendering to the ultimate.[51]

But on what ground do we surrender? We believe the ultimate ground on no ground whatsoever. Rather, we believe the ultimate *as* ground, as the origin and foundation of all grounds, as the real and only place to stand. By committing ourselves entirely and wholeheartedly to this ultimate foundation, it becomes its own evidence for its own ultimacy. That foundation is, as the rationalist might say, self-evident, because it is its own evidence. It makes itself evident, through commitment, to faith. The original foundation, through commitment to that foundation, reveals itself in faith.

In this way and as an ultimate foundation, an original foundation imposes on our knowledge (through faith) the ultimate limits of all that can be known. And because what we grasp in faith has a certain belief content—a core of creedal beliefs in which we articulate our faith—faith through these beliefs can serve as ultimate ground for our basic propositions, i.e., for believing them.

By saying the ultimate is self-evident, I mean it produces its own evidence for itself. It does this by fulfilling the claims it makes about itself to those who have faith and act upon it. The evidence is acceptable only for those who are committed believers. They live in hope, and they live to see the promises made by the ultimate fulfilled. Only faith will accept such evidence of fulfillment of hope. Faith rooted in commitment hears what the ultimate reveals to it.

Thus, the ultimate foundation of even basic propositions turns out to be what is self-evident and, because of commitment, incorrigible for the believer. However, if we articulate what is then believed, we are not uttering propositions. We are confessing what has become known in faith and consequently stated in creedal beliefs.[52] This remains true even when our ultimate reliance is on propositions, inference, observation or rationality. Self-evident propositions are then self-evident *to* reason *through* ultimate reliance *on* reason. But there is not a single rational procedure that would establish the ultimacy of rationality for the unprejudiced (also for the rationally unprejudiced) observer. At best, we can have faith in such ultimacy through commitment to reason.[53]

Is There a Priority of Faith over Reason or of Reason over Faith?

When we answer this question, much depends on the flexibility of our conceptual scheme. Does it allow various sorts of priority relations? For example, between two entities *a* and *b* there could be the following relationships: *a* is rooted in *b*, based on *b*, founded on *b*, dependent on *b*, conditioned by *b*, etc. Suppose that in some of these relations we concluded that *b* has priority over *a*. Might it still be possible for the very same *a* and *b* to sustain other relationships in which *a* might have priority over *b*? We might say that in one way *a* is founded on *b*, whereas in another way *b* is rooted in *a*. We would then have two different relationships, each establishing priority of one relation over the other in a different direction. Such, I believe, may be the case with the relationship between rationality (or rational understanding) and faith (or commitment).

How are we to see a relationship between the confessed content of faith (creedal beliefs) and the conceived content of rationality (propositions) in which they are mutually prior with respect to one another? This can readily be grasped once we see on the one hand how *all* beliefs, whether propositional (of conceived order) or creedal (of the grasped ultimate), are still beliefs, and as such matters of trust and not matters of rationality. Functionally speaking, all beliefs as beliefs have an ultimate foundation in commitment to the ultimate. For this reason the creedal commitment beliefs concerning the ultimate foundation are grounds for all other beliefs. On the other hand, all our beliefs do have a basis in propositions, i.e., in our understanding of the nature of things. This basis is required if our faith is not to be without understanding, even though in essentials it may also pass understanding.[54] For this reason, we can say propositional beliefs are basic to our faith. And thus our faith has a basis in rational understanding.

We might express the difference between a creedal statement of commitment and a rational statement of understanding as follows. A proposition can be conceived without being believed (although not without having some beliefs), whereas ultimate creedal statements cannot become intelligible without being believed first.[55] Belief in the ultimate must always guide our understanding of it. Ultimate creedal beliefs can be rendered intelligible only when we believe them.[56] In keeping with this we might thus formulate the relationship of mutual priority as follows: insofar as people reach out, in the belief content of their faith, to what is revealed to them as ultimate for their commitment, all human functioning (including all rational functioning) is rooted in commitment. But insofar as people need to understand what it is they are committed to, confessional beliefs must be based on a conceptual framework of believed propositions about the world. These confessional beliefs are in this way based on conceptual beliefs. They are both, equally, beliefs. But whereas confessional beliefs reach out to the ultimate, conceptual beliefs reach out to grasp general structures. We will never understand what we are committed to and what that implies unless our knowledge has a rational basis. And we will never know what our commitment reveals to us unless our knowledge has fiduciary grounds. Our faith leads our knowledge; our understanding clarifies our knowledge.

Two related questions now arise. Are there confessional beliefs that are essentially ultimate, and are there rational beliefs that are never capable of being legitimate confessional beliefs, at least for a Christian?[57] Earlier I said beliefs can be of all sorts. Not all of them can be treated as though they were genuine propositions, even when they are stated in forms that appear propositional. The belief content of our faith is more than propositional. What I now want to clarify further is that all propositional beliefs are ultimately rooted in commitment because they are being controlled by or grounded in beliefs of faith that are not propositional.[58] In these confessional ground beliefs of commitment we grasp what is revealed to us as the foundation of all things, the origin of everything. Believing propositions is not itself an act of rationality such as inference would be. What is rational is the forming or conceiving of a proposition, understanding it, rendering it intelligible. Consequently, when we say something is the case, we only sometimes mean we *understand* it is the case or we understand what it is that is said to be the case. Then we speak of rational knowledge. But when we mean that we have *accepted* it to be the case, and we *believe* it to be the case, then we are dealing with belief as a species of faith, i.e., fiduciary knowledge.

So when we believe propositions, then the fiduciary or certitudinal dimension of knowledge always plays an important role. And this dimension of our knowledge always has, as one of its constituent elements, beliefs that are directly rooted in commitment. These are confessional beliefs. They are articulated in terms of confessed statements which are not genuine propositions—although they can still be true statements. (Truth is then, of course, not defined as propositional or semantic.)[59] These ultimate assumptions or ultimate beliefs are vindicated, not by their test of rationality, but by their authenticity in relation to the commitment out of which they arise.[60] And these ultimate beliefs, rooted in commitment, ultimately guide and control us in deciding whether any proposition is true or even believable, and they help us to know what a proposition may mean.

Such guidance and control is not always related directly or immediately to the acceptance of any particular proposition. Knowledge of this kind is very dependent on a framework. Propositions are elements of larger theories, which in turn fit the theoretical climate and framework of some historical period. In its turn, this historical period finds a rationale in some philosophical outlook. And it is usually on this philosophical level that commitment beliefs begin to play a more visible role.[61] However, when paradigms are uncertain and the times are unsettled, we can detect philosophical differences even in our immediate theoretical analysis. In addition, the philosophical outlook is itself an articulate form of the world-view of a community, which in turn has its own creedal foundations. And via this long chain, no proposition is ultimately free from the control of ultimate beliefs.

In this sense we can say the acceptance of all propositions is ultimately rooted in commitment, and certain beliefs directly rooted in commitment are what they are by their very nature. These beliefs are essentially beliefs of commitment. They are essentially ultimate. In this way the confession that God is the sovereign Creator of all things visible and invisible is essentially an ultimate belief. It can only be known in faith. Our understanding of this belief must follow the lead of faith. Its meaning cannot finally be decided on the basis of inference.[62] And no proposition will be *accepted* or be acceptable if it is not ultimately compatible with such ultimate beliefs. We function in this manner even though our culture's age-old commitment to rationality has made all of us insensitive to the role played by such ultimate beliefs in the way we form our theories. Western culture has conditioned us not only to accept simultaneously some Christian beliefs and some rationalist beliefs that are mutually incompatible, but also to reject Christian beliefs in favor of rationalist beliefs.

I am not saying, of course, that different propositions might not be compatible or appear to be compatible with the same ultimate beliefs. (This could be true even for propositions that are mutually incompatible.) Conversely, I am not saying that the same propositions might not be compatible with different ultimate beliefs. All I am saying is that the propositions we do in fact hold, we hold in some (direct or indirect) relation to certain beliefs of commitment that are not propositional, that are essential to that commitment, and that are essentially creedal beliefs of commitment. On the other hand, every belief rooted directly in commitment can only be *understood* on a propositional basis. But in this case, the basis I have in mind is not the root dependency on commitment but the structural basis for the possibility of any articulate belief. No articulated belief can possibly be held unless we have some understanding of its articulation. The belief that God is our father cannot be reduced to a propositional belief. It does (sur)pass the understanding.[63] But it would also not be possible to believe that God is our father unless we had some rational understanding of what is involved or logically implied, from a conceptual point of view, in being a father.

Let me elaborate on my earlier example. We believe God is our father. This does not mean God is a creaturely instance of being a father. God is not, for example, a male. Yet our belief is based on our understanding of such instantiation. And in this sense faith not only seeks understanding but requires understanding. At the same time the nature of propositions forbids us, as Christians, from ever reaching out in the ultimate commitment to what is conceptual and propositional in nature.

I have talked in this section mostly about beliefs, i.e., creedal beliefs and propositional beliefs as the content of faith. I should now also say that the articulation of our commitment in faith—the creedal part of our belief content of faith, as well as all other beliefs we hold—is not all there is to our commitment and certainly not to our faith as it is rooted in commitment. The core of faith cannot be reduced to articulate knowledge. Its core is a yielding, an accepting and trusting which transcends both understanding and articulation. It is a giving of ourselves in surrender.[64] Thus, someone might go even further than I have in this essay. All believed propositions are not only grounded in confessional beliefs, which in turn are rooted in commitment. In addition, those commitment beliefs are founded in faithful surrender and trusting acceptance. However, in regard to surrender we must say it is made possible by the structure of human experience. Even the mystery of surrender is not an irrational surrender of all of our faculties, but the action of an understanding creature. And this in turn implies that surrender has its own basis in rationality.[65]

Does Faith Have Common and Constant Elements?

To answer this question I must explore a little further the nature of ultimate confessional beliefs rooted in commitment. As I noted above, the connection between ultimate confessional beliefs and propositional beliefs is somewhat indirect. The realities of confession, world-view and philosophy, with all their complexity and immensity, form links here. This has an immediate consequence. A fund of shared ultimate beliefs will not necessarily show up in terms of equally shared propositions at the level of minor analytic detail. This is especially true because ultimate beliefs depend, for being understood, on their own sub-layers of propositional beliefs. These sub-layers may differ greatly between people holding similar ultimate convictions. Thus, some Christians may become nominalists based on one of their central ultimate beliefs, while others on account of the same reason become realists. What can be made of this?

The biblical testimony suggests the nature of commitment is communal; it brings people into communion with one another. Of course, even in the institution designed to foster the communion of believers—the church—we have known division rather than unity. However, this lack of unity may be partly due to the way our culture has rationalized and intellectualized faith. It seems we have thereby allowed the rational-propositional differences in our analysis of basic beliefs to prevail over unity of commitment. Indeed, with our rational idea of truth, we tend to fight for the truth primarily in terms of our articulation of insight, rather than in terms of our common commitment. All too easily we accept differences in formulation as differences in commitment. Could we also go the other way? Is there a way in which unity in commitment can be made to foster unity in a rational framework?

Rationality, as we have seen, can never form a truly ultimate foundation for our knowledge. As a result of this the rationalist foundation of our culture has encouraged a diversity of intellectual communities within the unity of our faith. As Christians we have allowed all of the diversity fostered by a mistaken commitment to rationality to enter into our community. Is this necessary? I am thinking here about our heritage of rationalism in relation to matters of faith and theology. In these realms Western Christianity has seldom explored with any conviction and endurance the possible control and leading of rationality by our ultimate Christian beliefs. Instead, in our thinking we have too often let ourselves be guided by theoretical and rational considerations alone. Nor have we fully realized that the core of our beliefs is not itself rational. So we have failed to understand that we must not let rationality have the last word even in matters rational, let alone in determining what is the meaning of our ultimate beliefs. Thus, here is at least one possible reason for the utter division among Christians. We have not sufficiently realized how the ultimate meaning of our ultimate beliefs cannot be articulated rationally. If we realize this, then the faith we all have in our unity and in our unity of commitment may in fact begin to play its intended role, namely, to lead and control all of our experience, including our rational experience.[66]

Now, if unity is first of all born from unity of commitment and not from unity of understanding, and if unity of understanding must be rooted in unity of commitment, then experienced unity of confession may (if we let it) have much more power than we have experienced to date. It could lead to unity in our world-view and thence to unity in basic philosophical ideas. It would lead us away from the rationalist idea of truth as agreement in articulation. Instead we could move toward a more biblical idea of truth as the unity of submission to the Word in unity of spiritual direction.

A possible objection might be raised here. Might we end up having our propositional beliefs so fully grounded in faith that any meaningful mention of verifying our beliefs by argument, test or observation could seem unrealistic? I believe the opposite is actually the case. In a rationalistic climate, the test for the truth of anything lies in its observable rationality. Recent history has demonstrated, however, that truth locked into rationality is ultimately unachievable. No general proposition can be proven by a finite observation of particulars. Inductive arguments fail for the same reason. And valid inference is dependent on basic beliefs that cannot be tested rationally.

But suppose we have a framework of ultimate beliefs that includes beliefs in a creation with constancy and continuity, as well as belief in the ultimacy of commitment to a reliable Creator. Then both inductive arguments and observational testing can be believed to provide reliable indicators of the truth of a theory. We must not expect observation, of course, to yield neutral or impartial results. Observation, too, has its roots in commitment. But it is not for that reason untrustworthy. Rather, a hidden commitment to rationality, which hides its own character as commitment, is what is rationally unreliable. And where these commitments force us to accept observation as impartial, the distortions can be much greater and less detectable than where both observation and argument are openly rooted in commitment.

Notes

N.B. All the literature found in the notes will also be found in the bibliography which follows them. Brief citations in the notes refer to the complete references in the bibliography.

1. My own orientation is primarily to the continental tradition, especially to the work of neo-Kuyperian philosopher Herman Dooyeweerd.
2. Wolterstorff refers to such foreign elements within Christian thinking in *Reason Within*.
3. See Plantinga, "Is Belief in God" and Alston, "Religious Experience."
4. See Hart, "On the Distinction" and Wolterstorff, "Once Again."
5. Although *reason* might well be taken in a broad sense here, the narrow sense remains the core. Thus, rational justification would in any case be a form of justification through valid reasoning or argumentation.
6. The whole enterprise of the justification of "belief" (as such) seems irrational to me. Why does it need to be justified? And by whom? What does seem appropriate is to justify some particular belief for which some claim is being made, apparently without ground or in the face of some other defect. We might wish to have a justification for the belief that the United States is appropriately involved in suppressing the uprising of the oppressed in El Salvador. But it is hard to see how such a belief would be rationally justified. Obviously the problem with Ronald Reagan is not just that he has been rationally deluded in accepting certain propositions.
7. See the end of Alston, "Religious Experience." My use of *rational* in this

paper is the same as his in "The Role of Reason."

8. I have discussed these ideas at length in "The Impasse of Rationality Today" (Revised) and in "The Re-cognition of Science as Knowledge."

9. The doctrine of the autonomy of reason has been a major theme in the work of Herman Dooyeweerd, notably in his *New Critique*. That work has been a major inspiration for my own thinking. Section 2 of this paper is, in fact, an exploration of his notion of the concentric direction of thinking upon the human heart or selfhood and of his claim that all human behavior is guided by faith. That section explores the religious root unity of the human person in relation to two functions of human experience, viz., the pistic function and the analytic function (to use Dooyeweerd's own terms). This exploration especially concentrates on the relation between the pistic anticipations within analysis and the analytic retrocipations within pistis. But I have attempted to develop this exploration in such a way that no knowledge of the Dooyeweerdian framework or of its terminology are needed for an understanding of the points I wish to raise.

10. I hold that there can be no certainty in rationality. In saying this I do not only refer to the widespread conviction in our time that neither empirical verification nor inference can establish with certainty that something is the case. I also refer to the fact that accepting something in trust, in reliance or by yielding (which does result in certainty) is rationally always subject to doubt or subject to the consideration that something else is conceivably possible. Although we accept something for certain, there is always a logical possibility to see it differently. Formally we can conceive of something else as being the case. If reason is autonomous, the only route to certainty is through rationality, and that route is itself always subject to doubt.

11. One definition (among many) of rationalism would be: a commitment to the ultimate authority of reason as the road to cognitive certainty and practical autonomy. Even with this definition, however, many different versions of rationalism would be possible. We could stress various dimensions of rationality in our ultimate commitment to it: universality, necessity, law conformity, objectivity, logicality, etc. In addition, the authoritative procedure for final appeal to reason may also differ from case to case. Some might appeal to the finality of empirical evidence and verification. Others may rest their case on inference.

12. I will later distinguish faith from commitment. Other problems come to the fore once this relation is discussed again. One is that much contemporary thought in the English-speaking community, for all its precision and clarity, has been lacking in critical self-examination on this point. This is due in part to its tendency to reduce philosophy to analysis and analysis to its analytic functions only. As a result, the analytic tradition seems to have more problems than other traditions in entering into the renewed discussions. Many of the conceptual approaches needed at this stage present themselves as vague concepts and metaphors to philosophers trained in that tradition.

13. Perhaps the earliest modern introduction of faith into philosophy has come from existentialist Karl Jaspers, first with his *Der Philosophische Glaube* as early as 1947, followed by his major work *Der Philosophische Glaube angesichts der Offenbarung* in 1962. Prior to that, and in a radical departure from rationalism, Michael Polanyi introduced the function of fiduciary experience into rationality. His work was very influential outside mainline English-speaking philosophic circles, mostly as a result of *Personal Knowledge*, published in 1958. Probably the most widely read contemporary introduction of a fiduciary element into North American scholarly thought has been Kuhn's *The Structure of Scientific Revolutions* of 1962. A very helpful discussion of the upheaval caused by the recent investigations of rationality and science is Gerard Radnitzky's *Contemporary Schools*, which started to appear in 1968. The historic function of the Christian faith in science as we know it has been exhaustively explored in many works by Stanley Jaki. His most succinct and recent work dealing with this theme is *The Origin of Science*, his 1977 Fremantle lectures at Oxford.

    Many Dutch philosophers in the Calvinian tradition have reflected on these problems on an ongoing basis for over a century, centered in institutions for higher education in Amsterdam, Potchefstroom and Grand Rapids. A recent renewal of this mode of reflection gave rise to the Institute for Christian Studies in 1967 in Toronto, Canada. That institution was designed especially to concentrate full-time on the problems of rationality in ways that would be rooted in biblical revelation. At the Calvin Center for Christian Scholarship, in Grand Rapids, Michigan, established in the mid-70s, the same aims prevail. And in 1979 the Free University of Amsterdam opened a Reflection Center for a similar purpose. Among recent publications issuing from this movement are Wolterstorff's *Reason Within the Bounds of Religion*, Klapwijk, Groenewoud and Griffioen's *Vrede met de Rede? (Peace With Reason?)*, VanderStelt's *Philosophy and Scripture* and Plantinga's "Is Belief in God Rational?"

    A great deal of communal reflection has occurred recently at conferences dealing with rationality, both in Christian and secular humanist settings. Examples are Ottawa ("Rationality Today," 1977), MIT ("Faith and Science in an Unjust World," organized by the World Council of Churches in 1979), Amsterdam ("Concern about Science," 1980), Wheaton (1980), and Toronto ("Rationality in the Calvinian Tradition," 1981).

14. Examples would be the unabated rationalism of Chisholm and the fiduciary rationality of commitment in Michael Polanyi.

15. The analytic tradition remains quite convinced that philosophy is to be characterized as clear and precise thinking. Polanyi, by contrast, believes that "we have no clear knowledge of what our presuppositions are" and that what we "gain in exactitude . . . is accompanied by a loss in clarity . . . ." This has much to do with his conviction that "only words of inde-

terminate meaning can have a bearing on reality . . . ." For this reason he "would eliminate precision as an ideal . . . ." (*Personal Knowledge*, pp. 59, 119, 231) By pointing this out I am not, of course, signaling my opposition to either analysis or clear thinking.

16. Many of those who reject rationalism find it difficult to see how their continued devotion to rationality can often be explained only if they are committed in some way to rationality as an ultimate. It is even harder for many to put into practice what in fact they may theoretically accept, namely, that knowledge is richer and more complex than rational knowledge.

17. We often find evidence of circularity in coming to terms with the reality of beliefs and propositions. Beliefs are defined as accepted propositions, while propositions are defined as what can be believed. That makes a belief the acceptance of what can be believed, which materially speaking says little, if anything at all.

18. We certainly find this in the work of Dooyeweerd, Polanyi, Plantinga and Wolterstorff.

19. Jaki, Polanyi and Radnitzky make a strong case for that and in so doing appeal to work done by Gödel and Tarski on the incompleteness of formalisms.

20. Radnitzky quotes Hempel as saying that "it appears quite doubtful whether the basic tenets of positivism and empiricism can be formulated in a clear and precise way" (*Contemporary Schools*, p. 112). Laszlo complains that increase in rigor in philosophy has resulted in a decrease in information (*Introduction to Systems Philosophy*, p. 3). A recent issue of *The Chronicle of Higher Education* (January 12, 1981) gives the impression that according to many philosophers the majority of analytic philosophers do not think of their tradition as a school next to other schools, but see their approach simply as the only right way to think.

21. This is recognized, while at the same time no one abandons the view that science is by nature reductionist, i.e., seeks to reduce conceptual multiplicity to conceptual simplicity as much as possible. Many theorists also see that in this respect a difference must be honored between philosophy as an integrating, totalizing and unifying discipline, and the sciences which take a limited and specializing point of view (cf. Radnitzky and Laszlo).

22. Dooyeweerd, Laszlo and Radnitzky.

23. If the final authority for all truth is found in rationality, then it would seem reasonable to demand the rational justification of all knowledge (cf. note 6, above). This raises a difficult question, however: how can we claim that everything be rationally justified? This question certainly lands us in trouble. For if the claim that all must be rationally justified is rationally justified, that claim would be self-justified. Surely this form of justification cannot normally be accorded much respect. But if the claim cannot be rationally justified, it could presumably not be true. Any independent wit-

ness (evidence?) would itself need to be justified as well. So, even in the case of the ultimacy of rationality, we find that the rationality of the claim of such ultimacy rests on commitment. Or, to put it differently, non-circular justification of rationality (or of any irreducible mode of consciousness) is an impossibility (see Alston in "Religious Experience"). As a result, it is not surprising that in traditional concepts of reason, the intuition of the nature of things (without inferential or evidential justification) was a natural endowment of reason. In a foundationalist approach to commitment to rationality, the evident or incorrigible or immediately certain beliefs (which were unfounded foundations for other beliefs) played their role so well because they were certain or evident to reason, i.e., to reason committed to itself. This is what we mean when we say we are unable to grasp such a truth without believing it. The grasping is done by a committed person, whose commitment is to that very grasping. Thus, the grasping which is said to precede belief is itself founded in belief.

24. The analytic tradition is highly committed to clarity and precision and for that reason to the study of details more or less abstracted from context (cf. notes 12 and 15, above). Therefore I do not believe the tools of that tradition are best suited to the development of a theory which can serve as a contextual paradigm for explorations in commitment. Such explorations need to be focused on the themes of totality and context. On the other hand, within such a paradigm the analytic tradition can probably do more than most other traditions to explain the meaning of special concepts (see my "The Re-cognition").

25. There is a great deal of available literature which documents the need for a renewed view of knowledge. And this literature is written from many different points of view. Laszlo pleads for it as a systems thinker, Jaki as a traditional Thomist, Polanyi as a practicing scientist, Radnitzky as an astute student of contemporary debates in theory of theory, Piaget as a pedagogue, Habermas as a neo-Marxist, Pannenberg as a theologian, Gibson as a student of perception and Merleau-Ponty as a phenomenologist. The dominant current of thought about knowledge and perception or sensation in English-speaking circles of philosophy does not seem to be deeply in touch with this modern literature. It is impossible, however, to make some of the new research fruitful unless old frameworks are at least relativized.

26. To be rational is to meet the norms for rationality, which are mostly the rules of inference, at least insofar as the essential inner structure of rationality is concerned. The normative procedure of rational experience is studied in logic. This normative structure will, if we observe it, lead us to an understanding of conceptual relations, which in turn are our grasp of general structures. Logical possibility, in this respect, is conceivable possibility. Such possibility is limited by the possibility of conception *(not imagination)*. Thus it is limited by the rules of inference as well as by the given order of what is conceived. Conception is mostly limited to general structures. Not all things are conceivable, although all things are know-

able. I will not use *rational* to mean sensible, meaningful, appropriate or similar things. I will always use it to refer to the inner structure of the rational-analytic functional dimension of human experience. What I have in mind here is similar to what Alston has in mind in the opening paragraph of "The Role of Reason." This is how I understand this inner structure: when I gain a clear understanding of something through inference, the essentials of rationality are present. Whether I will also believe what I understand or whether my understanding is justified—these are matters outside the inner structure of rationality.

27. Believing, at least from a functional point of view, is not taken to be a rational activity or state, although it would be wrong to view it as irrational. Believing and conceiving (or understanding) are irreducibly different. We can, of course, also believe a proposition or a theory. In this case it will help to know whether the proposition or theory meets the norms for rationality. But there is no peculiar privileged connection between believing and conceiving. Thus, the belief content of our faith is not necessarily propositional in its entirety. Propositions are among the things we can believe. But other things besides propositions can also be believed. So belief, in this sense, does not need to be rational in the sense in which inference needs to be rational. In fact, as we will see later, when belief is an integral part of faith it will be able to grasp mysteries which surpass the understanding. In this sense, then, belief must not be interpreted as thinking with assent (cf. James H. Olthuis).

28. The best contemporary literature on commitment is to be found in Polanyi.

29. The nature of truth is thus not limited to rationality. One sort of truth (viz., where an act or its result corresponds to the norm in question) occurs on every human functional level where the functioning and its results are according to their norms. Truth is also not limited to propositions. My view of truth does not limit truth to either conceptual or semantic realities. And a sentence, in order to be true, does not need to express a proposition. Scientific truth, courtroom truth or artistic truth are known kinds of truth. They show us how one single semantic or correspondence conception of truth is not rich enough to do justice to the great variety of truth encountered in experience.

30. Within the short compass of a few sentences it is hardly possible to give a satisfactory account of my views on these crucial matters. I can only give some indication of my uncommon usage, in the hope that the actual functioning of the terms in the text will then be more intelligible and, through that functioning, also be more clear.

31. My basic beliefs on these matters will imply not only certain basic propositions (cf. Plantinga in "Reformed Objections" and in "The Evidentialist Objection"), but these in turn will also have a foundation that is non-propositional (cf. Plantinga in "The Evidentialist Objection"). In some cases Plantinga seems to ground a basic belief on commitment (cf. "Is

Belief in God Rational?"). I believe Gödel's incompleteness theorem implies that a person's complete rational-noetic system is dependent for its truth on extra-propositional foundations. These foundations could be empirical-perceptual as well as fiduciary-revelational. This would not make so-called basic propositions any less basic, since they are basic only because they are not based on other propositions. They can be based on foundations other than propositions.

32. For example, in "Is Reason Enough?" In his "Justified Belief" rationality is the norm for justification of belief, even though reasons are not all that will justify a belief. Rationality, for Wolterstorff, seems to be a norm that in principle does not need to be connected with reasoning or inference.

33. It is clear to me that even when a term is well defined, this does not guarantee we will see or hear that meaning. The writer or speaker may have given it this meaning, but if it is a crucial term and well established with another meaning, the novel usage may not be rejected, it may simply not be heard.

34. Can commitment to a basic proposition be rational (cf. note 23)? The proposition may be rational. But can the commitment be rational?

35. Plantinga does not seem to hold that some beliefs are immune to argument (cf. "The Evidentialist Objection").

36. I believe that not all articulations of our commitment can be propositional in nature. Faith cannot be reduced to understanding. So I do not mean something propositional when I use the term *statement* here.

37. Ultimate rational demonstration of all rational beliefs would be impossible without circularity and would be lacking in independent evidence (see note 23, above). Even beliefs evident to reason or to rational intuition would not be so evident unless they were grounded in a prior commitment to the ultimacy of rationality. On the basis of the same commitment we decide that some propositions are not questioned by reason because this seems unreasonable. What is said here is not intended, of course, to characterize faith as irrational. In fact, I believe faith itself has rational foundations which are even more integrally connected with beliefs of faith than Wolterstorff's concept of control belief would suggest (see his *Reason Within*).

38. Both Jaki and Polanyi discuss Gödel extensively (cf. also Popper, pp. 209-210). Before I read about it in the literature, I had intuited the epistemological and ontological implications of Gödel when the theorem was pointed out to me in 1965 (cf. *Challenge*, p. 56). Nevertheless, the proof itself is beyond my comprehension. It seemed to me then, as others have since pointed out, that if Gödel's theorem holds for formal systems it holds even more conclusively for complex and informal systems of rationality.

39. The rational-noetic system of a group would be all its propositional beliefs that are consistent and coherent, or that are held to be so, and that are so held in common by most of the members.

40. Plantinga's exploration of the nature of basic beliefs (most explicitly in

"Reformed Objections") ends with this conclusion: belief structures are linear when it comes to the relation of beliefs based on beliefs. Therefore he seems committed to a propositional belief that is ultimate to other propositional beliefs. This is acceptable, of course, only relatively speaking within the limits of rationality. Within human consciousness such a basic belief is itself supported by non-propositional grounds. The latter point is more clearly stated in "The Evidentialist Objection."

41. This seems to be supported by the end of Wolterstorff's "Justified Belief."
42. The relation of both rationality and commitment to (the rest of) reality is an important one, but it cannot be discussed here.
43. Wolterstorff establishes a link between rationality and commitment when he understands some of the belief content of a person's commitment to be in control of his or her rational-noetic structure (cf. *Reason Within*). Plantinga says that belief in God, although it is founded on commitment, cannot for that reason be rejected as irrational (cf. "Is Belief in God Rational?"). As will be clear from this essay, I think both approaches need to be taken further. Readers must appreciate that I am here not inquiring into possible *proximate* grounds for basic propositions outside rational-noetic systems and inference. Such grounds could be perception, memory, authority, etc. Here I am interested in an *ultimate* grounding of basic propositions.
44. By *statement*, we will recall, I do not necessarily mean the assertion of a proposition.
45. A basic proposition (i.e., basic in the sense of having no other proposition as its basis) may nevertheless have a basis elsewhere in, for example, sense experience, testimony or other sources. But this is not what I have in mind here. Rather, I am referring to someone thoroughly committed to the ultimacy of rationality as final epistemic authority or norm. This person would likely say that a proposition is rational for some person only if it is either self-evident to that person, evident to the senses, incorrigible or supported by propositions (through inference) which meet these conditions. But how should we view this conviction? Does it meet the criteria it sets forth? Probably it does not meet them in any straightforward sense. However, someone previously committed to rationality would, upon understanding this criterion, also immediately believe it as evident (see note 23, above).
46. Although perception is not ultimate in the sense of the ultimate authority for cognitive states of affairs, perception is, of course, irreducible to other cognitive sources. Perception is an irreducible epistemic practice (see note 23, above).
47. Once again I remind readers that by *statement* I do not necessarily refer to something inherently propositional (cf. notes 36 and 44, above).
48. This also makes inference possible with respect to confessional pronouncements. However, these inferences must be firmly bounded by the whole of

our commitment and cannot be guided solely by logical considerations.

49. What we grasp in faith may surpass our understanding, but it does not come about without understanding. Whatever we do not understand at all cannot be believed. The core confession of commitment, although not rational in its inner nature, must nevertheless find a context in some rational-noetic system.

50. See James H. Olthuis.

51. The ultimate, although known in faith, also remains a mystery, i.e., we cannot explain or account for the origin of all explanation. The ultimate, viewed as the origin of all that is, makes known whatever can be known. The ultimate can be known only in terms of what it makes known. But in transcending all things of which it is the origin, it remains a mystery.

52. Thus, statements and terms of commitment cannot be subjected with the same confidence to inference as can straightforward concepts and propositions. Inference concerning the belief content of commitment requires independent validation by faith, in subjection to the Scriptures as the norm of faith. The articulated confession of the known mystery of faith is only partially understood. In terms of ultimates, every language "breaks down at some stage or other" (Popper, p. 210).

53. Wolterstorff and Plantinga seem to treat all belief as propositional (cf. note 43). They establish the appropriateness of certain ultimate beliefs by testing their implications through inference in relation to other beliefs. Using this procedure they both miss, I believe, one important fact: when they thus correct initial intuitions of the faith they do not seem to allow basic confessional beliefs to control their inference. Instead they let inference first control what can be believed (see Plantinga in *Does God*, Wolterstorff in *On Universals* and Hart in "On the Distinction").

54. Beliefs of commitment can be analyzed legitimately and the ordinary rules of inference apply. But such analysis is limited. What can and cannot be legitimately concluded is not just determined on the basis of logical considerations, but on the basis of what our whole faith allows us to think. Inference cannot take the mystery out of fiduciary knowledge.

55. The teaching concerning the Trinity is a good example. So is our belief in the authority of Scripture. From a purely logical point of view, the Bible is far from consistent and at essential points would be seen to contradict itself. But once the Bible is believed *as* a document of faith, its authority and essential unity can also be understood. Many more examples can be given. The relation of human responsibility and divine sovereignty is logically impenetrable. But once believed it can be understood quite adequately.

56. Compare notes 23 and 37 above. Self-evident beliefs are sometimes characterized as concepts or propositions which, upon being understood, must be believed. I am here suggesting that the compulsion to believe such a proposition comes from faith in rationality.

57. For Wolterstorff no control belief is essentially a control belief, depending on its role in inquiry (see *Reason Within*).

58. Thus, I here differ significantly from Wolterstorff (see *Reason Within*). Creedal beliefs and creedal statements can be disguished from genuine concepts and propositions precisely when we discover how the former do not, while the latter do, behave normally in inference. Creedal beliefs of commitment not only ground basic propositional beliefs, but they also derive their meaning from faith in revelation. Our faith intuitions (a Plantinga-Wolterstorff term) serve to correct inferential conclusions. Ultimate intuitions of faith will be corrected by inference only if an equally ultimate commitment to rationality prevails over faith.

59. At least, it is not defined in the way that is traditionally referred to by calling truth propositional or semantic.

60. Compare note 53.

61. It is especially those commitment beliefs that are essentially basic and ultimate that I have in mind here. Inference open to commitment will filter these beliefs into its procedures. It does this through certain philosophic assumptions constructed into fundamental categorial frameworks. They are paradigm organizers on perennial questions.

62. This could be called fideism, which I would then understand as follows: if our commitment to God's sovereignty, for example, would conflict with certain purely rational (i.e., formal logical) considerations, then those considerations would have to be reformed through control by essential beliefs of commitment.

63. It will not help to make a distinction between God as he is in himself and God as he is known to us or as he has revealed himself to us. Sometimes this distinction is introduced in order to clarify matters: whereas we may not know or fully understand the former, the latter is fully accessible in a univocal way to our analysis. The distinction is, however, quite meaningless and superfluous. If there is a God who is not known to us or who has not revealed himself to us, then that would end the matter right there; we would not have any awareness of him. Rather, it is the God who has revealed himself to us. It is also this very same God who transcends our understanding of him. A God who is not related to us is a God we do not know. God, the God we know through his revelation, is in relationship to us. We know no other God. The introduction of the distinction can only serve to make us doubtful of whether we truly know the true God.

64. And since our giving of ourselves always involves that sense of mystery about who it is to whom we give ourselves, conversion does involve an element of a leap into the unknown. The knowledge and the certainty come only after the surrender or, at best, in the surrender. They cannot precede it.

65. A mystery, of course, means that what we know is not fully accessible to our explanatory powers. But it is not thereby wholly inaccessible. We do,

in some important senses, know what we are doing when we believe, even in the sense of understanding what we are doing.

66. Thus there could be more visible manifestation than is now the case of the mystery of the one holy catholic church, which all Christians confess.

Bibliography

Alston, William P. "Religious Experience and Religious Beliefs." Unpublished.

Chisholm, Roderick M. *Theory of Knowledge*. Englewood Cliffs, N.J.: Prentice-Hall, 1966.

Concern About Science: possibilities and problems. Materials for the academic congress for the centennial of the Free University of Amsterdam. 1980.

Dooyeweerd, Herman. *A New Critique of Theoretical Thought*. Philadelphia: The Presbyterian and Reformed Publishing Company, 1954-1958. 4 vols.

Fowler, James W. *Stages of Faith*. New York: Harper and Row Publishing Company, 1981.

Geraets, Theodore F. *Rationality Today / La Rationalité Aujourd'hui*. Ottawa: Ottawa U.P., 1979.

Gibson, James J. *The Senses Considered as Perceptual Systems*. Boston: Houghton Mifflin, 1966.

Habermas, Jürgen. *Knowledge and Human Interests*. Boston: Beacon Press, 1971.

Hart, Hendrik. *The Challenge of Our Age*. Toronto: Wedge, 1967.

______. "On the Distinction between Creator and Creature: Discussion of a Central Theme in Wolterstorff's *On Universals*." *Philosophia Reformata*, 1971, pp. 183-193.

______. "The Re-cognition of Science as Knowledge" in *Concern About Science*, (see above) pp. 17-24. 1980.

______. "The Impasse of Rationality Today" in *Wetenschap Wijsheid en Filosoferen*. Assen: Van Gorcum, 1981 (Revised), pp. 174-200.

______. "Critical Reflections on Wolterstorff's *Reason Within the Bounds of Religion*." Unpublished ICS mimeo.

Hook, Janet. " 'Analytic' vs. 'Pluralist' Debate Splits Philosophical Association." *Chronicle of Higher Education*, January 12, 1981.

Jaki, Stanley L. *The Origin of Science and the Science of its Origin*. South Bend: Regnery/Gateway, 1979.

Jaspers, Karl. *Der Philosophische Glaube*. Fischer Bücherei, 1958.

______. *Der Philosophische Glaube angesichts der Offenbarung*. München: Piper, 1962.

Klapwijk, J., Griffioen, S. and Groenewoud, G., eds. *Vrede met de Rede?* (Peace with Reason?). Assen/Amsterdam: Van Gorcum, 1976.

Kuhn, Thomas S. *The Structure of Scientific Revolutions*. Chicago: Chicago University Press, 1970.

Laszlo, Ervin. *Introduction to Systems Philosophy*. New York: Harper and Row Publishing Company, 1972.

Merleau-Ponty, Maurice. *The Primacy of Perception*. Northwestern University Press, 1964.

Olthuis, James H. "Worldviews: Integrators between Faith and Praxis." Toronto, 1982. ICS mimeo, unpublished.

Pannenberg, W. *Theology and the Philosophy of Science*. Philadelphia: The Westminster Press, 1976.

Piaget, J. *The Psychology of Intelligence*. Totowa, N.J.: Littlefield, Adams & Co., 1973.

Plantinga, Alvin. "Is Belief in God Rational?" in *Rationality and Religious Belief*. C.F. Delaney, ed. Notre Dame: University of Notre Dame Press, 1979.

______. *Does God Have a Nature?* Milwaukee: Marquette University Press, 1980.

______. "The Reformed Objection to Natural Theology" in *The Journal of the American Catholic Association*, 1980.

______. *The Evidentialist Objection to Theistic Belief*. Fremantle Lectures, Oxford University, 1980.

Polanyi, Michael. *Personal Knowledge*. London: Routledge and Kegan, 1958.

Popper, Karl R. *Conjectures and Refutations*. New York: Harper and Row Publishing Company, 1968.

Radnitzky, Gerard. *Contemporary Schools of Metascience*. Chicago: Regnery, 1973.

Schinn, Roger L. and Abrecht, Paul. *Faith and Science in an Unjust World*. 2 vols. Geneva: World Council of Churches, 1980.

Tarski, A. "The Semantic Conception of Truth and the Foundations of Semantics." *Philosophy and Phenomenological Research*. 1944, pp. 341-376.

Vander Stelt, John C. *Philosophy and Scripture*. Marlton, N.J.: Mack Publishing Company, 1978.

Wolterstorff, N.P. *On Universals*. Chicago: Chicago University Press, 1970.

______. *Reason Within the Bounds of Religion*. Grand Rapids, Michigan: Eerdmans Publishing Company, 1976.

______. "Once Again, Creator/Creature," in *Philosophia Reformata*, 1981.

______. "Is Reason Enough?" in *The Reformed Journal*, April, 1981.

______. "Rational Belief." Unpublished.

______. "Justified Belief." Unpublished.

______. "Introduction" in *Rationality and Fidelity* (forthcoming).

Present Positions on Key Problems

Part Three:

The Nature of Philosophy

The Nature of Philosophy*

Henry Pietersma

LET US BEGIN BY SAYING THAT PHILOSOPHY is a mode of rational inquiry. This definition may not do complete justice to the nature of philosophy, but it can serve as a start. And it has the advantage of putting philosophy in a wider context: there are also non-philosophical modes of rational inquiry. I would not like to begin by placing philosophy somewhere in a domain that it has all to itself. We may be led to distinguish it from other things, but I think this should be a conclusion we are forced to accept by rational considerations, i.e., by considerations that derive their force from a universe of discourse which includes more than philosophy alone. Philosophy, then, as a mode of rational inquiry stands in the midst of other modes of rational inquiry, e.g., natural science.

Now, philosophy has been around for a long time, so one would expect that after centuries of philosophizing we are now fairly clear about its nature. If one said, as one is certainly inclined to say, that philosophy is the oldest form of inquiry, it would seem strange if we were not clear about its nature. As a matter of fact, I am inclined to say that, although progress in philosophy is not always clear, we have made some progress on the question of the nature of philosophy. It seems to me that we are now clearer about the nature of philosophy than in previous centuries. We are, to be sure, far from having reached agreement, but I think there is now more clarity about the sources of disagreement. And this does seem to indicate progress.

If there has been progress in the understanding of the nature of philosophy, this progress has been in large part the result of the growth of various kinds of rational inquiry which have proved themselves distinguishable from philosophy. More and more ques-

---

*I wish to express gratitude to my colleagues, J.A. Graff, P.H. Hess, and F.E. Sparshott, for their helpful comments on a previous version of this paper.

tions, initially thought to belong to the domain of philosophy, have in the course of the ages been recognized as questions to be handled in specifically different ways. As time went on, different questions seemed to call for distinctively different treatment. And as such peculiar treatment continued to seem appropriate, independent sciences developed. Thus fewer questions were left to philosophy, the presumption being that these remaining questions should be taken to define the nature of philosophy.

What I have just sketched as a history may be, at least in part, mythology. Yet I think that, as time passed, philosophers were less and less likely to mistake a scientific question for a philosophical one. To say, however, that this necessarily resulted in a clearer awareness of the peculiar nature of philosophy is still a simplification. For one could also say that philosophers became increasingly less clear as to the rightful place of philosophy. Several in recent times envisaged the complete demise of philosophy. Hopefully or despairingly they asked this question: hasn't it become clear that so-called philosophical issues can be much better dealt with by this or that scientific discipline? The theories of the Logical Positivists in the early part of this century are a good example of this kind of reaction. While at present there are not many that adopt their attitude, I think it is nonetheless true that there is still enough uncertainty about the nature of philosophy to make some philosophers wonder whether philosophy does represent an abiding disposition and inquiry. The puzzling utterances of Wittgenstein are, in this regard, significant. Is there a distinctive job for philosophy?

A good deal of what we call modern philosophy has been preoccupied with the human mind. Was the inquiry into other matters seen to be adequately represented by other disciplines, e.g., such a discipline as physics with regard to the material universe? Was the inquiry into the human mind seen to be necessary in order to give an adequate foundation to other disciplines? To the extent that the former was the case, philosophy appeared to be a mode of inquiry additional to others, e.g., investigating the mental alongside other disciplines that investigate matter. Such a view made good sense in the absence of a supposedly scientific psychology, so philosophy flourished until the end of the nineteenth century. If, on the other hand, the view prevails that sciences lack adequate insight into their own foundations, philosophy's preoccupation with the human mind requires a different interpretation. Then philosophy does not simply stand alongside other modes of inquiry, adding to our scientific knowledge. What it contributes is not more factual knowledge in the way in which one science can be said to add knowledge of facts to another science.

This second view seems to have prevailed, and to some extent one may be happy about this turn of events. Philosophy ought not to be confused with a science like psychology, whatever your view of psychology might be. One reason I have for expressing appreciation here is that this development toward a philosophy distinct from the sciences safeguards what we might call the *universal scope* of philosophical inquiry. Philosophy retains the vision of itself which it had possessed, certainly since Plato. In distinguishing itself from all the sciences it was in a position to discuss all of them from its own distinctive vantage point. It refused to be assigned a limited domain within the whole, however important that domain might be. However we may want to construe the critical function of philosophy, one thing at least remains clear: its scope is fairly wide. My expression of appreciation is not unqualified endorsement. We should remember that what is in question is a turn of philosophical inquiry toward the experiencing subject, even if this subject be construed in a non-psychological fashion. It is still a quest for the foundations of the sciences *in that subject*. As I hope to show, this turn should give us pause to reflect; but to restate my earlier point, the development in modern philosophy that gradually led to a distinction between philosophy and human sciences like psychology may be appreciated positively.

Kant's philosophy occupies pride of place in this development. I am not saying that historically it marks the final phase in that development; I *would* be inclined to say that later phases in the development of a distinction between the philosophical preoccupation with the mind and other types of inquiry into the mental tended, again and again, to appeal to a broadly Kantian perspective. I have already confessed that I have some appreciation for this perspective. My strategy in the remainder of this chapter will therefore be to discuss philosophy by considering the scope and limits of transcendental philosophy.

Now, I want the designation "transcendental philosophy" to be understood rather broadly, namely as a philosophy that views everything in relation to a subject experiencing it. And it insists on this perspective so strongly that any inquiry which comports itself as exclusively object-directed, abstracting from the subjective for the sake of objectivity, is branded as incomplete, although perhaps justified in view of its own direction of inquiry. The philosophical point of view demands that everything whatsoever should ultimately be seen in the context in which it is "subjectively constituted." That is to say, an object whose properties and relations may already have been determined in some inquiry or other should not be accepted as such and used, let us say, to construct an interpretation of other things, e.g., the mental acts directed upon it. (It makes no essential difference whether the philosopher articulates this context in terms of mental acts or the uses of words.) This kind of reflection, as it is usually stated, uncovers the *a priori* conditions for the possibility of experience. Taking the label this way I would apply it to a fairly wide range of philosophies. Let us now try to give a more precise characterization of this so-called transcendental philosophy.

As we would expect, it is a way of philosophizing that shows an intense awareness of the natural sciences and, particularly in its later post-Kantian manifestations, of other forms of systematic inquiry, e.g., the social sciences. In fact, as might already be clear from ideas I set forth earlier, it calls itself "transcendental" because it wants to mark the difference between itself and those other modes of rational inquiry, to which it nonetheless addresses itself. Philosophy no longer enters into direct competition with the sciences for knowledge of facts, as it is often stated somewhat ambiguously. A better way to put it would be to say that the philosophers concern themselves with scientific factual knowledge from a different point of view, namely a second-order point of view. Instead of asserting facts of that sort on the basis of evidence, the philosopher is concerned with questions about how there can be such a thing as factual knowledge based on evidence. It is in this sense that philosophy does not give new information or make discoveries, to quote some more slogans.

Besides, one point has to be made separately, even if it is already implied by what I just noted: philosophy no longer sees itself as concerned in a straightforward way with what earlier philosophy spoke of as the first principles of being. If philosophy still claims the title of ontology, this concern with being is carefully redefined. Ontology can be understood as setting out the first principles of being, if we are clear that these principles are in the first instance the principles of our experience. They do not necessarily reflect the way things are in themselves, but rather the way they are experienced. Philosophy, if you prefer, is concerned with the meaning of being. What do we mean when we say that something exists or has being? One might say this kind of philosophy expresses a deep sense of the fact that man's shadow lies heavy on whatever he claims to know as facts or being. Philosophy sees a problem here that calls for a solution, to be given by that rational mode of inquiry called transcendental philosophy. The problem is one that affects the sciences, engendering skepticism where the progress of inquiry seemed assured. This problem also affects philosophy, which reacts to it by reinterpreting itself. The questions that philosophy can and must face demand that inquiry be directed to the subject who is engaged in inquiry.

The problem just alluded to is of course in a certain sense most familiar: we often stand in the way of seeing things as they are. We acknowledge this whenever we suggest that we must avoid subjective bias, be on the alert for distortions due to irrelevant interests, recognize limitations placed on us by a certain situation, etc. In short, we acknowledge this by holding that truth is a matter of search; error something we must always try to avoid. In order to grasp things as they are we should be careful, circumspect, make an effort to avoid what could stand in the way. The effort required may be small. It may require of us simply to walk up to an object and fix our eyes on it. The effort may also be great, as when we carefully devise hypotheses and conduct elaborate, time-consuming experiments to see if there are things that would falsify those hypotheses. Whatever the case may be, we know we have to do certain things, or at least actively resist certain things (e.g., inattention), if we want to know something. (Such knowledge, of course, need not always be held desirable for its own sake or concern very lofty matters. It may be knowledge we need in order to act effectively and/or responsibly. And it may concern very ordinary, everyday things.)

But in all this we still presume to be able to succeed. We are confident that by doing, or refraining from, certain things we can escape our own shadow, directly confront reality, and say what it is. Even if we speak falsifying rather than verifying hypotheses, we still take it for granted that in some situations we can tell what we have in front of us and see that it falsifies the hypothesis we had formed. We believe that in one way or another we can make our statements accord with the facts; in other words, our efforts are not in vain.

Transcendental philosophy, however, seems to deny what I would call this realism of the truth-seeker. It expresses the view that, even after we have done all we can to remove what hinders a clear vision, we still do not confront things as in themselves they really are. Even in optimal situations (i.e., situations in which we have exhausted our cognitive powers), the thing-in-itself still eludes us. To put it more strongly and precisely, even when no one can indicate to us either powers we have not yet exercised or powers we might be able to acquire and then exercise, there remains a sense in which reality transcends our reach.

Such a bald statement can hardly be convincing, but philosophers who hold such a view present arguments worth attending to. They might begin by reminding us of the point Plato made in the *Meno*, namely that we can only find something if we approach it with a concept of that thing already in mind. Finding is recognizing something as being such and such, when the concept we have in mind sets out what it is to be a such and such. It is true that many of these concepts under which (at a given level of inquiry) we subsume particular things *have* at another level been formed, as we say, on the basis of experience. The concept of a swan was shown by experience not to include whiteness. This need not be disputed by a transcendental philosopher. What he will dispute, however, is that *all* our concepts are thus empirical in origin. The traditional triad of space, time, and causality, are not empirical concepts. They cannot be thought of as having been formed on the basis of experience; and they are not held to be either confirmable or deniable by experience. We already have them when we enter into experience.

The reasoning in which the transcendental philosopher here engages will in fact yield many more concepts which do not clearly originate from experience, i.e., in response to the way reality presents itself to us. We confront reality, for example, with all those concepts whose possession must be granted to us, inasmuch as we use that elaborate network of meanings we call language. When we use a language, we engage an understanding not just of space, time, and causality, but of an entire world. As we use words we imply a way of looking at things. Knowing a language is knowing *what* to say *when*, i.e., in what sorts of situations. All meanings form a kind of network. They are related to one another by contrasts and similarities, so one can say that by the use of a certain expression on a given occasion the speaker implies a contrast or a similarity. Calling something a human act, for instance, implicitly marks a contrast with other occurrences, e.g., purely natural occurrences. The use of language, then, consists in the use of a whole, internally articulated scheme of concepts; if some were eliminated, the meaning of those that remained would be altered.

Although these remarks do not sound Kantian, they are faithful to the spirit of transcendental philosophy. Now, it might be said by way of an objection that we do apply to reality the concepts we use. In the sort of optimal situation mentioned earlier (when we pronounce on the facts after most careful investigation), we feel that what we are presented with in that situation warrants, or calls for, the application of just those concepts we are applying to it. As is clear, this objection springs from a determination to adhere to the truth-seeker's realism and a sense of unease about the destructive implications of transcendental philosophy. Let me add yet another objection, distinct but closely tied in with the first. In finding that a concept has application, we think we extend our knowledge. We can now assert what the mere possession of a concept did not allow us to assert, namely that there exists an item of the kind specified in the concept. Isn't such an existential assertion a case of extending our knowledge beyond concepts and their relations to one another? Isn't this a case of confronting concepts with reality, the facts? And isn't it clear that there must be such a thing, if we are still to speak of verification in the broad sense of finding out whether or not something is true?

That such objections should be addressed to the transcendental philosopher is understandable, when we realize how much use the latter makes of an argument from the necessity of antecedently available concepts. No experience is possible except by virtue of such and such concepts, he argues. No knowledge of things in themselves is possible, he concludes, because we always confront reality armed with a conceptual framework. Let us now try to sketch what answer he might give to the objections. To begin, there is a sense in which the objections simply formulate what is incontrovertible. The sorts of situations envisaged have a phenomenological status that is above suspicion. We do at times find ourselves in epistemic situations similar to those indicated in the objections formulated above. To be sure, as Husserl's admirable phenomenology of epistemic levels shows, there is a lot more that could be said about such situations. But the point I want to make is that the transcendental philosopher is not likely to counter the objection by denying its phenomenological basis. Therefore he will, in a sense, accept those features of the objection that simply reflect a phenomenological description. His rejoinder will come in the form of a reinterpretation.

What he essentially argues is this: when we think we confront the facts, we actually find ourselves in a situation whose cognitive value is contextual. It is, of course, true that there are situations which we think will establish definitively whether something is the case. And this is not just a matter of fact—psychological and/or sociological. There is something like a right, or even an obligation, to regard certain situations in this way. And it seems phenomenologically true to say that, in those situations, what we are presented with calls for the application of the concepts we in fact apply to it. The way one would justify that application, for instance, would include talk of the object's mode of givenness—something to the effect that here the object *itself* is met with (the emphatic pronoun indicating the subject's awareness of less favorable epistemic situations).

Having granted all this, however, our philosopher will proceed and show that the type of situation in question has its privileged status only within a wider context. This context comprises, in addition to matters mentioned earlier (e.g., linguistic practices), all those sorts of activity that constitute the human search for truth; and as their objective correlate, the context comprises various categories of objects whose truths can be established by means of those various forms of search. Within this context, there corresponds to any given category of objects a type of inquiry appropriate to objects of that category. Finding that a concept applies, or that a statement is true because the corresponding fact obtains, is part and parcel of this same context. The situations envisaged may in some sense be optimal, but that sense should not blind us to the fact that they are embedded in the context of those activities, namely as their result.

A simple example will illustrate the kind of thing I have in mind. Suppose I want to find out something specific about the gorillas in the zoo. The context of this little inquiry takes for granted that I have a general idea of what gorillas are like. It likewise takes for granted what is the appropriate way to find out what I want to find out—for instance, whether they have babies. When I say the context takes this for granted, I mean I take all that for granted; it is a context I understand as such. This means I know where I am and where the gorillas are, and in order to bring my inquiry to a successful conclusion I have to travel a certain distance in a certain direction. In other words, I do not expect to see the gorillas simply by looking up from my typewriter. If I happened to look up and seemed to see one, I would reject it as an hallucination. It is only after I have traveled to the zoo, walked to the appropriate pavilion, and directed my eyes in a certain way that I will see a gorilla with a baby; this counts as confirmation of the fact I was to determine. If this confirmation was not experienced as the outcome of certain quite specific activities, I would not claim to have established the truth. Without this awareness of context, seeing a gorilla would have to be given a different epistemic value. Even if on the strength of seeing a gorilla in a different context I somehow concluded what was in fact true, I would consider this a miracle and myself as lucky. But I would not consider myself as having found out in the usual sense—the sense that defines the human search for truth.

On the other hand, granted the background, the search *is* finished when I look and see. The gorilla *herself* is there in front of me (using "herself" in the sense in which Husserl liked to talk about "seeing the object itself"). And she has a baby, no doubt about it. What I set out to investigate is the sort of thing about which further investigation is clearly inappropriate; I don't need either a telescope or a microscope. Hence the feeling that this confirmation is optimal. And because the activity of inquiry stops at this point and nothing further remains to be done (I merely have to look and see), we can perhaps give a certain amount of sense to that very old view according to which a knower is not active but passive, simply contemplating what is. And in the same spirit one might grant, as did Kant himself, that truth is to be defined as correspondence with reality. For in the kind of situation illustrated by my example, do we not confront reality and form our statements in accord with it?

As we can see, the transcendental philosophy can appear very generous to the realism of the truth-seeker. Yet in the final analysis he will insist that we have here only an internal aspect of our conceptual, transcendental framework. Whatever sense he may be willing to give to the correspondence-idea of truth will, in the final analysis, be defined fully by the inquiring activities that go into the establishing of correspondence. The relata of that relation lie *both* within the scope of inquiry. The recognition of reality and truth is validated from within the conceptual context of the search for truth.

We have to agree, I think, that this answer to the objections mentioned is impressive, as is the scope and importance of such transcendental philosophy. That so much philosophical work since Kant has been done on the topics suggested by him is not surprising. The transcendental point of view opens up before the philosopher a range of things which it is important to investigate and which, it would seem, can only be investigated by him. It may be a philosophy of reflection (in contrast to earlier philosophy), but this change of orientation does not seem to have affected its universal scope. In Kant's terms, philosophy may be an analytic of the understanding, but it is still an ontology; it still addresses itself to all of reality. Is this, in fact, correct?

Kant himself wasn't sure, as he showed by mentioning the thing-in-itself. His rational inquiry had laid bare what could be called the foundations of scientific inquiry. And inasmuch as they coincide with the very conditions of experience, Kant had secured those foundations. Experience is not possible without objects about which we can come to know things, the sorts of things the sciences claim to investigate. It makes no sense to want to cast doubt on the existence of an external world of knowable objects by arguing from experience, as Hume seemed to be doing. For, experience itself is a unitary scheme, one feature of which is precisely the existence of objects, which are external at least in the sense that they call for scientific inquiry (this is what we mean when we say they are distinct from any particular experiencing subject). But this success of his philosophy, Kant felt, was attainable only by paying a certain price, which is what he hinted at by his reference to the thing-in-itself which eludes us. It looked as though one form of skepticism could be eliminated only by inviting another.

Many later philosophers viewed Kant's position this way: as a position which, in spite of everything said by him to the contrary, is subjectivist and open to skeptical attack. And so they asked a reasonable question: does it make sense for rational inquiry to present, ostensibly as a conclusion from an argument, such a self-limiting idea? Hegel and those who followed his lead more or less believed that, if reason indicates a limit, it has *ipso facto* transcended that limit to a point of vantage beyond it. If reason constructs the subject-object distinction we find within the transcendental framework (as Kant's own philosophy had demonstrated), talk of a thing-in-itself could only make sense as an act of reason by which that distinction is cancelled from a more ultimate point of vantage, one already attained by reason. Thus if doubt is cast upon the metaphysical status of the transcendental framework, it must be doubt which evinces the power of thought, not a doubt that threatens it. I won't explore Hegel's philosophy beyond this point, since my concern is only to suggest the general character of such a response to Kant, a response which one also finds in contemporary positions that do not consider themselves idealist, e.g., some of Wittgenstein's followers.

For my present purposes the essential point is this. What is established in a descriptive analysis of our transcendental framework (some highlights of which I presented above) can be valued in a different way from Kant. He continued to wonder about the thing-in-itself and was therefore in some sense skeptical about this transcendental framework of forms and categories. As I hope I have made clear, a certain justifiable realism is an internal feature of this framework: the subject thinks he gets to know things as they really are, an idea the transcendental analysis showed to be not entirely absurd. Kant's wonder, however, considers the framework externally, although the very notion of adopting such an external point of view is beset with problems, as philosophers since Kant have never tired of pointing out. (How often have we been assured in recent years, particularly by Wittgensteinians, that such skepticism is pointless?) Now if we could only cease to wonder, the metaphysical status of the framework would be assured, given the way it is understood from the inside. As my brief allusion to Hegel was meant to suggest, the power of thought is then reinstated as being co-terminous with the domain of real being. And one may adopt such a view without sharing the Hegelian conviction that this power leads us to an ultimate point of view beyond, where subject and object are one.

As to the nature of philosophy, it would seem to be clear that, having exorcized the thing-in-itself (as well as the evil genius of Descartes), philosophy can settle down and be descriptive of conceptual or linguistic frameworks. (The use of the term "framework" may in fact be argued to be inappropriate, since its use suggests an external point of view.) If philosophy makes any discoveries, they will be due to the circumstance that a user of a framework tends to forget it is there, being preoccupied with all the things that appear by virtue of his using it (a point exploited by Heidegger in the development of his concept of being). Philosophy serves to recall what we know but had forgotten.

Philosophy still understands itself as the broadly reflective analysis of experience. What it "discovers," if we do say that it discovers something, is still interpreted subjectivistically, e.g., as rules of linguistic practices or grammar. What non-philosophical people forget and thus overlook, however, is not understood by them that way. (Understanding must in this case, of course, be implicit.) They will understand all that as being, at least for the most part, the general way in which things exist in relation to one another and to us. Because the rules are so general, they do not constitute the focus of our everyday preoccupations, but they are still taken to make up the world, rather than the general structure of our linguistic practice. Philosophy, as I said, still comports itself as a reinterpretation when it marks them as rules followed in a practice.

On the other hand, philosophy seems to be animated by a remarkable confidence, as typically shown by the confidence vis-à-vis the skeptic who wonders whether it is really so apparent that we know things as they are. The kind of philosopher I have in mind thinks he has adequately responded to skepticism by showing that in the terms of what we all believe (alternatively, the way we all act) the only doubts which make sense are those that can be removed by specific modes of inquiry. As to other doubts, namely those that cannot be so removed, he confidently calls them senseless. Such a skeptic, he might add, sets standards other than those we all use, so it is not surprising that what we all do does not satisfy them (cf. Strawson).

But I would then like to ask a question: whence that confidence about our standards, i.e., those laid bare by descriptive philosophy?

Is it really obvious that epistemic practices in which we all engage can reveal the truth about things other than themselves? I think we can only dismiss this question if we adopt an idealist stance. By opting for such a stance we take a position that has no external point of view. There is no point of view in which the transcendental framework as a whole can be related to reality in a way that causes us to wonder. Is it apparent that this is impossible? Perhaps this raises questions that cannot be answered, but that does not mean they cannot be asked. We may have to grant further that the formulation of such questions is difficult. Our formulations are vague and halting. There is hardly one that is not open to the charge of making use of questionable metaphors and models. If in spite of that such a question remains alive, I think its source must lie in some deeper level of our being.

We are, of course, tempted to say that this sort of question arises from the sciences, because they seem to be placing man in the kind of wider context to which I alluded earlier. Besides, it is true as a matter of history that the kind of radical skepticism at issue here has often felt itself to be nourished by science. What if our so-called transcendental categories are no more than biologically necessitated modes of comportment (Nietzsche)? But it is clear that skepticism seriously argued on that kind of basis is absurd, as has often been pointed out (e.g., by insisting on distinguishing reasons and causes). The grounds for such a doubt are derived from a scientific view assumed to have been demonstrated by human thought; so these grounds presuppose a certainty which this skepticism wants to cast doubt on. Scientists have at times their doubts, but those doubts can be removed by further research. The kind of doubt connected with the wondering I spoke of cannot be grounded in science nor answered by further science. If this kind of skeptic vaguely gestures in the direction of a wider context of being and wonders what place human thinking has within it, we cannot articulate that context by means of a certain body of scientific knowledge. In this respect a transcendental philosophy like that of Husserl seems to me to have made a valid point by insisting on what he called a transcendental-phenomenological reduction.

I think we have to admit that the radical skeptic, who attacks the self-confidence of philosophy in the form I characterized above, has no grounds for saying it is mistaken, but is a skeptic who insists we have no grounds for saying it is well-founded. And given this state of affairs his attitude is one of distrust. That wider context of being he hints at does not give him a source for confidence; it is silent like Pascal's infinity of space. It is no use arguing against him, except when he succumbs to the temptation to cast his doubt into the form of an argument. But since his real doubt is not a matter of having grounds and arguments, it will survive the refutation of any argument he might on occasion offer.

I bring up the matter of skepticism because it can lead us into the final stages of my discussion of the nature of philosophy. Skepticism gives prominence to the issue of the metaphysical status of the subject, the place of man in the totality of being. The skeptic wonders how well-founded is the confidence of the philosopher who thinks that the categories we use in experience are also the categories of being itself, so that we can say we know the general principles of being. Do we know this? What is our metaphysical status in being? As I tried to suggest, rational inquiry as exemplified by the kind of philosophy I sketched cannot answer this question, although the philosopher who carries out the inquiry may adopt an attitude that is not open to this question. The radical skeptic, by contrast, is open to this question but despairs of an answer. The Christian philosopher, however, is open to the question and he believes he has received an answer. And by virtue of that answer he confronts the skeptic with a new confidence in rational inquiry.

For reasons that should be clear by now, this answer cannot itself be an outcome of the rational inquiry of philosophy. It is rather a matter of having received a gift, in the religious-confessional sense in which that word has been used in the Bible. I think it is important to say that the Christian philosopher stands in the same "place" as the skeptic: without the gift of faith he would also be without a basic orientation and unable to trust. His confidence is therefore quite different from that of the philosophers discussed earlier.

The Christian philosopher proceeds from the belief that his metaphysical status has been made clear to him. He feels he is part of a whole and has been given a part. He feels part of an order of being created by God for a purpose, and therefore in principle he is able to fulfill that purpose. And within this created whole he has been given certain parts to play, one of which consists in rational inquiry. The crucial point here is the idea of purpose or design. Man's cognitive capacities, when used aright, can be relied upon to give us knowledge of things other than themselves, because God made them adequate for that role. In slightly different terminology, the basic principles of inquiry, the adherence to which entails a specific use of capacities, are such that following them makes sense with regard to our cognitive goals: reality can become known in that way.

There is such a thing as a Christian standpoint in philosophy, inasmuch as the confidence spoken of is not shared by every philosopher. To be sure, one might say that a philosopher like Aristotle also had this confidence. And one might also think of Jewish philosophers whose source for confidence would be very similar to that of Christians. As regards Aristotle, the decisive difference consists in the fact that the source of his confidence does not lie in revelation (unless we want to introduce the idea of natural revelation at this point). I am not at all sure I do justice to the matter, but I am inclined to think that this confidence (which is not peculiar to Aristotle) represents a kind of blind dogmatism, unaware of its own precariousness. As to the difference between Jewish and Christian philosophy, the central question has to do with the difference in Messianic outlook. I will again have to deal with the issue in a manner that may be inadequate. What the Jew and the Christian share is the belief in God as Creator. And the common element in their respective Messianic views is the belief that God reaffirms his creative purpose in the face of evil by sending a Messiah. Now, for the Christian this renewal has in principle already occurred with the Christ-event, but the Jewish faith insists that the Messianic age is in every respect still in the future. What relevance does this difference in outlook have for the status of man as a knower? In the Christian view, a Christian is a new creature and his rational capacity participates in this newness. But God's act of renewal is also operating in the world at large: men participate in it, even if they do not acknowledge Christ. Now, if one believes that kind of thing, it does seem to me to qualify the Christian confidence in a way that, if I am right, sets it apart from the Jewish point of view. I repeat, however, that what I have said on this issue is vague, tentative, and possibly quite wrong.

To return to my principal train of thought, there is such a thing as a Christian standpoint in philosophy, because the specifically Christian confidence is not shared by every philosopher. And the acknowledgment of revelation gives an aspect to reality that not every philosopher appreciates. I am here thinking of the idea of a new creation, spoken of in the Bible. But stressing that such things set a Christian apart is only a half-truth. Precisely those things that have (as yet) only been revealed to him and that small community we call the church are in principle accessible to all. Ideas like creation and the kingship of God refer to things that are objective; they are truths, even if concealed from many. If the Christian philosopher believes his capacity for rational inquiry is able to reveal truth, then this capacity is shared with all men. Therefore, he will exercise that capacity and engage everybody in it, confident that this is not a hopeless enterprise. There are truths that can in principle be discovered.

This may sound somewhat like a naive confidence, not at all a true reflection of the concrete situation we are in. Such an objection is fair and compels me to add to the point I just made. The confidence I have in mind is tempered by an awareness of the manner in which it was gained. It has its source in a revelation that does not permit us to expect ready agreement or assent from other philosophers. This source speaks of blindness, hardness of heart, sinful passions, a very profound unwillingness on the part of human beings. It speaks of a necessary change in us which our own powers are unable to bring about. The language reflects what we might be tempted to call without qualification the real situation, from which even the Christian philosopher himself is not free. In other words, more than rational inquiry is needed.

This is probably the most profound reason why Christian philosophy is flanked by Christian theology. I am not going to propose a general way of distinguishing those two disciplines. However it does seem useful at this juncture to say that theology is closely linked in its central concerns with the community of believers—for instance, with the purity of preaching. This community of believers is characterized by such activities as preaching and evangelizing. In such activities, theology addresses itself and those not part of it. And it does address people at what I will call (for lack of a better term) the existential level. In biblical language, it calls for conversion. And these things must continue (till the end of the ages, as the Bible has it), because there will always remain the necessity for conversion.

The Christian philosopher, himself a member of that community, knows that the new creation is not yet present. He will therefore not be afraid to take a position that does not immediately command the agreement of others, nor be puzzled if he often stands alone in his philosophizing. He knows that rational inquiry is not taking place in a vacuum. It is not something absolute, in possession of a life of its own and operating in obedience only to its own intrinsic laws. How could he fail to realize this, seeing that his own life as a Christian springs precisely from a de-absolutization of rational inquiry?

But he will nonetheless not comport himself as though he were really alone (or only addressing the believing community to which he belongs). He will address all philosophers by engaging them in rational inquiry, doing this in the justified hope that the nature of things will be discovered in this way. In fact, doesn't such an attitude amount to a formal definition of rationality? I think it is important to emphasize that the Christian philosopher is bound by his religious convictions to continue the discussion, no matter what opposition he may encounter. After all, we are not sure how much can be attained by such discussion, are we?

A frequently asked question (which in the past I often found unnerving) is this: how does one's Christian commitment show itself in one's philosophizing? What I just said is part of the answer. We show it by showing faith in rational inquiry. The other part of the answer has to do with what I would call a certain sensitivity to the existence of such things as commitments. Because of his own commitment, a Christian philosopher has a developed sense for noticing commitments. He is accordingly prepared to find them and often does, in which case he feels bound by his own allegiance. That is to say, when he encounters affirmations that spring from what he can only regard as an unwillingness—perhaps an inability—to listen to God, he will repudiate such affirmations.

It seems important to stress that such a readiness to stand by one's conviction should be combined with a readiness to engage with others in a rational argument. When the former predominates, we get a style of Christian philosophizing that tends to become isolated, in the end communicating only with a certain believing community. Everything one says as a philosopher tends to be said in a spirit of repudiation and antithesis. One feels that everything must have stamped upon it the clear imprint of one's Christian commitment. For this reason the readiness to stand firm by one's commitment ought to be tempered by a readiness to see where rational inquiry may lead us. There is yet another reason. Unless we do engage with other philosophers in rational inquiry, we cannot with certainty identify the issues we are really confronting in an antithetical commitment. What may seem to be an antithetical commitment may turn out to be a case in which some agreement can be reached by argumentation and inquiry. It would then be absurd to formulate a position on such an issue supposedly on the strength of one's Christian commitment.

I am inclined to think that this chapter illustrates the point I just made. Just where and how I would affirm my Christian conviction in the broad area of epistemological and metaphysical issues did not become clear to me until I had engaged a large number of philosophers in a discussion. If I have illustrated that point, I will feel somewhat less guilty about my preoccupation with those matters in what was to be discussion of the nature of philosophy. Indeed, my discussion of the nature of philosophy reflects the things I spent some time thinking about in recent years. If I had worked in ethics or the philosophy of history, the discussion would no doubt have been very different. Let me conclude by affirming that philosophy is a many-splendored thing whose beauty can only be sung by many different voices.

The Nature of Philosophy

D.F.M. Strauss

Introductory Remarks

WHEN DISCUSSING *RATIONALITY* IN THE CALVINIAN tradition, any account of the nature of philosophy should naturally pay attention to the role of rationality in the area of philosophical reflection. A mere glimpse at the vast number of publications dedicated to the problem of "paradigms" since Kuhn's work on the structure of scientific revolutions appeared in 1962 emphasizes that the scope and limits of rationality are now being subjected to an extensive re-evaluation. Studies in the history of science have contributed greatly to our understanding of the role of underlying theoretical constructs ("paradigms"). These function as a necessary theoretical frame of reference in order to account for the regularities and law-conformity of factual reality.

In this context I want to start with an examination of the typical and unique structure of theoretical (i.e., scientific) thought.

The Uniqueness of Theorizing

To come to grips with this problem, it is necessary to draw a distinction between non-distinctive characteristics and that which can be considered to be the distinctive feature of any truly scientific activity. Features like systematization, verification/falsification, method (and the so-called relation between a knowing subject and a studied object) are all non-distinctive, since various non-scientific forms of human behavior may display the same properties. (If a housewife wants to bake a cake she has to *make sure*—"verify"—that she uses the correct ingredients; then she has to proceed *systematically*, strictly following the *method* described by the recipe she has *studied* in order to achieve the desired result.) Clearly, one can distinguish between scientific and non-scientific subject-object relations, methods, verification and falsification, and systematization.

To be sure, any concrete entity ("object") *functions* concretely in different *modes of being* (modalities), such as the numerical mode (aspect), the *spatial* modality, the sensitive sphere (sometimes passively as a *sensed* object), the logical aspect (for instance as something analyzable, i.e., identifiable and distinguishable), the sign-aspect (its name), etc. The fundamental question, therefore, is not "What object is scientifically studied" but "From what angle (aspect, mode) is this or that entity approached?" Certain things, events, or societal relationships always allow us to approach them from diverse angles or modal perspectives; different *modalities* may serve as special scientific points of entry to concrete reality.

To think scientifically, one has to focus one's attention on a specific modal perspective, disregarding other modal points of entry. What is at stake here is the abstraction of modal aspects. Because abstraction occurs frequently in non-scientific daily life, it should not be used in an unqualified sense as the distinctive feature of scientific activities. The remarkable fact is that *abstraction* and *analysis* imply each other reciprocally. To analyze something always implies an act of identification and distinguishing, and abstraction concerns the lifting out or identification of something or at least some property of it by disregarding it or distinguishing it from non-relevant things or features. In a similar way the two legs of analysis imply each other: identifying something requires the necessary distinction between what is identified and what is distinguished from it, and vice versa.

Although we may be inclined to think that non-theoretical concepts are not abstractive,[1] the reciprocity of analysis and abstraction implies quite the contrary. The identification of *a human being* or *a car* presupposes the prior general *abstract* concept, for otherwise no one would have been able to place *this* man or *that* car within the conceptual category of human beings or automobiles. Consider the little child seeing for the first time a particular bird. To answer her question about what it is, her father replies: it is a *pigeon*. A few days later she encounters an *owl*, but then she calls it a pigeon. What happened is that she singled out certain common characteristics of birds —such as having feathers, having a bill, having wings, having legs—by disregarding those particular features that show the differences between a pigeon and an owl. In other words, she formed the concept *bird* by means of abstraction, i.e., by lifting out and disregarding, identifying and distinguishing, but she designated this concept with the wrong word *pigeon*. This example illustrates the difference between concept and word.

Since our normal everyday concepts are directed toward the typical total representation of things and events without articulating specific modes as opposed to and distinguished from others, we may call this kind of abstraction (analysis) "entitary directed" or even "concrete." Abstract concepts like "man," "car" and "bird" are not concerned with specific aspects or functions of entities *apart* from the entities experienced. Number will always in non-theoretical experience be related to some entities or parts of an entity that can be *counted*, spatial configurations to some entity *measured*, physical mass to some entity *weighed*, etc. Surely "concrete abstraction" is not the only kind of abstraction.

Scientific activities display a specific kind of analysis, namely *modal analysis* (abstraction). Although the various aspects of reality are implied in our non-scientific experience of things and events, only scientific analysis reflects on the universal nature of the modal aspects as such. For this reason, every special scientist implicitly or explicitly has to answer the following *philosophical* basic question of his special science: what is the delimiting angle of approach of my special science? To answer this question one has to *identify* the relevant modality, which implies that one must simultaneously distinguish it from other modalities. The mutual cohering presence both of identification and distinguishing stresses the necessity of a philosophical view on the cohering diversity of modal aspects: a view that transcends the boundaries of any modally delimited special scientific viewpoint. In other words, the very nature of modal abstraction (analysis) reveals the philosophical dependence of the special sciences.

Moreover, the nature of philosophy is fundamentally tied up with modal abstraction, since the task of taking into account all possible distinguishable and identifiable modes of reality is peculiar to its theoretical approach.

From discussions with students and other philosophers, it is clear that the notion of modal abstraction still causes some misunderstanding. The crucial point to observe is that we do not claim that *any* philosophers or *any* special scientists not acquainted with our analysis have in fact coined modal distinctions and then explicitly used them to account for whatever they studied. However, not sharing our specific analysis does not mean that philosophers and special scientists did not actually, albeit implicitly, *use* modal notions in theoretical expositions. We do want to claim that not being aware of or not actually being engaged in explicitly developing modal distinctions does not at all detract from the transcendental limiting nature of the modal aspects for theorizing. Furthermore, it also does not mean that theoretical analysis, i.e., modal analysis, is divorced from the concrete entities of our daily life. On the contrary, it might still be concerned extensively with various kinds of entities—but then always from the modal perspective of some point of entry. What is at stake here may be framed in terms of the following subsection.

The "Coherence of Irreducibles"

Perhaps one can claim that a most basic philosophical problem concerns the "coherence of irreducibles." One may consider all *monistic* approaches in philosophy and the special sciences as implicitly answering this question in the negative. Monistic pan-psychism (for example, the view of Th. de Chardin) wants to reduce every phenomenon to a psychic perspective. In a similar way, the classical mechanistic approach in physics, following Galileo's discovery of the kinematical law of inertia, has tried, at least in its main trend, to view all physical bodies exclusively in terms of *mechanical movement.*[2] However, Planck's discovery of the quantum and the establishment of the second main law of thermo-dynamics, i.e., the law of non-decreasing entropy (which indicates the irreversibility of physical processes) revealed the untenability of this monistic mechanistic approach in modern physics.

What is normally referred to as "primitives" in logic and foundational studies pertain to the "irreducibles" mentioned above. These primitives also reflect the inherent limitations of concept-formation and definition; in the final analysis every definition can only define something in *indefinable terms*. Whenever one tries to *define* a truly primitive notion, the inevitable result is (antinomic) *reduction*. Zeno's classical reasoning against the reality of movement is nothing but an attempt to define pure movement (a primitive notion in kinematics) solely in static spatial terms—as if a moving body possesses from moment to moment a definite place in space. In his fourth fragment one reads: "something in motion neither moves in the space it is occupying, nor in the space it does not occupy" (Diels-Kranz, B Fr.4). When a moving body is, at every moment of its "movement," in one specific place, it is after all at rest, since "being in one place" simply means "not being in motion." It is not of any help to define movement in terms of *change of place*, as Descartes has tried to do.[3]

One of the two substances distinguished by Descartes is characterized by the essential feature of *extension*. However, in one sense the extension of a body is nothing but its *place*. But if extension, i.e., its place, is the very essence of a body (cf. *Med*.II), then the definition of movement as a *change of place* is antinomic: being essentially its place, no body could ever change place—at least not without simultaneously eradicating its very essence!

Let us consider another example, that of *historicism*. According to historicism, everything (law, morality, art, faith, language and so on) is taken up in the flow of historical change and is everywhere only comprehensible as elements of an historical process. Contrary to this claim we are used to speaking about legal history, art history, economic history, and so on. But if law, art, and economics *are* nothing but history, we in fact must deal with the contradiction of an *historical history*. Whatever is history, cannot have a history; and whatever has a history, cannot itself be history. The irony is that historicism, reducing every facet of reality to the historical mode, has thus eliminated the very meaning of history; if everything is history, there is nothing that can have a history!

Thus far we have emphasized the irreducibility of primitive terms residing in the different universal modalities or aspects of reality. Of course they also display a remarkable *coherence*. To account for these inter-relationships, we provisionally have to overlook other differences between the natural aspects (number, space, movement, and the physical, biotical and sensitive aspects) and the typical human modalities (the logical, historical, sign-mode, social, economic, aesthetic, juridical, ethical and certitudinal aspects).

The coherence between the various aspects of reality can already be seen from a number of expressions used in everyday life, such as: legal feeling, social justice, historical causality and economic trust. Let us consider the following two expressions: social life, and biotic life. Clearly, there is a *moment of similarity* present between them: the term *life*. However, life in a biotic sense differs fundamentally from life in a social sense. Therefore, *in* this moment of similarity the difference between the social aspect and the biotic aspect reveals itself. It sounds almost paradoxical to say that two aspects show a similarity precisely in that moment which reveals the difference between them. This kind of a "difference in terms of similarity" may be called a *modal analogy*. Surely modal analogies are not the only kind of analogies that one can distinguish, since entities also evince differences in their moments of similarity. These *entitary analogies* are very common in ordinary (and even scientific) language where they are designated by *metaphors*.

Depending on the specific place of an aspect, one may detect a number of anticipatory and retrocipatory analogies within its structure. Legal feeling represents a sensitive retrocipatory analogy within the structure of the juridical aspect; social justice is an anticipatory juridical analogy within the social aspect; historical causality is a retrocipation from the cultural mode to the physical aspect; and economic trust represents an economic anticipation to the fiduciary (certitudinal) aspect of reality.

In a certain sense one can say with Dooyeweerd that through its analogies a specific aspect reflects its coherence with all other aspects of reality. Consider the following analogies within the structure of the social aspect: social unity and multiplicity (numerical analogy); social sphere, coherence and stratification (spatial analogy); social endurance (kinematic analogy); social dynamics (physical analogy); social growth, differentiation and integration (biotic analogy); social sensitivity (emotional analogy); social consensus and conflict (logical analogy); social power (cultural analogy); social meaning and interpretation (sign-analogy); social style (aesthetic analogy); social justice (juridical analogy); social integrity (ethical analogy); and social security or certainty (certitudinal analogy).

This representation might give the impression of a static scheme. However, the analysis of any analogy is a dynamic concern which constantly refers to other (not yet analyzed) analogical moments. To illustrate this state of affairs, we might consider the sociological basic concept: *social order*. This concept implies a *unity* in the *multiplicity* of the social norms that constitute a specific social order. To attain such a unity, the relevant office-bearer, as the *competent organ*, should *constantly* take care that, within his *sphere* of competence, the necessary reformational *changes* take place in order to ensure the internal stability and solidarity of the *life-form* concerned, amidst whatever *external* changes that might occur. To explain what is at stake in the concept *social order*, it is therefore necessary to use terms that stem from other modal points of entry. The italicized words refer successively to the numerical (the first two), the formative, the biotic, the kinematic and the spatial (both the terms *form* and *external*) aspects. It is only in this indissoluble coherence with other analogical moments within the social aspect that one can effectively analyze a specific analogy.

Later analogies also enable one to specify the meaning of earlier ones in a more precise way. For instance, in terms of the numerical analogy in the social aspect we are allowed to think of a specific life-form as a social *unit*. The spatial analogy provides a closer precision formulated for this analogical moment by saying that every life-form in its unity is a real social *whole*. The kinematic analogy adds yet another specification to the analysis, for in terms of this moment one is entitled to say that the unity of every social whole is *relatively constant*. At least some life-forms allow for a continuous *flow* of their members without any effect on the identity, durability or totality-character of the life-form concerned. In this moment we meet an analogy of thermo-dynamic open systems in the social aspect. An analysis of the biotic analogy allows the following formulation: every *differentiated* social unit ought to be an *integrated* whole. Without extending this brief reflection, the point should be clear: every analogical moment reciprocally determines the meaning of every other analogy in the structure of the social aspect, thus underlining the inherent dynamics demanded by this kind of (transcendental-empirical) analysis.

A confrontation with modern sociological theory reveals that no single trend can ignore the fundamental philosophical question: in what specific sense are the different basic concepts of sociology used? What do we understand when we use concepts like social order, social sphere, social endurance, social dynamics, social life, social competence and social significance and interpretation? Important sociological theories have emerged from an over-estimation of certain analogical moments, mostly understood in an original, instead of analogical, sense. One need only think about the mechanistic school, the physicalistic approach, organicism and functionalism (both over-emphasizing the biotic viewpoint), behaviorism, conflict-theory, the historicism of Mannheim and other representatives of the sociology of knowledge, and the (at least seven) variants of modern symbolic interactionism to come to some understanding of the various *systematic emphases* in the history and contemporary situation of sociology.[4]

From this brief discussion it should be clear that the problem of the coherence of irreducibles not only pertains to the core of philosophy but simultaneously confronts the various special sciences with inescapable *philosophical* basic problems. We may extend this analysis by paying special attention to a well-known and time-honored philosophical problem.

Universality and the Individual Side of Entities

We have seen that any act of "concrete abstraction" yields general concepts. The subsequent identification of any individual entity, for example, *this* human being or *this* car, is accomplished through the recognition of those universal characteristics implied (or combined) in the concept of the respective entity. However, to be a *human being* or a *car*, the entities concerned necessarily have to conform to the structural conditions for *being* human or *being* a car. These conditions are to be seen as the *structures for* the existence of an entity, whereas the law-conformative structuredness of a given entity reveals the universal way in which such an entity reflects its being subjected to the relevant conditioning structures-for. In other words, there is a strict correlation between the universal *conditioning order for*, and the universal *conditioned orderliness of* entities. Every entity displays both an individual and a universal side, in subjection to the universal conditioning order.[5]

Concept-formation is always bound up with the universal order for, and the universal orderliness of things. This implies, as already discovered by Aristotle, that one cannot comprehend conceptually the individual side of an entity. To save the possibility of (scientific) concept-formation, Aristotle had to introduce next to his primary substance (indicating something *individual*) the secondary substance as the *universal* substantial form of things (needing for its actualization *matter*). Unfortunately, he identified knowledge with conceptual knowledge (see *Metaphysics*, 1036 a 2-9). Contrary to this view, we must recognize that everybody has *knowledge* of things in their individuality, i.e., has knowledge of the individual side of things, even though this kind of knowledge is not conceptual. Rather it is of a limiting and approximating nature, referring to the individual side of entities in terms of universal features. But this is precisely what "idea-knowledge" is all about: an idea concentrates a conceptual diversity upon (or refers it to) that which transcends the limits of all concept-formation.

Aristotle leaves no room for *idea-knowledge*. This kind of approach is defined as *rationalistic*. Rationalism always elevates the universal (or universality) as the only source of knowledge. Irrationalism, on the other hand, always wants to pay tribute to the contingent uniqueness of the individual side of things or events which, as we saw, transcends the limits of concept-formation. Irrationalism leaves no room for real conceptual knowledge.

It is tempting to define this divergent appraisal of the relationship between the universal and the individual in terms of the opposition between universalism and individualism. But I have reserved this opposition to indicate alternative basic denominators for the cosmic diversity of aspects and entities.

Individualism always uses the discrete nature of the aspect of number (or analogies of number in later cosmic aspects) to explain cosmic reality in its entirety. Everything is reduced to a discrete multiplicity of elements (sometimes thought of as being in interaction; cf. sociological individualism). Universalism, on the other hand, rejects this "additive" approach by claiming that some kind of a whole precedes every individual, which is simply a dependent part of the larger whole. This use of the spatial whole-part relation (or analogies of this relation in other aspects) has many possibilities. Mostly it is associated with an organic whole and its parts, although it is possible to think organicistically in an individualistic way (by emphasizing the discrete numerical analogy in the biotical aspect). Here one may mention Spencer who, in spite of his organicism, advocated a more pronounced individualism instead of a more pronounced nationalism. In his *Politics*, Aristotle gave one of the classical formulations of universalism: "The state is, clearly, by nature prior to the household or to the individual human being; for the whole must be prior to the part" (1253 a 19-20).

The individuality of an entity can never be derived from any modal aspect. To be sure, any entity functions concretely within the universal cadre of different modalities, keeping in mind that the term *concretely* encompasses both the individual and the universal side of an entity. Viewed from the angle of the modal aspects, one therefore encounters various forms of *individuality* and *orderliness* within each modality. The typical structure of an entity *specifies* (but never individualizes) the universal modal structure of an aspect. It is preferable to speak in this context of modal specificity instead of modal individuality. Thermo-dynamics, for example, is a general and fundamental physical discipline, abstracting completely both from the individuality and the specificity of physical entities. It therefore uses modal function concepts such as volume, entropy, specific heat, etc., without reference to any entitary specification. In statistical physics this abstraction can no longer be maintained, since here one has to account for the *relation* between the physical micro-structures constituting macro-systems, and thermo-dynamics. This implies that the typical totality-character of physical entities should be recognized. Therefore, specific heat is dealt with differently in statistical physics according to the physical state of physical entities (compare the solid state with the gaseous state). In thermo-dynamics, however, the expression "specific heat" is used in a purely modal-functional sense, without any specification of the nature of a solid state, fluid state, or gaseous state.

The individuality and identity of entities are more than functional. This is why we have to distinguish the dimension of entities from that of the modalities. One cannot first break up an entity's unity in different modal functions, and then, in retrospect, seek *unity* in an entity. The transcendental idea of the individual whole precedes the theoretical analysis of its modal functions. For example, the well-known wave-particle duality is a direct outcome of the typical totality-character of physically qualified entities. The experimental difference between interference-phenomena and the Compton-effect, allowing for two mutually exclusive descriptions which cannot simultaneously be confirmed in an empirical way, in fact refers to irreducible aspects and their analogies within the structure of physically qualified entities. The concepts *particle* and *wave* are indeed modal functional concepts of physics, referring to two different retrocipatory analogies within the kinematical aspect, namely, movement-multiplicity and movement-extension. Number, space and movement, in their structural physical specification, remain mutually irreducible aspects of physical entities, fitted by means of modal analogies into an inter-modal coherence. Therefore it is impossible to reduce the functionally distinguished concepts *particle* and *wave* to each other—a state of affairs indeed confirmed by experiment!

The Conditioning Function of Modal Aspects in Theorizing

The unique structure of every aspect conditions theorizing in such a way that basic statements about reality can only use "point-of-entry-concepts." In the history of Western philosophy terms like retrocipatory and anticipatory analogies, derived from various modal perspectives, were used in connection with concrete, sensorily perceptible things. These terms even served the metaphysical theories developed to account for their existence.

From the fact that every entity functions within the universal structure of the numerical (arithmetical) aspect, the Pythagoreans drew the metaphysical conclusion that everything *is* number. In this way they wanted to account for the *order* in the cosmos. If we replace *order* with the Greek word *nomos*, and combine it with the term *cosmos*, we may say that the Pythagoreans used the modal meaning of number to express their fundamental *cosmonomic idea* about reality. In this sense modal arithmetical notions were used in the context of an *idea* concerning the diversity and unity in reality. Clearly, numerical notions may be used conceptually to express modally abstracted states of affairs, or they may be used to speak about things, or even reality in its entirety transcending the limits of the aspect of number; then we encounter an *idea*-use of such notions. Every modal aspect allows such a two-directional employment of its meaning.

Parmenides and his school were not interested in a pure

geometrical analysis, since they simply used these spatial notions to develop their metaphysical theory of *being*. Nevertheless, in doing this, they discovered and used crucial features of spatial extension (for instance, the implied whole-part relation, revealing the infinite divisibility of something continuous, cf. Zeno's B Fr.3). T.G. Sinnige correctly points out that Parmenides' description of *being* has been bound up to a high degree with "spatial images."[6] He also clearly sensed the two-directional use of a modal point of entry:

> . . . it is fairly clear that Parmenides gives us two distinct descriptions of Being. The first of these is intended to be understood in a metaphysical sense: Being is determined in all respects (B Fr.8 verses 26-42), the second is formulated in cosmological terms: Being is a spatial whole, kept in balance from within and not bordered upon by another Being (vs. 42-49). The two descriptions overlap to a certain extent, which means that most terms have at the same time a metaphysical and a spatial connotation (p. 86).

What Sinnige calls the *metaphysical* description is equivalent to our indication of an idea-usage of spatial terms, and what he calls a cosmological description is equivalent to our indication of a conceptual use of spatial terms.

The kinematic modality provides us with an *idea* about the *identity* of an entity—its persistence amidst all the changes it may experience. In confrontation with Heraclitus' concern with the problem of constancy and change, Plato realized that *changes* can only be detected on the basis of something which is *constant*. We would refer in this respect to the foundational role of the kinematic modality for physical change. Plato, however, explained this insight in a metaphysical way by identifying the *constant* with his transcendent realm of ideas (forms).

Without extending this analysis, we can formulate four positive statements about crucial elements of our own cosmonomic idea in terms of the first four modal aspects: (a) everything is unique; (b) everything coheres with everything else; (c) everything remains identical to itself; and (d) everything changes.[7] Idea-statements like these do not exclude, but imply and presuppose each other!

Without making modal distinctions in a *systematic* way, modern philosophy might also be analyzed to show in which way the modal aspects fundamentally conditioned its development.

Historicism as a Descendant of Modern Nominalism

The realistic metaphysics of St. Thomas tried to synthesize the

Aristotelian *lex naturalis* (with its dual teleological order) with certain fundamental biblical motives. The result was an idea partly inspired by St. Augustine which related the *lex naturalis* to a transcendent *lex aeterna* as the plan of creation in the divine Mind. The true being of things are given as ideas in God's Mind. In a derivative and limited form, individual things participate in the being of God; for every individual thing there is a corresponding idea in God (*Quest. Disp. de Ver.*, III, 8). Furthermore, Aquinas considered universals *(universalia)* to have a threefold existence: *universalia ante rem* (the real existence of ideas, before the creation, in God's Mind); *in re* (in the things as their universal substantial forms) and *post rem* (their subjective existence in the human mind as universal concepts).

Emphasizing the primacy of the will over St. Thomas' choice for the primacy of the intellect, Ockham only acknowledged the subjective existence of universals in the human mind *(mens humana)*, encompassing both words *(voces)* and general concepts *(conceptus)*. Since every universal is a purely mental quality, no universal can really exist outside the mind (*Summa logicae* I, 14). Nothing but individual things exist in reality. Science, however, is still concerned with universals but then only as the subjective universal image of the real individual entities. Consequently, nominalism shifted the criterion of truth (for realism given in the *adequatio intellectus et rei*) to the inner activity of the human mind; truth concerns the compatibility of concepts.

Recalling the definition which we have given for rationalism and irrationalism, we might ask the question: is *nominalism* rationalistic or irrationalistic? With respect to the typical structure of entities, nominalism does not accept any conditioning order (universal structures for), or any orderliness of (universal structuredness of) such entities. Every entity is strictly individual. In terms of our mentioned distinction, we might say that nominalism surely represents an irrationalistic view in connection with the structure of entities, since every entity is completely stripped from its universal orderliness (law-conformity) and conditioning order. This characteristic applies to both moderate nominalism, *viz.*, conceptualism (Ockham, Locke, Leibniz and others), and to extreme nominalism that rejects all general and abstract ideas and accepts only general names (Berkeley, Brentano).

This irrationalistic side of nominalism, however, does not exhaust the multifaceted nature of nominalism, because universals are fully acknowledged in the human mind, at least as general words in the case of Berkeley's and Brentano's extreme nominalism. This restriction of knowledge to universals is typical of rationalism in the sense defined by us. Therefore, it is possible to see nominalism as being simultaneously rationalistic in terms of the universals (concepts and words) in one's mind, and irrationalistic in terms of the strict individuality of entities.

This dual nature of nominalism forms the starting-point of two diverging philosophical developments in modern philosophy. On the one hand, it provided rationalism with the possibility to elevate human reason to the level of the creator of a rational order in reality. This follows from the fact that nominalism transposes the universal side of entities into the human mind. But, as we have indicated, the universal side of entities is nothing but the manifestation of the conditionedness of entities by the relevant universal order for their existence. Consequently, if an entity is stripped of its orderliness, its universal side, it is simultaneously stripped of its being subjected to a universal creational order. What is left is factual reality in its unstructured chaotic individuality and particularity. Driven by the new motive of logical creation, this very feature of nominalism enabled modern philosophy from Descartes onward to reconstruct all of reality in terms of natural scientific thought—characterized by Husserl as the rationalistic science-ideal.

Only the extreme consequences of this natural science-ideal, canceling in principle even human freedom, were questioned by Kant. Within the limited domain of the science-ideal, however, Kant drew the ultimate rationalistic conclusion of nominalism. The way in which he worked this out was strongly influenced by Galileo.[9] In relation to the natural scientific meaning of constancy and change, we have explained how Plato already realized that changes can only be detected on the basis of something which is constant. Galileo explored this insight in a natural scientific way in his formulation of the law of inertia (using a *thought*-experiment). In other words, out of the pure subjectivity of man's understanding, without taking any sense experience into account, he derived this law and prescribed it to moving entities. This represents the crucial epistemological turn in modern philosophy in ascribing the primacy not to the object, but to the *subject*. Kant drew the radical humanistic conclusion: the laws of nature are *a priori* contained in the subjective understanding of man: ". . . understanding creates its *(a priori)* laws not out of nature, but prescribes them to nature."[10]

Indeed, Kant tried to consolidate and strengthen the preceding natural science-ideal, albeit in the restricted form of the rationalistically elevated understanding. Although this understanding is limited to sensibility in order to save a separate super-sensory domain for the practical ethical freedom of man, it is considered to be the *a priori* law-giver of nature! Nominalism created a vacuum by leaving factual reality in its individuality *unstructured*. In order to fill up the lack of determination thus created, Kant introduced human understanding in order to take hold of this vacant position. To be sure, Kant did not merely transpose the universal side of entities into human understanding, but in fact elevated human understanding to the level of the (formal) *conditioning order for things*.

On the other hand, nominalism also provided a starting-point for all those trends in modern philosophy which, in an irrationalistic fashion, wanted to take seriously the unique and contingent character of reality (often designated as: *historical* reality). This avenue opened up by nominalism was followed by a variety of historicistic designs in modern philosophy—from the fourth phase of Fichte up to pragmatism, existentialism and contemporary neo-Marxism. If reality is stripped of both its orderliness and of its being subjected to a conditioning universal creational order, it seems to be a "self-evident historistic truth" that everything is ultimately historical and therefore taken up in the dynamic and contingent flow of historical events. (Ignoring the universal *structure* of the historical mode, historicism did not realize that historical continuity, i.e., historical constancy, is the foundation of all historical change [the kinematic analogy is foundational to the physical analogy]. Those inclined to use a historistic mode of expression, mostly to uphold the image of being *dynamic*, simply don't realize that their explanations are always accompanied by the conditioning and foundational kinematical mode, as evidenced in the use of terms with the meaning of constant [enduring, per sisting, everlasting, and so on]. Consider the following phrases: history testifies to the fact that everything is *constantly* changing; we are part of an *ongoing* process; every age is a fusion of *ever*-changing horizons; our life-world is *continuously* subject to *alterations*.)

Rationality and Our Thinking about God

It is clear that many philosophers are caught up in the prevailing rationalistic identification of *knowledge* with *conceptual* knowledge. Although I am in full agreement with H. Hart's notion of knowledge, I don't want to support his restriction of *rational* knowing to *conceptual* knowing. Our knowledge of God is not *irrational*, although we have to say that it is *not conceptual*.

If concept-formation (identified with rationality) refers

necessarily to the universal order for or the universal orderliness of something or some modal subject, then it necessarily implies that we can *know* God only as conforming to some universal order. This explains why, in the context of this traditional fusion of knowledge with conceptual knowledge, it is so easy to postulate a universal rational *order* encompassing God as well. (This implies that God must have an essence and must conform to necessary truths, such as: to be and not to be cannot both be true at the same time and in the same circumstances.)

As soon as we free our notion of knowledge from this restriction, and account for true *idea-knowledge*, transcending the limits of concept-formation, then we do not have to postulate a rational order encompassing both God and man in order to be able to speak rationally about God.

The traditional distinction between God in himself and God as he revealed himself to us (compare the contribution of R. Clouser) is nothing but an outcome of the traditional metaphysical substance concept. The substance concept itself, in turn, is nothing but a metaphysical answer to the problem of *constancy* and *change*. For example, Plato postulated his transcendent *eidè* to account for the element of constancy, while Aristotle started from the (conceptually unknowable) primary substance as the central point of reference for all its accidents. The constant element was mostly identified with the intelligible *essence* of something (Aristotle's secondary substance), whereas the element of change was seen as the (unreliable) *appearance* of something. (Kant used the same metaphysical substance concept, but reversed its order to save human freedom; if appearances were things in themselves, said Kant, then freedom was not to be saved [*CPR*, B, 564].)

Theologically the substance concept was used, in a theo-ontological way, to differentiate between (a) *in-communicable* (essential) properties (attributes) and (b) *communicable* properties (God's appearance as revealed). Any serious attempt to defend (a) must end up in a complete *negative* theology, precluding any knowledge ("rational" or "irrational") of God "in himself." Surely then we are forced to explore (b), saying for example that we know God only in terms of the created relations used by God to reveal himself. But then we have to say that God has revealed his *relations* and not himself to us.

Contrary to this tradition, it is perfectly meaningful to say that God uses creational terms to reveal *himself* (and not his created relations) to us. Due to the fact that we conceptually know the universal orderliness of *living* entities, such as plants, animals and human beings, we are able to understand, i.e., to *know*, what is meant when the Bible says that God *is* life (leaving aside for the moment the fact that knowing God ultimately transcends the sphere of rational knowing). This does not mean that God is a plant, an animal or a human being! But still the *biotic* term *life* is used in an idea-context to refer our rational knowing *beyond* the limits of the universal orderliness of living things (and therefore also beyond the universal order for these entities) to God himself, which transcends our conceptual knowledge and can therefore only be approximated in our idea-knowledge. The same applies to terms which have their original seat in other aspects of reality. For example, when we say God is omnipresent, almighty, and faithful, we are once again using universal creational features (modal properties, in this case coming from the spatial, the historical and the fiduciary modalities) to speak about God in the context of an idea of God. The Bible, furthermore, in addition to the employment of modal terms, also uses "entitary directed terms," such as *metaphors*, in an idea-context to speak about God. The two crucial metaphors used in the Bible are seen in the expression that God is the *King* almighty, on the one hand, and in the revelation that God is our *Father*. If the term "Father" was *not* used in an idea-context, we would have been justified in drawing the logical conclusion: then God must be male (this example is taken from Hart's paper).

Theo-ontology traditionally approached this problem with an implicit *duplication* of the diversity in creation. God is said to be "Father" in such an original and eminent way that our experience of what fatherhood implies is nothing but a faraway and imperfect image of what God himself as *Father* is. Similarly, all modal terms used by the Bible to speak about God might, theo-ontologically, be explained away from creation and transposed into God where they are supposed to have their original and eminent seat. This whole approach is still in the grip of the platonic philosophy of being, which elevated the universal order for creation to his realm of ideas, later on identified with the Ideas in God's Mind, in which created entities participate in a derivative and limited form. The fundamental difference between God as Creator and Redeemer on the one hand, and creaturely reality (subjected to God's law-Word as his command for the existence of all created subjects) on the other hand, is completely leveled out in this perspective—giving free play to the doctrine of *analogia entis* which claimed an essential *continuity* between God and creature.

Concluding Remark

From the distinctive feature of *modal abstraction* we concluded, among other things, that the modal dimension of reality ultimately conditions the theoretical use of concepts and ideas. We discovered that our experience of entities and events is also conditioned by these modal points of entry to reality. Even the distinction between the orderliness, i.e., the universal side, of entities and their individual side (their uniqueness) cannot but use the spatial and numerical points of entry (cf. also our earlier circumscription of individualism and universalism). And we have tried to show that modern philosophy cannot be understood without acknowledging the specific way that nominalism accounted for the relation between universality and individuality. Surely the problem of universality and individuality is as old as philosophy itself, which simply accentuates the fact that modal analysis conditioned philosophical reflection from its very beginning. The same applies to the other fundamental philosophical problem used in our text to explain the nature of philosophy, namely that between constancy and dynamics. In a certain sense, therefore, one could explain a good deal of our philosophical legacy in the West in terms of its wrestling with the angles of approach provided by the first four aspects of reality, even though none of them developed a *theory* of modal aspects as such. Although the other facets of reality are also relevant, it seems that these *foundational* modes really played a crucial role.

Descartes posited the maxim that our ideas should be clear and distinct—considering *clarity* to be more fundamental than distinctness (see *Principles*, XLVI). If we want to connect this perspective with the place of rationality in philosophy, our qualification should be as follows: to think clearly, the philosopher has to use philosophical concepts and ideas, framed by means of modal abstraction and true to the conditioning order-diversity of created reality; yet the philosopher must not become a victim of metaphysical elevations or dialectically opposed disjunctions. Accepting the inherent limits of rationality, philosophy should stick to the created world-order as it is given, without attempting to reconstruct it after philosophy's own desire. Only then can we claim to continue the main thrust of the Calvinian tradition in rationality, as well as in philosophy. The *choice* for any kind of rationality is directed by the supra-rational root of our existence.

Notes

Acknowledgment: The reading of this paper at the conference on rationality held in Toronto was made possible by a grant from the South African Human Sciences Research Council.

1. Cf. the view of Roy Clouser: "A Critique of Descartes and Heisenberg," *Philosophia Reformata*, 1980, p. 163.
2. The most comprehensive, but perhaps last, attempt to reduce all physical phenomena to kinematical movement is found in the mechanics of H. Hertz. He was the first to broadcast and receive radio waves and established that light and heat are electromagnetic waves.
3. Cf. *The Principles of Philosophy*, part II, XXIV.
4. I have analyzed a number of these approaches in "Philosophy and Sociology," published in *Philosophia Reformata*, 1979, pp. 150-182.
5. In his stimulating and instructive discussion of the problem of universals, W. Stegmüller unfortunately still denies the universal side of concrete entities, cf. *Das Universalienproblem einst und jetzt* (Darmstadt, 1965), pp. 51, 53, 58, 62, 70, 75, 116. Also Dooyeweerd only speaks about the concrete as something individual.
6. Cf. Sinnige, T.G.: *Matter and Infinity in the Presocratic Schools and Plato* (Assen, the Netherlands, 1968).
7. Cf. my contribution "The modal aspects as points of entry to our experience of and reflection on created reality" to the Van Riessen *Festschrift* (Nov., 1981).
8. Cf. *Die Krisis der europäischen Wissenschaften und die Transzendentalen Phänomenologie* (1936); *Husserliana*, vol. VI (1956), p. 119.
9. Cf. Holz, Fr.: *Die Bedeutung der Methode Galileis für die Entwicklung der Transzendentalphilosophie Kants, Philosophia Naturalis* (1975), pp. 345-358.
10. *Prolegomena zu einer jeden künftigen Metaphysik die als Wissenschaft wird auftreten können*, part II, par. 36, p. 320 (originally published in 1783).

Present Positions on Key Problems

Part Four:

Rationality and Scripture

Rationality and Scripture

John M. Frame

THIS PAPER WILL DEAL, FIRST, WITH THE RULE OF SCRIPTURE over the Christian life as a whole. I shall then seek to show, at least in broad terms, how this rule applies specifically to our use of reason, concluding with a discussion of how reason, so understood, functions in our interpretation of Scripture itself. Obviously, these discussions are interdependent: as I seek to interpret Scripture's teachings at the beginning of this paper, I will be presupposing the hermeneutical points made at the end, as well as the epistemological points made in the middle, and naturally the middle and end also presuppose the beginning. Such circularity is common in theology and philosophy, and I know of no way to avoid it. God's truth is an organism.

I. Scripture as Our Rule of Faith and Life

I think it is important for us to recognize that reasoning is one of many human activities, one of many aspects of human life. Scripture therefore governs our reasoning, first of all, as it governs life as a whole. We ought, therefore, to give some attention to the way in which Scripture is intended by God to rule human life in general. I shall assume, here, that "the Bible is the Word of God inscripturated" and thus is "the supreme standard for all of human life." But some reflection is needed on *how* Scripture functions as "supreme standard."

A. Scripture and the Organism of Revelation

First, although Scripture is the Word of God, it is not the whole of God's revelation to us. It has often been pointed out (especially, in recent years, by thinkers oriented to the cosmonomic idea philosophy)[1] that in Scripture, "Word of God" applies not only to spoken and written revelation, but also to that divine speech which created[2] and directs[3] the world, and to Jesus Christ himself[4] as the supreme self-expression of the Father. Thus, God makes himself known to us, not only through the Bible, but through everything in creation.[5] We ourselves, made in God's "image,"[6] constitute an especially important form of God's self-disclosure.[7]

God never intended that any of these forms of revelation should function without the others. From the very beginning of Adam's existence, he was confronted by a world which revealed God, a spoken Word which defined his nature and task,[8] and his own nature as God's image. Clearly, God intended Adam to interpret the world and himself consistently with the spoken revelation; Adam was to accept his status as the image of God and to regard the world as properly subject to his godly dominion. Thus the spoken Word was to determine Adam's interpretation of the revelation of God in creation.

But, on the other hand, Adam's knowledge of the creation surely also influenced his understanding of and response to God's spoken words. It is hard to imagine Adam understanding the spoken revelation of Gen. 1:28-30 without some understanding of the world independent of that particular revelation. For him to understand that Word of God, he had to understand the language in which it was spoken; he had to have some idea what it meant to "be fruitful and multiply," to "replenish and subdue"; he had to know what the "earth" was. Possibly some of that information might have been given to him by additional verbal revelations, but such an assumption would be gratuitous. Surely such procedure does not occur today, at least, when the need for it would seem to be identical. And it is in any case impossible to teach anyone language through words alone; the words must be tied to the world about which they speak.[9]

Further, it is also the case that Adam could not *obey* the command of Gen. 1:28-30 without some additional knowledge of himself and the world. How, after all, does one go about "subduing the earth"? Surely this is a technological feat of enormous complexity, requiring a careful study both of the earth and of one's own capacities. Such study was essential if Adam and his descendants were to learn *concretely* and *specifically* what it meant to replenish and subdue the earth. And surely we must ask: if we understand God's Word only in general terms and not in its specific requirements, can we claim to understand it at all?

The same situation exists today. To understand and apply Scripture, we must know something about the world and about ourselves. Understanding Scripture is never merely a matter of memorizing words and locations of verses. A parrot or a computer could be taught to do that. The Jews of Jesus' day had a good rote-knowledge of Scripture; but Jesus accuses them of ignorance of the Word of God, since they failed to see the *relationships* between the old covenant documents and the crucial redemptive events of their own time.[10] To understand Scripture is to understand its bearing on our lives, upon our world. But, if this is so, then we cannot claim to understand Scripture unless we also understand things other than Scripture. Not even theology may restrict its attention to Scripture alone; for theology aims not to reproduce the Bible, but to put Scripture into different words, words designed to communicate its truth into a new context. Theology seeks to answer people's questions about the Bible, to meet people's needs from the Bible. As such, it must understand those needs, those questions, that present context into which the truth must be spoken.[11]

Thus, revelation is an organism. Revelation in Scripture, world and self presuppose and supplement one another; we cannot understand one of them without reference to the others. However, we may not stop with such observations. From what I have said so far, the distinctive role of Scripture within this organism is not apparent. Until now, I have communicated no sense of the *prominence* of Scripture in the believer's life. Indeed, at this point, it may seem as though Scripture is just one of a number of sources for revelation to be considered on an equal basis; so that when apparent conflicts arise, e.g., between my understanding of Scripture and my understanding of the natural world, I might, with equal sense of responsibility before God, go either way. Such an attitude, however, would scarcely do justice to the sharp distinctions in Scripture itself between the Word of God on the one hand and the word of man on the other. On such a view, what practical distinction could be drawn between the Word of God and my own wisdom, imagination, reasoning? Why wouldn't Abraham have had the option of acting on the evidence of his eyes rather than of the promise (Rom. 4:18-21)?

The question, then, of Scripture's *distinctive* role within the "organism" must be faced. I suggest that Scripture is distinctive in at least three ways.

1. *Subject-matter:* Scripture is distinctive, first of all, in that it tells a story that would not otherwise be available to us, the story of Jesus Christ and how he saved his people from their sins. The purpose of Scripture, then, is not to give us miscellaneous information on all sorts of subjects. It has a specific focus, a direction. It is directed toward a particular human need, the need of redemption, rather than other needs, such as the need for a cancer cure or the need for an adequate theory of geologic strata. This focus is reflected in the *style* of

Scripture: it is written, generally, in the language of everyday life, rather than in the technical style of scientists and philosophers.

Much has been written by reformed authors in recent years concerning this focus (*"scopus"*) of Scripture.[12] Essentially the same point has been made in various different terminologies: that Scripture is a "book of faith,"[13] that it is "confessionally qualified,"[14] that it is "Christologically theocentric."[15] In itself, the point is neither new[16] nor controversial. Controversy does arise, however, concerning certain conclusions which have been drawn from this principle. Jack B. Rogers, for instance, takes issue with Van Til's statement that "the Bible has much to say about the universe," giving as his sole argument the redemptive focus of Scripture.[17] Quite a large logical jump here! The focus on redemption proves that Scripture does *not* say anything much about the universe? Why? Does Christ have nothing to do with the universe? Does redemption? Even if redemption has nothing to do with the universe, does a "focus" on such redemption exclude incidental reference to things in the universe? The universe is a big place, and the Bible is a big book. It's a bit hard to conceive of the latter avoiding the former to the extent that Rogers conceives! Similarly, A. DeGraaff reflects on the soteriological focus of Scripture and, again from that fact alone, concludes:

> . . . that the references to God's creating do not answer our scientific, biological or geological questions, just as little as the Bible answers the questions of the historian or the anthropologist. The Bible is just not that kind of a book.[18]

Again, it sounds as though redemption takes place somewhere other than in the world! DeGraaff writes as though it were perfectly obvious that a focus on redemption excludes *anything* of interest to the sciences. And Dooyeweerd tells us that since Scripture deals with concepts of faith, it can have no interest in the chronological relations among the days of creation.[19]

The question of *scopus* is, of course, a serious one, not to be ridiculed. But it ought to be plain that arguments on the issue need to be constructed with more care than has been common to this point. We need particularly to take into account (a) that the gospel message is a message about events which took place in time (space history): the incarnation, crucifixion, resurrection and ascension of Jesus, and the filling of the church with the Spirit. These events are crucial to any account of history, "scientific" or otherwise.[20] And also: (b) that the gospel message is a message of cosmic importance about the creation, fall and redemption not only of man, but of all things,[21] and that it makes a demand upon all areas of human life[22] including, of course, his science. And: (c) if Scripture is "the Word of God written," then surely what God teaches us therein must be accepted, not only in its central thrust, but also in its *obiter dicta*. It is blasphemous for us to tell God that we will honor only what we regard as the "main drift" of his words.

Having said all of this, I still would not expect to find in Ezekiel predictions of the invention of the airplane, or in Proverbs a formula for converting mass into energy. But I do expect to find in Scripture those religious assumptions about the cosmos which Christians ought to hold and with which they ought to bring their scientific theories into conformity.[23] And, especially in regard to Scriptural teachings about creation, miracle, resurrection, I would not be at all surprised to find in Scripture *some* detailed factual assertions which would conflict with *some* assertions of *some* scientists. On specific questions (e.g., whether Gen. 5 contradicts the common scientific view of the antiquity of mankind), I know of no *a priori* theological or philosophical principle by which an answer can be found by way of deduction from the *scopus* of Scripture as a whole. Rather, the passage in question must be studied individually to determine its own *particular scopus*, that *scopus* being consistent, to be sure, with what II Tim. 3:16ff. and other passages say about the purpose of Scripture as a whole. The fact that Scripture has a redemptive focus gives us a rough-and-ready guide, a general rule, as to what we should expect to find in Scripture. But this focus does not answer all detailed questions about Scripture's contents: it does not make exegesis unnecessary; it does not immunize us against the power of God's Word to surprise.[24]

Thus it will be understood that for purposes of this paper, the chief importance of *scopus* is not that it limits the subjects which Scripture may address, although it does set some rough limits of this sort. Rather, the importance of *scopus* is that it gives Scripture a centrality for all thought and life. Since Scripture contains the message of redemption, we must have continual recourse to it in all areas of life. As sinners saved by grace, struggling with the remnants of sin in all our thinking and living, we must hunger and thirst constantly for the written Word of God, seeking in it the means by which God wishes to sanctify each area of life. First in importance for every part of life must be the implications of the biblical message. And since it is in Scripture, not nature in general, that this saving message is to be found, this principle necessarily gives to Scripture a certain primacy within the total organism of revelation. It is Scripture that shows us how to use the other revelation obediently, how to repent of sin in our use of creation. Scripture must be allowed to *correct* that thinking which is based on natural revelation. But how can Scripture have such primacy without destroying the organic character of revelation? How can Scripture correct our understanding of creation when, as we mentioned earlier, creation also often helps us to correct our understanding of Scripture? I will deal with these questions presently, but I must first move on to other aspects of Scripture's "distinctive role" within the organism.

2. *Soteric Function:* Scripture not only contains a distinctive subject-matter; it also has a distinctive kind of *power*. As the apostle says, the gospel, the message of Scripture, is "the power of God unto salvation."[25] In Scripture we not only find the *information* needed to reform, to sanctify our lives, we also find there the *ability* to do so; for the Holy Spirit of God works in and with the Word, and he works in saving power.[26] Thus we have an additional motive to return again and again to Scripture. It is there that we find the strength to change, to reform our ideas and life-decisions in obedience to God. The words of Scripture and the Spirit therein work together (not, of course, independently); thus by the Spirit's work the words "captivate" us, "grip" us.[27] We find them memorable, penetrating, profoundly true. We find that we cannot avoid taking them into account.

It is often pointed out that the soteric "grip" of Scripture upon us is not to be equated with theoretical insight.[28] It is a "heart-knowledge."[29] Indeed, the regenerating and sanctifying power of the Word operates on children as well as adults, on ordinary people as much as scholars. That much truth, at least, may be found in the assertion that this knowledge of God is "beyond . . . scientific problems" and "not a question of theoretical reflection."[30] Further, it is right to point out that the product of this saving power is knowledge of God, not a mere knowledge of miscellaneous facts, theological or otherwise. Such observations, however, ought more often to be balanced by two considerations. (a) The power of the Spirit energizes *all* of Scripture, for all of Scripture is God's redemptive message, God's gospel.[31] The Spirit drives home to God's people, therefore, all of Scripture's implications, its applications for our lives.[32] As observed earlier, our responsibility to Scripture is not merely to its "general drift," but to its full range of meaning—"*every* word that comes out of the mouth of God," "*all* Scripture."[33] Thus the implications of Scripture for theoretical work come under the empowering, illuminating ministry of the Spirit, although the work of the Spirit is certainly not limited to that. (b) Therefore, although every Christian is in the "grip" of the Word, not every Christian has experienced illumination with respect to the same scriptural contents. A theologian may be convicted by the Spirit as to the relevance of Rom. 6 to the doctrine of sanctification, while his ten-year-old son may have no idea what the questions even are. To summarize: the *scopus* of the Spirit's work in and with Scripture is as broad as the *scopus* of Scripture itself (see I,A,1).

So, as we return to the question of the place of Scripture in the organism of revelation, we find that the importance of the Spirit's work does not lie in any limitation of the *scopus* of Scripture in addition to those limits noted earlier. Rather, the soteric function of Scripture is important in that it shows us how Scripture can have a primacy among the other forms of revelation, even while being in some ways dependent on them. We must have continual recourse to Scripture, not only that we might be rightly informed of God's truth, but so that we may gain power to reform our ways of thinking and living. Scripture rightly understood (with the inevitable help of general revelation!) can cut through our falsehood in a way that nothing else (even general revelation seen in the light of Scripture!) can.

3. *Covenantal Status:* Scripture is also distinctive in that it is the constitution of the covenant between ourselves and God. Suzerainty covenants in the ancient Near East were governed by written documents. The document was authored by the "great king" and laid down as law before the "vassal king," the lesser king who became, by covenant, the servant of the great king. Kline[34] argues persuasively that written divine revelation should be viewed as falling under that genre; that Scripture is a "covenant document." As such, it is by Scripture, by the covenant document, that our faithfulness to the covenant is to be tested. To disobey the document is to disobey the covenant, and *vice versa*. When God, through the prophets, conducts his "covenant lawsuit" against Israel, it is the treaty, the covenant document, which serves as the standard of judgment. Thus the document has a special status: it is placed in the ark of the covenant, the holiest place in Israel. It is to be read publicly, to be taught to children, to govern all areas of community life.

Fundamental to the covenantal status of Scripture is its divine authorship. The covenant document, we recall, was authored by the great King himself, written in the first person. The same pattern is found in the decalogue which is, according to Kline, the first covenant document in Israel. So strongly does Scripture emphasize the divine authorship of the decalogue that it is said to be "written by the finger of God."[35]

Whatever we may think of the details of Kline's argument, it certainly presents a useful model of scriptural revelation emphasizing concerns which reformed theology has always had—with the divine authorship of Scripture and with its unique office as the "supreme standard of faith and life." Nature does not have this kind of status. Although created and directed by God, it does not consist of words divinely authored. (Nature is governed by God's Word, but it is not the Word.) And nature is not our covenant document; Scripture is.

All our thought and life, therefore, must be tested by Scripture. Although general revelation aids us in interpreting Scripture, once we are assured of Scripture's teaching that assurance ought to take precedence over any opinions gained from any other source.

Thus the fact that general revelation helps us interpret Scripture, indeed that it often moves us to correct our interpretations of Scripture, does not make the two forms of revelation equivalent in function. To put the matter somewhat schematically: (a) Scripture does not correct general revelation, nor *vice versa;* the two are equally authoritative, equally true. (b) Scripture does often correct our *interpretation* of general revelation, but the reverse is also true. All of our interpretations are subordinate to every form of divine revelation. (c) But there is also an important asymmetry: we must believe Scripture even when it appears to contradict information available from other sources. We are not to accept information apparently derived from other sources which seems to us to contradict Scripture. Or to put it more concisely: what we interpret as the teaching of Scripture must prevail, in event of conflict, over what we interpret as the teaching of general revelation. I am, of course, talking about *settled* interpretations; certainly information derived from general revelation can correct our interpretation of Scripture, as I have said earlier. But once we are convinced that Scripture teaches x, we must believe it, even if general revelation appears to teach not-x. This formulation is only an attempt to systematize the teaching of Rom. 4 regarding the faith of Abraham. So far as Abraham could tell, the data of natural revelation (his great age, the condition of Sarah) rendered the divine promise impossible. Yet be believed the promise and was commended for his faith.

If, therefore, we try to maintain (a) and (b) without (c), we can make no meaningful distinction between walking by faith and walking by sight. Without (c), Scripture and general revelation are equivalent in function, and Scripture is in no unique sense the covenant document of the people of God. No distinction, then, becomes possible between the Word of God and the opinions of men, so far as their practical authority is concerned.

Therefore, when we formulate the doctrine of the sufficiency of Scripture, it is important to say that it contains *all* of the divine norms to which principle (c) applies. This is not to say that Scripture contains all truth or all of God's revelation; it does not.[36] It is to say that only Scripture stands in this particular relation to our decisions.

The first point, then, as to how Scripture rules human life in general is that it functions interdependently with other forms of God's revelation, but with a primacy among them necessitated by the nature of God's redemptive covenant with his people.

B. Scripture and Sanctification

We noted earlier (I,A,2) that one aspect of Scripture's rule over us is its role as a locus of soteric power: we go to Scripture not only to gain information concerning God's will, but also to receive strength to obey. But there is also another, seemingly opposite fact that must be noted about the relation between Scripture and sanctification. Not only is Scripture necessary to our sanctification, but sanctification is necessary for a right use of Scripture. For a person to "prove what is the will of God," he needs not only the intellectual ability to relate the biblical message to his situation (I, above), he also needs to offer his body as living sacrifice, to be transformed by the renewing of his mind[37] to live as a child of light[38] to *love* in a way that abounds in knowledge.[39] According to Heb. 5:11-14, the deeper truths of Scripture (in context, the Melchizedek priesthood) are available only to the spiritually mature "who by constant use have trained themselves to distinguish good from evil."[40] To properly apply Scripture, then, requires not only intellectual capacities, but moral and spiritual maturity as well. There is an inevitable circularity here: we go to Scripture in order to become more obedient, and as we become more obedient we come to understand Scripture better. How do we break into this circle? We don't; we enter the circle by the grace of regeneration, by the power of the Holy Spirit.[41]

C. The Richness of Scripture's Pedagogy

We have discussed the rule of Scripture in relation to other forms of revelation and in relationship to our growth in grace. At this point, we shall focus more sharply on the language of Scripture to learn something of the *methods* by which God in Scripture instructs his people.

There has, I think, often been a tendency among us, both as theologians and as simple believers, to think of Scripture as containing only one type of language. We tend sometimes to read the Bible as if it consisted exclusively of propositional truths, bits of true information. (And yet we are not consistent: when in a different mood, we tend to read Scripture as a collection of ethical commands!) We know, of course, that Scripture does not consist only of one kind of language; but the usual goals of Bible study (ascertaining doctrinal truths, and finding ethical principles) often lead us to read *as if* Scripture were all of one or two sorts. And our tendency to see theology exclusively as an academic or "theoretical" discipline has certainly not helped matters in this respect.[42]

Yet the variety of language in Scripture is rich indeed. Its grammatical moods include not only indicative and imperative, but also significant interrogatives[43] and exclamations.[44] Our God teaches us not only by informing, but also ("Socratically!?") by asking penetrating questions and by shouting at us—rousing us out of our complacency. The "illocutionary" and "perlocutionary" functions[45] of biblical language are manifold: asserting, commanding, but also questioning, expressing, promising,[46] praising, cursing, lamenting, confessing, instructing, edifying, comforting, amusing, convicting. There are also many literary genres: historical narrative, law, prophecy, poetry, proverb, romance, letter, apocalypse. And many more specific things could be said under the category of *Formgeschichte*. And we should note also what David Kelsey says about the many different ways in which Scripture may function in a theological argument.[47]

To speak of Scripture, therefore, as "propositional revelation" is misleading, although against the mystical concepts of revelation prevalent in our day it is important to stress that Scripture does have *some* propositional content.[48] And, since we must consult the whole Bible in determining the propositional content of God's revelation, it is legitimate to say that all of Scripture is propositional in that it all has a propositional function; it all serves to inform us. But we should remember that the same can be said of the imperative, interrogative and exclamatory functions: all Scripture binds our conduct, questions us, awakens us. All Scripture is a hymn of praise to our great God and Savior; all Scripture is the faithful response of redeemed sinners. All is law; all is prophecy; all is wisdom. Thus, all Scripture is propositional in a sense, but Scripture is far *more* than propositional.[49, 50]

It will be important for evangelical theologians in the future to work out a concept of scriptural authority that does justice to this variety in biblical pedagogy. Too often our formulations make it sound as if acceptance of scriptural authority simply amounts to believing a certain set of propositions taught by Scripture. It is important for us to consider how not only the propositional function but also the other functions of Scripture serve as "authority" for us. For instance, what does it mean to say that a poem or a Psalm, let us say, is authoritative? Certainly not merely that we should accept whatever propositional teaching can be extracted from an analysis of it. Somehow, there is a difference between an authoritative *poem* (a *canonical* poem), and other poems. Surely the authoritative poems are to become the songs of our hearts, are to rule our inner life in some peculiar way. Much more work needs to be done on this kind of question.

II. Scripture as a Rule for Human Reasoning

To avoid trespassing on ground to be covered by other papers in this series (and to avoid getting beyond my depth!), let me define "reason" in a simple, quasi-dictionary fashion: "A person's capacity for forming judgments, conclusions, inferences." "Reasoning," then, will be the process of forming those judgments, conclusions, inferences. So understood, reasoning is a part of life, and therefore we have been talking about it implicitly all along in this paper. Now we need to show the applications of the preceding generalities to the specific topic of human reason.

The word "reason," defined as above, does not appear in English translations of Scripture (any more than does the word "Trinity" or phrases like "personal God" or "Christian labor union"). Yet it is evident that Scripture addresses the subject. First, as we have argued, Scripture addresses redemptively all of human life, and reason is part of that.[51] Second, Scripture has much to say about human qualities and activities which presuppose and involve the ability to reason: wisdom, teaching, discernment, etc.[52] Third, Scripture commands actions which involve making judgments, conclusions, inferences: obeying, understanding the Word, loving others as Jesus loved us, etc.[53] Fourth, Scripture itself contains any number of judgments, conclusions, inferences which it calls us to accept.[54] To accept these is in itself a rational activity, a forming of a judgment, conclusion, inference. To say these things is *not* to say that Scripture is *primarily* concerned with reasoning or that the "rationality" of Scripture is its most important quality. Scripture is not "qualified by the analytical aspect," to use Dooyeweerdian language.[55] But it is concerned with human reasoning, as it is concerned with everything we do before God. Let me summarize some of the important applications of Scripture to the rational enterprise under two headings: first, the status of reason, and second, the practice of human reasoning.

A. The Status of Reason

1. Its Importance

(a) *Reasoning pervades human life.* The forming of judgments, conclusions and inferences is not limited to academic or theoretical activities.[56] It does not occur only when we are composing syllogisms; nor is it limited to "thinking," if by "thinking" we mean puzzling ourselves about some problem or other. We often form judgments, etc., unconsciously or subconsciously. A woman sees a military officer coming toward her front door with a solemn expression on his face: she concludes immediately that he has brought bad news about her soldier husband. This is reasoning, drawing a conclusion by inference from data. It may very well be excellent reasoning, but there is no period of inward dialogue, no making of a syllogism. A football quarterback sees a tell-tale movement in the defensive backfield: he moves instinctively to avoid the defensive play which he knows is coming. This, too, is reasoning. He has formed a conclusion by inference. But there is nothing academic about it; it is more like a reflex mechanism, but a mechanism inwrought by much training and study of the game. Such a one we call an "intelligent" quarterback; but such intelligence is different from the intelligence one hears in a lecture hall.[57]

Reasoning, therefore, is something that everyone does, in every area of life. It is certainly not limited to those who have studied logic or epistemology. Those disciplines only seek to map *some* of the conditions which distinguish good from bad reasoning.[58] Reasoning is so pervasive, because it is involved every time we respond voluntarily to a situation in our experience. Thus, inevitably, our response to Scripture involves reasoning. When I seek to obey Scripture, e.g., by showing more love to Christian brothers and sisters in my church, I do this because (consciously or not) I have reached the *conclusion* that such activity is a proper application of Scripture. (Scripture does not tell me specifically to love Mr. Jones; my obligation to love Mr. Jones is a conclusion based on inference.)[59]

(b) *Scripture demands a rational response.*[60] Since *any* voluntary response to Scripture involves reasoning (good or bad), we must say that Scripture requires a rational response; the alternative is to claim that Scripture requires no voluntary response at all. Furthermore, since Scripture demands a *proper* response, we conclude that it requires of us not only reasoning, but good reasoning. Reasoning is a crucial aspect of our responsibility before God. God *cares* that we make the right judgments, conclusions, inferences; he cares about this because he cares about our *obedience*. Reason has its limitations and its dangers, as we shall see, and from those dangers some have concluded that it is somehow impious to apply human reason to the things of God.[61] Surely our use of reason must be responsible, subject to God's lordship. But to deny altogether the legitimacy of reasoning from scriptural data is to deny the legitimacy of obedience, for it is to deny the application of Scripture to the world in which we seek to obey the Lord. Irrationalism is not pious; it is ungodly, Satanic. God *commands* us to apply his Word to our world, and in doing so, he commands us to reason and reason well. That is the basic point: reasoning is part of obedience.

In addition, it is also worth noting that Scripture contains a great many arguments—reasonings—which it expects us to appreciate. But it is not only these that demand a rational response; it is the whole Scripture. Thus the position of the Westminster Confession of Faith, I, vi, which finds the "whole counsel of God" not only in the express statements of Scripture but also in what may be deduced from Scripture by "good and necessary consequence," is inescapable. Our obligation before God consists not of the bare words of Scripture, but of the *bearing*, the *application* which these words have on our decisions.

If anyone objects that this principle exalts human wisdom (e.g., humanly formulated laws of logic) to the status of divine revelation, I would repeat what I said earlier,[62] that *every* obedient response to Scripture involves a knowledge of creation and of self as well as a knowledge of Scripture. This fact does not erase the "primacy" of Scripture;[63] Scripture retains the prerogative to judge any system of logic that we use to interpret it. But we must face the fact that whenever we *use* the Bible, some human reasoning is involved.

2. Its Limitations

Since reasoning is part of life, and part of our total responsibility before God, it is never something "neutral." As a part of human life, reasoning is something that we can do in a godly or an ungodly way, obediently or disobediently, competently or incompetently. Such sciences as logic, mathematics and epistemology may usefully be classified as "ethical" sciences;[64] for they seek to help us determine what we *ought* (ethical "ought") to believe, granted certain data or certain other beliefs. But we must also say that not only the conclusions but also the premises, the presuppositions, the starting points of these sciences are subject to ethical—ultimately religious—evaluation.

The idea that human reason, or at least the "laws of logic," are a neutral, even infallible basis for human decision-making is an idea that dies hard. Here, it would be wise to remind ourselves briefly of various specific limits on the ultimacy, the powers and the reliability of reason in general and logic in particular. (a) The law of non-contradiction is only "necessary" to those who acknowledge a practical ("ethical") necessity to think logically.[65] (b) Logic presupposes that those using it are able to agree on the nature of and criteria for truth and falsity; but these concepts are controversial, and religiously so. The agreement to say that "*p* may not be both true and false in the same respect and at the same time" is a formal (and thus in an important sense meaningless) agreement unless there is agreement on the meaning of "true" and "false." (c) The disciplines of mathematics and logic, far from consisting of truisms, are riddled with controversy.[66] (d) No one has succeeded in justifying induction from within the discipline of logic; yet all non-deductive reasoning presupposes it.[67] (e) We do not know all the "laws of logic"; in fact our systems fail to account for many everyday forms of inference, such as the examples above under II,A,1,(a).[68] (f) The discovery of one fact apparently contrary to one's belief, or even an apparent contradiction within that belief, does not serve to refute it. When faced with such a challenge, one may simply treat it as a "problem" to be worked out within one's already-existing system of thought. One cannot specify in precise terms *how much* unresolved discrepancy will, or ought to, cause someone to reject a belief; the point at which "refutation" occurs will depend greatly on practical, personal—even religious—factors.[69] And generally such discrepancy will produce modifications in one's position rather than abandonment of it. (g) Logical rigor by itself does not guarantee truth; one also needs true premises. And our knowledge of the truth of premises is always conditioned by our fallibility.[70] (h) The principle of non-contradiction states that "A is A and not non-A *at the same time and in the same respect*"; thus it is limited in its application to aspects of reality which are unchanging.[71] (i) Logical syllogisms generally require some restatement of an argument, some translation from ordinary language into the technical language of logic. There are acknowledged discrepancies which enter here: the logical "if-then" (material implication), for example, is generally not equivalent to the use of "if-then" in ordinary language. Thus an otherwise adequate argument may fail by inadequately translating the ordinary language which it purports to test.

Thus it is evident that we do not find in human reason alone, even in logic, an infallible criterion of truth that might compete with Scripture as our ultimate covenant rule. Scripture, indeed, must be seen to rule over our reasoning as over every other aspect of life.

B. The Practice of Reason

How does Scripture rule our reasoning? As it rules all of life. Let us refer back to the principles discussed under (I) above.

1. *The Organism of Revelation:* We get the premises of our argument, as well as the principles of reasoning, by a godly, obedient correlation between Scripture, the world and ourselves, with Scripture having "covenantal primacy." The triad "Scripture, world and self" corresponds roughly, not perfectly, to the epistemological triad, "law, object and subject."[72] The correlation is imperfect, because as we have seen, we discover laws (of thought and life) by *correlating* Scripture, world and self; and we learn of objects and subjects similarly. Indeed, every item of experience functions in all three ways, as law, object and subject: everything has a law-function, since any such item may be involved in an application of Scripture to a situation (God expects us to take account of, and thus to be governed by, all that is, to the extent that this is possible for us); everything has an object-function, since everything (in experience, again) is a possible object of knowledge; and everything in experience has a subject-function, because it is *my* experience, part of my inner life. Items of experience, then, can be seen from what I would call "normative, situational and existential perspectives." But no item functions in only one or two perspectives; each functions in all three.[73] Without normativity, an item cannot be understood; without objectivity, it cannot be real; without subjectivity, it cannot be known.

This triadic scheme illumines some ways in which epistemologists have tried to justify the holding of a belief: (a) by showing that this belief follows from a sound application of the laws governing reasoning, (b) by showing that the belief "corresponds to reality" (often conceived in empirical terms), and (c) by showing that the belief is subjectively satisfactory, that it leaves one at peace, with no further inclination to question. Some have attempted to reduce two of these to the third. (a) It can be argued that law is fundamental, since "correspondence" and "satisfaction" presuppose *criteria* for correspondence and satisfaction. (b) It can be argued that correspondence is fundamental, since "law" and "satisfaction" are suitable criteria only to the extent that they are grounded in *reality*. (c) It can be argued that satisfaction is primary, since we *acknowledge* only those "laws" and alleged "correspondences" which leave us satisfied.

But if we assume the teaching of Scripture and of Calvin concerning the interdependence between our knowledge of God's law, the creation and ourselves, we do not need to elevate any of the three perspectives above the others. Since God has established all three, and established them in a coherent, wise order, we can start with any perspective, as long as we do not neglect the principles emphasized by the others. We can justify our beliefs by reference to God's laws for thought, as long as we recognize that these must be applied to the creation and to ourselves. We can justify our beliefs by reference to the objectivity of creation, as long as we accept God's criteria for objectivity and recognize the problematics of approaching that objective world through a fallible subjectivity. And we can justify our beliefs subjectively, as long as we recognize God's criteria for legitimate subjective satisfaction and the fact that we are not alone in God's world.

Thus our reasoning, as all of life, is founded on the full richness of God's organic revelation: law, object and subject interpenetrate and interpret one another. But we should also note that here, as in the rest of life, Scripture is primary. From one point of view, Scripture is a rather small "item." From the normative perspective, it is only part of the "organism of revelation" by which we determine our obligations. From the situational perspective, it is only one part of creation. From the existential perspective, it is only one item of our subjective experience. Yet it is, in each case, the definitive part. As I said earlier, our settled beliefs about Scripture's teaching (however influenced those beliefs may be by extra-scriptural knowledge) must prevail, in the event of conflict, over beliefs drawn from any other source. As this is the case in all of life, it is the case in the area of reasoning. And so when Scripture teaches that human reasoning is subject to God's law, that it is subject to the fallibilities of sin and finitude, that God and his plan are incomprehensible, then it is to be believed. Scripture is not a textbook of logic any more than it is a textbook of biology or geology; but what it says about logic and reasoning in general must be respected.

2. *Sanctification:* The subjective basis of reasoning ("existential perspective," above) underscores the important fact that one cannot reason or understand unless he has the capacity to do so. One cannot see unless he has "eyes to see." One cannot, therefore, make adequate use of the organism of revelation unless he is subjectively qualified by virtue of regeneration and sanctification. And growth in sanctification leads to a more adequate use of revelation. What of the unregenerate? Are they unable to reason at all? Scripture speaks of them both as "knowing God"[74] and as "not knowing God."[75] To distinguish adequately between their "knowledge" and their "ignorance" would take up too much space here. Their knowledge, at

least, is an ironic, paradoxical sort of knowledge-in-ignorance which exists only by virtue of God's common grace, which restrains the effects of sin. We are, however, considering reason as it *ought* to operate, i.e., regenerately.

I should, however, address the question: are the most sanctified people always the best reasoners? No. (a) For sanctification is not the only factor bearing on reason. A person's intelligence, his access to data, his education and training, his experience in reasoning, all these play a role as well. (b) For sanctification bears on all areas of human life, not only reasoning. And it affects these areas of life sometimes unevenly: a person may show his holiness by helping the poor, while not being as faithful in other areas of life. Yet sanctification *can* be an epistemological advantage, for it opens our eyes to relate our experience to God.

3. Richness of Pedagogy

Scripture teaches us about reason by describing (at least implicitly) the importance, limits and practice of reason (above), by providing examples of godly reasoning to govern our thought, but also in many other ways. Remember the examples of "informal logic" cited earlier (II,A,1,a): the woman observing the soldier, the quarterback observing the defensive players. In Scripture, God wants us not only to draw conclusions from arguments, from propositional teaching; he wants us to respond rationally to poems, to parables, to the events described in the narratives. And he wants us to recognize the multiplicity of uses to which Scripture can ("rationally!") be put. This point is of hermeneutical importance. The allegory of Hagar and Sarah (Gal. 4:21-31) is baffling if we believe the Old Testament story is written only to inform us of a significant event. But no, God also gave us that story as an illustration of New Testament truth. That, too, is a legitimate use of Scripture, a use by which people can be taught, by which their understanding can be illumined.

The richness of Scripture's pedagogy also implies that to apprehend what Scripture teaches we need *all* our faculties, not only logical skills, but imagination, emotional empathy with the text, the will to obey, etc. We need these faculties if we are to respond rightly (and therefore "rationally") to all the richness of Scripture.[76]

III. Reasoning about Scripture

Having discussed some points about Scripture and about reasoning, I now will state a few conclusions of a "hermeneutical" sort, concerning the role of reason in the use of Scripture. Much of this has been said already, but a summary will be helpful.

First, there can be no question but that reason has a legitimate application to Scripture. To say there is something wrong about drawing inferences from Scripture is to deny that Scripture can be *used*, that it can be *applied* to our situations, that it can be *obeyed*. Obedience always involves (consciously or unconsciously) a rational correlation between the words of Scripture and some present human decision.

Still, we must remember that human reason is limited, fallible. We do make mistakes, in our use of Scripture as well as in everything else. And in one sense, the limits of reasoning are especially evident when we seek to apply it to Scripture. For God is incomprehensible, his thoughts are not our thoughts, and his understanding is unsearchable.[77] We should recognize that theologians have historically found it difficult to speak of God without at least "apparent contradiction."

My own conclusion (argued more fully elsewhere[78]) is that we must simply "hang loose" to our current standards of what is logical or rational. We must, in reasoning about God, be especially sensitive to the limitations of our logic, opening ourselves even more than usual to catch the practical "informal logic" of Scripture's teachings. When our logical deductions lead to more and more flagrant "apparent contradictions," when they lead us to deny things that are plainly taught in Scripture, then we should "back off," acknowledge an unresolved "problem,"[79] and direct our thinking elsewhere until we get a new insight. But such problems must never lead us to abandon (if such were even possible) the use of logic altogether in the appropriation of Scripture. To abandon logic is to abandon our responsibility before God.

We gain a rational understanding of Scripture in the same way we gain a rational understanding of anything else: by correlating Scripture, world and self (and thus law, object and subject); by receiving from the Holy Spirit the grace to understand; by recognizing the richness of scriptural pedagogy and the corresponding richness of the response demanded (a response of the whole person, involving all his capacities).[80] Scripture has the primacy even here, even in its own interpretation *(Scriptura ipsius interpres)*. But this primacy is not threatened by the use of reason if our reasoning is carried out in a godly way.

Notes

1. Note, e.g., Olthuis, J. and Zylstra, B., "Confessing Christ in Education,"

International Reformed Bulletin 42 (Summer, 1970), 41ff; Zylstra, B., "Thy Word Our Life," *International Reformed Bulletin* 49-50 (Spring/ Summer, 1972), 57-68. On p. 68 Zylstra says that, "A number of leaders in the orthodox protestant community have lately insisted that the Scriptures are the Word of God, *only* and *exclusively*." If this means that these leaders deny the existence of the other forms of divine speech we have noted, then I am at a loss as to which leaders Zylstra is referring to.

2. Ps. 33:6 (cf. Gen. 1:3, 6, 9, etc.), John 1:1-3, II Pet. 3:5.
3. Ps. 119:89-92, 147:15-18, 148:8.
4. John 1:1-14, I John 1:1, Rev. 19:13.
5. Ps. 19:1ff, Rom. 1:18ff. Note also that the Bible does not exhaust even the total of oral and written revelation God has given to men. There were prophecies, words of Jesus, probably even Pauline epistles, which in God's providence did not find their way into the canon of Scripture. Since, however, I believe that oral and written revelation (with the status of covenant law) has ceased, I would maintain that Scripture contains all the revelation of that type available to *us*. So, for simplicity, I will speak as though "Scripture" is equivalent to "oral and written revelation."
6. Gen. 1:26ff.
7. The assertions of this paragraph have always been central to reformed (or "Calvinian," if you will!) theology. Calvin, more than any of the other reformers, was impressed by the stamp of God on the whole creation, and with man as a reflection of God's glory. Note the remarkable first pages of the *Institutes* where he correlates the knowledge of God with self-knowledge, and then (contrary to what we might expect from a Calvinist) tells us he doesn't know which comes first.
8. Gen. 1:28-30; see also 2:16ff, 19.
9. If one does not know English, for example, it will not help him to define one English word by means of synonyms or definitions in English. The teacher must, at some point, speak a language which the student *knows*. You cannot learn a language (through verbal teaching, at least) unless you already know one. So I assume that God did not teach language to Adam merely by speaking to him. There must have been some other means. Thus when Adam received the verbal revelation, he understood it partly in reference to what he already knew.
10. Matt. 22:29-32, John 5:39ff; cf. Luke 24:25.
11. For more considerations as to why general and special revelation presuppose and supplement one another, see Van Til, C., "Nature and Scripture," in Stonehouse, N., and Woolley, P., eds., *The Infallible Word* (Grand Rapids: Eerdmans, 1946), pp. 255-293.
12. Important in this development has been Berkouwer, G., *Holy Scripture* (Grand Rapids: Eerdmans, 1975). Cf. also the study committee report, "The Nature and Extent of Biblical Authority" (Grand Rapids: Board of Publications of the Christian Reformed Church, 1972).

13. Dooyeweerd, H., *In the Twilight of Western Thought* (Nutley, N.J.: Craig Press, 1968), pp. 132-156.
14. Spykman, G., "A Confessional Hermeneutic," *RES Theological Bulletin* I, 3 (Dec., 1973), 9.
15. Klooster, F., "Toward a Reformed Hermeneutic," *RES Theological Bulletin* II, 1 (May, 1974), 5.
16. In response to the charge that such theologians as Hodges and B.B. Warfield neglected this truth, N. Shepherd (in an unpublished lecture, "The Nature of Biblical Authority") cites Warfield, *The Inspiration and Authority of the Bible* (Phila.: Presbyterian and Reformed, 1948), p. 161: "If the 'inspiration' by which Scripture is produced renders it trustworthy and authoritative, it renders it trustworthy and authoritative only that it may the better serve to make men wise unto salvation." Cf. also C. Van Til's response to Jack B. Rogers in Geehan, E., ed., *Jerusalem and Athens* (Nutley: Presbyterian and Reformed, 1971), pp. 165-171.
17. Rogers, J., "Van Til and Warfield on Scripture in the Westminster Confession," in Geehan, E., ed., *op. cit.*, pp. 162ff.
18. DeGraaff, A., and Seerveld, C., *Understanding the Scriptures* (Toronto: AACS, 1968), p. 12. Earlier in the paragraph, however, he says that "the creation story serves as the religious basis and directive for the Christian biologist's and geologist's theorizing." Thus, apparently, Scripture does, after all, answer biological and geological questions, namely questions about the religious basis of those disciplines. Possibly DeGraaff is working with some highly precise concept of a "biological or geological question"; but, if so, why does he not tell us about it?
19. Dooyeweerd, H., *op. cit.*, pp. 149ff.
20. Shepherd, *op. cit.*; Packer, J., *Beyond the Battle for the Bible* (Westchester, Ill.: Cornerstone Books, 1980), pp. 54ff.
21. Cf., e.g., Gen. 3:17ff, Rom. 8:18-22, Col. 1:19.
22. I Cor. 10:31, Rom. 14:23, Col. 3:17, 24. Note also Van Til, C., in Geehan, E., ed., *op. cit.*, pp. 165ff. (vs. Rogers), Shepherd, N., "Bible, Church and Proclamation" (response to Prof. J.A. Heyns), *International Reformed Bulletin* 54 (Summer, 1973), pp. 60ff.
23. DeGraaff seems to recognize this (above, note 18), but I cannot regard this recognition as consistent with his later statement that Scripture answers no scientific questions. For one thing, I see no reason to say that questions about the religious direction of a science are not "scientific." Furthermore, if this religious direction exists, then surely it influences in some way the specific assertions of that science. Thus if one challenges that religious direction, one simultaneously challenges some of the specific assertions of the science in question. Thus if Scripture answers the question about religious direction, it answers at least some specific questions as well.
24. The same must be said about statements to the effect that Scripture is a

"naive" or "pre-theoretical" book as opposed to a "theoretical" book. I have criticized the common naive/theoretical distinction as taught by the cosmonomic philosophy in my pamphlet, "The Amsterdam Philosophy" (Phillipsburg, N.J.: Harmony Press, 1972), pp. 6-14. I find the distinction unclearly defined, its persuasiveness built on vivid but unexplained metaphors. I find no justification for the apparent denial of any continuum between the "naive" category and the "theoretical," especially since each seems able to include elements of the other. I see no basis for saying that naive thinking is somehow beyond the scope of philosophical or scientific criticism or that theoretical thought must be strictly limited to the cosmos. Thus, I do not find it helpful to discuss Scripture in terms of such a dichotomy. Certainly Scripture is generally written in the language of ordinary life as opposed to that of the academic world. But there are large diversities of language within Scripture itself (e.g., between the Psalms and Romans). I don't, again, expect to find $E = MC^2$ in the Bible; the connection of this formula with redemption is remote, and I don't think Scripture gets to be *that* theoretical. But to say that "Scripture speaks the language of ordinary life" gives me, again, only a rough, general guide to Scripture's contents. It gives me no *a priori* basis for excluding any exegetical possibilities.

25. Rom. 1:16; cf. II Tim. 3:15, John 6:63, etc.
26. I Thess. 1:5. For more discussion of this point, see I,B, below.
27. The metaphors of "gripping," etc., introduce a helpful vividness into our formulations. We must be careful, however, that we do not regard the power of the Word as a kind of "blind force" which influences us apart from the linguistic meanings of scriptural words and sentences. "Being gripped" by the Word must involve a conviction as to its truth and a desire to obey.
28. Dooyeweerd, H., *op. cit.*, pp. 115, 120, 125.
29. Klooster, F., *op. cit.*, 4.
30. Dooyeweerd, H., *op. cit.*, p. 125.
31. II Tim. 3:16ff.
32. For the correlation between meaning, implication and application, recall what was said above, second and third paragraphs of section I,A.
33. Matt. 4:4, II Tim. 3:16; emphasis mine, of course.
34. Kline, M., *The Structure of Biblical Authority* (Grand Rapids: Eerdmans, 1972).
35. Ex. 31:18; cf. 24:12.
36. I would say the doctrine entails that every human obligation is an application of Scripture. Otherwise no distinction could be made between divine doctrine and "commandments of men" (Matt. 15:9, Col. 2:22). This does not mean, however, that our duty is exhausted by the specific, explicit injunctions of Scripture. As we have seen, application involves both scrip-

tural and extra-scriptural premises since it seeks to relate Scripture to our situations.

37. Cf. Rom. 12:1ff.
38. Cf. Eph. 5:8.
39. Cf. Phil. 1:9ff.
40. Heb. 5:14.
41. Hence another good reason for saying that "heart-knowledge" of God transcends theoretical problems (Dooyeweerd, H., *op. cit.*, p. 120, 125). But none of this implies that theoretical knowledge of Scripture is irrelevant to, or unhelpful for, becoming obedient.
42. My own (radical) suggestion is that we define theology simply as "the application of Scripture to all of life." Broad as this notion may be, I think it is virtually equivalent to the *didache, didaskalia* of the Pastoral Epistles.
43. Cf. Gen. 3:9, John 21:15, Rom. 6:1, 15, 7:1, 7, 13, etc.
44. Cf. Rom. 6:2—*me genoito!*
45. For this terminology, see Austin, J., *How to Do Things with Words* (Cambridge: Harvard University Press, 1962).
46. Austin (above, note 45) argues that a promise is not the same as an assertion. An assertion may predict that something will happen in the future, but a promise commits the speaker to accomplish what is promised.
47. Kelsey, D., *The Uses of Scripture in Recent Theology* (Phila.: Fortress, 1975). My review of the book appears in the *Westminster Theological Journal* XXXIX, 2 (Spring, 1977), 328-353.
48. Dooyeweerd rightly emphasizes the variety of content communicable in language (in Geehan, E., *op. cit.*, pp. 84ff.). But I fail to understand why he finds it necessary to deny the existence in Scripture of "conceptual thought-contents." Or does he have some technical definition of "conceptual" which he has failed to share with the uninitiated reader? Clearly, in the usual sense, Scripture is quite full of "conceptual thought-contents."
49. The suzerainty-treaty pattern (above, I,A,3) illuminates this unity in diversity. Kline *(op. cit.)* shows how the covenant structure necessarily includes history, law, curse, blessing and administrative regulation. If Scripture is a covenant of this sort, we should expect such many-facetedness. Note also the Westminster Confession of Faith, XVI, ii, which stresses the different kinds of language in Scripture and the consequent variety in the human response solicited by it.
50. The other major criticism of "propositional revelation" in our circles is found, e.g., in Zylstra, B., *op. cit.*, p. 67. There, Zylstra argues against "*rationalistic* propositionalism" (emphasis his) which holds, he says, that Scripture contains "*verbal statements that are true in and of themselves.*" As is often the case, Zylstra's language is a bit too obscure to do his point justice. (One wants to know: is "Washington is the capital of the U.S." such

a statement? If not, what is? Are there any? If the Washington statement *is* the type of thing Zylstra is speaking of, what prevents statements of this kind from being in the Bible?) The discussion is clarified somewhat when Zylstra quotes from Zuidema, who argues against "prying off a text from the whole." Apparently, "rationalistic propositionalism" is the view that biblical sentences can be adequately interpreted with no regard to their context. Well, perhaps there is some danger of this; the reader can judge for himself.

51. Cf. the discussion of *scopus* above, I,A,1.
52. These qualities are not *merely* rational; they involve elements other than reason, but they do involve reason.
53. See II,A, below.
54. Thus, in a sense, we are called to "think God's thoughts after him." Why Dooyeweerd objects to this idea is utterly beyond me. See Geehan, E., *op. cit.*, p. 84.
55. I get the impression that when someone says, for example, that Scripture is "rational," those trained in the cosmonomic philosophy immediately assume that he is asserting what they would call an "analytic qualification" to Scripture. This is the only assumption by which I can make any sense at all out of Dooyeweerd's and Knudsen's articles in Geehan, E., ed., *op. cit.*, or out of John Vander Stelt's *Philosophy and Scripture*. But if so, then the cosmonomic thinkers are guilty of enormous and culpable misunderstanding. No one except a Dooyeweerdian would ever dream of using a mere adjective to express a "modal qualification." In fact, no one but a Dooyeweerdian would believe that there are such things as modal qualifications. It is totally without justification for cosmonomists to read their own idiosyncratic technical meanings into the words of people who obviously hadn't the slightest intent of using them that way.
56. Cf. Spier, J., *An Introduction to Christian Philosophy* (Phila.: Presbyterian and Reformed, 1954), pp. 71ff.
57. One could argue that a lecture-hall type of intelligence presupposes the ability to react intelligently to stimuli.
58. I emphasize *some*, not all. See below, II,A,2,e.
59. We saw earlier (I,A) how *every* application of Scripture, every act of obedience, involves some extra-scriptural knowledge.
60. Again, the response is "rational," but not "merely rational" or "primarily rational."
61. It is interesting that Van Til, criticized in cosmonomic circles for being something of a rationalist, is also applauded in other circles for being opposed to the use of reason in religious matters. See my review of White, W., *Van Til—Defender of the Faith* (New York: Nelson, 1979), *Westminster Theological Journal* XLII, 1 (Fall, 1979), 198-203. But neither rationalism nor fideism is to be applauded. We must seek to avoid both

through a careful and biblical delineation of the powers and limits of reason. And for that task Van Til's writings are immensely helpful.

62. Above, I,A.

63. Above, I,A,3.

64. Of course, this is not the *only* helpful or legitimate way to classify them.

65. Cf. Holmes, A., *All Truth is God's Truth* (Grand Rapids: Eerdmans, 1977), pp. 87ff.

66. *Ibid.*, p. 92. Cf. Poythress, V., "A Biblical View of Mathematics," in North, G., ed., *Foundations of Christian Scholarship* (Vallecito, CA: Ross House, 1976), pp. 159-188. See also his treatment of logic in *Philosophy, Science and the Sovereignty of God* (Nutley: Presbyterian and Reformed, 1976), pp. 199-205.

67. Cf. Wolterstorff, N., *Reason Within the Bounds of Religion* (Grand Rapids: Eerdmans, 1976), pp. 34-36.

68. Cf. Ryle, G., "Formal and Informal Logic," in his *Dilemmas* (Cambridge: Cambridge University Press, 1954), pp. 111-129.

69. Cf. Kuhn, T., *The Structure of Scientific Revolutions* (Chicago: University of Chicago Press, 1970).

70. Holmes, A., *op. cit.*, pp. 90ff.

71. *Ibid.*, pp. 89ff.

72. Spier, J., *op. cit.*, pp. 125ff. His argument that knowing involves not only subject and object but also law, I find cogent and important. Cf. my previous comments on knowing as an ethico-religious response to revelation.

73. Thus we are saved from various philosophical dilemmas, such as the tendency in secular philosophy either to absorb all reality into the self or to lose the self altogether in a quest for "objectivity."

74. Rom. 1:21.

75. II Thess. 1:8.

76. "Emotion" and "intellect" are mutually dependent. For example, if I had no emotional reactions to the issues about which I am writing, it is unlikely that I would form any opinions, or even think the project worth spending time on.

77. Cf. Isa. 55:8, Rom. 11:33.

78. Cf. my "The Problem of Theological Paradox" in North, G., ed., *op. cit.*, pp. 295-330. Also published as a pamphlet, "Van Til, the Theologian" (Phillipsburg, N.J.: Pilgrim, 1976).

79. Cf. above, II,A,2,f. An apparent contradiction does not always render a doctrinal formulation useless. It is useful to note the "informal logic" by which the biblical writers use doctrines (like divine sovereignty and human responsibility) which often seem contradictory to us. We may seek to employ the doctrine of divine sovereignty, for example, in contexts

similar to those in which the biblical writers used it, without necessarily being able to reconcile it with human responsibility. A contextually limited use may be a possible answer (either temporarily or permanently) in such cases.

80. Note above under II,B,3 for a hermeneutical application of this point.

Rationality and Scripture: Outline of a Philosophical Approach

N.T. van der Merwe

I. Introduction

THE TOPIC OF "RATIONALITY AND SCRIPTURE" can be treated from various angles. My contribution as a philosopher to the discussion of this theme, which is so important for Christian scholarship, will focus on "Rationality and Scripture," not on its profound correlate "Scripture and Rationality." Consequently my essay will be limited to a few *philosophical* facets which seem in need of further clarification and more thorough study. It will, moreover, be a sketch rather than a full-fledged exposition. To delineate the scope of the philosophical problems I am about to identify, my approach to the subject will proceed in three phases.

In the first instance I shall give a brief exposition of some essential features of rationality. Next I shall try to indicate an intrinsic connection between my philosophical analysis of rationality and certain basic issues of epistemology and the methodology of science. In conclusion I shall apply a few basic insights acquired along this route to the more complex question of Scripture and rationality.

The crucial issue, of course, is to discover the point of intersection between Scripture and rationality. My assessment of the matter is that this intersection is pinpointed in the intrinsic relation between divine revelation (primarily through the medium of Scripture) on the one hand and human (religious control) beliefs on the other hand. In essence I mean the effect of faith commitments, through the presence of the Holy Spirit in the heart of man, on all concrete cognitive acts. Accordingly, I would invite criticism of my working hypothesis in the concluding section.

In contrast to the growing volume of literature on rationality appearing in periodicals, the theme of "rationality and Scripture" does not seem to interest scholars particularly at present—if published material could serve as a yardstick. The number of references to this theme, both in the literature on rationality and on Scripture, is minimal. A much keener interest is shown in specific facets of rationality and the function of reason in expositions of the "authority of the Bible," for example, or of "science and Holy Scripture." As far as examples of the latter are concerned, one can refer to B. Ramm, *The Christian View of Science and Scripture*, or to W. Keller's *Und die Bibel hat doch recht.*

Scholarly periodicals, moreover, frequently screen the topic of the "rationality of belief(s)," including the rationality (or irrationality) of religious belief, which dovetails with the problem of the plausibility of arguments or proofs for the existence of God. George I. Mavrodes, for example, has an interesting section on the latter topic in his *Belief in God: A Study in the Epistemology of Religion*. And Alvin Plantinga competently exposes the "intellectual imperialism on the part of the foundationalist" in his article "Is Belief in God Rational?"—one of several important chapters in the book *Rationality and Religious Belief*, edited by C.F. Delaney. Perhaps I may be permitted to quote, as an illustration of what I have in mind, Plantinga's conclusion on p. 26: "So far we have found no reason at all for excluding belief in God from the foundations; so far we have found no reason at all for believing that belief in God cannot be basic in a rational noetic structure." Expositions like these do not treat the theme of rationality and Scripture as such, but they are very much a part of the total "problem area."

The same can be said of investigations like Michael Polanyi's "The Stability of Beliefs." Consider, for example, the following thesis from this article (1952, p. 230):

> Science and magic are both comprehensive systems of beliefs, possessing a considerable degree of stability, and a comparison of the two systems has shown that the convincing powers of both are derived from similar logical properties of their conceptual frameworks. I hold that we have good reasons for preferring science to magic or astrology or . . . to the perversion of science imposed by Stalinism on the territories under Communist rule. But I suggest that these reasons can never be adequately stated without a personal affirmation of belief on the part of the speaker.

If Polanyi is correct, it seems that we will have to compare the "belief system" of not only science, magic and ideologies as mentioned by Polanyi, but also of world-views and of faith as well as its correlate, namely the effect on faith of literature of a special category listed as "holy" or "sacred," as well as of divine revelation.

At this point a legitimate question might be whether our investigation has hereby moved squarely into the province of theology proper. And is it now time to hand the task over to our colleagues in the theological branch of science? This does not prove to be the case, however. To mention just one aspect, language is an essential component of faith and revelation, and involves intrinsic philosophical problems. McDougall made the point aptly in his paper in *Mind* (1972, p. 523):

> . . . what kind of work religious language is doing, how statements about God and his existence are "verified" or otherwise justified, what the concept of "God" means, are as much theological as philosophical questions. Consequently, the very interpretation which the philosopher puts upon the function of religious language will condition his view of whether religious belief as a whole can be justified.

Perhaps someone is not convinced that this is quite pertinent to the topic of rationality. Let me then finally quote Bennett (1964, p. 93): ". . . the possession of a language is necessary for rationality; and it follows from the whole line of argument of this essay that the possession of a language is not sufficient for rationality."[1]

My first remark, therefore, is that the significance of the theme "rationality and Scripture" is not evident from bibliographical indices. The explanation is that there are many facets to the theme, and only if they are taken together do the pieces of the puzzle fit into their proper position. Accordingly a narrow reduction to the philological components of "rationality" and "Scripture" hardly allows one to sense the real parameters of the inner dynamics of this theme.

My second remark is that one thus has no option but to distill the essential features of the theme "rationality and Scripture" from the various contexts in which the topic is treated. So I shall commence with a philological and philosophical analysis of "rationality," progressively move on to the other component of the theme of my essay, and finally attempt to conclude with a kind of synthesis.

II. Rationality

A. Rationality in Contemporary Thought

Concise expositions of the "anatomy of rationality" in all its ramifications are scarce.[2] It is also remarkable that although various scholars have been dissecting the knotty problems connected with rationality, and have written extensively in scholarly articles and books during the past decades, the outcome has hardly filtered through to the level of encyclopedias and philosophical dictionaries. Even P. Edward's influential *Encyclopaedia of Philosophy* (1967) did not consider rationality a full-fledged philosophical topic. This surely is an indication that this theme is still in the process of initial analysis, and the "synthesizing" concluding phase is not yet in sight.

A study of the relevant literature shows moreover that a large amount of discussion is still centered on two points: (1) attempts to vindicate rationality against the onslaught of irrationalism, while salvaging a new face of rationalism in this process;[3] or (2) on analyses of the various claims of skepticism (inasmuch as this presents a threat not merely to dogmatism but even to rationality) on the one hand, and probing the merits and intricacies of its irrationalistic correlate "commitment" on the other hand.[4]

It is obvious that a "single-minded alignment" to reason, as one encounters in rationalism, must in one way or another entail "pointers" to the role and essence of rationality. It is surprising, however, that on the whole the grand period of rationalism was concerned more with issues of reason than rationality.[5] In the final analysis the concern with rationality in the 20th century can be traced to the problematic notion of reason and science (so-called "eternal truths"). This issue forced the philosophers of the age of the enlightenment, of positivism and of contemporary thought to investigate the possibilities of and obstacles to the emancipation of reason in correlation with the ideal of human freedom. Nevertheless it was the implications of an incisive reaction which triggered the 20th-century interest in the philosophical dimensions and significance of rationality.[6]

B. The "Logical Geography" of Rationality

With this background material in mind, we can now move on to the philosophical issue of rationality. The most obvious procedure for a philosopher is to pose the central question: what is the meaning of the term rationality. In this essay we will not be able to indulge in a proper conceptual or linguistic analysis of this topic. But we cannot avoid exposing a few roots in a summary fashion either. Lewis and Short's well-weathered Latin dictionary (1879) translates "rationalitas" as reasonableness or rationality. It is interesting to note that the reference is to that exceptional molder of early Christian idiom, and that unique specimen of an acute rational mind—Tertullian! In fact, the reference is to his *De anima*, 38: "habet anima rationalitatem." The related adjective "rationalis" highlights two facets of this elusive term: (1) belonging to accounts, and also (as a noun) indicating an accountant, a treasurer; (2) belonging to reason, rational, endowed with or depending on reason.

What a modern ring, indeed, one encounters in "rationaliter": in a reasonable manner, reasonably, rationally. If one persists in tracing the family history of next of kin like "rationarium," "ratiocinium," "ratiocinatio," "ratiocinor" and "ratio," one discovers the embryonic stages of science as a theory, doctrine or system based upon reason. We also encounter the quadruplet offspring: business accountancy (calculation), computing science (reckoning), statistics (statistical table or schedule) and explanative and instructive reasoning. (The latter has its Janus' face of order, rule and law—as exhibited in either syllogistic logic and reflective thought, or considerative and understanding judgment which is inherent in interrogative reasoning, rhetorical argumentation and inference.)

In this early emphasis clearly on the powers of the mind rather than reason itself, a marked affinity with the contemporary interest in rationality presents itself. But taking into account the dual origins of Western thought—Roman practical ingenuity in legal and moral matters and Greek intellectual subtlety and encyclopedic versatility in theoretical inquiry—let us check the Greek correlate. "Logos" and related terms show to a large extent the same differentiation in connotation, although perhaps not always so clear cut as in Latin usage. There seems to be one exception: the lingual facet echoes the dominant melody, "logos" being the word by which the inward thought is expressed. Accordingly Greek usage is in a position to strike a superb balance between word or language and thought or reason as illustrated in "logikos" (belonging to speech or to reason). Two interesting related terms are "logimos" (worth mention, remarkable) and "logion" (a declaration, oracle).[7]

As far as the philosophical architecture of rationality is concerned, the relevant literature presents abundant evidence that "rationality" as a philosophical topic is steadily seeping through to all spheres of philosophical inquiry. Stimulating material has been written on rationality and logic, analysis, inquiry, method, criteria and standards, research, understanding and interpretation, science, theory, assumptions, beliefs, presuppositions, commitment, actions, praxis, evidence, truth, verification, certainty, etc.[8] The same is true of the contrasting relationship between "rational" and "irrational" with reference to the problem of rationality.[9]

J. Kekes' *A Justification of Rationality* (1976) clearly marks an advanced stage of the growth of philosophical knowledge regarding rationality.[10] I can put forward this statement rather categorically because any attempt to justify rationality presupposes access to a "basic construction kit" of the structure of rationality, including of course the "bricks of the wall," as well as to a full-fledged theory of rationality. I have a special reason, moreover, for referring specifically to Kekes' instructive analysis of rationality. Within the spectrum of possible options, Kekes allots preferential treatment to rationality as a method, a method for solving problems. My own approach proceeds in a similar direction, at least in essential respects, but, at the same time entails some important modifications.

To keep this essay within reasonable bounds I shall therefore concentrate on this issue and refrain from developing a systematic treatment of the topic. I will not trace the main contributions in the history of Western philosophy,[11] nor the influential ideas of 20th-century thinkers like Ayer, Carnap, Habermas, Kuhn, Popper, Russell and Trigg, to mention but a few.

My rationale for this choice is based on two other supporting pillars. First, Kekes does not seem to have an acceptable explanation for the growth of kowledge, or for the rationality of problem solving, that really comes to grips with Feyerabend's mood "against method." Feyerabend contends that the growth of knowledge often tramples on rational procedures, and often ignores important methodological rules. So I would like to further the discussion of this important issue by suggesting a possible explanation for the "rationality of rationality" in the face of anarchism, and in the midst of the collapse of a rationalistic and positivistic ideal of a perfect and consistent scientific method.

My second rationale for focusing on Kekes involves some questions. How novel and original is Kekes' rationalization of rationality? Is the concern with the justification of rationality perhaps still a far-off legacy of positivistic ties with rationality?[12] Yes or no, what are the implications of a Christian commitment with regard to this topic? What answers have been and should be forthcoming within the Calvinian tradition? Without anticipating any responses to this essay, I shall limit myself to what is attainable at this stage.[13] I would also like to indicate briefly how the philosophical problematics of rationality and Scripture do open up new vistas on this crucial issue of contemporary thought.

"Pointers" toward the above-mentioned goal will be (1) the epistemological framework of rationality, (2) the methodological implications of rationality, (3) rationality, commitment and a life and world-view, and (4) rationality and revelation.[14]

III. Human Knowledge and Rationality

A. Rationality and the Human Mind

The result of my exposition regarding the spectrum of connotations of the term "rationality," as far as its roots are concerned, can be summarized as follows: rational—belonging to reason or depending on reason, thought and speech; reasonable—the capacity and the responsibility to render an account, acting as a treasurer, calculating (credits and debits), reckoning and computing; explanative and instructive reasoning. Somewhat further removed one can discern a notion like an inquiry proceding in a methodical manner, which has as its major offshoots theorizing and justification of beliefs.

For many centuries the scientific enterprise was considered the example *par excellence* of such a methodical procedure. One could say that science and rationality exhibit two sides of the same coin. It is quite understandable that Feyerabend's (1976) challenge regarding the irrationality of scientific endeavors should have caused concern and even alarm, touching as it did faith in the very essence of scientific inquiry.

The rather naïve identification of science and rationality, no less than the anarchistic isolation of science and rationality, demand a response from Christian scholars. Certainly this issue is relevant to the Calvinian tradition, which has through the centuries tried to avoid the Scylla and Charybdis of rationalism and intellectualism on the one hand, and mysticism and pietism on the other hand.

It is important to remember that the tradition of Western philosophy is characterized by an inherent trust in the functions of the human intellect, in the mastery achieved by the innate powers of the human mind. In modern times reason was even proclaimed by many to serve as the foundation and guarantee of all true knowledge; this evoked a major reaction in the 20th century. Nonetheless, in the course of the history of Western philosophy several alternative theories of knowledge were developed by penetrating minds, from Parmenides to Popper. One important facet of this process is the scale indicating the differentiation between maximizing and minimizing epistemologies. Some thinkers regard perfect knowledge as truth in contradistinction to error; knowledge thus implies certainty which produces subjective confidence. Others oppose belief or mere opinion to ideal knowledge. Meanwhile a third party considers perfect knowledge unattainable and suggests that skepticism is the most prudent council.

An excellent example of a maximizing theory is to be found in

Plato's epistemology. Especially in his later writings, the notion of an intelligible world was introduced. Here Plato explored the potentialities of a realistic theory of knowledge which could transcend the realm of permanent change, situational sensual awareness and slippery illusion and error. It is significant that Plato introduced the notion of a supra-human element to knowledge in his *Theaetetus*, to which I shall later give more specific attention. This fact is important as it presents already at the initial stages of philosophy an alternative to a rigid immanentistic theory of knowledge. In Parmenides, Plato, Aristotle and other pagan philosophers, the supra-intellectual element is of course tinged by Greek mythology, or more correctly stated, by pagan philosophical theology. But the philosophical problems involved, including the acknowledgment of limits to knowledge and the search for a criterion of valid knowledge, are legitimate, and treated by Christians like Augustine, Anselm and others in their own way.

In the third instance, the special function of the intellect as "dianoia" entails the basic concept of "meaning" (of an entity). The notion of meaning, together with the inner relation between knowledge and wisdom (i.e., the ability and skill to use one's mind in a sensible way in practical affairs) add up to four challenging aspects of rationality. To these the Calvinian tradition has given a distinct response. But I should not forget to mention a fifth factor of immense importance, which is closely connected with the distinction between good and evil—truth. This is crucial not only for a sound perspective on critical independence and an open-minded attitude in daily life as well as in scientific endeavors, but also as an antidote against verificationism.[15]

I think one can state by way of summary that the rationality of knowledge operates within the limits of an ideal of perfect, valid, and trustworthy knowledge on the one hand, and the reality of non-perfect but sound and useful knowledge—exposed to the grip of error and mistake—on the other hand. Within this context a significant philosophical problem is that of knowledge and belief. This theme is intended to sort out the optimum developmental point of equilibrium between normative and factual facets of human cognitive endeavors, and is of such importance that I shall soon devote further attention to it.

In the third instance, if the anthropological issues involved receive due attention, the philosophical concern with cognitive beliefs will stimulate a philosophical analysis *and* assessment of rationality. I stress this point because rationality entails not only logical intelligibility but especially the aspect of giving an account of the meaning of knowledge—explaining the reasonableness of human cognitive activity. In short, the "rationality of rationality" can be described in this context in familiar terms as "the justification of rationality."

Now this is something different from mere analysis. I find a theory of modal functions and analogical terms—as developed in Calvinistic philosophy[16]—very helpful in understanding this complicated issue. This theory should be complemented, however, by a methodology which takes into account the various factors inherent in what is called "method" and which affect all cognitive acts, including the scientific enterprise. For this reason I shall devote special attention to this facet of rationality. This will furthermore open up avenues to approach the complex problem of cognitive frameworks and the function of beliefs in that context.

One of the most important trends in contemporary philosophy of science is the recognition that beliefs have a much more incisive function in scientific inquiry than had been surmised in the past.[17] An accompanying development is the closer attention devoted to the investigation of presuppositions and the anatomy of human understanding in contemporary hermeneutics. At the same time there has been a growing tendency to solve philosophical problems inherent in scientific beliefs within the field of the philosophy of science itself. I shall disregard this trend on account of its reductionistic tendency, and soon pay attention to some basic issues like that of knowledge and belief as well as to a few important parameters of a Christian theory of knowledge.

In conclusion, I have referred above to the role of beliefs in the context of frameworks. This entails, briefly, that a "paradigm" can be viewed as a cognitive construct emerging from a world-and-life-view. This construct determines the perspective from which theoretical and practical tasks in life are approached, and operates on an intellectual level—often in a scientific context.

B. Knowledge and Belief

It is general knowledge that the first substantial philosophical inquiry concerning knowledge and belief is to be found in Plato's *Theaetetus*—at least if one approaches the matter in the Anglo-Saxon tradition.[18] I add the latter remark because, in contrast to "episteme" as authentic knowledge, belief is considered in this philosophical tradition to be the obvious equivalent of the Greek term "doxa" (i.e., on the positive side, the negative being often taken to be "mere opinion" or "a mistaken notion"). Now the Greek term "doxa" means basically a notion, opinion, or mere opinion, a sentiment or judgment, a fancy or vision, one's reputation (the opinion and expectation others have of one), thus credit, honor, glory. In applying one's notion of knowledge and belief to Plato, one should thus be on guard against the modern overtones in the use of the term "belief."

It is sometimes said (see Quinton, for example, 1967, vol. 4, p. 347) that in the *Theaetetus* three definitions of knowledge are examined, and in the end all are rejected. This statement is an oversimplification of the matter. This is, of course, not the venue for a detailed analysis of Plato's epistemology, and so I shall mention only a few particulars without paying attention to the logic of the argument.

Plato's essay on knowledge contains in actual fact seven definitions or descriptions of theories of knowledge. The first refers to a specific type of knowledge or skill in a certain area acquired by an expert, whose word is accepted and who is capable of noticing resemblances and common features. Or in a slightly different variation, "knowledge" amounts to a definition of various forms of knowledge, a collection of various items like numbers under one heading.

The second approach describes knowledge as a skill or proficiency, like that of the artisan ("hai toon demiourgoon technai"), which can be learned and taught (the opinion of the Sophists). It is the proficiency of midwifery, the maieutic art as a task conferred by a god, which brings to birth in the souls of men the distinction between true and false, and tests the genuineness of the fruit.

The third approach identifies knowledge with perception ("aesthesis") of qualities, in the way individual things appear ("phainetai") to a person. Perception covers both existing things on the one hand and the subject of perception in a process of becoming on the other hand.

The fourth discussion identifies some problems with perception (for example, in a dream, illusion, illness) and defines knowledge as the hidden truth of the thought of an important person. Knowledge concerns that which cannot be seen. This is clear from the fact that memory ("mneme") presupposes correct perception but is more complex than a "phenomenon."

The fifth attempt concentrates on true thinking ("alethes dianoia") in contrast to false opinion ("pseudes doxa") and illustrates the point by reference to a few examples (like the "channel theory," cognitive consciousness, the theory of exclusion, the "inner speech" theory and the memory theory).

A sixth approach describes knowledge as true opinion plus definition and explanation, i.e., opinion with a bodyguard, a notion that has been corroborated and confirmed; or to use a famous phrase, "belief accompanied by a rational account . . . ."

The concluding definition pulls the threads together: knowledge is wisdom, i.e., no pretence about knowing what one doesn't know! Under the aegis of Delphi, epistemology and anthropology are united. But wisdom also presupposes the maeutic technique as a divine gift. Thus knowledge as a skill has a supra-human dimension.

It is clear that Plato distinguishes "episteme," "dianoia" and "doxa." Together with "dianoia" (knowledge of real things), "doxa" clears the hurdle of perception, but as a function of the soul it nonetheless does not fully qualify as knowledge—it needs an extra. In this sense, belief as a well-founded opinion, as a notion supported with sufficient reasons, approximates real knowledge.

We are now in a position to highlight a few important facets of Plato's *Theaetetus*. In this dialogue Plato not only applies "knowing that" (propositional knowledge), "knowing what" (suppositional, interrogative or dialectical and communicative knowledge), "knowing how" (technical knowledge) and "acquaintance with" (personal knowledge) to the exposition; he also applies evaluative (or estimative), essential (knowing the "what" and the "how" of the "that") and philosophical knowledge (wisdom).

Plato also discusses several important epistemological problems in this book without mentioning their respective relations. One could mention subjects like (1) different kinds or types of knowledge; (2) the nature and essence of knowledge; (3) the origin and growth of knowledge; (4) the validity of knowledge; (5) knowledge and subjective certainty; (6) didactic facets of knowledge (whether knowledge can be learnt and taught); (7) the relation of art, skill and technique to knowledge; (8) the interrelationship between sense perception and thought; (9) the problem of cognitive universals (common features and generality); (10) the limits to knowledge; (11) human knowledge and the divine factor; and (12) various epistemological theories.

We can now broach an important question. Where does the problem of knowledge and belief fit in? It seems to me that this philosophical issue can be regarded as a combination of various aspects of a theory of knowledge mentioned above, especially items (1), (2), (4), (5) and (8). Though Plato touched on several essential components of knowledge, there is a missing link in his brilliant exposition of facets of knowledge: a thorough analysis of the general *structure* of knowledge. Accordingly Plato is not in a position to indicate the actual contribution of each single facet to epistemological theory as such. If my conjecture about "a combination of aspects of knowledge" is correct, the relevance of "a point of equilibrium between normative and factual facets of human cognitive endeavors" (mentioned above in my summary) becomes apparent. And so does the importance of the theme of knowledge and belief!

C. Some Basic Epistemological Implications

Notwithstanding the profound insights and obvious merits mentioned above, Plato's theory of knowledge and, for that matter, the Platonic tradition as such, afflicted rationality with an inner conflict and tension between rational thought and sense perception. It pointed to the role of definition, explanation, technique and a supra-human factor; but it left in the dark what exactly this function should be.

Can one learn from Plato and move a step ahead? Let's try. In the first instance, Plato made an important distinction and intrinsic connection between "episteme" and "dianoia." In this way he approached knowledge from the perspective of thought or intellect or mind. This approach shows that the latter, although it is a necessary criterion, is not a sufficient criterion of knowledge.

Moreover, a window is opened to a "supra-human" element. A different approach to this element is present in Aristotle, Zeno, Epicurus and others. Very intriguing statements were made also by Christians such as Augustine, Anselm and Bonaventure, to mention just a few.[19] Anselm's concept of what cannot be understood and what transcends human thought deserves careful scrutiny. But "dianoia" is important in a second sense: it also points to the sense or meaning of something. The 20th-century thinkers in particular have come to realize the importance of meaning as far as philosophical analysis is concerned—and rationality as well![20]

In the second instance, Plato discerned the limits of human knowledge and found the solution in wisdom. This approach entails a severe blow to unfounded human pride and self-esteem. I think this is an important contribution, although the idea and ideal of self-knowledge should be put in a Christian perspective. What, then, is the inner connection between knowledge and wisdom? Briefly stated: the necessity to use one's mind in a sensible way in practical matters, to have insight into what should be done and what can be done—from the perspective that "the fear of the Lord is the fount of wisdom."[21] The grace of God is the basis of life.

This perspective demands that attention be paid to the function of truth in this context, taking into account both the epistemological and religious dimensions of truth—Christ being the Way, Truth and Life. The common sense of faith equips one with a basic view of life, a vision in which the most fundamental beliefs act as a girdle of surety to human knowledge. The common-sense tradition in philosophy is not stupid; it should simply get on track and not seek a final hide-out in philosophy or science.

Within a pagan context, Plato had a brilliant insight when he pointed to the distinction between true and false in the soul as a result of a technique that should be considered a divine gift. Do Christians in the modern secularized world make a maximum use of the means that God—the real, living, personal God—has put to their disposal to discern true and false, good and evil in the sphere of knowledge? Or do they use these means to consider and accept the grace of God as the daily ration to life? This is philosophically very important, for truth liberates, sets one free, creates wide vistas, eliminates narrow-mindedness.[22] Truth is thus normative for human action.

A very important facet, as far as the objective and the result of human action are concerned, is the way in which human actions are performed. Accordingly we should at this stage switch over to the role that "method" plays in cognitive matters.

IV. Method and Rationality

A. A General Analysis of Method

The English term "method" is derived from the Greek "methodos," which means basically a passage or a route from a point of departure to a specific goal. Greek words with a related connotation show that method can be viewed as a pursuit, a hunt in which something (like truth, for example) is chased, as an investigation or inquiry, and thus also as intellectual research (see Liddell & Scott, 1843). In modern times two facets of the meaning of method have received special attention: (1) the route one follows to achieve a certain result, and (2) a program that regulates how a series of actions should be executed to achieve a specific result.

It is interesting to note that method shows as great a diversity as human life itself. In the area of human praxis one finds methods to organize a conference, to grow fruit trees, to train horses for a gymkana show, methods to communicate with people, to paint a picture or to compose a melody, to invest sensibly, to acquire knowledge, etc.

The next task is to look into the constitutive elements of method and then single out the characteristics of the scientific method which the scholar applies in his specific field of study.[23]

Method is a procedure, a course of action, the way in which an action is performed. As examples of procedures one can mention the way in which bees gather pollen, or ants grass, the procedure of the formation of stalagmites in grottoes, or the process in which the propagation of mushrooms comes to pass.

Method is, however, a more complicated procedure; it presupposes *human* activity or at least a process which has been initiated by human intervention (as in modern technology). Activities like eating and drinking, traveling to one's work, etc., are events, human events. It is possible to discover the nature of method by paying attention to the procedure involved in such similar activities. Let us point this out briefly. In contrast to the dominant positivistic methodological tradition,[24] it seems to me that one has to reckon with at least seven different factors which are essential to a methodical procedure. This does not imply a chronological order from (1) to (7), nor that each is equally important in every instance.

(1) Inherent in those activities which are relevant to an investigation of method is in the first instance a goal that is being pursued—say, for example, cleaning a car. If the action succeeds in a specific instance, the objective is attained.

(2) The result obtained is of course dependent on the actual performance of the action (wishful thinking is of no use!) as well as on the execution of the procedure through all phases right up to the ultimate conclusion.

(3) The success of the action is also dependent on the proper planning of the procedure, especially the successive phases of the procedure. In this respect human thought is essential. It is interesting to note that in actual practice, logical rigor concerning successive steps to be taken is nonetheless compatible with some measure of zig-zag deviation from the main route. Scientific work, especially when viewed retrospectively, shows some similarity to cross-country driving.

(4) It is not only important *that* a certain action be performed but also *how* a certain procedure is executed.

(5) As has already been hinted at in (3), method presupposes a human person endowed with thought who is able to get into action, or alternatively some kind of apparatus which has been manufactured by man and operates under human supervision.

(6) A procedure like cleaning a car requires, in addition to

"elbow grease," certain available material that needs cleaning, and (7) appropriate tools or instruments to aid the cleaning process.

With this brief summary of its essential features, we are a step closer to a provisional definition of method. It is the procedure that unites in the best possible manner the seven above-mentioned constitutive elements in one total activity. As the *combination* of these factors is unique in each specific instance according to the contingent circumstances involved, it seems obvious that a diversity of possibilities will be encountered. The measure of success will accordingly vary, too. Moreover, when one takes into account the various ways in which the final combination may be produced by circumstances, it is obvious that any practical decision will entail a kind of compromise, a normative approximation to the ideal standard.

Even a superficial reflection on the issues involved in method will prove that it is far from easy to find a flawless and concise definition of method. The following description highlights some of the difficulties involved. Method is a procedure planned to attain a specific goal as far as possible in an economical rational way. It presupposes both an entity (material of some kind, even facts) as object of the planned activity and a subject to execute the process in its various phases with a view to the goal in mind. In other words, a human person is intentionally focused on a certain objective and tries to attain the goal as efficiently as possible by means of appropriate "tools" or "instruments." In some instances a specially designed apparatus—fabricated, operated and controlled by a human agent—may act as a substitute for a human subject.

The question remains how one can determine the efficiency and success of a specific method. The least complicated criterion to use in this case is to investigate in what measure the specific method proves to be a suitable means for attaining the specific goal. It is clear that no more than an "approximative" norm is to be expected, i.e., a rule which determines the measure of success in attaining the goal. We can expect to find the extent to which the method can be considered an ideal "passage" from the point of departure to the intended objective.

My description of the "anatomy of method" has thus far focused on method in general. The diversity of methods include cognitive methods, methods to increase, corroborate, and integrate one's knowledge, even to get rid of exploded notions and to get one's basic working knowledge up to date. Whereas the positivistic tradition furthered the gathering and reproduction of facts, the 20th century has shown an increasing focus on the contingent facet of methodological procedures: growth and change.[25] It is necessary, however, to mention some aspects of the scientific enterprise in order to understand the interesting developments taking place in this area. Although the difference between knowledge in the everyday life situation and scientific knowledge is relative in several respects, scientific knowledge does have some unique features. Therefore, methodological procedures of science will now receive brief attention.[26]

B. Method within the Scientific Context

As an introduction I would like to mention seven aspects of the problem area which have some reference to the seven features of method mentioned earlier. Subsequently I shall discuss briefly a few additional facets, linking up the discussion a bit closer with the problem of rationality.

(1) The scientific enterprise applies the scientific method as a *systematic procedure geared* to a *theoretical goal*, i.e., it is a means toward scientific knowledge, scientific theory and explanation in a specific area of investigation.

(2) Scientific method requires that scientific research be carried out in coordinated phases and that the planned project be executed in a (flexible) logical order of consecutive steps.

(3) The planned systematic procedure inherent in scientific inquiry often necessitates a research program, even a strategy to handle the research program efficiently.

(4) The manner in which the investigation is carried out is particularly important and requires the specialized cognitive experience, the "know-how" and skills of

(5) an educated scholar—or a group of scholars, as is the case with various scientific projects. Naturally it can be presumed that such a scientist possesses an acute mind and some experience in planning the necessary layout correlating the various phases. Quite often, appropriate "extensions" to bodily organs have to be designed, produced and used to cope with special circumstances.

(6) The scientist launches an inquiry into one or more scholarly *problems* which require attention or further study.

(7) The scientist handles data and furthers his investigation by using scientific *instruments* designed for specific purposes as aids to perception, measurement and control functions. In many instances this facet of method has been simplified, standardized and perfected

to appropriate *techniques*.

It is true that everyday cognitive life entails observation, distinction, identification, generalization, communicative description, etc. Typical of the scientific endeavor is that these human activities are linked to a specific field of study, which entails a specific kind of abstraction. The relevant facts and data are traced in a certain context and handled within the framework of a chosen perspective or "paradigm"; scientific results are verified, explained and sorted into their appropriate "box" in the classification system of the specific discipline. The hypotheses or theories thus obtained, and the character of the inherent basic beliefs (as well as their degree of objectivity and explanatory "power"), are then checked and tested (by designing manageable experiments, for example) and criticized within a "context of justification."

Scientific method is far more complex than the positivistic tradition would like us to believe and also more intricate than my brief description could point out. But this should be sufficient to show what is meant by the rationality of science, which to my mind finds expression especially in the rational procedures of the scientific method. In this perspective it is also quite sensible to talk of "progress in science" or the "growth of knowledge."[27] Bronowski's (1978) well-known indicator "the common sense of science" admirably highlights this aspect of the rationality of science.

From a philosophical and contemporary point of view it seems to me that one should be highly critical of rationalism and rationalistic theories of rationality. But I see no reason why we should not as Christian scholars elaborate a theory of rationality which honors the ordered intelligibility of intellectual life and acknowledges the rationality of knowledge in everyday life as well as in the sphere of scientific inquiry. I would only add one proviso: the concept of experience and logic which we apply in science should stretch to the limits of the human horizon and not suffocate within a reductionistic framework.[28] As a result, I suggest that method be considered an exceptional indicator to illumine the worth of rationality in human life. I shall explain in the next section what this entails.

V. Rationality, Commitment and a World-and-Life-View

What has been stated in the previous section does not, of course, imply that method is recommended as a modern absolutized idol on the scientific market. Neither does it entail rationalizing pet ideas in a dogmatic fashion. It does require investigating in a serious academic way what our calling as present-day Christian scholars implies.[29]

Perhaps we should also consider applying the basics of a Christian philosophy of history to this task. And we should pay special attention to the scope of Christian scholarship in the modern world as well as to our basic commitments and our communal responsibility in regard to our principles, beliefs and style of life in theory and practice. For that is the quintessence of our "reasonable service and spiritual worship."

But does this not expose the Christian academic to irrationalism? This is an important issue for Christian scholars because commitment to the Christian faith is often considered to be primarily a matter of the heart of man rather than his mind. Confession of faith is therefore sometimes labeled an irrational decision and a performative act, which defy logic and a rational account. Of course, one can and should distinguish between beliefs in the sphere of confessional faith and beliefs inherent in scientific theories. But what is of greater importance is to gain insight into the nature of beliefs as such. In that context the question still remains whether the specter of irrationalism does not also touch intellectual beliefs as well. We might end up all the same with that uneasy feeling of being "unscientific," and far adrift from an "objective" attitude.

Let us tackle this knotty problem by first stating that there are many facets to irrationalism and many kinds of irrationalism as well.[30] It would be fatal not to discern the umbrella function of this term. But let us ignore the philosophical subtleties for a moment and concentrate on what seems to be the crux of the matter. Scholars like Trigg (1977) outlined the philosophical problematics connected with the swing to commitment and the associations with subjectivism and relativism. Moreover, the outlook of people like Kuhn and Feyerabend is often labeled "irrational." So there can be no argument about the actuality of the matter. Even though Kuhn has not been all that consistent in his expositions, he nonetheless posed a serious challenge to traditional ideas about rationality and furthered the discussion with interesting perspectives on the role of paradigms in science.[31] Feyerabend for his part drew the issue to sophistical (Dadaistic!) ultimate limits.[32] So the basic decision seems to be whether one should cross the Rubicon and say farewell to rationality, or perhaps call a mental "epoche" to one's aid. How serious is the situation?

Feyerabend substantiated his claim that "anything goes" with penetrating historical analyses. Indeed, the history of science records many instances where basic methodological rules were contravened. Moreover, on an instrumental level, beliefs *are* operational factors involved in theory construction. Does this prove, however, that the rationality of science is a mistaken notion, and that modern science's commitment, even devotion, to rational procedures is an abortive attempt?[33]

I suggest that one should not be in a hurry to exorcize science on account of obvious defects and lack of "consistency." That would be mere sophistry and aesthetic redundancy. I think one should rather try to understand the rationale for science *and* the obvious discrepancy between ideal and praxis. Feyerabend's "Anarchism" has brilliantly exposed the fact that the much praised rationality of science is not so rational after all.[34] Certainly, scientific inquiry shows blemishes and does not always justify the amount of energy and money spent; but "some does not imply all," that is elementary logic. Did Feyerabend really justify his claim that "anything goes"? One does not write off a Jaguar because it has a couple of dents, does one? But let us not quarrel about the merits and failures of science; it is after all just a "slice of life." Let us rather counter Feyerabend by indicating *why* the practical application of the scientific method cannot be absolutely consistent, and why the scientific endeavor cannot evade flouting methodological rules occasionally.

In my description above I have given some indications that *scientific* method is a combination of at least seven basic factors in respect to a selected problem or number of problems in a specific field of study. Now consider for a moment a further complication of the matter: the close liaison between scientific method and the scientific enterprise as such, especially the role, for example, of scientific thought; scientific terms; hypotheses, theories and models; the strategy of research programs; the justification of theories, paradigms and beliefs; the integrity and responsibility of scholarly activities and the influence and effect of cultural attitudes and the scientific ideal of the academic community at large; etc. Then also take into consideration the enormous diversity of areas of investigation and multiply this by seven different combination ratios inherent in scientific method—with the possibility in each instance that the desired optimum compromise may not be reached. Then one arrives at a triumphant justification of the sweet chance of continual failure inherent in the scientific enterprise!

It is rather remarkable that science does leave a faint impression of rationality after all! But who would be so rash as to denounce the anatomy of the human body on account of variations in structure and function of individual limbs and organs? If one keeps in mind this simple fact, it seems to me that anarchism and methodological pluralism lose much of the impact and academic glamour attained in certain circles.

Kuhn made interesting comments on the incommensurability of theories, each theory creating its own context. Thus, to understand and utilize a theory presupposes the potential and limits of that context, which is determined by a so-called "Gestalt switch." Now the challenge that Kuhn's intriguing theory poses will function on another level than the problem area discussed in the previous paragraph. For scientific research is "theory laden" and thus bound to a specific paradigm, framework or perspective that determines which facts can be discovered and acknowledged. Basically no criterion for comparing theories can be found according to this point of view; the "Gestalt switch" assumption effectively eliminates any such possibility.

I suggest that this influential theory be countered by a few important adjustments. Kuhn did move away from the older positivistic tradition, but not far enough. There are indeed no "bare facts," but there are no "bare paradigms" like 20th-century monads either. A paradigm functions as a cognitive framework and is embedded in a cultural and intellectual context. And this context refers to both the ontological dimensions of science and the anthropological bases of the intellectual environment of the scholar.

Kuhn's holistic and historicistic approach to prime cultural units, and his attachment to the sociology of science, stressed the unique and "solipsistic" character of paradigms. This prevented him from pricking the system and developing a (philosophical) meta-theory which could reflect on the ontological, anthropological and epistemological bases of paradigms and also evaluate their characteristic features within the context of a specific period. It seems an important task indeed to find such a vantage point. In this connection I would like to offer the following proposal. If one is prepared (1) to take a "realistic" stance in the philosophy of science, (2) to develop a "meta-theoretical" roots-probing "arche-ological" method which transcends the limits and the scope of transcendental and phenomenological approaches, and is a method capable of analyzing presuppositions in science, I see no objection to finding (3) a criterion for comparing and criticizing theories, paradigms and beliefs. This criterion would at the same time present a platform to evaluate the justifications offered. It would also uncover the intimate inherent inter-relation between knowledge (science), commitment to ultimate beliefs, and the basic role of a world-and-life-view.

In retrospect I think it is clear that rationalism, with its concomittant foundationalism, is not a feasible option today. But it is equally obvious that a Christian scholar need not subscribe to nor fear irrationalism in order to account for the "subjective" element in science and its total context.[35]

The result obtained in the previous paragraph enables us to move on to the third phase of our exposition: the role of religious beliefs in science—and more profoundly still of Scripture's role.

VI. Rationality and Scripture

A. Scripture and Science

I take the term "Scripture" to signify the canonical books of the Old and New Testaments as the scriptural lingual testimony of God's good news for man and the proclamation of his kingdom. As such it presents to man God's revelation of his will and intention with creation. Holy Scripture also functions as a criterion of faith.[36] Scripture directs itself as a rule of faith to each individual in his historic situation. At the same time it broadcasts a universal message transcending the historic set-up of its original oral and literary context. The crux of the matter—discussed today primarily within the framework of biblical hermeneutics—is the point of intersection between *man's* understanding of God's Word and the "autonomy" of *Scripture* as a *divine communication*, which is not restricted to one specific historical era.[37] This is also the major reason why I have laid stress on the intrinsic role of revelation in a (Christian) theory of knowledge.

The crucial question which should now be considered is this: can science utilize Scripture? Is Scripture relevant to modern science? This is a wide ranging and difficult problem, and I do not intend to offer more than a few cursory comments.[38] My first statement is: Scripture does put many facts at the disposal of the *scholar*.[39] These facts are of various kinds: linguistic, sociological, medical, legal, historical, theological, etc. As a book of ultimate concern, Scripture is also essential for the philosopher. Apart from the broader issue of the basic ideas prevalent in various epochs and cultures and the logical procedures and thought patterns of Semitic peoples (see Boman, 1965), the Bible also offers exquisite material for a logic of "question" and "answer," obligations, commitments, etc. Compare, for example, the interesting logical pattern of Matthew 12:30 and Mark 9:39. But apart from "facts," the Bible is also relevant in a normative sense to logic and other disciples, i.e., the Bible provides a unique illumination of what straight and crooked thinking entails.

Here is my second thesis. Although I think the thesis of scholars like Ramm (1967, p. 86)—that the Bible anticipated science—is only in a limited sense true, I fully agree that the Bible provided essential directives for the development of a scientific mind as well as powerful stimuli for scientific research.[40] Scripture provides a perspective on many issues. This is especially important insofar as the Christian view of life and the world, for example, has a direct bearing on scientific beliefs and paradigms.[41]

My third thesis follows. In principle the Bible is utilized legitimately by orthodox Christians, but abused for ideological objectives by heretics and hyper-orthodox Christians alike. The former expect too little of the Bible (subversively exchanging the scope of Scripture for an immanentistic philosophical system of one or another kind); the latter expect too much (demanding that the Bible conform to "Farisaic" requirements or make assertions outside its central scope).[42] Steering a steady course entails, moreover, that the Christian scholar need not (should not!) quote a biblical passage just to prove or decorate every statement made, or to "score a point." Scripture should guide the scholar and not make him a fallible man, who sustains himself by usurping the Bible for subjective and selfish needs.[43] He should refer to Scripture where his Christian commitment is *crucial* to the beliefs that underpin his main ideas and theory. In other words the scholar should give some indication at the proper moment and in a correct fashion how Scripture guides his heart and mind as an intellectually trained academician. This is the more profound level of the influence of a world-and-life-view in the sphere of science.

Here is my fourth thesis. Scripture is rejected without sufficient scholarly attention by various scientisms on account of reductionistic methodologies or anti-religious ideological commitments.[44] The popularity of scientisms of various strains adds to the embarrassment of Christianity as well as to the crisis and the predicament of modern man. As far as the Christian is concerned it is obvious that the authority of Scripture should be acknowledged with sincerity. The core of the matter is the role accorded to the kingdom of God. In the Reformed tradition this implies that Scripture is relevant to all spheres of life, including intellectual endeavors. Scripture offers a unique perspective on many problems with which the scholar, as well as the philosopher, is engaged.

In my fifth thesis, I would suggest that typical of "the modern mind" is a religious commitment to science.[45] This commitment effectuates the loss of perspective and meaning so characteristic of modern times. An accompanying feature of "the modern mind" is materialism or, to quote Dijksterhuis, the "mechanization of the world picture." This attitude is disastrous, because the relevance of Scripture is neutralized artificially.

My sixth thesis relates to knowledge. The special and unique feature of Scripture is not limited merely to relevant facts and perspectives "supplied" to the Christian scholar. The special circumstance is that the Bible is the *Word* of *God*, thus furnishing as divine revelation a supra-human dimension to knowledge.[46] Christian scholars should come to grips with the Western tradition (especially the Platonic and solipsistic projection theories) and indicate the necessity and implications of acknowledging a divine dimension to human knowledge.[47]

As a seventh thesis, I would suggest that in the world of science, the following "voices" should resound.

(a) A proper Christian theological hermeneutics that can handle the basic philosophical assumptions involved. Such a hermeneutic theory should not only present indications (rules) to understand the message of the Bible, and to understand the text of Scripture; this theory should also indicate its relevance to modern life and to scholarly endeavors.[48]

(b) A Christian philosophy—loyal to the Bible—that can develop a theory of creation (nature), of man, society and history, and of human knowledge and the scientific enterprise.

(c) Christian special sciences that really come to grips with the basics of their disciplines and are able to counter anti-religious propaganda aired in the name of "science."

Beliefs, suggests my eighth thesis, have been viewed and treated for too long as a kind of faith chameleon. Christians active in the sphere of the philosophy of science should pay special attention to a penetrating analysis of a typology of beliefs—and thus indicate common and differentiating features. Typical of *scientific* beliefs are the following qualities: such beliefs are cognitive commitments; they do not operate simply on the level of propositional deductions; they *do* imply various kinds of reasoning which function in various modal spheres; they are motivated by basic assumptions; and they bring certainty in their trail.[49]

My ninth thesis offers an alternative. To counter a foundationalist attitude to beliefs, Christian scholars could consider giving priority to a logic of commitment. This would entail probing the characteristics of belief, the kind of commitment entailed by belief, the conceptual "containers" and symbolism of belief, operational interests inherent in beliefs, the integrity of belief and the challenge presented to skepticism. It is also important to bear in mind the link between the divine Holy Spirit and the heart and mind of man.

As a tenth and final thesis, I believe that Christian scholarship can advance the perennial issue of faith (or Scripture) and science by means of an integrated approach. Such scholarship can also indicate a criterion to pinpoint the role of beliefs in scientific thought.[50] It is obvious that a Christian philosophy of religion can also provide valuable perspectives in this context, especially regarding the nature and the scope of revelation in human life. This entails that beliefs, as indicators of ultimate concern, will manifest themselves in science to the extent that the scholar is part of the scientific method. (This circumstance has, in fact, been explained earlier in this essay.)

B. Rationality and Revelation

In conclusion I would like to present as a working hypothesis the following perspective on rationality and Scripture.

The debate on knowledge and belief is still going strong, although the discussions are not always directly related to the problematics of science. A Christian approach can stimulate insight in the area of epistemology with research on the nature of knowledge—outside the bounds of rationalism and irrationalism—and by pinpointing the role of beliefs in human cognitive processes. As well, this research can also show the interdependence of belief, certainty, and trust. This is of great importance to understanding the significance of commitment in theory and praxis, and the problem of "loyalty" to viewpoints and (radical or gradual) conceptual shifts.

Four basic requirements should be met in this context:

(a) An analysis must be made of the inner connection between beliefs, commitment and the "common sense" of a world-and-life-view.

(b) An inquiry must be undertaken into the nature of presuppositions as related to beliefs and cognitive commitments.

(c) Acknowledgment must be made of the crucial missing link in influential epistemologies: the function of revelation in human life.

(d) Understanding must be directed toward the peculiar nature of the logic of faith assertions. The logic of the Bible does not eliminate "ordinary elementary logic." But in utilizing everyday logic, the Bible nonetheless functions on the level of belief, with its own philosophical problematics, including the basic notions of mystery, wonder and divine reconstruction.

The significance of such an approach can be illustrated by an analysis, for example, of the biblical notion of proof.[51] Christian scholars with a knack for abstract thought and expertise in the area of faith-beliefs might find a full-fledged "logic of commitment" a worthwhile enterprise. I feel that such an approach can also contribute its share to an increasing recognition that "the Bible in the Age of Science" is not an outdated notion but the one indispensable key to "the growth of knowledge" as well as the liberation of mankind from cognitive error and misleading beliefs. The Christian faith is also a stimulus to the "production" of valuable theoretical and practical knowledge. Christians can be motivated by the insight that the fear of the Lord is the principle of knowledge, that knowledge and love are closely related, and that in the light of the Word of God man attains understanding, insight and wisdom. This requires the peace of mind that accomplishes all understanding. The rationality of knowledge has these very qualities; and if it does not, then beliefs are not reasonable, of no use and profit, and Christian scholarship is futile.

In conclusion, I will offer a kind of "synthesizing" summary by linking the subjects of rationality and revelation to those of human knowledge and method. I have already mentioned that human cognitive acts display many facets. Let us now have a closer look at a few important aspects of the structure of human knowledge. To know or "cognize" is an intellectual feat which presupposes the *biological* function of brain processes; these, in their turn, display *physical* forces of electric current detectable in brain waves. *Psychic* awareness ensures that we are emotionally prepared and linked by means of our senses with a cognitive object, as well as able to associate ideas. Conceptualizing moves us onto the universal plane, i.e., a concept like "book" has a general reference to any book anywhere, abstracting as it does from time and space attachments of sense perception.

Logical distinctions and identifications accordingly fit into a category of their own, transcending a loose and sometimes even random association of ideas. A concept can furthermore be used, even misused, as a means to an end. Such a *technical* use of a concept involves the concept being applied for a specific purpose and not merely in its referential function "representing" an object. On the basis of conceptualizing, judgment confronts us with the intricacies of predication. Two interesting facets of this aspect of knowledge are the significant constructive role of creative thought and the disclosive function of *lingual* signs and symbols, which enable the knowing person to reach out beyond the immediately given. Therefore signs and symbols naturally have a constitutive value for "the meaning of meaning." Analysis and reasoning as higher level species of logical judgment depend on language. In addition, analysis presupposes assumptions as well as givens, data or facts. The inner structure of reasoning also determines the limits of relevant cognitive communication in a *social* context.

For reasons of space I shall mention only briefly a few of the more complex components of the cognitive process: intellectual inquiry and theorizing; description; evaluation, systematizing and classification of knowledge on the basis of (economic) human interests and aspirations; cognitive strategy planning, ("political") policy and decision making, and comparison of basic convictions as well as intersubjective cooperation in the communal task of responding to the intellectual problems in the development of God's creation. Other features of the cognitive process include: criticism and justification of basic views held; attachment to or shifts and changes in basic attitudes and perspectives; the (ethical) responsibility as far as the integrity and veracity of cognitive acts are concerned; and the role of beliefs, commitment to ultimates and the surety of conviction or the uneasiness of skeptical doubt.

Method is intricately woven into all these dimensions of human cognizing. Or, stated differently, each dimension of human cognitive acts exerts a specific effect and influence on the use of method in various contexts. I shall limit myself to one illuminating example. Basic beliefs play a decisive role in all human cognitive acts—not as foundation, but as motivating perspective, steering the cognitive process in a specific direction. Here the role of a cognitive framework or paradigm becomes apparent. On the one hand it has ramifications in a human view of life; on the other in an intellectual and sometimes philosophically deepened basic perspective. We need and use the control mechanisms of our view of life and the world for all our beliefs as such, not only our religious beliefs and faith commitments. In this connection divine revelation is of prime importance in helping us to obtain clarity in the process of transforming sensual experience by means of conceptualizing acts.[52] Revelation can be characterized more or less as the integrative factor of a human basic perspective, precisely because it is no mere immanent component of human cognitive acts.

On the ultimate level, beliefs confront one with the problem of dogma, basic convictions *and* intellectual independence, mental "openness" and individual cognitive freedom. One of the interesting problems in this area is the question whether one can climb onto one's own back and peep into one's control beliefs. Personally I think this is one of the most challenging tasks of philosophy—probing the influential ideas of our times and ourselves. I think it can be shown that the Calvinian tradition has at least made a fair start in grinding special tools to accomplish this specific task of probing the origins and motives of the human mind. In this connection reference can be made to various applications of a transcendental critique. Perhaps one could also try one's hand at a reflective archeological method.[53] Helpful in any case, I think, is a further development of a logic of commitment which can spell out the details of what intellectual commitment actually entails. Here I am thinking of a supra-immanentistic and transcending element, as already indicated by Plato and interestingly corroborated by such thinkers as Augustine and Anselm. We see through a glass darkly. We should, moreover, leave the mystery of creation intact and not try to exalt ourselves to the position of an intellectual *deus ex machina*. But the most exhilirating thing is that the light of God's Word is sufficient to direct the human mind to fulfill its basic tasks.

This mandate does not imply that a *Christian* scholar possess a kind of esoteric method with entrenched privileges, nor maintain an ascetic retreat somewhere between heaven and earth. The Christian scholar, and the methods and techniques he utilizes, are part and parcel of scientific human endeavors and linked to the tradition of Western civilization. But each facet of the scientific method is molded by the unique contribution made by the cognitive acts of a scholar whose total intellectual approach is conditioned by his Christian beliefs, assumptions and presuppositions. Indeed this scholar is impregnated and integrated by the perspective of his faith in Scripture and by the revealing light of God's creative Word.

Thus the person engaged in intellectual inquiry, and the way in which the facts are approached and assessed, and even the tools developed for this purpose, are all intrinsically related to the rationality of Christian scholarship as an authentic human enterprise. Accordingly the integration of all separate aspects of method as discerned above will condition human thought on every level of cognitive awareness and in all its theoretical and practical applications. This is equally true of the multi-dimensional process of reasoning[54] and of the role that faith plays in such a concrete human cognitive act.

It is therefore rather senseless to search for and display isolated elements of prize Christian achievements. For Christian scholarship is a human enterprise which can to my mind only be assessed in its total setting and as a continually evolving research program. Thus Christian scholarship cannot be expected to produce different and unique results on every single occasion. But where the total combination of factors involved in methodical procedure does make a difference, it is crucial. Religious (control) beliefs do not manifest themselves merely externally on rare occasions of basic philosophical dispute over controversial problems of society. These beliefs are inherent in the rational procedures of the scientific enterprise itself.

Therefore solid scholarly work is, at the most incisive juncture, an intrinsic part of the relevant contemporary task of the Christian in the kingdom of God. Only Scripture, with its divine message of hope and ultimate trust, can supply this basic perspective. And only Scripture can link the rationality of Christian intellectual endeavors with revelation as a unique criterion of fallible, sometimes falsifiable, yet worthwhile and useful human knowledge.

Notes

Note: Complete references will be found in the bibliography, which follows the notes. Dates in parenthesis indicate an author's particular text, where more than one is listed in the bibliography.

1. The context of Bennett's essay is predominantly that of comparative psychology. See also the criticism of Bennett's main thesis by R. Kirk (1967), "Rationality without Language." An excellent introduction to the general problematics of rationality—and more thorough in dealing with various relevant facets of rationality than Bennett's essay—is Kekes (1976).
2. One of the few exceptions is A.A. Derksen's (1980/81) discussion of problems and relevant literature within the context of the philosophy of science. Stimulating studies on a larger scale and within quite different contexts include Kekes (1976), Wilson (1970), Geraets (1979) and Derksen (1980).
3. Particularly important in this respect is the 20th-century contribution of scholars associated with "Critical Rationalism" such as K.R. Popper, H. Albert and others. Popper's variety of rationalism is characterized by the crucial role accorded to criticism, which he finds lacking in irrationalistic tendencies like historicism. See, for example, Popper 1966 (1945), 1966 (1957) and 1979, p. 82: ". . . the testing of scientific theories is part of their critical discussion; or, as we may say, it is part of their rational discussion, for in this context I know no better synonym for 'rational' than 'critical.' " It is interesting to note that the new brand of rationalism advocated by these writers, although critical of many facets of "Early Modern Rationalism," nonetheless exhibits a special sympathy toward the "positive aspects of the Enlightenment (see Albert 1976, pp. 38ff.). Harnessing the

Enlightenment to 20th-century interests is, of course, not typical of "Critical Rationalists" exclusively. Well known and important is the interpretation of J. Habermas and other contemporary writers.

4. Cf. the expositions of Hamlyn (1977, pp. 10ff.), Nielsen (1973) and Popkin (1967, pp. 449-461) in general and Agassi & Jarvie (1979), Kekes (1976, especially the conclusion, pp. 254ff. and 1971) as well as Agassi (1974) and Nielsen (1979) in particular on the former, and Bartley (1962), Trigg (1977) and Polanyi (1952) on the latter subject. The use of the terms rational(ism) and irrational(ism) as well as the contexts considered appropriate for applying these terms are unfortunately by no means clear and distinct; cf. the general introductions of Williams (1967, 7: pp. 69-75) and Gardiner (1967, 4: pp. 213-219), as well as Kekes (1972 & 1976), Eisler (1927, I. Bd., "Irrational": pp. 780-783; 1929, II. Bd., "Rationalismus": pp. 579-584, & "Rationalität": p. 584; 1930, III. Bd., "Vernunft": pp. 395-406), Rücker (1976, pp. 583-588), Gadamer (1979), Fethe (1972), Fohr (1972) and Hollis (1970).
5. Rationality was taken for granted by and large, and the "counterfactuals" were considered as exceptions to the rule; cf. the interesting findings of Van den Berg (n.d.) and Foucault (1967).
6. An accompanying feature of the reaction to rational*ism* is a marked new interest in and approach to rational*ity*. Important contemporary views on reason and the function of reason within the context of rationality are Apel (1979), Dufrenne (1979), Gadamer (1979), Habermas (1979), Nielsen (1979), Ricoeur (1979) and Vuillemin (1979). As far as Christian philosophy is concerned, the interest shown in rationality by scholars at Calvin College (Calvin Center for Christian Scholarship), the Free University of Amsterdam (Klapwijk, 1976) and the Institute for Christian Studies (Hart, 1980) has highlighted the need for Christian academics to engage in the contemporary debate.
7. Further differentiations in connotation can be checked in Liddell & Scott (1843).
8. Cf. Delaney (1979), Frankel (1968), Habermas (1979), Hempel (1979), Kekes (1972 & 1979), Kisiel (1979), Kockelmans (1979), Lukes (1970), McMullen (1974b), Perelman (1979), Popper (1972 & 1979) and Winch (1976).
9. Cf. Szabados (1979) and the literature on the terms "rational" and "irrational" mentioned in note 4 above.
10. Cf. also especially Derksen (1980) and Geraets (1979).
11. A detailed analysis of Plato, Aristotle, Augustine, Boethius, Anselm, Aquinas, Descartes, Leibniz, Hume, Kant and especially the positivistic movement would be worthwhile.
12. Part of this problem (and the "justification tradition") has been competently analyzed by Radnitzky (1979).
13. A few of the important issues discussed at the Toronto Conference on Ra-

tionality which have a special bearing on the topic treated in this essay are (1) the nature and limits of rationality, (2) common sense and rationality, (3) reason and religious beliefs, (4) the significance of knowledge of God as well as a biblical notion of creation, revelation and Scripture for scholarly studies, and (5) the authority of the Bible and the nature of legitimate appeal to Scripture.

14. Treatment of these four topics dovetails with the three phases of my approach mentioned in paragraph one of my Introduction.
15. Cf. Vrielink (1956), Brümmer (1975 & 1978/79) and Popper (1972 & 1979). An important facet is the issue of constructive communication between philosophical schools of diverse background.
16. Well known in larger circles through the translation of H. Dooyeweerd's *De Wijsbegeerte der Wetsidee* (1935) as *A New Critique of Theoretical Thought* (1953). I have made an application of the theory of modal functions in "Aspekte van 'n funksionele beskouing van verbeelding en 'n tipologie van teorieë oor die verbeelding," *Philosophia Reformata*, 34, 1969, pp. 147-178.
17. Some aspects of this problem are treated with insight in Radnitzky (1973); cf. also Ackermann (1972, esp. chap. 3), Quine & Ullian (1970) and Wolterstorff (1976). My remarks, of course, also hold for religious belief; cf. Delaney (1979), Mavrodes (1970) and McDougall (1972).
18. For contemporary discussions of the topic, see Brown (1977, especially pp. 145 ff.), Griffiths (1967), Kassmann (1973), Pailthorp (1969).
19. I have touched on a few facets of this subject in a paper read at the first South African Calvin Congress at the University of Pretoria, August 1980: "Augustinus totus noster" (Calvyn) en "Nulli nobis quam isti (= Platonici) propius (Augustinus)—enkele gedagtes oor Augustinus en Calvyn." My epistemological acknowledgment of a "supra-human" element is, of course, on quite another track than the problematics which Krzesinsky (1953) mentions.
20. See also Lehrer (1970), Blanshard (1964, pp. 189ff., although his assessment of Peirce does not seem to be incisive and adequate), and Gipper (1971, pp. 757-759 s.v. "Bedeutung," and pp. 760-761 s.v. "Bedeutungslehre").
21. Recognized as philosophically important by Christian scholars like J.P.A. Mekkes, H. Hart and H.W. Rossouw. Cf. also the humanistic criticism of Schut (1962, pp. 151ff.).
22. Cf. Stoker (1944-45), Vrielink (1956), in a general sense the classics Russell and Gadamer (1965) and in the context of rationality Albert (1978). Reddiford (1975) has a few interesting remarks on the relation between rationality, understanding, beliefs and truth.
23. Instructive studies on various facets of method include Adorno (1975), Black (1952), Blake (1968), Bocheński (1954), Caws (1965 & 1967), Cohen & Nagel (1934), De Bruyne (1959), Dewey (1967), Feigl (1949), Feyera-

bend (1976 & 1978), Hart (1968), Hook (1967), Kern (1975), Lakatos (1970), McKeon (1966), Menne (1980), Nagel (1974), Nielsen (1967), Poincaré (1946), Popper (1972a), Quine (1974), Russell (1950), Sachsse (1974), Stoker (1961 & 1970), Weisheipl (1967). My own views on method have been developed in close association with my colleague and friend H.G. Stoker's (1961) and later (1965, republished 1970) studies. I could also take advantage of criticisms of my B.Phil. students of the past decade.

24. Well described in Kemeny (1959), pp. 85ff.

25. Important issues are discussed in Lakatos & Musgrave (1970).

26. During the discussion of my paper at the Toronto Conference on Rationality in August, 1981, the important question was raised whether several of the following points (e.g., 1, 4, 5) do not entail a circularity in definition. I still do not think the differentiation between scientific knowledge and non-scientific knowledge of everyday life is basically circular—provided the seven factors mentioned are not taken separately in isolation. The real problem seems to be that of describing adequately the distinguishing features without jeopardizing the relative similarity; a complicating factor is the fact that scientific procedures, views and jargon have already infiltrated most spheres of daily life.

27. Cf. Radnitzky & Andersson (1978) and Lakatos & Musgrave (1970).

28. Even empiricism, which generally considers itself "down to earth," "objective" and "broad-minded," often utilizes a reductionistic concept of experience.

29. The basic premise substantiating this statement is that there is more to Christian scholarship than Christian theology (even though the importance and relevance of theology for scholarship should be acknowledged without bias). Many writers do not know or do not see the importance of this distinction which is so crucial to Christian scholarship in the Reformed tradition. H. Albert, for example, identifies acknowledgment of revelation with dogmatism, the stifling of a critical scientific mind and a halt to scientific progress. True, too much faith in a specific branch of science ("regina scientiarum") certainly is risky and an all too human error. But one can hardly miss the positivistic roots of Albert's generalization and his pet philosophical notion of the history of science in his easy identification of scholarly work by Christians with theology.

30. See especially Gardiner (1967, 4: pp. 213-219) and other studies mentioned in note no. 4 above.

31. See in particular Kuhn (1970), pp. 1-23, 231-378. Although I admit that Kuhn's philosophy is part of 20th-century irrationalistic thought, I have queried the label "irrational" attached to him in my essay "Paradigm, Science and Society" (1975, pp. 328-358). I think the concomitant association with relativism is not as simple as that in his writings. See also Spiegel-Rösing (1973), pp. 69ff.

32. It should be evident from my exposition that although I do not agree with Feyerabend, I do take his opinions seriously—exactly because even his humorous "Dialogue on Method" (1979) attempts to test the limits of rationality in a rational way.
33. It is interesting to note that Feyerabend himself (re)phrases his basic contention somewhat more carefully in an earlier work (1978), pp. 39ff.
34. A most dramatic exposition is found in Feyerabend (1976); see also his subsequent text (1978).
35. I believe that a "theory-laden approach" involving the total human person (conscious of his ultimate beliefs) can preclude utilizing an absolutized reason as a "deus ex machina." (Here I am thinking of an intrinsic source of illumination, i.e., of "natural" revelation, as well as a catalyst for the universal process of pedagogic enlightenment and emancipation.) This approach can *also* move well beyond irrationalistic limits.
36. Cf. Du Toit (1941), Olthuis (1976) and Zylstra (1972).
37. Cf. J.C. Coetzee, B.J. de Klerk & L. Floor (1980), Rossouw (1979 & 1980), Seebasz (1974, pp. 124ff.), Vorster (1979) and Olthuis (1979).
38. Cf. Ramm (1967), Richardson (1968), various articles in *Koers* (1979, 44, no. 1) and Dippel & De Jong (1966 & 1967).
39. I stress this point as I believe that Scripture is of prime importance to the theologian but not exclusively to the theologian; it is relevant also for scholars in other areas of science. Scripture is also basic and relevant to all those people in daily practical life who trust God on account of his revelation in Scripture and believe in him. One approach in the Calvinian tradition acknowledges that the Bible contains essential facts for various scientific disciplines, although that is not the basic intention and thrust of Holy Scripture. Another approach denies the appropriateness of "facts" for the modern scholar and stresses normative directives. I think that both possess a kernel of truth. Another instructive approach is the impact which the 16th-century Reformation had on academic life on account of the relevance of the Bible for the totality of human life and society (see Hooykaas, 1972).
40. The implications for various scientific disciplines are explored in Dippel & De Jong (1966 & 1967).
41. See Hart (1969). Interesting comments are offered in quite another context in Hooykaas (1972), Gilson (1940) and Sertillanges (1941).
42. Cf. the elucidating remarks of Klapwijk (1975, p. 2) and Ramm (1967, pp. 23ff.).
43. This idea presupposes a quite outdated "justification theory" of proof and a rationalistic epistemology.
44. Notoriously reductionistic are various strains of logical positivism. But it is also interesting to note how several outstanding scholars of our time have been waging endless polemics against Christianity without arriving

at a final assessment; Russell is one of the classic examples, Sartre another.

45. A very lucid account is found in Horrobin (1969); see also Alexander 1972, pp. 185ff.) as well as the contributions of Cronjé (pp. 1ff.), Rossouw (pp. 17ff.) and Murray Janson (pp. 55ff.) in Cronjé (1972), and Dippel & De Jong (1966, pp. 121ff.).
46. Cf. Baillie (1965) and Du Toit (1941). Baillie's study is particularly instructive on various attitudes to revelation.
47. I have treated a few aspects of the relevance of a divine dimension to human knowledge in a paper on "Augustine, Calvin and Platonism" at the South African Calvin Congress, August 1980, and would especially like to draw attention to important contributions in this regard of scholars such as Bavinck (1908), Stoker (1965 & 1970), Van Til (1969) and Vollenhoven (1967). I consider this facet important in countering not merely solipsistic but especially immanentistic philosophies and epistemologies of various strains.
48. Rossouw (1963), (1979) and (1980) present an exceptionally clear picture of the basic problems involved in this area; see also Coetzee, De Klerk & Floor (1980).
49. The discussions at the Toronto Conference on Rationality (August, 1981) pinpointed various interesting facets of the rationality of belief; see the conference papers as well as Wolterstorff (1976), Plantinga (1979), Mavrodes (1970) and Suppes (1969, pp. 407ff.) to mention just a few elucidating treatments of the topic.
50. Several aspects are well discussed in Klapwijk (1978); see also Van Riessen (1960), Runner (1960) and Mekkes (1961).
51. The way in which the apostle Paul proves "from the Scriptures" is unique and much more complex than ordinary logical proof, although not incompatible with basic logic. Interesting remarks can be found in Berkouwer (1959); see also Van der Merwe, D.C.S. (n.d.).
52. The influence of Scripture on rationality should, of course, be distinguished from the problem of the rationality of Scripture and the reading of Scripture as a rational process. Here we should also distinguish the hermeneutical problem of interpreting and understanding Scripture as divine revelation.
53. Interesting analyses which can serve as pointers are found in Dooyeweerd (1953) and Foucault (1977).
54. Different types of reasoning include logical reasoning, handling of information, "sales talk," rhetorical reasoning, ethical reasoning, etc. In each instance the whole human person is involved.

Bibliography

Ackermann, R.J. *Belief and Knowledge*. New York: MacMillan, 1972.

Adorno, T.W., et al. *Der Positivismusstreit in der deutschen Soziologie.* Darmstadt & Neuwied: Luchterhand, 1975 (1969).

Agassi, J. "Criteria for Plausible Arguments." *Mind*, 83:406-416, 1974.

Agassi, J. & Jarvie, I.C. "The Rationality of Dogmatism." Geraets, T.F., ed. *Rationality To-day.* Ottawa: Univ. of Ottawa Press, 1979.

Albert, H. *Rationaliteit in wetenschap en samenleving: opstellen over wetenschap, ideologie en politiek, geredigeerd en ingeleid door F.D. Heyt.* Alphen aan den Rijn: Samsom, 1976.

———. "Science and the Search for Truth." Radnitzky, G. & Andersson, G., eds. *Progress and Rationality in Science.* Dordrecht: Reidel, 1978.

Alexander, D. *Beyond Science.* Berkhamsted: Lion, 1972.

Anderson, R.S. "Theology as Rationality." *Christian Scholar's Review*, 4(2): 120-133, 1974.

Apel, K.O. "Types of Rationality Today: The Continuum of Reason between Science and Ethics." Geraets, T.F., ed. *Rationality To-day.* Ottawa: Univ. of Ottawa Press, 1979.

Baillie, J. *The Idea of Revelation in Recent Thought.* New York: Columbia University Press, 1965 (1956).

Bartley, W.W. *The Retreat to Commitment.* New York: Knopf, 1962.

Bavinck, H. *Wijsbegeerte der Openbaring: Stone-lezingen voor het jaar 1908, gehouden te Princeton, N.J.* Kampen: Kok, 1908.

Bennett, J. *Rationality: An Essay towards an Analysis.* London & New York: Routledge & Kegan Paul and Humanities Press, 1964.

Berkouwer, G.C. "Het bewijs in de theologie." *Het bewijs in de wetenschap: Interfacultaire voordrachten.* Kampen: Kok, 1959(?).

Black, M. *Critical Thinking.* Englewood Cliffs, N.J.: Prentice-Hall, 1952 (1946).

Blake, R.M., Ducasse, C.J. & Madden, E.H., eds. *Theories of Scientific Method: The Renaissance through the Nineteenth Century.* Seattle: Univ. of Washington Press, 1968 (1960).

Blanshard, B. *Reason and Analysis.* La Salle, Ill.: Open Court, 1964 (1962).

Bochenski, I.M.J. *Die zeitgenössischen Denkmethoden.* Bern: Francke, 1954.

Boman, T. *Das hebräische Denken im Vergleich mit dem griechischen.* Göttingen: Vandenhoeck & Ruprecht, 1965.

Bronowski, J. *The Common Sense of Science.* London: Heinemann, 1978 (1951).

Brown, H.I. *Perception, Theory and Commitment: The New Philosophy of Science.* Chicago: Precedent, 1977.

Brümmer, V. *Wijsgerige begripsanalyse.* Kampen: Kok, 1975.

———. "Verificatie en feitelijkheid." *Wijsgerig perspectief op maatschappij en wetenschap*, 19(4):91-95, 1978/79.

Caws, P. *The Philosophy of Science: A Systematic Account*. Princeton, N.J.: Van Nostrand, 1965.

———. "Scientific Method." *The Encyclopaedia of Philosophy*, 7:339-343. New York: MacMillan & Free Press, and London: Collier-MacMillan, 1967.

Coetzee, J.C., De Klerk, B.J. & Floor, L. "Die hermeneuse van die Skrif." *Koers*, 45(1):18-36, 1980.

Cohen, M.R. & Nagel, E. *An Introduction to Logic and Scientific Method*. London: Routledge, 1934.

De Bruyne, E. *Grondproblemen van de wijsgerige logica*, 2 vols. Brussel: Paleis der Academiën, 1959.

Delaney, C.F., ed. *Rationality and Religious Belief*. Notre Dame & London: Univ. of Notre Dame Press, 1979.

Derksen, A.A. *Rationaliteit en wetenschap*. Assen: Van Gorcum, 1980.

———. "Angelsaksische Wetenschapsleer in de zeventigerjaren: rationaliteit, realisme en wetenschapsgeschiedenis." *Wijsgerig perspectief op maatschappij en wetenschap*, 21(4):114-119, 1980/81.

Dewey, J. "The Supremacy of Method." Konvitz, M.R. & Kennedy, G. *The American Pragmatists*. Cleveland & New York: Meridian Books, 1967.

Dippel, C.J. & De Jong, J.M., eds. *Geloof en natuur wetenschap*, 2 vols. The Hague: Boekencentrum, 1966 (1965 & 1967).

Dooyeweerd, H. *A New Critique of Theoretical Thought*, trans. by D.H. Freeman & W.S. Young, vol. I. *The Necessary Presuppositions of Philosophy*. Amsterdam, Paris & Philadelphia: Presbyterian and Reformed Publ. Co., 1953.

Dufrenne, M. "La raison aujourd'hui." Geraets, T.F., ed. *Rationality To-day*. Ottawa: Univ. of Ottawa Press, 1979.

Du Toit, J.D. *Die Bybel is die Woord van God*. Stellenbosch: Pro-Ecclesia-Drukkery, 1941.

Eisler, R. *Wörterbuch der philosophischen Begriffe*. Berlin: Mittler. 1:780-783, s.v. Irrational, Irrationalismus, 1927.

______. Ibid. 2:579-584, s.v. Rationalismus, Rationalität, 1929.

______. Ibid. 3:395-406, s.v. Vernunft (Ratio), 1930.

Feigl, H. "Operationism and Scientific Method." Feigl, H. & Sellars, W., eds. *Readings in Philosophical Analysis*. New York: Appleton-Century-Crofts, 1949.

Fethe, C.D. "Rationality and Responsibility." *The Personalist*, 53(1):193-198, Winter, 1972.

Feyerabend, P. *Against Method: Outline of an Anarchistic Theory of Knowledge*. London: NLB, 1976 (1975).

———. *Science in a Free Society*. London: NLB, 1978.

———. "Dialogue on Method." Radnitzky, G. & Andersson, G., eds. *The*

Structure and Development of Science. Dordrecht: Reidel, 1979.

Fohr, S.D. "The Non-Rationality of Beliefs and Attitudes." *The Personalist*, 53(1):63-70, Winter, 1972.

Foucault, M. *Madness and Civilization*. London: Tavistock, 1967.

———. *The Archaeology of Knowledge*, trans. from the French by A.J. Sheridan Smith. London: Tavistock, 1977 (1972).

Gadamer, H.G. *Wahrheit und Methode*. Tübingen: Mohr (Siebeck), 1965 (1960).

———. "Historical Transformations of Reason." Geraets, T.F., ed. *Rationality To-day*. Ottawa: Univ. of Ottawa Press, 1979.

Gardiner, P. "Irrationalism." *The Encyclopaedia of Philosophy*, 4:213-219. New York: MacMillan & Free Press, and London: Collier-MacMillan, 1967.

Geraets, T.F., ed. *Rationality To-day*. Ottawa: Univ. of Ottawa Press, 1979.

Gilson, E. *Christianisme et philosophie*. Paris: Vrin, 1949.

Gipper, H. "Bedeutung & Bedeutungslehre." Ritter, G., ed. *Historisches Wörterbuch der Philosophie*. Band 1:757-759 & 760-761. Darmstadt: Wissenschaftliche Buchgesellschaft, 1971.

Griffiths, A.P., ed. *Knowledge and Belief*. Oxford: University Press, 1967.

Haberman, J. "Aspects of the Rationality of Action." Geraets, T.F., ed. *Rationality To-day*. Ottawa: Univ. of Ottawa Press, 1979.

Hamlyn, D.W. *The Theory of Knowledge*. London: MacMillan, 1971 (1970).

Hart, H. *The Challenge of Our Age*. Toronto: Guardian, 1968.

———. "The Impasse of Rationality Today," revised ed. Toronto: Institute for Christian Studies, 1980.

———. "The Impasse of Rationality Today," Blokhuis, P., et al, eds. *Wetenschap, wijsheid, filosoferen*. Assen: Van Gorcum, 1981.

———. "The Re-cognition of Science as Knowledge: An Attempt to Contribute to the Recovery of Rationality from Its Present Crisis." Toronto: Institute for Christian Studies, 1980.

Hempel, C.G. "Scientific Rationality: Analytic vs. Pragmatic Perspectives." Geraets, T.F., ed. *Rationality To-day*. Ottawa: Univ. of Ottawa Press, 1979.

Hollis, M. "The Limits of Irrationality." Wilson, B.R., ed. *Rationality*. Oxford: Blackwell, 1970.

Hook, S. "The Centrality of Method." Konvitz, M.R. & Kennedy, G., *The American Pragmatists*. Cleveland & New York: Meridian Books, 1967.

Hooykaas, R. *Religion and the Rise of Modern Science*. Edinburgh: Scottish Academic Press, 1972.

Horrobin, D.F. *Science Is God*. Aylesbury, Bucks: Medical and Technical Publishing, 1969.

Janson, M. "Religie in die moderne wereld." Cronjé, G., et al. *Die mens en die moderne wereld*. Johannesburg & Kaapstad: Tafelberg, 1972.

Kassmann, A. *Knowledge and Belief*. Bletchley, Bucks: Open University Press (Problems of Philosophy, units 19-20), 1973.

Kekes, J. "Fallibilism and Rationality." *American Philosophical Quarterly*, 9 (4):301-309, October, 1972.

Kekes, J. *A Justification of Rationality*. Albany: State Univ. of Albany Press, 1976.

Keller, W. *Und die Bibel hat doch recht: Forscher beweisen die historische Wahrheit*. Düsseldorf: Econ, 1957 (1955).

Kern, I. *Idee und Methode der Philosophie: Leitgedanken für eine Theorie der Vernunft*. Berlin & New York: De Gruyter, 1975.

Kemeny, J.G. *A Philosopher Looks at Science*. Princeton: Van Nostrand, 1959.

Kirk, R. "Rationality without Language." *Mind*, 76, 369-386, 1967.

Kisiel, T. "The Rationality of Scientific Discovery." Geraets, T.F., ed. *Rationality To-day*. Ottawa: Univ. of Ottawa Press, 1979.

Klapwijk, A. "Het mensbeeld in de Angel-Saksische wijsbegeerte." *Radix*, 1(1):25-36, January, 1975.

Klapwijk, J., Griffioen, S. & Groenewoud, G., eds. *Vrede met de rede? Over het vraagstuk van rede en religie, van autonomie en heil*. Assen & Amsterdam: Van Gorcum, 1976.

Kockelmans, J.J. "Reflections on Lakatos' Methodology of Scientific Research Programs." Radnitzky, G., & Andersson, G., eds. *The Structure and Development of Science*. Dordrecht: Reidel, 1979.

Krzesinski, A.J. "The Immanency and Transcendency of Our Knowledge." Proceedings of the XIth International Congress of Philosophy, vol. II, Epistemology. Amsterdam: North-Holland Publ. Co., and Louvain: Nauwelaerts, 1953.

Kuhn, T.S. "Logic of Discovery or Psychology of Research?" and "Reflections on My Critics." Lakatos, I. & Musgrave, A., eds. *Criticism and the Growth of Knowledge*. Cambridge: University Press, 1970.

Lakatos, I. "Falsification and the Methodology of Scientific Research Programmes." Lakatos, I., & Musgrave, A., eds. *Criticism and the Growth of Knowledge*. Cambridge: University Press, 1970.

Lakatos, I. & Musgrave, A., eds. *Criticism and the Growth of Knowledge*. Cambridge: University Press, 1970.

Lehrer, A. & Lehrer, K., eds. *Theory of Meaning*. Englewood Cliffs: Prentice-Hall, 1970.

Liddell, H.G. & Scott, R. *A Greek-English Lexicon*. Oxford: Clarendon Press, 1951 (1943).

Lukes, S. "Some Problems about Rationality." Wilson, B.R., ed. *Rationality*. Oxford: Blackwell, 1970.

McDougall, D.A. "Religious Belief and Philosophical Analysis." *Mind*, 81:519-532, 1972.

McKeon, R. "Philosophy and the Development of Scientific Methods." *Journal of the History of Ideas*, 27(1):3-22, January-March, 1966.

McMullin, E. "Logicality and Rationality: A Comment on Toulmin's Theory of Science." Cohen, R. & Wartofsky, M., eds. *Boston Studies in the Philosophy of Science*, vol. 11, 1974.

Mavrodes, G.I. *Belief in God: A Study in the Epistemology of Religion*. New York: Random House, 1970.

Mekkes, J.P.A. *Scheppingsopenbaring en wijsbegeerte*. Kampen: Kok, 1961.

Menne, A. *Einführung in die Methodologie: Elementare allgemeine wissenschaftliche Denkmethoden im Überblick*. Darmstadt: Wissenschaftliche Buchgesellschaft, 1980.

Nagel, E. *The Structure of Science: Problems in the Logic of Scientific Explanation*. London: Routledge & Kegan Paul, 1974 (1961).

Nielsen, H.A. *Methods of Natural Science: An Introduction*. Englewood Cliffs: Prentice-Hall, 1967.

Nielsen, K. *Scepticism*. London: MacMillan, 1973.

———. "Reason and Sentiment: Sceptical Remarks about Reason and the 'Foundations of Morality.' " Geraets, T.F., ed. *Rationality To-day*. Ottawa: Univ. of Ottawa Press, 1979.

Olthuis, J.H. *The Word of God and Biblical Authority*. Potchesftroom: Instituut vir die bevordering van Calvinisme (Reeks Fl: Studiestuk no. 101), 1976.

———. *Towards a Certitudinal Hermeneutic*. Kraay, J. & Tol, A., eds. *Hearing and Doing: Philosophical Essays Dedicated to H. Evan Runner*. Toronto: Wedge, 1979.

Pailthorp, C. "Knowledge as Justified, True Belief." *The Review of Metaphysics*, 23(1, issue 89):25-47, September, 1969.

Perelman, C. "The Rational and the Reasonable." Geraets, T.F., ed. *Rationality To-day*. Ottawa: Univ. of Ottawa Press, 1979.

Plantinga, A. "Is Belief in God Rational?" Delaney, C.F., ed. *Rationality and Religious Belief*. Notre Dame & London: Univ. of Notre Dame Press, 1979.

Poincaré, H. *The Foundations of Science: Science and Hypothesis, the Value of Science, Science and Method*. Authorized trans. by G.B. Halsted with a special preface by Poincaré and an introduction by J. Royce. Lancaster: Science Press, 1946.

Polanyi, M. "The Stability of Beliefs." *The British Journal for the Philosophy of Science*, 3(11):217-232, 1952.

Popkin, R.H. "Skepticism." *The Encyclopaedia of Philosophy*, 7:449-461.

New York: MacMillan & Free Press, and London: Collier-MacMillan, 1967.

Popper, K.R. *The Logic of Scientific Discovery*, sixth impression revised. London: Hutchinson, 1972 (1959).

———. *Objective Knowledge: An Evolutionary Approach*, revised ed. Oxford: Clarendon Press, 1979 (1972).

Quine, W.V. "On Popper's Negative Methodology." Schilpp, P.A., ed. *The Philosophy of Karl Popper*, vol. I:218-220. La Salle, Ill.: Open Court, 1974.

Quine, W.V. & Ullian, J.S. *The Web of Belief*. New York: Random House, 1970.

Radnitzky, G. *Contemporary Schools of Metascience*. Chicago: Regnery, 1973 (1968).

Radnitzky, G. & Andersson, G., eds. *Progress and Rationality in Science*. Dordrecht: Reidel (Boston Studies in the Philosophy of Science, vol. 58), 1978.

———. *The Structure and Development of Science*. Dordrecht: Reidel (Boston Studies in the Philosophy of Science, vol. 59), 1979.

Ramm, B. *The Christian View of Science and Scripture*. Exeter: Paternoster, 1967 (1955).

Reddiford, G. "Rationality and Understanding." *Philosophy* (The Journal of the Royal Institute of Philosophy), 50:19-35, 1975.

Richardson, A. *The Bible in the Age of Science: The Cadbury Lectures in the University of Birmingham, 1961*. London: SCM Press, 1968 (1961).

Ricoeur, P. "La raison pratique." Geraets, T.F., ed. *Rationality To-day*. Ottawa: Univ. of Ottawa Press, 1979.

Rossouw, H.W. *Klaarheid en interpretasie: Enkele probleemhistoriese gesigspunte in verband met die leer van die duidelikheid van die Heilige Skrif*. Amsterdam: Jacob van Campen, 1963.

———. "Hoe moet 'n mens die Bybel lees?" *Koers*, 44(1):18-37, 1979.

———. *Wetenskap, interpretasie, wysheid*. Port Elizabeth: Univ. of Port Elizabeth (Seminare, Simposia en lesings B 7), 1980.

Rücker, S. "Irrational, das Irrationale, Irrationalismus." Ritter, G. & Gründer, K., eds. *Historisches Wörterbuch der Philosophie*, 4:583-588. Darmstadt: Wissenschaftliche Buchgesellschaft, 1976.

Runner, H.E. *The Relation of the Bible to Learning*. Pella: Pella Publ. Co. (Christian Perspective, 1960), 1960.

Russell, B.A.W. "On Scientific Method in Philosophy." Russell. *Mysticism and Logic, and Other Essays*. London: Allen & Unwin, 1950.

Sachsse, H. "Methode, Verfahren, Zugangsweisen." Rombach, H., ed. *Wissenschaftstheorie, 2: Struktur und Methode der Wissenschaften*. Freiburg: Herder, 1974.

Schut, P. "Rede en Religie." Van Praag, J.P. et al. *Rede en religie in het humanisme*. Amsterdam: De Bussy, 1962.

Seebasz, H. *Biblische Hermeneutik*. Stuttgart: Kohlhammer, 1974.

Sertillanges, R.P. *Le Christianisme et les philosophies*. Paris: Aubier, 1941.

Spiegel-Rösing, I. *Wissenschaftsentwicklung und Wissenschaftssteuerung. Einführung und Material zur Wissenschaftsforschung*. Frankfurt am Main: Athenäum, 1973.

Stoker, H.G. "Die waarheid maak vry." *Die Kerkblad*, 22-9-1944; 6-10-1944; 3-11-1944; 17-1-1945; 6-4-1945; 18-5-1945; 20-7-1945; 3-8-1945; 7-9-1945.

———. *Beginsels em metodes in die wetenskap*. Potchefstroom: Pro Rege (2d ed., 1969; Johannesburg: De Jong, 1961).

———. "Outlines of a Deontology of Scientific Method." *Philosophy and Christianity: Philosophical Essays Dedicated to Prof. Dr. H. Dooyeweerd*. Kampen: Kok, and Amsterdam: North-Holland Publ. Co., 1965.

———. "Een en ander oor metode." *Bulletin van die Suid-Afrikaanse Vereniging vir die bevordering van Christelike wetenskap*, no. 23 & 24, 1970.

Suppes, P. *Studies in the Methodology and Foundations of Science: Selected Papers from 1951 to 1969*. Dordrecht: Reidel, 1969.

Szabados, B. "A Note on Irrationality." Geraets, T.F., ed. *Rationality To-day*. Ottawa: Univ. of Ottawa Press, 1979.

Trigg, R. *Reason and Commitment*. Cambridge: Cambridge University Press, 1979 (1973).

Van den Berg, J.H.G. *De dingen en hun wetenschap: Een metabletisch onderzoek van het vervreemdingsproces tussen natuur en wetenschap*. Nijkerk: Callenbach.

Van der Merwe, D.C.S. "Moderne sending en antieke denkwette." Floor, L., ed. *Die saailand is die wereld*. Hammanskraal: Die Hammanskraalse Teologiese Skool, 1973(?).

Van Riessen, H. *The Relation of the Bible to Science*. Pella: Pella Publ. Co. (Christian Perspectives, 1960), 1960.

Van Til, C. *A Christian Theory of Knowledge*. Philadelphia: Presbyterian & Reformed Publ. Co., 1969.

Vorster, W.S., ed. *Scripture and the Use of Scripture*. Pretoria: Univ. of South Africa, 1979.

Vrielink, J.H. *Het waarheidsbegrip*. Nijkerk: Callenbach, 1956.

Vuillemin, J. "La raison au regard de l'instauration et du développement scientifique." Geraets, T.F., ed. *Rationality To-day*. Ottawa: Univ. of Ottawa Press, 1979.

Weisheipl, J.A. "Scholastic Method." *New Catholic Encyclopaedia*, 12:1145-1146, 1967.

Williams, B. "Rationalism." *The Encyclopaedia of Philosophy*, 7:69-75. New York: MacMillan & Free Press, and London: Collier-MacMillan, 1967. 1967.

Wilson, B.R., ed. *Rationality*. Oxford: Blackwell, 1970.

Winch, P. *The Idea of a Social Science and Its Relation to Philosophy*. London: Routledge & Kegan Paul, and New York: Humanities Press, 1976 (1958).

Wolterstorff, N. *Reason Within the Bounds of Religion*. Grand Rapids: Eerdmans Publ. Co., 1976.

Zylstra, B. "Thy Word Our Life." *Will All the King's Men . . . .* Toronto: Wedge Publ. Foundation, 1972.

Present Positions on Key Problems

Part Five:

Thinking About God

The Reformed Objection to Natural Theology

Alvin Plantinga

SUPPOSE WE THINK OF NATURAL THEOLOGY as the attempt to prove or demonstrate the existence of God. This enterprise has a long and impressive history—a history stretching back to the dawn of Christendom and boasting among its adherents many of the truly great thinkers of the Western world. One thinks, for example, of Anselm, Aquinas, Scotus and Ockham, of Descartes, Spinoza and Leibniz. Recently—since the time of Kant, perhaps—the tradition of natural theology has not been as strong as it once was; yet it continued to have able defenders both within and without officially Catholic philosophy.

Many Christians, however, have been less than totally impressed. In particular, Reformed or Calvinist theologians have for the most part taken a dim view of this enterprise. A few Reformed thinkers—B.B. Warfield, for example—endorse the theistic proofs; but for the most part the Reformed attitude has ranged from tepid endorsement, through indifference, to suspicion, hostility and outright accusations of blasphemy. And this stance is initially puzzling. It looks a little like the attitude some Christians adopt toward faith healing: it can't be done, but even if it could it shouldn't be. What exactly, or even approximately, do these sons and daughters of the Reformation have against proving the existence of God? What *could* they have against it? What could be less objectionable to any but the most obdurate atheist?

I. The Objection Initially Stated

By way of answering this question, I want to consider three representative Reformed thinkers. Let's begin with the nineteenth century Dutch theologian Herman Bavinck:

> A distinct natural theology, obtained apart from any revelation, merely through observation and study of the universe in which man

> lives, does not exist. The knowledge of God called "natural theology" is not a product of human reasoning.
>
> Scripture urges us to behold heaven and earth, birds and ants, flowers and lilies, in order that we may see and recognize God in them. "Lift up your eyes on high, and see who hath created these." Is. 40:26. Scripture does not reason in the abstract. It does not make God the conclusion of a syllogism, leaving it to us whether we think the argument holds or not. But it speaks with authority. Both theologically and religiously it proceeds from God as the starting point.
>
> We receive the impression that belief in the existence of God is based entirely upon these proofs. But indeed that would be "a wretched faith, which, before it invokes God, must first prove his existence." The contrary, however, is the truth. There is not a single object the existence of which we hesitate to accept until definite proofs are furnished. Of the existence of self, of the world round about us, of logical and moral laws, etc., we are so deeply convinced because of the indelible impressions which all these things make upon our consciousness that we need no arguments or demonstration. Spontaneously, altogether involuntarily: without any constraint or coercion, we accept that existence. Now the same is true in regard to the existence of God. The so-called proofs are by no means the final grounds of our most certain conviction that God exists. This certainty is established only by faith; i.e., by the spontaneous testimony which forces itself upon us from every side.[1]

According to Bavinck, then, belief in the existence of God is not based upon proofs or arguments. By "argument" here, I think he means arguments in the style of natural theology—the sort given by Aquinas and Scotus and later by Descartes, Leibniz, Clarke and others. And what he means to say, I think, is that Christians do not *need* such arguments. Do not need them for what?

Here I think Bavinck means to hold two things. First, arguments or proofs are not, in general, the source of the believer's confidence in God. Typically, the believer does not believe in God on the basis of arguments; nor does he believe, on the basis of arguments, such truths as that God has created the world. Second, argument is not needed for *rational justification;* the believer is entirely within his epistemic right in believing, for example, that God has created the world, even if he has no argument at all for that conclusion. The believer does not need natural theology in order to achieve rationality or epistemic propriety in believing. His belief in God can be perfectly rational even if he knows of no cogent argument, deductive or inductive, for the existence of God—indeed, even if there *isn't* any such argument.

Bavinck has three further points. First, he means to add, I think, that we cannot come to knowledge of God on the basis of argument; the arguments of natural theology simply do not work. (And he follows this passage with a more or less traditional attempt to refute the theistic proofs, including an endorsement of some of Kant's fashionable confusions about the ontological argument.) Second, Scripture "proceeds from God as the starting point," and so should the believer. There is nothing by way of proofs or arguments for God's existence in the *Bible;* that is simply presupposed. The same should be true of the Christian believer then. He should *start* from belief in God, rather than from the premises of some argument whose conclusion is that God exists. What is it that makes those premises a better starting point anyway? And third, Bavinck points out that belief in God relevantly resembles belief in the existence of the self and of the external world—and, we might add, belief in other minds and the past. In none of these areas do we typically *have* proofs or arguments, or *need* proofs or arguments.

Suppose we turn next to John Calvin, who is as good a Calvinist as any. According to Calvin, God has implanted in us all an innate tendency, or nisus, disposition to believe in him:

> 'There is within the human mind, and indeed by natural instinct, an awareness of divinity.' This we take to be beyond controversy. *To prevent anyone from taking refuge in the pretense of ignorance, God himself has implanted in all men a certain understanding of his divine majesty.* Ever renewing its memory, he repeatedly sheds fresh drops. Since, therefore, men one and all perceive that there is a God and that he is their Maker, they are condemned by their own testimony because they have failed to honor him and to consecrate their lives to his will. If ignorance of God is to be looked for anywhere, surely one is most likely to find an example of it among the more backward folk and those more remote from civilization. Yet there is, as the eminent pagan says, no nation so barbarous, no people so savage, that they have not a deep-seated conviction that there is a God. So deeply does the common conception occupy the minds of all, so tenaciously does it inhere in the hearts of all! Therefore, since from the beginning of the world there has been no region, no city, in short, no household, that could do without religion, there lies in this a tacit confession of a sense of deity inscribed in the hearts of all.
>
> Indeed, the perversity of the impious, who though they struggle furiously are unable to extricate themselves from the fear of God, is abundant testimony that this conviction, namely, that *there is some God*, is naturally inborn in all, and is fixed deep within, as it were in the very marrow . . . . From this we conclude *that it is not a doctrine that must first be learned in school*, but one of which each of us is

> master from his mother's womb and which nature itself permits no one to forget.[2]

Calvin's claim, then, is that God has created us in such a way that we have a strong tendency or inclination toward belief in him. This tendency has been in part overlaid or suppressed by sin. Were it not for the existence of sin in the world, human beings would believe in God to the same degree and with the same natural spontaneity that we believe in the existence of other persons, an external world, or the past. This is the natural human condition; it is because of our currently unnatural sinful condition that many of us find belief in God difficult or absurd. The fact is, says Calvin, one who does not believe in God is in an epistemically substandard position—rather like a man who does not believe that his wife exists, or thinks she is like a cleverly constructed robot which has no thoughts, feelings or consciousness.

Although this disposition to believe in God is partially suppressed, it is nonetheless universally present. And it is triggered or actuated by a widely realized condition:

> Lest anyone, then, be excluded from access to happiness, he not only sowed in men's minds that seed of religion of which we have spoken, but revealed himself and daily discloses himself in the whole workmanship of the universe. As a consequence, men cannot open their eyes without being compelled to see him.[3]

Like Kant, Calvin is especially impressed in this connection by the marvelous compages of the starry heavens above:

> Even the common folk and the most untutored, who have been taught only by the aid of the eyes, cannot be unaware of the excellence of divine art, for it reveals itself in this innumerable and yet distinct and well-ordered variety of the heavenly host.[4]

And Calvin's claim is that one who accedes to this tendency and in these circumstances accepts the belief that God has created the world—perhaps upon beholding the starry heavens, or the splendid majesty of the mountains, or the intricate, articulate beauty of a tiny flower—is entirely within his epistemic rights in so doing. It isn't that such a person is justified or rational in so believing by virtue of having an implicit argument—perhaps a version of the teleological argument. No, he does not need any argument for justification or rationality. His belief need not be based on any other propositions at all. Under these conditions he is perfectly rational in accepting belief in God in the utter absence of any argument, deductive or inductive. Indeed, a person in these conditions, says Calvin, *knows* that God exists.

Elsewhere Calvin speaks of "arguments from reason" or rational arguments:

> The prophets and apostles do not boast either of their keenness or of anything that obtains credit for them as they speak; nor do they dwell upon rational proofs. Rather, they bring forward God's holy name, that by it the whole world may be brought into obedience to him. Now we ought to see how apparent it is not only by plausible opinion but by clear truth that they do not call upon God's name heedlessly or falsely. If we desire to provide in the best way for our consciences—that they may not be perpetually beset by the instability of doubt or vacillation, and that they may not also boggle at the smallest quibbles—we ought to seek our conviction in a higher place than human reasons, judgments, or conjectures, that is, in the secret testimony of the Spirit.[5]

Here the subject for discussion is not belief in the existence of God, but belief that God is the author of the Scriptures. I think it is clear, however, that Calvin would say the same thing about belief in God's existence. The Christian does not *need* natural theology, either as the source of his confidence or to justify his belief. Furthermore, the Christian *ought* not to believe on the basis of argument; if he does, his faith is likely to be "unstable and wavering," the "subject of perpetual doubt." If my belief in God is based on argument, then to be properly rational and epistemically responsible I shall have to keep checking the philosophical journals. I will need to see whether, say, J.L. Mackie has finally come up with a good objection to my favorite argument. This could be bothersome and time consuming; and what do I do if someone does find a flaw in my argument? Stop going to church? From Calvin's point of view, believing in the existence of God on the basis of rational argument is like believing in the existence of your spouse on the basis of the analogical argument for other minds—whimsical at best and unlikely to delight the person concerned.

The 20th century theologian Karl Barth is particularly scathing in his disapproval of natural theology. *That* he disapproves is overwhelmingly clear; his *reasons* for thus disapproving, however, are much less clear. His utterances on this topic, as on others, are fascinating but Delphic in everything but length. Sometimes, indeed, he is outrageous, as when he suggests that the mere act of believing or accepting the Christian message is a manifestation of human pride, self-will, contumacy and sin. Elsewhere, however, he is both more moderate and thoroughly intriguing:

> Now suppose the partner in the conversation [i.e., natural theology] discovers that faith is trying to use the well-known artiface of dialec-

> tic in relation to him. We are not taking him seriously because we withhold from him what we really want to say and represent. It is only in appearance that we devote ourselves to him, and therefore what we say to him is only an apparent and unreal statement. What will happen then? Well, not without justice—although misconstruing the friendly intention which perhaps motivates us—he will see himself despised and deceived. He will shut himself up and harden himself against the faith which does not speak out frankly, which deserts its own standpoint for the standpoint of unbelief. What use to unbelief is a faith which obviously knows different? And how shocking for unbelief is a faith which only pretends to take up with unbelief a common position . . . . This dilemma betrays the inner contradiction in every form of a "Christian" natural theology. It must really represent and affirm the standpoint of faith. Its true objective to which it really wants to lead unbelief is the knowability of the real God through Himself in his revelation. But as a "natural" theology, its initial aim is to disguise this and therefore to pretend to share in the life-endeavour of natural man. It therefore thinks that it should appear to engage in the dialectic of unbelief in the expectation that here at least a preliminary decision in regard to faith can and must be reached. Therefore, as a natural theology it speaks and acts improperly . . . . We cannot experiment with unbelief, even if we think we know and possess all sorts of interesting and very promising possibilities and recipes for it. We must treat unbelief seriously. Only one thing can be treated more seriously than unbelief; and that is faith itself—or rather, the real God in whom faith believes. But faith itself—or rather, the real God in whom faith believes—must be taken so seriously that there is no place at all for even an apparent transposition to the standpoint of unbelief, for the pedagogic and playful self-lowering into the sphere of its possibilities.[6]

We must try to penetrate a bit deeper into these objections to natural theology, and suppose we start with Barth. Precisely what is the objection to which he is pointing? That somehow it is improper or un-Christian or dishonest or impious to try to prove God's existence; but *how* exactly? Barth speaks here of a *dilemma* that confronts the natural theologian. Dilemmas have horns, so what are the horns of this one? The following, I think. In presenting a piece of natural theology, the believer must either adopt what Barth calls "the standpoint of unbelief" or he must pretend to his unbelieving interlocutor to do so. If he does the former, he deserts his Christian standpoint; but if he does the latter, he is dishonest, in bad faith, professing to believe what in fact he does not believe. But what is the standpoint of unbelief and what is it to adopt it? And how could one arrive at this standpoint just by working at natural theology, just by making a serious attempt to prove the existence of God?

Perhaps Barth is thinking along the following lines. In *arguing* about the existence of God, in attempting to prove it, one implicitly adopts a certain stance. In adopting this stance one presupposes that it is not yet known whether there is a God; this remains to be seen, and is up for discussion. In adopting this stance, furthermore, the natural theologian implicitly concedes that what one ought to believe here depends on the result of the inquiry. If there are good arguments *for* the existence of God, then we (the believers and unbelievers who are together engaged in this inquiry) ought to accept God's existence. If there are good arguments *against* the existence of God, we ought to accept its denial. And if the arguments on both sides are equally strong, or equally weak, then perhaps the right thing to do is to remain agnostic.

In adopting this stance one concedes that the rightness or propriety of belief and unbelief depends on the outcome of a certain inquiry. Belief in God is right and proper only if there is, on balance, better reason to believe than not to believe—only if, that is, the arguments for the existence of God are stronger than those against it. But of course an inquiry has a starting point and arguments have premises. In supposing the issue thus dependent on the outcome of argument, one supposes the appropriate premises are available. What about these premises? In adopting this stance, the natural theologian implicitly commits himself to the view that there is a certain set of propositions from which the premises of theistic and anti-theistic arguments are to be drawn—a set of propositions such that belief in God is rational or proper only if it stands in the right relation to that set. He concurs with his unbelieving interlocutor that there is a set of propositions that *both* can appeal to, a set of propositions accepted by all or nearly all rational persons; and the propriety or rightness of belief in God depends on its relation to these propositions.

What are these propositions and where do they come from? We shall have to examine that question more deeply later; for the moment, let us call them "the deliverances of reason." Then to *prove* or *demonstrate* that God exists is to show a deductive argument whose conclusion is that God exists, and whose premises are drawn from the deliverances of reason. Moreover each of the steps involved must follow an argument whose corresponding conditional is among the deliverances of reason. Aquinas' first three ways would be attempts to demonstrate the existence of God in just this fashion. A demonstration that God does not exist, of course, would be structurally isomorphic. It would meet the second and third condition just mentioned but have as its conclusion the proposition that there is no such person as God.

An alleged example would be the deductive argument from evil: the claim that the existence of evil is among the deliverances of reason and is inconsistent with the existence of God.

Of course it might be that the existence of God does not thus follow from the deliverances of reason but is nonetheless *probable* or *likely* with respect to them. One could then give a probabilistic or inductive argument for the existence of God, thus showing that theistic belief is rational or epistemically proper in that it is more likely than not, with respect to the deliverances of reason. Perhaps Aquinas' fifth way and Paley's argument from design can be seen as falling into this category. And perhaps the probabilistic argument from evil—the claim that it is unlikely that God exists, given all the evil there is—can then be seen as a structurally similar argument for the conclusion that unbelief is the proper attitude.

According to Barth, then, the natural theologian implicitly concedes that the propriety of belief in God is to be tested by its relationship to the deliverances of reason. Belief is right, or rational, or rationally acceptable only if it stands in the proper relationship to the deliverances of reason—only if, for example, it is more likely than not, or at any rate not unlikely, with respect to these deliverances.

Now to adopt the standpoint of unbelief is not, as Barth sees it, to reject belief in God. One who enthusiastically accepts and believes in the existence of God can nonetheless be in the standpoint of unbelief. To be in that standpoint it is sufficient to hold that belief in God is rationally permissible for a person *only if he or she has a good argument for it.* To be in the standpoint of unbelief is to hold that belief in God is rationally acceptable *only if it is more likely than not, with respect to the deliverances of reason.* One who holds this belief, says Barth, is in the standpoint of unbelief; his ultimate commitment is to the deliverances of reason rather than to God. Such a person "makes reason a judge over Christ," or at any rate over the Christian faith. And to do so, says Barth, is utterly improper for a Christian.

The horns of the Barthian dilemma, then, are bad faith or dishonesty on the one hand, and the standpoint of unbelief on the other. Either the natural theologian accepts the standpoint of unbelief or he does not. In the latter case he misleads and deceives his unbelieving interlocutor, and thus falls into bad faith. In the former case he makes his ultimate commitment to the deliverances of reason, a posture that is for a Christian totally inappropriate, a manifestation of sinful human pride.

> And this attempt to prove the existence of God certainly cannot end

> in any other way than with the affirmation that even apart from God's grace, already preceding God's grace, already anticipating it, he is ready for God, so that God is knowable to him otherwise than from and through himself. Not only does it end with this. In principle, it begins with it. For in what does it consist but in the arrogation, preservation and affirmation of the self-sufficiency of man and therefore his likeness with God?[7]

Now I think the natural theologian has a sound response to Barth's dilemma: he can execute the maneuver known to dialectician and matador alike as "escaping between the horns." As a natural theologian, he offers or endorses theistic arguments; but why suppose that his own belief in God must be based on such argument? And if it isn't, why suppose he must pretend that it is? Perhaps his aim is to point out to the unbeliever that belief in God follows from other things the unbeliever already believes, so he can continue in unbelief (and continue to accept these other beliefs) only on pain of inconsistency. We may hope this knowledge will lead him to give up his unbelief. But in any event the believer can tell him quite frankly that his belief in God is not based on its relation to the deliverances of reason. Indeed, the believer can follow Calvin in claiming that belief in God *ought* not to be based on arguments from the deliverances of reason or anywhere else. So even if "the standpoint of unbelief" is as reprehensible as Barth says it is, the dilemma of the unbeliever seems to evaporate.

What is most interesting here is not Barth's claim that the natural theologian faces this dilemma; here he is probably wrong, or at any rate not clearly right. More interesting is his view that belief in God need not be based on argument. Barth joins Calvin and Bavinck in holding that the believer in God is entirely within his rights in believing as he does even if he does not know of any good theistic argument (deductive or inductive), even if he does not believe there is any such argument, and even if in fact no such argument exists. Like Calvin, Kuyper and Bavinck, Barth holds that belief in God is *properly basic*. It is rational to accept belief without accepting it on the basis of any other propositions or beliefs at all. In fact, they think the Christian ought not to accept belief in God on the basis of argument; to do so is to run the risk of a faith that is unstable and unwavering, subject to all the wayward whim and fancy of the latest academic fashion. What the Reformers held was that a believer is entirely rational, entirely within his epistemic rights, in *starting with* belief in God, in accepting it as basic, and in taking it as a premise for arguing to other conclusions.

In rejecting natural theology, therefore, these Reformed thinkers mean to say first of all that the propriety of rightness of belief in God in no way depends on the success or availability of the sort of theistic arguments that form the natural theologian's stock in trade. I think this is their central claim here, and their central insight. As these Reformed thinkers see things, one who takes belief in God as basic is not thereby violating any epistemic duties or revealing a defect in his noetic structure; quite the reverse. The correct or proper way to believe in God, they thought, was not on the basis of arguments from natural theology or anywhere else. The correct way is to take belief in God as basic.

Now suppose we understand classical foundationalism as the view that incorporates the following three theses:

(1) In every rational noetic structure there is a set of beliefs taken as basic—that is, not accepted on the basis of any other beliefs.

(2) In a rational noetic stucture, non-basic belief is proportional to support from the foundations.

(3) In a rational noetic structure, basic beliefs will be self-evident or incorrigible or evident to the senses.

Now I think these three Reformed thinkers should be understood as rejecting classical foundationalism. They may have been inclined to accept (1); they show no objection to (2); but they were utterly at odds with the idea that the foundations of a rational noetic structure can at most include propositions that are self-evident or evident to the senses or incorrigible. In particular, they were prepared to insist that a rational noetic structure can include belief in God as basic. As Bavinck put it, "Scripture . . . does not make God the conclusion of a syllogism, leaving it to us whether we think the argument holds or not. But it speaks with authority. Both theologically and religiously it proceeds from God as the starting point." And of course Bavinck means to say that we must emulate Scripture here.

In the passages I quoted earlier, Calvin claims that the believer does not need argument—does not need it, among other things, for epistemic respectability. We may understand him as holding, I think, that a rational noetic structure may very well contain belief in God among its foundations. Indeed, he means to go further, and in two separate directions. In the first place, he thinks a Christian *ought* not to believe in God on the basis of other propositions. A proper and well-formed Christian noetic structure will *in fact* have belief in God among its foundations. And in the second place Calvin claims that one who takes belief in God as basic can nonetheless *know* that God exists. Calvin holds that one can *rationally accept* belief in God as basic; he also claims that one can *know* that God exists even if he has no argument, even if he does not believe on the basis of other propositions. A foundationalist is likely to hold that some properly basic beliefs are such that anyone who accepts them, *knows* them. More exactly, he is likely to hold that among the beliefs properly basic for a person *S*, some are such that if *S* accepts them, *S* knows them. He could go on to say that *other* properly basic beliefs cannot be known, if taken as basic, but only rationally believed; and he might think of the existence of God as a case in point. Calvin will have none of this; as he sees it, one needs no arguments to know that God exists.

II. Is Belief in God Properly Basic?

According to the Reformed thinkers discussed in the last section, the answer is "yes indeed." I enthusiastically concur with this contention, and in the following pages I shall try to develop this view and defend it against some objections. I shall argue first that one who holds that belief in God is properly basic is not thereby committed to the view that almost *anything* is basic. I shall then argue that when belief in God is accepted as basic, it may nonetheless be *grounded.* And I shall argue finally that one who accepts belief in God (or another belief) as basic may nonetheless be open to arguments *against* that belief.

A. The Great Pumpkin Objection

It is tempting to raise the following sort of question. If belief in God is properly basic, why can't *just any* belief be properly basic? Could we not say the same for any bizarre aberration we can think of? What about voodoo or astrology? What about the belief that the Great Pumpkin returns every Halloween? Could I properly take *that* as basic? Suppose I believe that if I flap my arms with sufficient vigor, I can take off and fly about the room. Could I defend myself against the charge of irrationality by claiming this belief is basic? If we say that belief in God is properly basic, won't we be committed to holding that just anything, or nearly anything, can properly be taken as basic, thus throwing wide the gates to irrationalism and superstition?

Certainly not. What might lead one to think the Reformed epistemologist is in this kind of trouble? The fact that he rejects the criteria for proper basicality purveyed by classical foundationalism? But why should *that*, however, commit him to such tolerance of irrationality? Consider an analogy. In the balmy days of positivism, the positivists went about confidently wielding their verifiability criterion and declaring meaningless much that was obviously meaningful. Now suppose someone rejected a formulation of that criterion, the one to be found in the second edition of A.J. Ayer's *Language, Truth and Logic*, for example. Would that mean he was committed to holding that, contrary to appearances, the following makes good sense:

(1) "T was brillig; and the slithy toves did gyre and gymble in the wabe"?

Of course not. But then the same goes for the Reformed epistemologist; the fact that he rejects the criterion of proper basicality purveyed by classical foundationalism does not mean he is committed to supposing just anything is properly basic.

But what then is the problem? Is it that the Reformed epistemologist not only rejects those criteria for proper basicality, but seems in no hurry to produce what he takes to be a better substitute? If he has no such criterion, how can he fairly reject belief in the Great Pumpkin as properly basic?

This objection betrays an important misconception. How *do* we rightly arrive at or develop criteria for meaningfulness, or justified belief, or proper basicality? Where do they come from? Must one have such a criterion before one can sensibly make any judgments—positive or negative—about proper basicality? Surely not. Suppose I do not know of a satisfactory substitute for the criteria proposed by classical foundationalism. I am nevertheless entirely within my rights in holding that certain propositions in certain conditions are not properly basic. Some propositions seem self-evident when in fact they are not; that is the lesson of some of the Russell Paradoxes. Nevertheless it would be irrational to take as basic the denial of a proposition that seems self-evident to you. Similarly, suppose it seems to you that you see a tree. You would then be irrational in taking as basic the proposition that you do not see a tree, or that there are not any trees. In the same way, even if I do not know of some illuminating criterion of meaning, I can quite properly declare (1) meaningless.

And this raises an important question, one which Roderick Chisholm has taught us to ask.[8] What is the status of criteria for knowledge, or proper basicality, or justified belief? Typically, these are universal statements. The modern foundationalist's criterion for proper basicality, for example, is doubly universal:

(2) For any proposition *A* and person *S*, *A* is properly basic for *S* if and only if *A* is incorrigible for *S* or self-evident to *S*.

But how could one know a thing like that? What are its credentials? Clearly, (2) is not self-evident or just obviously true. But if it is not, how does one arrive at it? What sorts of arguments would be appropriate? Of course a foundationalist might find (2) so appealing that he simply takes it to be true, neither offering argument for it, nor accepting it on the basis of other things he believes. If he does so, however, his noetic structure will be self-referentially incoherent. For (2) itself is neither self-evident nor incorrigible. Hence if he accepts (2) as basic, the modern foundationalist violates the condition of proper basicality he himself lays down in accepting it. On the other hand, perhaps the foundationalist will try to produce some argument for it from premises that are self-evident or incorrigible. It is very hard to see, however, what such an argument might be like. And until he has produced such arguments, what shall the rest of us do—we do not find (2) at all obvious or compelling? How could he use (2) to show us that belief in God, for example, is not properly basic? Why should we believe (2), or pay it any attention?

The fact is, I think, that neither (2) nor any other revealing, necessary, and sufficient condition for proper basicality follows from clearly self-evident premises by clearly acceptable arguments. And hence the proper way to arrive at such a criterion is, broadly speaking, *inductive*. We must assemble examples of beliefs and conditions in which the former are obviously properly basic in the latter, and examples of beliefs and conditions in which the former are obviously *not* properly basic in the latter. We must then frame hypotheses as to the necessary and sufficient conditions of proper basicality and test these hypotheses by reference to those examples. Under the right conditions, for example, it is clearly rational to believe that you see a human person before you: a being who has thoughts and feelings, who knows and believes things, who makes decisions and acts. It is clear, furthermore, that you are under no obligation to reason to this belief from others you hold; under those conditions that belief is properly basic for you. But then (2) must be mistaken; the belief in question, under those circumstances, is properly basic, although neither self-evident nor incorrigible for you. Similarly, you may seem to remember that you had breakfast this morning, and perhaps you know of no reason to suppose your memory is playing you tricks. If so, you are entirely justified in taking that belief as basic. Of course it is not properly basic on the criteria offered by classical foundationalists; but that fact counts not against you but against those criteria.

Accordingly, criteria for proper basicality must be reached from below rather than above. They should not be presented *ex cathedra* but argued to and tested by a relevant set of examples. But there is no reason to assume, in advance, that everyone will agree on the examples. The Christian will of course suppose that belief in God is entirely proper and rational. If he does not accept this belief on the basis of other propositions, he will conclude that it is basic for him and quite properly so. Followers of Bertrand Russell and Madelyn Murray O'Hare may disagree, but how is that relevant? Must my criteria, or those of the Christian community, conform to their examples? Surely not. The Christian community is responsible to *its* set of examples, not to theirs.

So, the Reformed epistemologist can properly hold that belief in the Great Pumpkin is not properly basic, even though he holds that belief in God is properly basic and even if he has no full-fledged criterion of proper basicality. Of course he is committed to supposing that there is a relevant *difference* between belief in God and belief in the Great Pumpkin, if he holds that the former but not the latter is properly basic. But this should prove no great embarrassment, for there are plenty of candidates. These candidates are to be found in the neighborhood of the conditions that justify and ground our belief in God—conditions I shall discuss in the next section. Thus, for example, the Reformed epistemologist may concur with Calvin in holding that God has implanted in us a natural tendency to see his hand in the world around us. The same cannot be said for the Great Pumpkin, there being no Great Pumpkin and no natural tendency to accept beliefs about the Great Pumpkin.

B. The Ground *of Belief in God*

My claim is that belief in God is properly basic; it does not follow, however, that this belief is *groundless*. Let me explain. Suppose we consider perceptual beliefs, memory beliefs, and beliefs ascribing mental states to other persons. Let's examine such beliefs as

(3) I see a tree.

(4) I had breakfast this morning.

and

(5) That person is in pain.

Although beliefs of this sort are typically taken as basic, it would be a mistake to describe them as *groundless*. Upon having experience of a certain sort, I believe I am perceiving a tree. In the typical case I do not hold this belief on the basis of other beliefs; it is nonetheless not groundless. Having that characteristic sort of experience—to use Professor Chisholm's language, my being appeared treely to—plays a crucial role in the formation of that belief. It also plays a crucial role in its *justification*. Let us say that a belief is *justified* for a person at a time if (a) he is violating no epistemic duties and is within his epistemic rights in accepting it then, and (b) his noetic structure is not defective by virtue of his then accepting it. Thus, my being appeared to in this characteristic way (together with other circumstances) is what confers on me the right to hold the belief in question; this is what justifies me in accepting it. We could say, if we wish, that this experience is what *justifies* me in holding it; this is the *ground* of my justification, and, by extension, the ground of the belief itself.

If I see someone displaying typical pain behavior, I take it that he or she is in pain. Again, I do not take the displayed behavior as *evidence* for that belief; I do not infer that belief from others I hold, nor do I accept it on the basis of other beliefs. Still, my perceiving the pain behavior plays a unique role in the formation and justification of that belief. As in the previous case, it forms the ground of my justification for the belief in question. The same holds for memory beliefs. I seem to remember having breakfast this morning; that is, I have an inclination to believe the proposition that I had breakfast, along with a certain past-tinged experience that is familiar to all, but hard to describe. Perhaps we should say I am appeared to pastly. But this might not distinguish clearly the experience in question from the experience of accompanying beliefs about the past, which are not grounded in my own memory. The phenomenology of memory is a rich and unexplored realm, and unfortunately I cannot now explore it. In this case as in the others, however, there is a justifying circumstance present, a condition that forms the ground of my justification for accepting the memory belief in question.

In each of these cases, a belief is taken as basic, and in each case *properly* taken as basic. In each case there is some circumstance or condition that confers justification; there is a circumstance that serves as the *ground* of justification. So in each case there will be some true proposition of the following sort

(7) In condition *C*, *S* is justified in taking *p* as basic.

Of course *C* will vary with *p*. For a perceptual judgment such as

(8) I see a rose-colored wall before me,

C will include my being appeared to in a certain fashion. No doubt *C* will include more. If I am appeared to in the familiar fashion but know that I am wearing rose-colored glasses, or that I am suffering from a disease that causes me to be thus appeared to (no matter what the color of the nearby objects), then I am not justified in taking (7) as basic. The same holds true for memory. Suppose I know that my memory is unreliable and it often plays tricks on me. In particular, when I seem to remember having breakfast, more often than not I *have not* had breakfast. Under these conditions I am not justified in taking it as basic that I had breakfast, even though I seem to remember that I did.

So being appropriately appeared to, in the perceptual case, is not sufficient for justification. Some further condition—a condition hard to state in detail—is clearly necessary. The central point, here, however, is that a belief is properly basic only in certain conditions. These conditions are, we might say, the ground of its justification and, by extension, the ground of the belief itself. In this sense, basic beliefs are not, or are not necessarily, *groundless* beliefs.

Now similar things may be said about belief in God. When the Reformers claim this belief is properly basic, they do not mean to say, of course, there are no justifying circumstances for it, or that it is groundless or gratuitous. Quite the contrary. Calvin holds that God "reveals and daily discloses himself in the whole workmanship of the universe," and the divine art "reveals itself in the innumerable and yet distinct and well ordered variety of the heavenly host." God has so created us that we have a tendency or disposition to see his hand in the world about us. More precisely, there is in us a disposition to believe propositions of the sort *this flower was created by God* or *this vast and intricate universe was created by God* when we contemplate the flower or behold the starry heavens or think about the vast reaches of the universe.

Calvin recognizes, at least implicitly, that other sorts of conditions may trigger this disposition. Upon reading the Bible, one may be impressed with a deep sense that God is speaking to him. Upon having done what I know is cheap, or wrong, or wicked, I may feel guilty in God's sight and form the belief *God disapproves of what I have done*. Upon confession and repentance, I may feel forgiven, forming the belief *God forgives me for what I have done*. A person in grave danger may turn to God, asking for his protection and help; and of course he or she then forms the belief that God is indeed able to hear and help if he sees fit. When life is sweet and satisfying, a spontaneous sense of gratitude may well up within the soul. Someone in this condition may thank and praise the Lord for his goodness, and will of course form the accompanying belief that indeed the Lord is to be thanked and praised.

There are therefore many conditions and circumstances that call forth belief in God: guilt, gratitude, danger, a sense of God's presence, a sense that he speaks, perception of various parts of the universe. A complete analysis would explore the phenomenology of all these conditions and of more besides. This is a large and important topic, but here I can only point to the existence of these conditions.

Of course none of the beliefs I mentioned a moment ago is the simple belief that God exists. What we have instead are such beliefs as

(8) God is speaking to me.

(9) God has created all this.

(10) God disapproves of what I have done.

(11) God forgives me.

and

(12) God is to be thanked and praised.

These propositions are properly basic in the right circumstances. But it is quite consistent with this to suppose that the proposition *there is such a person as God* is neither properly basic nor taken as basic by those who believe in God. Perhaps what they take as basic are such propositions as (8)-(12), believing in the existence of God on the basis of propositions such as those. From this point of view, it is not exactly right to say it is belief in God that is properly basic. To be more exact, what are properly basic are such propositions as (8)-(12), each of which self-evidently entails that God exists. It is not the relatively high level and general proposition *God exists* that is properly basic, but instead propositions detailing some of his attributes or actions.

Suppose we return to the analogy between belief in God and belief in the existence of perceptual objects, other persons, and the past. Here, too, it is the relatively specific and concrete propositions, rather than their more general and abstract colleagues, that are properly basic. Let us examine such items as

(13) There are trees.

(14) There are other persons.

and

(15) The world has existed for more than 5 minutes. Perhaps these items are not in fact properly basic; it is instead the following propositions that deserve this accolade:

(16) I see a tree.

(17) That person is pleased.

and

(18) I had breakfast more than an hour ago.

Of course propositions of the latter sort immediately and self-evidently entail propositions of the former sort. And perhaps there is thus no harm in speaking of the former as properly basic, even though so to speak is to speak a bit loosely.

The same must be said about belief in God. We may say, speaking loosely, that belief in God is properly basic. Strictly speaking, however, it is probably not this proposition but such propositions as (8)-(12) that enjoy such status. But the main point, here, is this: belief in God, or (8)-(12), is properly basic. To say so, however, is not to deny that there are justifying conditions for these beliefs, or conditions that confer justification on one who accepts them as basic. They are therefore not groundless or gratuitious.

C. Is Argument Irrelevant to Basic Belief in God?

First, suppose someone accepts belief in God as basic. Does it not follow that he will hold this belief in such a way that no argument could move him, or cause him to give it up? Will he not hold it come what may, in the face of any evidence or argument with which he could be presented? Does he not thereby adopt a posture in which argument and other rational methods of settling disagreement are implicitly declared irrelevant? Surely not. Suppose someone accepts the following as basic:

(19) There is such a person as God.

It does not follow at all that he will regard argument irrelevant to this belief of his, or that he is committed in advance to rejecting every argument against it. It could be, for example, that he accepts (19) as basic, but also accepts as basic some propositions from which, by arguments whose corresponding conditionals he accepts as basic, it follows that (19) is false. What happens if he is apprised of this fact by being presented with an argument from those propositions to the denial of (19)? Presumably some change is called for. If he accepts these propositions more strongly than (19), presumably he will give up the latter.

Similarly, suppose someone believes there is no God, but also believes some propositions from which belief in God follows by argument forms he accepts. Presented with an argument from these propositions to the proposition that God exists, such a person may give up his atheism and accept belief in God. On the other hand, his atheistic belief may be stronger than his belief in some of his propositions or his belief in their conjunction. It is possible, indeed, that he *knows* that he accepts certain propositions to be true, but he believes some of them less firmly than he believes that there is no God. In that case if you present him with a valid argument from one of his accepted propositions to the proposition that God exists, you may cause him to give up a proposition he knows to be true. It is thus possible to reduce the extent of someone's knowledge by giving him a sound argument from premises he knows to be true.

So a person can accept belief in God as basic without accepting it dogmatically—i.e., in such a way that he will ignore any contrary evidence or argument. Now let us suppose the fact is belief in God *is* properly basic. Does it follow that one who accepts it dogmatically is within his epistemic rights? Does it follow that someone who is within his rights in accepting it as basic *remains* justified in this belief, no matter what counter-argument or counter-evidence arises?

Again, surely not. The justification-conferring conditions mentioned above must be seen as conferring *prima facie* rather than *ultima facie* or all things considered justification. This justification can be overridden. My being appeared to treely gives me a *prima facie* right to take as basic the proposition *I see a tree*. But of course this right can be overridden. I might know, for example, that I suffer from the dreaded Dendrological Disorder, whose victims are appeared to treely only when there are no trees present. If I do know that, then I am not within my rights in taking as basic the proposition *I see a tree* when I am appeared to treely. The same holds for the conditions that confer justification on belief in God. Like the theist noted above (19), perhaps I have been brought up to believe in God and am initially within my rights in so doing. But conditions may arise in which I am no longer justified in this belief. Perhaps you propose to me an argument that concludes it is impossible for trees to be such a person as God. If this argument is convincing for me, if it starts from premises that seem self-evident to me and proceeds by argument forms that seem self-evidently valid, then perhaps I am no longer justified in accepting theistic belief. Following John Pollock, we may say that a condition which overrides my *prima facie* justification for *p* is a *defeating condition* or *defeater* for *p* (for me). Defeaters, of course, are themselves *prima facie* defeaters, for the defeater can be defeated. Perhaps I spot a fallacy in the initially convincing argument; perhaps I discover a convincing argument for the denial of one of its premises; perhaps I learn on reliable authority that someone else has done one of those things. Then the defeater is defeated and I am once again within my rights in accepting *p*. Of course a similar remark must be made about defeater-defeaters: they are subject to defeat by defeater-defeater-defeaters, and so on.

Many believers in God have been brought up to believe, but then have encountered potential defeaters. They have read books by skeptics, been apprised of the atheological argument from evil, heard it said that theistic belief is just a matter of wish fulfillment or only a means whereby one socio-economic class keeps another in bondage. These circumstances constitute potential defeaters for justification in theistic belief. If the believer is to remain justified, something further is called for, something that *prima facie* defeats the defeaters. Various forms of theistic apologetics serve this function (among others). Thus the *Free Will Defense* is a defeater for the atheological argument from evil, which is a potential defeater for theistic belief. Suppose I am within my epistemic rights in accepting belief in God as basic and am then presented with a plausible argument—by Democritus, let's say—for the conclusion that the existence of God is logically incompatible with the existence of evil. (Let's add that I am strongly convinced that there *is* evil.) This is a potential defeater for my being rational in accepting theistic belief. What is required, if I am to continue to believe rationally, is a defeater for that defeater. Perhaps I discover a flaw in Democritus' argument, or perhaps I have it on reliable authority that Augustine, say, has discovered a flaw in the argument. Then I am once more justified in my original belief.

By way of summary, I have argued that the Reformed objection to natural theology, unformed and inchoate as it is, may best be seen as a rejection of classical foundationalism. As the Reformed thinker sees things, to be self-evident, or incorrigible, or evident to the senses is not a necessary condition of proper basicality. He goes on to add that belief in God is properly basic. He is not thereby committed to the idea that just any or nearly any belief is properly basic, even if he lacks a criterion for proper basicality. Nor is he committed to the view that argument is irrelevant to belief in God, if such belief is properly basic. Furthermore, belief in God, like other properly basic beliefs, is not groundless or arbitrary; it is grounded in conditions which confer justification.

Notes

1. *The Doctrine of God*, tr. Wm. Hendriksen (Grand Rapids: Eerdmans, 1951), pp. 78-79.
2. *Institutes of the Christian Religion*, tr. Ford Lewis Battles (Philadelphia: Westminster Press, 1960), I,iii, pp. 43-44.
3. *Ibid.*, p. 51.
4. *Ibid.*, p. 52.
5. *Ibid.*, p. 78.

6. *Church Dogmatics*, tr. G.T. Thompson and H. Knight (Edinburgh: T. & T. Clark, 1956), I/I, pp. 93-95.
7. *Ibid*., p. 135.
8. *The Problem of the Criterion* (Milwaukee: Marquette University Press), p. 14ff. See also Chisholm's *Theory of Knowledge*.

Religious Language: A New Look at an Old Problem

Roy Clouser

IN WHAT FOLLOWS, I WILL BE PROPOSING A VIEW of religious language which, so far as I know, has not been advocated in any of the recent discussions of that topic. The view I shall be defending is that talk about God as exemplified in Scripture, the traditional confessions, and even theology, should be regarded as quite ordinary language. It should not, in my view, be seen as requiring some sort of extended analogy, or special symbolism unique to itself, in order to understand the possibility of its truth. This should not be taken to mean that religious language is always to be taken literally so far as its meaning is concerned. Like all other ordinary language, it employs many styles and figures of speech, and occurs in many literary forms and types. Determining the intent of its author on linguistic and historical grounds is paramount for ascertaining the correct interpretation of such talk. But I will contend that neither its meaning nor the possibility of its truth require that it be treated as systematically different from other ordinary language universes of discourse.

The background inspiration for this view is found in the reformers of the 16th century. Luther, Calvin, and their associates laid great stress on the distinction between Creator and creature. I believe the evidence is that they regarded this distinction as exhaustive,[1] and placed it against the prevailing trend of medieval theology which they regarded as semi-pantheistic.

Now at first glance it may not appear that the Creator-Creature distinction has much, if anything, to do with that of religious language—especially with whether that language is to be regarded as analogical or ordinary. But I believe the position we take on the Creator-Creature distinction is in fact decisive for how we approach the religious language problem. Accordingly, the first task of this paper will be to investigate whether there is biblical warrant for regarding everything but God as dependent on God. Then we will proceed to consider the problem of religious language, which is to say how terms drawn from human experience can apply to God.

I. Universal Creationism

There cannot be much doubt that the biblical writers assert God's creatorship of the world of everyday experience. The visible heavens and earth, the sun, moon, stars, the life forms on earth—these are all explicitly said to have been brought into existence by God. Moreover, the biblical writers teach that this creating was not, at first, the mere forming of something already there. It was a matter of bringing into existence out of nothing, rather than cosmic interior decorating. Gen. 1:1 teaches this, and a host of other biblical passages echo it: God is the one who has created "all things."

But just how far does the expression "all things" extend? It obviously seems to include middle-sized and large objects of the universe clearly enough. But what of properties, propositions, laws, and the so-called host of abstract animals in the great corral of Plato's Other World? Assuming they exist, would a believer in the biblical Creator have to say God created them, too? Or could they exist independently from the God of Abraham as easily as they did from the God of Plato? More especially, are there any ***biblical*** grounds for answering such a question?

It is pretty clear that no biblical writer *specifically* answers such a question, any more than he specifically mentions the big bang or super novae among the stellar creations, viruses or spiny anteaters among the created life forms, or molecules and quarks among the tiny creatures. The reason is simple. No biblical writer ever raised questions about such entities. So if we are going to find their attitude on this issue we will have to look at how they use such expressions as "all things" and how they talk about God's creatorship in general. Then we will have to extrapolate from that talk in order to apply their attitude to those abstract animals—putative or real—whose separate existence neither Abraham nor Moses nor St. Paul seems to have suspected. Doing this can hardly take the form of a detailed hermeneutical analysis of each pertinent text, however; that would take a book all by itself. So what follows is a brief annotated index of several passages I think pertinent to the issue. Anyone who thinks my understanding of these passages to be seriously faulty will, no doubt, disagree with my conclusions. But we can hardly be wrong in starting with the biblical evidence, even if we do not end up agreeing on its meaning in every case.

1. Gen. 8:22. I believe this passage applies a general doctrine to a few specific examples, without *confining* the doctrine to those examples. Accordingly, this passage teaches that the law-like order of things is God's creation. The laws of nature depend on God since it is by God's guarantee that the regularities we observe and rely on will continue as long as the earth exists. There is nothing here to suggest that these regularities are self-existent or eternal, and that God is merely informing us of their inherent stability and reliability. On the contrary, it is God who is said to be stable and reliable and the laws are viewed as dependent on him; our reliance on natural laws is justified by God's promise, not anything in the laws themselves. In Ps. 119:89-91 and Jer. 33:25, natural laws are also spoken of as the means by which he rules creation, and they are termed his creations and his servants.

2. Gen. 22:16 and Heb. 6:13. These texts minimally teach that there is nothing greater than God. They do not go so far as to say nothing else is uncreated or that nothing else is on a par with God. But they do rule out anything to which he could be subjected in any sense, or else it would not be true that there is no greater reality by which he could secure his promise.

3. Isa. 44:24ff. God's sovereignty over all sorts of entities is asserted here, as is his uniqueness; he is the sole deity. Just what that entails is not spelled out, but it is significant that included among the "all things" which God is said to create are not just ordinary middle-sized and large visible objects, but also "darkness," events in the course of history, peace, evil, and human decisions.

4. Eph. 1:3-2:2. Again God is sovereign over "all things" where this expression includes the course of history and the election of those who believe. Eph. 3:9 and 10 extends "all things" to cover "principalities and powers," as does Rom. 8:38 and 39, which explicitly calls life, death, angels, principalities, and powers, "things present," and "things to come," *creations*. It is important to note how "height" and "depth" are also covered here as creations.

I say "important" because it is obvious by now that "all things" and "creatures" are used in Scripture in a very wide sense indeed. Powers, principalities, spatial extensions, human decisions, darkness, and the course of history are quite different sorts of entities.

5. Phil. 3:21 extends "all things" to the future renovations of believers' resurrected bodies, and Col. 1:16-20 emphasizes that immaterial and invisible realities are also to be understood under the rubric of "all things." These latter again include "dominions, principalities, and powers."

6. I Cor. 4:7, on any natural reading, seems to say quite clearly that any characteristic or talent which humans possess is given by God. I realize my critics may reply that God could see to it that people receive just the characteristics they do without his being the creator of those properties. But in the context of the biblical teachings so far, that is not the general drift or attitude we have found. In each case so far, God's sovereign control is linked to his creatorship; there are no exceptions. Unless some sort of hermeneutical special pleading is inserted here, the passage would appear to teach that the properties and dispositions of every human are God's creations. There is still some room to wriggle a bit, I admit. But to deny this general import to the passage seems strongly implausible at this point.

7. Compare what has been said so far with the treatment of wisdom in Prov. 8:22-31. There, in a personification, wisdom is represented as saying of herself:

> Yahweh formed me as the beginning of his way, the first of his works of old. I was set up from everlasting, from the beginning, before the earth was.

Here wisdom is spoken of as an abstract entity: a something existing before the earth or anything else; a something which is everlasting! This is perhaps as close as any Bible passage ever comes to saying that something has the status Plato ascribed to abstract properties, yet even here wisdom is declared to be God's creation! Even if everlasting, then, it is everlastingly dependent on God.

8. Finally, it is significant that in drawing the fundamental religious contrast between believers and unbelievers, St. Paul says the only options humans have are: (1) the service of God or (2) the service of something God created which is wrongfully accorded God's status (Rom. 1:25). It is hard to see such a remark as anything less than an explicit confirmation of what we have found so far everywhere else: everything whatsoever is either God or a creation of God's. There are no other alternatives.

St. Paul speaks this same way in other places as well. In Rom. 9:5 he says God is "over all" as though it means "all else. " And he shows that this is the way he uses "all" and "all things" by some even more explicit remarks in I Cor. 15:24-28. There Paul says that at the second coming of Christ, God will turn his kingdom over to Christ to rule it. At that time all other powers and authorities in the world will be abolished, including the power of death. At that point "all things" will be in subjection to Christ *except for God himself* (v. 27): clearly, this is an all-inclusive comment. The qualifier covers everything but

God, who is explicitly stated to be the only exception.

Now it might be replied that even if "all things" means everything but God, in the latter passage Paul only says that God *rules* all, not that all else creatively *depends* on him. But this reply will not do. For in Col. 1:17 Paul speaks of this same topic, uses the same expressions, and explicitly adds that the "all things" were created by God and are sustained by Christ.[2] Again, the language here gives every impression of *trying* to say that God created everything but himself. There is even a basis for suggesting the New Testament teaches that God created time (Titus 1:2, II Tim. 1:9, Rev. 10:5-7).[3]

On the basis of the foregoing considerations, I conclude it is a biblical teaching that the Creator-Creature distinction is exhaustive; all reality is either God or something that depends on God. So if there exist propositions, numbers, universals, relations, or any other abstract animals from Plato's great barnyard in the sky, they must be regarded, in the biblical scheme of things, as dependent on Yahweh the Creator.

If this is correct, it becomes totally unacceptable to regard anything else as uncreated. To do so is to regard it as being every bit as divine as Yahweh. The issue here is not only whether there exists something over which God would not have *control*. That is part of what is at stake, yes. But the additional issue at stake is nothing less than monotheism. For given the biblical position, the admission that anything besides Yahweh exists independently of him accords divine (uncreated) status to it, and is equivalent to a crypto-polytheism.

II. Analogy Theory

Now it is precisely this unbridgeable difference between the Creator and all creatures which gives rise to the problem of religious language. The problem which traditionally goes by that title in philosophy is the puzzlement as to how terms of any human language can be truly predicated of God. And the problem arises because the terms used of God connote and/or denote properties and relations which are known from our experience of creation. And this means that what is ascribed to God must also—in some sense—be true of creatures. So it appears we are driven to say either that something in (or about) the universe is uncreated, or something about God is created!

The traditional solution to this dilemma has long been some form of the analogy theory. In fact, the analogy theory has enjoyed such popularity for so long that recently its advocates have been claiming it is the only possible answer; that it has no conceivable alternative![4]

Essentially, the analogy theory attempts to resolve the issue by claiming that God does not really have *exactly* the same properties as creatures at all. Our words, to be sure, do connote and denote properties, relations, etc., in creation. But those are not univocally true of God. What God really has are super degrees of those properties, degrees not found in creation. In this way our language comes as close to the truth about God as is possible. It does not lead us to falsehood since God really does have, say, love or wisdom. But the level of love or wisdom he has (or as Aquinas put it: the *mode* in which he possesses these properties) is utterly different from anything created. In this way our language succeeds in stating something *like* what is true about God, but not exactly the truth, since God and creatures share no property exactly in common.

Now it seems to me that this move, for all its surface plausibility, simply fails to do an end-run around the problem. The failure as I see it lies in the *likeness* which is supposed to hold between what is true of God and what we can say. This likeness is essential to any notion of analogy, so it will not matter whether we are discussing Thomas Aquinas' version, Cajetan's version, Suarez' version, or Newman's version of the theory. The reason this theory fails is that "likeness" requires that something be univocally true of any two things which are alike. Let me elaborate.

For one thing, A, to be like another thing, B, they must have some element in common which is exactly the same for each. (And I do not merely mean that they have in common the property of being like one another.) There must be some *respect* in which they are alike. If A is red and B is green they are alike in being colors; neither is more truly a color than the other. If A is small and B is large, they are alike in having size; neither is more fully a size, or possesses the quality of size in a better way, than the other. It is simply impossible to conceive of two things being like one another, if it is supposed to be true that they have no property in common *univocally*. For that to be true, two things would have to be "alike" although there is no respect in which they are the "same." And, in fact, the analogy theory does not accomplish such a trick either.

Suppose we are talking of the love of God. In the analogy theory "love" has for its meaning the various senses of the word which are true of creatures. God is supposed to have something like what we know as love, while at the same time his mode or degree of love is one which does not occur in the universe.

But even if it is true that the divine mode of love is not possessed by any creature, in order for that mode of love to be *like* any creaturely mode of love there must be some respect in which they are really the same. There must be some element common to both in order for both to be cases of love. And whatever that element is, it will have to be univocally true of each: of divine love and creaturely love. In that case there must be a quality which is exactly the same in God's love and creaturely love. But this would mean that the original problem to be solved now recurs at another level. For the quality shared by divine and creaturely love cannot at the same time be uncreated (in God) and created (in the world). The problem is not resolved; it still appears we are driven to admit that either there is something about God which is created or something about the universe which is uncreated. The analogy theory takes the latter tack, and regards certain qualities of things in the universe as uncreated properties.

III. A New Proposal

Since the biblical teaching seems to be dead set against the latter of the two options, why not try the former? Is it really unbiblical to say of the properties and relations ascribed to God by Bible writers that they are entities he has created? I wish to suggest that there is not only nothing against this option in biblical teaching, but much in favor of it.

Consider, for example, the biblical doctrine of creation. This doctrine entails that once there was only God and then God brought the universe into existence out of nothing. But that would further entail that prior to creating the universe, God did not have the property of being Creator. He did not stand toward anything in the relation "being-the-creator-of," because there was only himself. However, simultaneously with creating the universe, God also created the relation "being-the-creator-of" and the property of standing in that relation; namely, the property of being the Creator. That property itself, then, is a created property, given the biblical account.

Why, then, cannot God's other properties be equally created? If God can take on one created property, stand in one created relation, then why not many? Why not, in fact, construe all of the personality properties of God this way? Terms such as "loving," "forgiving," "angry," "just," "merciful," "judgmental," "wise," "good," "powerful," etc., will all refer to created properties God has taken on in relation to creatures. And since these properties are the same as those which exist in the universe, we can know them as they are, not merely "something like" them. They can be just the characteristics we mean by the terms of our language as we ordinarily use them!

This is not to say that God possesses these characteristics with the same incompleteness, inconsistency, or other faults that people do. His love and wisdom are complete and faultless. But they are still what we mean by love and wisdom in ordinary language. We would not say that God's love is unlike what we ordinarily mean by "love" because his mode of loving is so extraordinary we cannot imagine it.

Even if it were granted that much God-talk could be construed in this way, it is fair to ask whether this interpretation is capable of being applied to *all* the talk about God. I must say that I think not. God's divine being (his non-dependence) and his ability to bring everything else into existence are not themselves created properties. They are not characteristics God has created. But I would contend they are not properties at all.

This is, of course, a complex and controversial issue which cannot be fully treated here. But in the ontology I am presupposing, properties fall into a number of basic kinds, and always correspond to the laws of their respective kind. Properties and laws exist in correlation; there are no properties which exist aside from every sort of order, nor does there exist a sort of orderliness which fails to govern anything.[5] In this view of properties they do not correspond to predicables in every case. Not everything which can be said of something denotes a property of that something. For example, we can speak of the individuality of an entity. But individuality is not one more property of a thing alongside its other properties.

In addition to arguing that individuality is not a property, I would contend that we have no *concept* of individuality. It is a fact encountered in our direct experience and approximated in a limiting *idea*. But a limiting idea is the best we can manage.

Now this situation holds also for talk about the uncreated Being of God. Speaking of his Being is not attributing to God a property which God possesses alongside, and in addition to, his other (created) properties. It is not a property at all. Neither is the fact he can bring all else into existence a created fact or a property—although it is a created property of all things in the world that they depend on God. As in the case of created individuality, we have only a limiting idea of God's divinity and creativity. God as he was prior to creating, and as he now is aside from the created properties he assumes, cannot be thought of as a thing with properties at all. For if God created all laws, and if properties are the ways things function under laws, then God prior to creating was not a thing with properties; and as the

Creator of all laws, he is not subjected to any of them.[6]

So far as God's Divine Being is concerned, then, there is nothing in the world that is even like it. So there is no way in which this position requires any property to be univocally predicated of God (as he was prior to creating) and creatures. At the same time, however, this position entails that God now shares many properties in common with creatures. Indeed, all God's personal characteristics, and all our knowledge of him which is truly conceptual, consists in the knowledge of these properties. And since these properties are created, they are subject to the same (created) laws which govern them in creatures. Thus they can be known and our language can carry its ordinary meaning for the terms used of them.[7]

As for the talk expressing the limiting idea of the Divine Being of that on which all else depends, this is also ordinary language. It is not a usual or common employment of language, to be sure. Especially the terms representing limiting ideas are a use which points to the limits of our thought and language and indicates a reality beyond them. But the language employed does not constitute a unique symbol-system, nor have a unique logic of its own, nor require an extensive analogy theory to understand its meaning.

As was remarked earlier, there appear to be grounds for thinking that the basis for this proposal (that religious language be regarded as ordinary language) was outlined by certain remarks Luther and Calvin made on the topic. While neither reformer makes quite the proposal I have made here, they do seem to have drawn a distinction between God's uncreated Being and the properties and relations God has assumed toward us. Luther said, for example:

> Now God in his own Nature and Majesty is to be left alone, in this regard we have nothing to do with him nor does he wish us to deal with him. We have to do with him as clothed and displayed by this word, by which he presents himself to us. That is his glory and beauty in which the Psalmist proclaims him to be clothed.[8]

Calvin also comments that in many passages of Scripture, ". . . God clothes himself with human affections and descends beneath his proper majesty" (*Inst.* III,XXIV,17). Elsewhere he expands this idea:

> . . . in the enumerations of his perfections (God) is described (in Scripture) not as he is in himself, but in relation to us, in order that our acknowledgment of him may be a more vivid actual impression than empty visionary speculation . . . *every perfection* set down (in Scripture) may be found in creation; and hence such as we feel him

> to be when experience is our guide, such as he declares himself to be in his word.[9]

These attitudes agree with my suggestion insofar as they seem to recognize that what Scripture reveals about God is not accomplished by prying into his uncreated Being. After asserting the truth of the Divine Being, Scripture is mainly concerned with clarifying the ways God relates to us.

However, there is a danger in putting this point in just this way. For when stated this way, it can sound as though we are saying that although God has taken on various created relations and properties and revealed them in his Word, in reality he is something quite different behind a mantle of assumed characteristics.

But that is not what I am suggesting at all, and it is clearly not what Luther or Calvin held. In the view of almost any Jewish or Christian theologian, there is certainly more to God than he has revealed, more than we can know. My position that the truths about God are all (with the exception noted) *created* truths does not make them any the less true of God. Remember, God's standing in the relation of being Creator and sustainer of the world is itself a created fact about him. But the fact that this relation is itself created does not make it any less true of God. Although he created that relation, he now *really* stands in it. It is not true that this relation is a ruse behind which he is really not the Creator! I suggest that this is so for the other relations and personal characteristics God has revealed of himself. The fact that he has created them does not mean that behind those relations and properties which he has taken on he really has other properties or is another sort of personality altogether. For "behind" what God has revealed, our concepts simply do not apply at all!

Perhaps it should be added at this point that nothing said so far is intended to prove that the biblical view of God is the true religion. Nor does my position offer a guarantee that God has not in fact misled us about his characteristics, even if he did cause Scripture to be written. But then I do not believe that any theory or argument is capable of ruling out such a fear as, for example, Descartes tried to do when he attempted to prove that "God *cannot* deceive us." The fact that Scripture is God's revelation rests squarely and solely on the believer's experience of its truth, not on arguments or inferences. In the face of that experience, running a theoretical credit check on God is not only unnecessary but sacrilegious!

To sum up, my suggestion about religious language is that it be purported to give univocal truth about God. It should not be seen as giving us something *like* what is true of God, while it is all really beyond our comprehension, as the analogy theorists maintain. Nor should it be understood as merely our resolve to talk about God *as if* he had such characteristics, as Kantians and pragmatists have maintained.[10] Rather it should be seen as quite ordinary language purporting to ascribe to God properties which he really has and relations in which he really stands. And although God may possess those properties more completely than creatures generally do, or stand in those relations more faithfully than sinful humans do, nevertheless it is the creaturely mode of those properties and relations which are true of him. Thus we are supposed to know those properties and relations as they are, not just know something vaguely like a superior property existing in a mode unknowable to us. Nor is such talk merely a matter of what we might hope for.

IV. Replies to Objections

But is the teaching that God created everything other than himself still plausible? Or does it lead to absurd consequences which should force us to reconsider whether that can really be the correct interpretation of the biblical writers? Several thinkers have suggested that all sorts of absurdities are generated by this position, and at least one defender of this position has admitted as much!

Most of these objections center on the contention that along with the other features of creation, God also created all the laws operative in the universe. The criticisms are intended to show that if this contention is taken to include logical and mathematical laws as well as, say, physical and biological laws, then absurdities do result. On the other hand if logical and mathematical laws are not included, then it is simply not the case that God alone is uncreated. (Logical and mathematical laws will then be accorded divine status as they were by Aristotle or Pythagoras respectively.) Since the criticisms I have encountered are mostly examples of alleged logical rather than mathematical absurdity, the discussion to follow will concentrate on the logical issues.

A. Logical Objections

The nub of all the examples of logical absurdity supposed to be generated by the creationist position is that it requires God himself not to be subject to the laws he has created. As we noticed earlier, Calvin drew that inference in a number of places, as did Luther. Later, Descartes also held that since everything but God was created by God, all logical and mathematical laws and truths were also created:

> The mathematical truths which you call eternal have been laid down by God and depend on him entirely no less than the rest of his creatures. As for the eternal truths, I say once more that they are true or possible only because God knows them as true or possible. They are not known as true by God in any way which would imply that they are true independently of him.[11]

Or as he puts it in his *Reply to Objections to Meditation VI:*

> . . . it is clear that nothing at all can exist which does not depend on Him. This is true not only of everything that subsists, but of all order, of every law, and of every reason of truth and goodness . . .[12]

But while I believe these remarks of Descartes to be expressing the position which Scripture supports, there is reason to object to the way he expresses this position at other points. For example, he says this position holds that God was free to "make it not be true that three angles of a triangle were equal to two right angles, or in general that contradictories could be true together." And again, he says in another place that "God could from all eternity bring it about that it should be untrue that twice four is eight . . . ." Descartes then recognizes that this means all sorts of absurdities are possible, and advises "we should not put these thoughts before our minds."[13]

Remarks such as these have led such critics as Alvin Plantinga to describe Descartes' position as "universal possibilism," and to understand that ". . . Descartes does not intend to say that for God, the logically impossible is possible; he means to say instead that nothing is logically impossible."[14]

Now it is not my intention to determine whether this is or is not a correct interpretation of Descartes. It seems to me Descartes does make remarks which warrant this interpretation while at the same time making others which would rule it out. But I am more concerned here with establishing that this cannot be the right interpretation of the claim that God has created everything other than himself. That claim, I contend, does not entail that nothing is logically impossible or logically necessary. Neither does it require that "God could bring it about" that contradictories be true together.

The error in such misunderstanding is subtle but important. It involves a shift of levels in the discussion which results in the assumption, at a meta-level, of precisely what is being denied at the initial level of the discussion. Let me first illustrate this point with another sort of case altogether, and then apply it to the issue of God and creation.

My sample case is a teaching found in scores of undergraduate logic textbooks. It concerns the claim that where the premises of an argument are logically inconsistent with each other, the argument will validly yield any conclusion whatever. This is regarded by some authors as "paradoxical." It has even been termed the "paradox of strict implication": that when it is logically impossible for all premises to be true, then everything validly follows.[16]

But there is more going on here than an isolated paradox. And it is not innocuous![17] For in every case of determining validity, we are always engaged in seeing what else would be true if the premises were true. It is not necessary that we believe the premises to be true in order to determine that an argument is valid; we need only see what would follow from them in case they were true.

If, however, the premises of an argument containing assertions of the form P and ∼ P were both true, the law of non-contradiction would be false and there would be no such thing as logical entailment at all! In other words, nothing logically follows from the truth of p .∼ p, because the truth of p .∼ p would vitiate all "logical following" whatever.

Thus the paradox that Copi and other writers feel uneasy about is neither mere allegation nor trivial. It arises because although advocates of this point are trying to see what would be true if p .∼ p were true at the initial level of dealing with an inference, as soon as the contradiction becomes explicit they shift their thought and speech to a meta-level where they retain belief in the logical laws. They then proceed to apply the laws to the argument by employing logical rules which presuppose those laws. At this meta-level, then, the fact is that they are no longer seeing what would be true if the premises were true. For if the treatment of the argument remained at that level, the rules of logic would cease to apply since the law of non-contradiction would be denied.

What really happens here is therefore an unconscious shift to a meta-level where the premises are assumed to be false, while the truth and applicability of logical rules and the logical laws are insisted on. It is this shift from initial level to meta-level, and the inconsistency between the two, which produces the feeling of paradox surrounding the (illusory) demonstration that if premises are impossible everything validly follows:

P
∼ P
P v anything (rule of addition)
anything (disjunctive syllogism)

Please do not misunderstand my point here. I am not for a moment attempting to defend the view that we should seriously maintain p .∼ p and give up the logical laws. What I am trying to point out is the tacit shift in the levels of thought and discussion which are introduced by the supposed demonstration that p .∼ p entails everything. But I do mean to maintain that this shift of levels needs to be acknowledged, and that when it is acknowledged it highlights two very important factors. First, we cannot consider the truth or falsity of a statement, or of the state of affairs it asserts, in isolation from the laws which we assume to govern it. And second, we cannot pretend not to be begging the question against the hypothetical truth of a claim at one level, while at the same time passing judgment on it from another level where what it denies is already assumed to be true.

Thus Descartes should not think that the dependency of things on God entails that God can make it true that p .∼ p *while the laws of logic remain what they are!* This is what he appears to say at points, and what Plantinga takes him to assert. This, of course, results in absurdity. To hold that all things are (logically) possible, including those things the laws of logical possibility exclude, is absurd.

But there is no absurdity in holding that although there really is necessity, impossibility, and possibility for creation, the laws which determine those conditions also depend on God. In that case the correct way of stating the consequences of a universal creationism is not to call it "universal possibilism"; it is not that anything is possible for God. Rather it is that God created all the senses of possibility.

To interpret universal creationism as "universal possibilism" is to think about and discuss the creationist claim by tacitly shifting to a meta-level of thought and discourse; there it is assumed that logical necessity and possibility are conditions which govern God as well as creatures. It is to argue at a meta-level which assumes that the laws of logic form an "environment" for all things, God included. And it is to assume, at the same time, that the claim of God's exemption from those laws must somehow entail that God can make some creatures exempt from the laws while the laws remain universal laws for creation.

But universal creationism need hold no such things. It can very well hold instead that God has created the laws which obtain in the universe, and the things which are governed by them, as *correlates*. To create an exception would mean that what was formerly a law would no longer be a law. Thus universal creationism does not hold that "God can make 2×4 = 8 false." If the laws of mathematics and logic were different from what they now are, then "×" and "=" as well as "2," "4," and "8" would not mean what they now mean. If these laws were different, reality would differ in ways not now imaginable by us.

But this does not require that reality would differ by *violating* the laws which now do obtain. If the law of non-contradiction did not obtain, nothing would be self-contradictory or absurd as we now understand "self-contradictory" and "absurd." For anything to violate a law, the law must hold. Thus God's sovereignty over laws means that God was under no compulsion to make just the laws he did; it does not mean that creatures as we now know them could violate logical laws. For as we now know them, all creatures are subjected to logical (and non-logical) laws. And these laws govern not only what created entities can be, but how we can conceive of them.

The position that there could be entities not governed by logical laws therefore amounts to saying that there could be creatures we cannot conceive of. And that is true just because there are no logical constraints on God's creativity. (At any rate the denial that there could be such creatures is pure dogmatism: how can it be shown there could not be things which we *cannot* conceive of?)

Moreover, there is another objection to construing universal creationism as universal possibilism. It is that every example of alleged absurdity supposed to follow from universal possibilism requires that we speak of what is supposed to be possible for God to do. They all take the form: "God could have . . . ," or "God can . . . ." But if all senses of possibility are God's creatures, possibility does not apply to God's own creativity! To apply logical possibility to God's creativity is to reintroduce at a meta-level just what the universal creationist's claim denied. It is therefore to beg the question against universal creationism.

This is why it is incorrect to interpret the position being maintained here as saying that God can violate the logical laws. Since "can" means "is logically possible," such a position would amount to holding that it is logically possible for God to do what is logically impossible! But that is not at all what is being maintained. For an entity to *violate* a law, the law most hold for that entity. And precisely what we are saying is that the laws do not hold for God. To interpret this position as saying God can violate the laws is therefore to beg the question against it. We would be making a meta-level assumption of its falsity, analogous to the meta-level assumption which generates the paradox of material implication.

In sum, God's sovereignty over laws means that they depend on him and that they are not to be applied to him except insofar as they apply to the created properties he has taken on.

Am I then suggesting that we cannot even say God *could* have made things differently? Surely that seems strange! How else can we express the import of declaring God's divine self-existence and creativity not to be bound by laws unless we do say this?

One way to reply to such a question is to point out that this sort of speech is much like another problematic case of God-talk noted by St. Augustine. In his commentary on Genesis, Augustine remarks that when we try to talk about the fact that God created time we have no adequate way to do it. The normal inclination is to say things like "before God created time . . . ," or "God existed before creating time," etc. But, says Augustine, "before" is itself a temporal word; it implies a moment of time prior to some other moment. In this way the normal expressions cannot be taken to mean what they literally say; "before" cannot mean "temporally prior." Still, if we qualify such talk in this way, it does then convey something true when we use that mode of speech. It means that God existed outside time, that he existed although time did not.

This is another case where we have only a limiting idea of something rather than a concept. Our thought and speech is time-bound so we cannot conceive what non-temporal reality would be. The limiting idea of God-beyond-time points beyond what we can grasp conceptually, and reminds us that the limit to what we can conceive is not the same as the limit of what can be.

So, analogously, our counterfactual talk about what God "could have done," or "could now be doing," or "could yet do," cannot carry the usual connotation of "could." None of the senses of possibility which exist in the universe are uncreated, including logical possibility; none applied to God prior to his creating. So none applies to his creating the law order that establishes the necessities and possibilities which hold for creatures and which supply the foundation for our "could"-talk.

At the same time, it should be clear that these remarks recognize how the laws of creation—logical laws especially—are really limits on our ability to think, conceive, and imagine. As creatures, we are bound to recognize those laws and conform our thought to them as completely as we are able. Saying that God is the Creator of those laws and not himself subject to them does not in any way release humans from subjection to them. We may not assert or believe what is contradictory on the excuse that God is not limited by the logical limits which hold for us. The upshot of the matter is that while recognizing that our subjection to logical necessity and possibility prevents us from excusing absurdity, at the same time it forces us to recognize that God's uncreated Being and God's creating of everything else exceed our ability to conceive. For talk of what God "could do" or "could have done" would apply logical possibility to him when in fact he is the Creator of every sort of possibility.

B. Religious Objections

Even if the logical objections lodged against universal creationism can be answered, the theory of religious language based on it must pass yet another test. It must pass the test of comparison with biblical teachings to see whether it is compatible with them. Obviously, there is no room to do that extensively here. So I will restrict my comments to three major biblical doctrines: (1) the image of God in man, common to Jews, Christians, and Muslims; (2) the doctrine of the trinity; and (3) the doctrine of the incarnation. It should be stressed, however, that I do not see all the interpretive innovations about to be suggested as *entailed* by creationism. Rather, they presuppose it. They are permitted by creationism and by the freedom it makes possible from Greek metaphysical concepts such as "scale of being," "substance," "analogia entis," "hypostatic union," etc.

1. Trinity

   Let us start with the doctrine of the trinity. The first thing to be borne in mind is that, from the universal creationist position, not only tri-unity but every other quantitative property ascribed to God must be regarded as a created property he assumes to himself. The laws and properties of quantity are characteristics of created things in the universe, and so are themselves also created. This point must be borne in mind, then, for the Jewish and Muslim doctrine that God is *one*, as much as for the Christian doctrine that God is one-in-three. In each case quantity is something created and assumed by God, and not intrinsic to God as he was prior to creating. The quantity should be understood, then, as true of the way(s) God relates to creation.[18]

   In this view, Greek metaphysical concepts such as "substance" and "person" are not needed. At the same time this construal guards against all theological modalism and subordinationism in the trinity: no one of the trinitarian distinctions is any more truly God than any other, nor is the unity basic to the diversity or vice versa.

2. Incarnation

   There are four classes of statements in the New Testament asserted of Jesus of Nazareth. The first are statements about him as a human being. These include reports of his birth, childhood, public ministry, teachings and death. They include startling accounts such as his walking on water and being resurrected, as well as very ordinary accounts of eating and sleeping. The second class of statements contains assertions pertaining to his office as Messiah. Among these are remarks of Jesus himself as well as others which are intended to explain his actions and teachings, and to demonstrate that he fulfilled the prophetic description of the role of Messiah. The third class of statements are those which speak of the special relation of God to Jesus in virtue of his office as Messiah. In this respect God is said to "indwell" Jesus (Jn. 14:10) as had been said of the prophets before him; that is, God has conferred on him special powers and authority (Luke 4:32, 36). By way of contrast with the prophets which preceded him, however, Jesus is said to be indwelt without limitation (Col. 2:9; Jn. 3:34) and so to have *all* God's power and authority conferred on him (Matt. 28:18; Jn. 3:34; I Cor. 15:24; Rev. 19:16).

Now whatever difficulties anyone may have with any of these classes of statements, it seems pretty clear that consistency with the biblical doctrine of God is not among them. But the fourth class of statements does raise the issue of consistency. It is the set whose members have traditionally—and, I think, correctly—been understood to assert the divinity of Jesus. Yet anyone who reads these statements in the light of the biblical doctrine of God transcendence will have to sympathize with the Jews who accused the early Christians of idolatry. For how, given the radical biblical sense of God's transcendence, can God be identified with anything in the universe, even the Messiah?[19] However, a closer look at the statements which assert Jesus' divinity uncovers a remarkable consistency if they are construed along the lines of the universal creationist view of religious language.

Consider some of the most direct of this set of statements: Jn. 1:1-14 refers to Jesus as the "Word" of God, and boldly asserts "the Word was God"; Col. 1:15, I Cor. 11:7, II Cor. 4:4 and Heb. 1:3 all call Jesus the "image of God"; and Phil. 2:6 says he was "in the form of God" so that it was not illegitimate for him to be regarded in some sense as "equal with God."[20] Now the expressions used in these passages appear almost as though designed to conform with the theory I have put forward! For in them the man Jesus is not said to be identical with the Divine Being as it was prior to creation, but to be the embodiment of God "as revealed," as "clothed in his Word." Jesus is said to be the "Word," the "form" and the "image of the invisible God"; that is, he is the very embodiment of the personal character God had taken on and had been revealing to Israel for centuries.

One of the bases for suggesting this interpretation is the attempt to take seriously what terms like "form," "Word," and "image" would mean to a pious Jew steeped in the Torah, Psalms, and prophets, rather than what they might mean to an educated pagan steeped in Plato, Aristotle, or Plotinus. Reflecting on this, I find no need for talk about different "natures" in a "hypostatic union" to explain the relation between Jesus' humanity and his divinity. For in my interpretation it is the very humanity of Jesus that *is* the embodiment of Yahweh as revealed. That is, Jesus really had (and has) the properties God had assumed to himself and revealed through the prophets; there is a real identity between the two sets of properties and therefore between the two personalities. The lovingness, faithfulness, compassion, goodness, etc., which were true of the ways God related to mankind (Israel in particular) prior to the incarnation, were the same as those possessed by Jesus during his earthly ministry and which he still possesses since his resurrection.

Thus Jesus could appear to a pious believer to be *literally* the incarnation of the (created and revealed) personality of the second person of the trinity. The man Jesus is not, therefore, to be regarded as *identical* with God the Son. God the Son is eternal, while Jesus was born about 2000 years ago. But Jesus is the man whose personality is identical with that of God the Son; he is the incarnation of God the Son.

All the same, this is not the whole story on the doctrine of Jesus' divinity. To be seen in its proper perspective, the point made above must be taken in conjunction with that third class of statements having to do with God indwelling Jesus and conferring power and authority on him. For, remarkably enough, there is precedent even in Judaism for the identification of a man with God-as-revealed in the sense of having God's power and authority. That precedent is the case of Moses. More than once the book of Exodus records that God told Moses that he, Moses, was to be regarded as God: he was to be God to Aaron, and God to the Pharaoh of Egypt (Ex. 4:16, 7:1).[21] In the contexts these remarks are grounded in the extent to which Moses was empowered to speak for God,[22] and to which God's authority rested on him. On this same basis it is also made abundantly clear that any and all criticism or disrespect directed to Moses is disrespect to God himself.

But there is even more to be said here than these two points, important as they are. For in addition to having all God's power and authority conferred on him, and besides being the living embodiment of the revealed personality of Yahweh, there are grounds for saying that God now bears his relations to creation through Jesus' relations to creation! Such remarks as "God was in Christ reconciling the world to himself" certainly suggest strongly that Jesus now stands in those relations to the universe which only God had prior to the incarnation. Thus even God's present relations of sustaining the universe in existence is now exercised through Christ (Col. 1:17).

It now becomes clear why the doctrine of Jesus' divinity does not contradict the doctrine of God's transcendence. If Moses could, in a sense, be identified with God because of the extent to which he carried God's authority, why not the Messiah who carries *all* God's authority? Moreover, if this Messiah is at the same time, in his human personality, the living embodiment of the personality of "God in relation to us," the completion of the revelation of this anthropomorphic character, *and also the creature through whom God actually bears his relations to the world*, there could be no more adequate way to express these facts other than to complete this sense of identification with God which Moses was said to have partially. In fact, this seems to be exactly the point which forms the background to the explicit contrast drawn between Moses and Jesus in Jn. 1:17. In that passage Moses is, for all his greatness, said to be merely the instrument through which the law was given, while Jesus "creates grace and truth."

But should any doubt remain as to whether this understanding of Jesus' divinity is a proper interpretation of the New Testament, the real clincher is that Jesus himself asserts it in just these terms! In replying to those who accused him of blasphemy for claiming to be divine, Jesus, according to Jn. 10:34-36, said:

> It is not written in your law that "I said, 'you are gods.' " If he called them gods to whom the word of God came, and if scripture cannot be broken, why do you say of the one the Father has made holy and sent into the world, "you blaspheme" because I said I am the Son of God?[24]

3. Image of God

By now it may be quite obvious how the universal creationist view of religious language will handle the doctrine of the image of God in man. Man will be understood to be in the image of the created personality of God, not God as he was prior to creating. And this means that the anthropomorphic depiction of God is not only the revelation of God's character (in the sense of the created properties he assumed and the created relations he bears us), and not only the revelation of the treatment we can expect from God. This depiction is also the revelation of the biblical idea of what it is to be fully human. It is because of this latter element in the doctrine that Jesus is said to be a perfect human (Heb. 4:15; Eph. 4:13) whom we should imitate (Rom. 8:28; I Cor. 15:49; I Pet. 2:21). It also makes sense of Jesus' statement that we should be "perfect as your Father in heaven is perfect" (Matt. 5:48).[25] Our interpretation is that in assuming to himself certain personal characteristics and relations, God has made these the model of what it is to be rightly human. He has taken on faithfulness, patience, kindness, goodness, justice, understanding, pity, mercy, righteous anger, etc. Thus he has not merely accommodated the language of revelation to us; he has accommodated *himself*, and taken on an anthropomorphic personality.

This interpretation of the image of God in man is a deliberate break with a long history of theologies which have identified the image with some faculty that humans are supposed to have in common with God (e.g., reason); or with some particular duty of life which humans supposedly share with God (e.g., to be loving or creative). Instead the imago Dei now turns out to mean the whole of what it is to be rightly human.

In summary, I think it has been shown that the universal creationist view of religious language is a genuine alternative to the traditional analogy theory. This view presupposes, and remains consistent with, the biblical doctrine of God's transcendence, while the analogy theory does neither. Moreover, this view is still able to maintain religious language as literally meaningful and religiously significant, thus avoiding the unrelieved agnosticism which the analogy theorist fears. And finally, it appears that the creationist view of religious language, when applied to several important biblical doctrines, turns out to be illuminating by the way it clarifies them and frees their interpretations from the distorting influence of pagan Greek philosophical theories.

Notes

1. Luther: "God is he for whose will no cause or ground may be laid down as its rule or standard; *for nothing is on a level with it or above it.* But it is itself the rule for all things." J. Dillenberger, ed. *Martin Luther* (New

York: Doubleday Anchor, 1961), p. 196.
Calvin: ". . . the Divine will . . . is itself . . . the cause of all that exists." *Institutes*, III, XXIII, 2.

2. Paul's express stipulation there that "all things" includes whatever is "visible or invisible" also quite literally covers everything whatever, leaving no exception (comp. also Eph. 1:21-23, and II Cor. 4:18).

3. The theme of God's secret plan for the course of history is common to three of these texts. The *Titus* and *II Tim.* passages assert that plan to have existed "before time everlasting." The *Rev.* text picks up the same theme and comments that at the point when the present world is destroyed (and prior to the creation of the new heavens and earth) "time shall be no more." More recent translations have rendered this "let there be no more delay" (οὐκ ἔστι Χρόνον). But I can find no precedent in the Greek language for using the verb "to be" with Χρόνον to mean delay, and the common theme supports the presumption that the comments about time likewise have a similar thrust—God's creative sovereignty over time (comp. I Cor. 2:7).

   Since I understand the creation of the new heavens and earth to include the re-creation of time, my sticking with the older reading of the text does not entail that the everlasting life promised to believers will be timeless. Compare Vos' remarks in *The Pauline Eschatology* (Grand Rapids, Mich.: Eerdmans, 1961), pp. 288-291.

4. Ross, J.F. "Analogy as a Rule of Meaning for Religious Language," *International Philosophical Quarterly*, vol. 1, no. 3, Sept. 1971, p. 476. Also John Macquarrie, *Principles of Christian Theology* (New York: Scribners and Sons, 1977), p. 138; and Paul Tillich, *Systematic Theology* (Chicago: University of Chicago Press, 1951), vol. I, part 2, p. 235.

5. See H. Dooyeweerd's *A New Critique of Theoretical Thought* (Phila.: Presbyterian and Reformed Pub. Co., 1955), esp. vol. II.

6. Comp. Calvin: "Not that God should be (regarded as) subjected to the law, unless insofar as He is a law to Himself" (*De Aeternal Praedestinatione* C.R. 36, 361). ". . . And therefore He is above the laws because He is a law to Himself and everything" (*Comm. in Mosis Libros* V C.R. 52, 49, 131). ". . . We do not imagine God to be arbitrary (exlex). He is a law to Himself. The will of God is . . . the law of all laws" (*Inst.* III, XXIII, 2). ". . . it is perverse to measure (the) Divine by the standard of human justice" (*Inst.* III, XXIV, 17).

7. It may be objected that in at least two places biblical writers speak of God as having thought and having planned the course of history prior to creating time (Titus 1:2, II Tim. 1:9). Those texts are not at odds with this theory, and need not be construed as attributing to God properties knowable by us which he cannot help but have. God could have created and assumed to himself those properties prior to creating the spatio-temporal universe in which creatures have them.

8. *Martin Luther*, op. cit., p. 191.
9. *Institutes*, I, Xiii, 1.
10. E. Kant, *Critique of Practical Reason* (Liberal Arts Press, 1956), pp. 105-106; and James, *Pragmatism* (New York: Meridian Books, 1959), pp. 185-186, 192-193.
11. Letter from Descartes to Mersenne, Apr. 15, 1630, in *Descartes Philosophical Letters*, tr. and ed. by A. Kenny (Oxford: Clarendon Press, 1970), p. 11.
12. *The Philosophical Works of Descartes*, tr. E. Haldane and G. Ross (Cambridge: Cambridge University Press, 1967), vol. II, p. 250.
13. *Ibid.*, p. 251.
14. *Does God Have a Nature?* (Milwaukee: Marquette University Press, 1980), p. 116.
15. Eg., I. Copi, *Introduction to Logic*, 5th ed. (New York: MacMillan, 1978), pp. 332-335.
16. *Ibid.*, p. 335.
17. Lemmon, *Beginning Logic* (Camden, N.J.: Thomas Nelson & Sons, 1965), p. ix.
18. Augustine had a feel for this point when he recognized that although the tri-unity talk is true it still somehow falls short of God's own Being. He says that we speak of "trinity" and of "three persons" in theology "not because the phrases are adequate (to God)—they are the only alternatives to silence" (*De Trinitate*, V. 9).
19. Muslims also make this charge. In Islam the sin of identifying any part of creation with Allah is called "shirk."
20. There are also indirect assertions of Jesus' divinity and equality with the God of Israel. I Cor. 2:8 and Jas. 2:1 call him the "Lord of glory," an obvious allusion to Ps. 24:7-10: ". . . the King of glory shall come in. Who is the King of glory? The Lord of hosts, he is the King of glory."
21. Moses' father-in-law also speaks of Moses as God to the people of Israel (Ex. 18:19).
22. This, of course, is the literal meaning of "prophet": not "one who fortells the future," but "spokesman" or "deputy."
23. Ps. 82:6.
24. Of course, there is also the teaching of the supernatural character of Jesus' conception and birth. This, too, sets off his humanity as unique and calls attention to its ability to reveal God as he is towards us; in addition to speaking and being God's Word, in addition to having the personality and power of God the Son (the second person of the trinity), he is also uniquely the Son of God.
25. Just what this could mean on the analogical theory is beyond me!

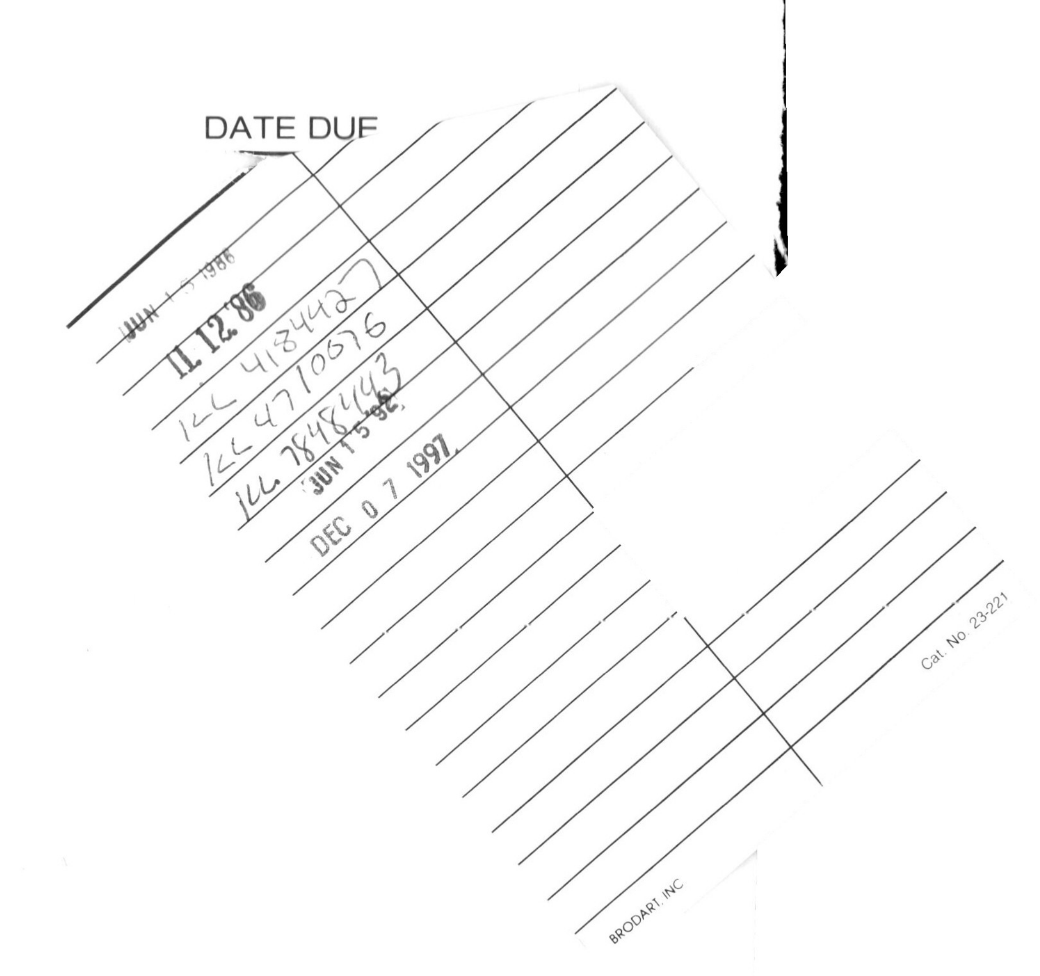
DATE DUE
JUN 1 5 1986
JL 12 '86
ILL 4184427
ILL 4710076
ILL 7848443
JUN 1 5 '92
DEC 0 7 1997
BRODART, INC
Cat. No. 23-221